KANSAS
IN THE GREAT DEPRESSION
Work Relief, the Dole, and Rehabilitation

Peter Fearon

University of Missouri Press   Columbia and London

Copyright © 2007 by
The Curators of the University of Missouri
University of Missouri Press, Columbia, Missouri 65201
Printed and bound in the United States of America
All rights reserved
5 4 3 2 1   11 10 09 08 07

Library of Congress Cataloging-in-Publication Data

Fearon, Peter.
    Kansas in the Great Depression : work relief, the dole, and
rehabilitation / Peter Fearon.
        p. cm.
    Summary: "Examines New Deal relief programs in Kansas
throughout the Depression from the perspective of recipients,
social workers, and poor commissioners. By focusing on the
relationship among the local, state, and federal governments,
Peter Fearon shows how the successful operation of work relief
depended on the effectiveness of those partnerships"—Provided
by publisher.
    Includes bibliographical references and index.
    ISBN 978-0-8262-1736-3 (hard cover : alk. paper)
    1. Public service employment—Kansas.   2. New Deal,
1933–1939—Kansas.   3. Depressions—1929—Kansas.
I. Title.
    HD5713.6.U542K24 2007
    362.5'84—dc22

                                                    2006102012

⊗™ This paper meets the requirements of the
American National Standard for Permanence of Paper
for Printed Library Materials, Z39.48, 1984.

Designer: Jennifer Cropp
Typesetter: The Composing Room of Michigan, Inc.
Printer and binder: The Maple-Vail Book Manufacturing Group
Typefaces: Palatino, Ink Pad, & Textile

FOR

Matthew, Simon, Sarah, Benjamin, and Alice

Contents

Preface

The Great Depression was a defining moment in United States history. Mass unemployment, severe deflation, bankruptcies, rising real debt, waves of bank failures, and a dramatic decline in investment led to a unique crisis that embraced both industry and agriculture. The prosperity of the 1920s was put sharply into reverse, and the sitting president, Herbert Hoover, was evicted from the White House by voters who had lost faith in the virtues of self-help and local effort as a means providing a safety net for those fallen on hard times. As economic confidence waned consumers stopped purchasing automobiles, or homes, or indeed anything not considered essential. Land values declined, banks ceased lending, and businesses fired workers in a desperate attempt to cut costs. As income fell, the budgets of all taxing units, which were heavily dependent upon the returns from taxes on property, moved into deficit at a time when the demands on poor funds rose. The nation was gripped in a vicious downward spiral of misery, which, it seemed, could only be reversed by governmental intervention on a scale not experienced before in peacetime.

This book examines the relief offered to the unemployed and to distressed farmers in Kansas from the onset of the depression until the New Deal was eclipsed by the demands of World War II. After a few years of hardship it was evident that the traditional methods of relieving distress, which depended heavily on private charities and county funding, were grossly inadequate. Obvious administrative inefficiencies combined with an increasing inability to raise sufficient funds to adequately care for the victims of depression, especially during the winter months, led to federal intervention. In 1932, the Reconstruction Finance Corporation was empowered to lend money to states whose governors could demonstrate that, in spite of exhaustive efforts, federal loans were essential to supplement local funds in order to avoid severe hardship. Beginning with the

Federal Emergency Relief Administration (FERA) in the spring of 1933, the New Deal embarked on a massive and highly diversified relief program in which grants replaced loans. Between 1933 and 1940, federal works programs or other forms of public assistance helped more than six million households each month. In early 1934, the households receiving aid contained more than twenty-eight million people, and even during the fall of 1937, the most favorable period, more than thirteen million fell into this category. As unemployment remained stubbornly above levels that had been achieved during the late 1920s, many victims of the depression asked for, and received, assistance. Because of the economic collapse, millions of Americans looked to Washington, D.C., for help where previously their local communities would have ministered to them. To the jobless we can add the many more who were victims of severe drought, low farm prices, and unmanageable debt.

Although federal involvement in welfare provision increased dramatically under the New Deal, the states and the localities still had a crucial role to play in caring for the destitute. Indeed, the relief programs can be seen as a partnership between Washington and state administrations. Starting with the FERA, New Dealers tried to impose good social work practices on the states. In the case of Kansas they were pushing at an open door. The Kansas legislature had anticipated the need to incorporate modern social work practices into relief delivery, and by mid-1933 the administration of relief in the state was held up, by informed outsiders, as an example of excellence. Kansas moved into this position under the leadership of John G. Stutz, the state's relief administrator, whose formidable talents helped craft an organization that combined efficiency with a high degree of social work professionalism.

It might be considered surprising that Kansas delivered New Deal relief programs so effectively, given that a Republican administration controlled the state from early 1933 to the end of 1936. Governor Alf Landon was first elected in 1932, and in 1934 he became the only re-elected Republican governor. Landon and his Republican colleagues shared the New Dealers' commitment to means-tested relief and their strong opposition to dole payments, which were viewed as a sure route to a dependency culture. Indeed, Kansas embraced much of the New Deal relief agenda, becoming an enthusiastic feeder at the federal feast. Landon's reliance on Congressional funding helps explain how he was able to balance the Kansas budget without the social costs becoming intolerable.

At the core of this volume is the evolving relationship between the state and Washington. The large number of relief initiatives necessitated the creation of a vast bureaucracy, not only in Washington, but also in the

states and the counties. The state relief administration, and by extension the county organization, had to implement federal policy. For example, individuals were declared eligible for relief after an investigation at a county relief office, but the engagement with the disadvantaged did not stop there. Local social workers were supposed to provide a continuing welfare service that would help clients to move from a state of dependence to one of economic self-sufficiency. Moreover, as the most important federal programs were seriously underfunded, these same social workers had to make difficult decisions about who would receive federal assistance and who would be allocated far less generous county relief. It was the poor commissioners and social workers who had to face the wrath of the angry unemployed who had been denied the help to which the believed they were entitled. Local officials also had to resist political pressure, especially during the run-up to elections. This study explains the organization of relief in Kansas and explores the reasons behind client–social worker tensions that periodically resulted in violence. The provision of an effective relief administration was crucial as the New Deal spawned a bewildering variety of relief-oriented initiatives, all of which had to be understood by officials and then introduced to potential clients.

A comprehensive state study can examine the minutiae of social and political life during this period of tremendous uncertainty and great change. There are advantages in knowing which parts of Kansas were most affected by the depression and drought, and in being able to examine what was done to relieve acute suffering. However, local studies also enable scholars to address issues of national significance, making it possible to obtain an insight into the rationale of the various New Deal initiatives, to analyze their implementation, and to account for their relative success and failure. The problems associated with gathering the information on which policy action could be based—or with the recruitment and training of staff to administer the programs, or the attempts to impose good social work practice in all of Kansas's 105 counties, or the sheer effort involved in keeping county officials informed of changes in rules and regulations—were not merely Kansas issues; they confronted officials in every state. Pungent criticisms of New Deal programs might appear misplaced or exaggerated when operational difficulties are taken into account. No local study which analyzes policy implementation should loose sight of the national picture. That is why, in this volume, Washington figures so prominently.

Acknowledgments

Any historian engaged in a long-term research project will accumulate debts, and my experience is not an exception. The work for this project, which took a long time to come to fruition, was made possible by periods of leave granted by the University of Leicester. Generous release from my teaching and administrative obligations presented me with the opportunity to undertake extensive archival research in the United States. A Fellowship from the American Council of Learned Societies was of tremendous value as it allowed me to spend considerable time exploring archival resources in Washington, D.C., and in Kansas. Visiting Fellowships at Clare Hall, Sidney Sussex College, and the Hall Center for the Humanities at the University of Kansas provided intellectual stimulation and an opportunity for writing in a collegial atmosphere. The manuscript was completed during late 2005 when I was privileged to spend a semester at the Institute for Advanced Study at La Trobe University. I have frequently marveled at the skill and patience displayed by archivists and librarians and, like countless numbers of historians, I have benefited from their professionalism. I must, however, single out for praise staff working in the Kansas Collection located in the University of Kansas Spencer Research Library. I am deeply appreciative of their efforts to support my work, which extended beyond the provision of a first-class archival service. The friendliness of the staff and their willingness to pursue even the most obscure or poorly framed request made working in the Spencer Library a truly rewarding experience.

I am also indebted to a number of scholars, in addition to those whose work I have consulted for this monograph. I am grateful to Tony Badger for, over a number of years, stimulating and broadening my interest in the New Deal. I gained an enormous amount of intellectual capital from attending many of the U.S. history seminars which Tony organizes at the

University of Cambridge. I benefited too from conversations with Bill Breen, Tim Minchin, John Wallis, and Ted Wilson, as well as the late John Clark, Dick Sheridan, and Don McCoy. Skilled practitioners themselves, John, Dick, and Don helped to foster, at an early stage, my interest in Kansas history.

I was very fortunate in persuading two outstanding historians to read the whole manuscript. The fact that both are friends did not dim their critical faculties. My colleague at Leicester, Richard Rodger, has provided the perceptive advice and friendly encouragement I have come to expect from him. Any New Deal historian would count himself fortunate to have John Salmond on his doorstep, as I did during my stay at La Trobe University. John not only provided a penetrating critique, but also suggested the University of Missouri Press as a publisher.

During my frequent research visits to Lawrence, Kansas, I have been very fortunate to have frequently stayed with Tom and Pat Weiss. Their generosity and friendship has been extraordinary, and I am very grateful to them. They tolerated, perhaps even came to terms with, my English humor and speech. I soon realized that Tom's ability to choose a restaurant and, indeed, a good wine is of the same superior quality as his scholarship. U.S. economic historians will know that this is high praise. Thanks to Tom and Pat, life in Kansas outside the archive for this scholar was always great fun, and I remember it fondly.

Finally, I am grateful to the editors of *Great Plains Quarterly* for granting me permission to reprint portions of this manuscript that first appeared in that journal as "Relief for Wanderers: The Transient Service in Kansas, 1933–35."

Abbreviations

AAA	Agricultural Adjustment Administration
CCC	Civilian Conservation Corps
CWA	Civil Works Administration
CWS	Civil Works Service
CCCorp	Commodity Credit Corporation
CERC	County Emergency Relief Committee
CFRC	County Federal Relief Committee
FCA	Farm Credit Administration
FSA	Farm Security Administration
FDIC	Federal Deposit Insurance Corporation
FERA	Federal Emergency Relief Administration
FSCC	Federal Surplus Commodities Corporation
FSRC	Federal Surplus Relief Corporation
KAW	Kansas Allied Workers
KERC	Kansas Emergency Relief Committee
KFRC	Kansas Federal Relief Committee
NYA	National Youth Administration
PECE	President's Emergency Committee for Employment
POUR	President's Organization on Unemployment Relief
PWA	Public Works Administration
RFC	Reconstruction Finance Corporation
RA	Resettlement Administration
SCDAA	Soil Conservation and Domestic Allotment Act
SERA	State Emergency Relief Administration
USES	United States Employment Service
WPA	Works Progress Administration

KANSAS IN THE GREAT DEPRESSION

1

The Storm Clouds Gather, 1929-1932

The United States economy began the slide that was to become the Great Depression in the seemingly prosperous summer of 1929. From that point business fortunes changed with dramatic rapidity, as a few months of declining profits led to diminished expectations for investors and brought to an end the vigorous consumer-led economic boom of the late 1920s. Prices on the New York Stock Exchange, which had been enthusiastically inflated by optimistic speculators, collapsed in October, and the ensuing Wall Street Crash gave the general public a first sign that a serious economic readjustment was taking place. A recovery in early 1930 flattered to deceive, raising hopes that were soon cruelly dashed. From mid-1930, but especially from the fall of 1931, the nation was gripped ever more tightly by an economic catastrophe that invaded all segments of society. Unemployment, estimated as less than 4 percent of the labor force on the eve of the depression, reached 25 percent before the worst was over. Moreover, many of those classified as employed were forced to accept a reduction in their working hours and substantial wage cuts. Pictures of destitute men and women, wrapped up to defeat the cold, patiently waiting in "breadlines" for food handouts, became one of the most harrowing images of the depression.

Bank failures engulfed the nation, especially during the fall of 1931, and again during the winter of 1932–33, adding to an uncertainty that often was transformed into fear. Savage deflation, a characteristic of this economic crisis, had a paralyzing effect on businesses that no longer saw the

advantages of investment, and on consumers who reduced their purchases to a minimum. Price falls also had a destabilizing effect on the farm community. Farm income was suddenly reduced, and the situation became especially serious for operators holding mortgages who found the real burden of their debt dramatically increased. Farm foreclosures and the desperate, even violent attempts to prevent them became increasingly common news. When Franklin Delano Roosevelt took the oath of office as president in March 1933, the country was as close to paralysis as was possible for a mature capitalist economy.

One frightening aspect of the economic slide was that its severity and its length were totally unexpected. In 1929, informed Kansans did not anticipate a major economic collapse nationally or locally. They did not foresee either rising unemployment or farm disaster, though Kansas, in common with other states dominated by agriculture, had a long history of periodic adversity. Indeed, the dramatic consequences which had followed the serious contraction of 1920–21 were fresh in the minds of many farmers. It is legitimate to ask at this point whether Kansas was well placed to withstand a serious economic shock. Was the state's economy in 1929 robust or fragile? Could those Kansans who became victims of the depression be cared for immediately and in a manner that would minimize their sense of failure and calm their anxiety? For how long could this care be provided? What actions could be taken by an individual state when confronted with the effects of a national, or in this case an international, contraction? How did Kansas leaders and institutions respond to the demands of this unfolding drama? Were they flexible, imaginative, efficient, and bold—or timid, conservative, and uncaring? What was the state's relationship with the federal government, and how did it develop as a result of this unprecedented economic crisis?

In order to provide answers to these questions, we must first examine the economic and social structure of the Sunflower State.

People and Employment

The *Fifteenth Census of the United States*, taken on April 1, 1930, recorded 1,880,999 Kansas residents. Of this total, 1,151,165 were rural dwellers (that is, they lived in settlements of less than 2,500 people) and the remaining 729,835 were classified as urban. The state's population had expanded by 111,742 since the previous census, taken a decade earlier. As in the rest of the nation, the number of urban dwellers had been increasing relatively for several decades, although in Kansas the rate of growth had

begun to slacken by the 1920s. Nevertheless, in this decade city expansion was far more vigorous than was noticeable for other rural or urban settlements, as is demonstrated by the following figures. While the urban population rose by approximately 18 percent between 1920 and 1930, during the same period Wichita expanded by 54 percent, Topeka by 28 percent, and Kansas City, Kansas, by 20 percent.[1] The attractions of urban life and the migration that it encouraged resulted in a net transfer of approximately 125,000 persons from rural to urban counties. This movement from some farms, villages, and small towns resulted in a population decline for 36 of the state's 105 counties during this decade.[2] However, the farm to city migration rate was below the national average because the creation of non-farm jobs in Kansas was relatively sluggish. Manufacturing and mining industries did not expand vigorously during the 1920s, and in both trade and industry the state's national position also declined. As a result, the fall in the farm population was relatively modest.[3]

The majority of Kansans were rural people. Indeed, 56 counties had no urban population whatsoever in 1930, and only 10 of the remaining counties had more than one incorporated city with more than 2,500 residents. The western third of the state had the lowest proportion of urban residents. During the 1920s the quality of rural life improved. Families for whom traveling had involved considerable effort benefited from the rapid spread of motorized transport and the construction of hard surfaced roads. They found it easier to market their goods, to shop, to visit neighbors, and to travel for work. It also became possible to operate a farm but live in a town some distance away. Rural isolation was further eroded by the spread of telephone ownership and by a more effective distribution of newspapers and magazines.[4] Between 1927 and 1929 there was a rapid expansion in the number of farms supplied with electricity from central stations. The most popular benefits were lighting in the home and the barn. However, although the growth in electricity connection during these years

1. U.S. Bureau of the Census, *Fifteenth Census of the United States: Population*, Vol. 1, 399. Urbanization did not guarantee growth. The state had twenty cities with a population of ten thousand or more in 1930, and of these Chanute, El Dorado, and Parsons had suffered a population decline since 1920. Numbers in Fort Scott, Leavenworth, and Pittsburg were virtually static during the same period. Ibid., Table 2, 400–401.

2. The largest declines, with percentages in parentheses, were: Butler (18), Crawford (20), Jewell (11), and Wilson (12). Thirty-two counties experienced population loss during the 1920s and in the decade that preceded it. Ibid., Table 3, 401–3.

3. Paul W. Zickefoose, *Kansas Income Payments, 1900–53*, 30–31, 34–38.

4. Ronald R. Kline, *Consumers in the Country: Technology and Social Change in Rural America*, 38. The use of telephones in Kansas was high; in 1930, 81 percent of farms possessed a telephone. S. W. Bell Telephone Co., *Economic Survey of Kansas*, 192–201.

was impressive, even by 1929 the number of farms affected was less than nine thousand.[5] Those who ran village and small-town businesses did not universally welcome the new freedom that rural residents enjoyed. They quickly realized that their previously loyal customers could now drive to large urban centers where they enjoyed a greater choice of goods and services, including banking.

An examination of farm and non-farm employment at the county level shows marked differences. For example, only 3 percent of the working population of Wyandotte County and 9 percent of Sedgwick County's was engaged in agricultural work. On the other hand, 49 counties had at least half of their gainful workers in agriculture, the majority being located in the western third of the state. It is important to remember that rural people are not necessarily employed on farms. Western Kansas had a mere 12 percent of its population classified as urban in 1930, but nearly half of its working residents had non-farm occupations. Many people had taken advantage of a range of employment opportunities made available in favorably located villages.[6]

Kansas had a relatively low proportion of foreign-born residents. In 1930 the national origins of the most prominent foreign-born communities were Germany (17,384), Mexico (11,183), Russia (8,781), Sweden (7,315), and England (5,272). Many migrants from Mexico were relatively recent arrivals, being exempt from the controls on immigration introduced by Congress during the early 1920s; they had been attracted by the possibility of working for the railroads or as unskilled farm labor. The 1930 census also identified just over eight thousand U.S.-born Mexicans, making the cohort from south of the Rio Grande a significant ethnic minority, but still only 1 percent of the total population.

Of the 66,344 African Americans recorded in 1930, 51,281 were urban dwellers. Most black Kansans lived in Kansas City, Kansas, Wichita, or Topeka, where they often competed with Mexicans for unskilled employment. In their comprehensive monograph, Clark and Roberts noted the differences in employment patterns between, on the one hand, foreign-born whites and native-born blacks, and on the other, native-born whites. A high proportion of foreign-born white families had no gainful worker because the group contained many retirees who had quit the labor force. However, this cohort also had a high proportion of families with two or

5. H. B. Walker, "Progress In Rural Electrification," 142–47; F. C. Fenton, "Progress of Rural Electrification in Kansas," 125–27; H. S. Hinrichs, "Twenty Years of Rural Electrification in Kansas," 68–79.

6. Carroll D. Clark and Roy L. Roberts, *People of Kansas: A Demographic and Sociological Study*, 189–91.

Table 1. Employment in Kansas (1930)

	Total	Male	Female
Employed work force	694,276	574,823	119,453
Main subgroups			
Agriculture	229,544	224,028	5,516
Mineral extraction	19,663	19,364	299
Manufacturing and mechanical industries	112,999	99,593	13,406
Transportation	80,481	73,421	7,060
Trade	103,846	80,737	23,109*
Professional service	54,316	24,318	29,998
Domestic and personal service	54,737	17,346	37,390

Source: U.S. Bureau of the Census, *Fifteenth Census of the United States, 1930: Population,* Vol. 3, Table 10, 829.
* Including 18,405 teachers

more wage earners. In African American families too, working wives were much more common than among the native-born white population.[7] In other words, these were low-income families who needed a regular financial contribution from more than one wage earner. There were also a small number (2,454) of Native Americans living in Kansas, of whom 26 percent resided in Jackson County and 18 percent in Brown County. The state's principal cities were home to very few Native Americans.

As Table 1 shows, agriculture offered employment to more Kansans that any other occupation. Indeed, 39 percent of all male workers worked in the farm sector. However, we should not forget that in Kansas more people were employed off the farm than on it. If the manufacturing and mechanical industries group, which includes not only construction but also the myriad of activities comprising trade, are taken together, they provided as much employment as did the farm sector. It is interesting to note the concentration of women's employment, particularly the large numbers working in low-pay domestic and personal service occupations.

There is a clear link between economic activity, especially non-farm economic activity, and urban growth. Apart from those cities that rose to prominence as trading centers, of which Dodge City is a prime example,

7. Ibid., 153–55.

urbanization was spurred on as a result of the exploitation of the state's extensive mineral resources and the development of its manufacturing industries.[8] The city of Hutchison, for example, benefited from the processing of salt, which was mined in Ellsworth, Reno, and Rice counties. Kansas was the nation's fourth largest petroleum producer, with its most important fields in Butler and Sedgwick counties. Petroleum refining was also a significant activity.[9] The state had extensive oil and natural gas fields extending over more than thirty counties, which provided a wide range of non-farm employment, especially when the market was buoyant. According to the 1930 census, nearly 10,000 were employed in gas and oil wells; the figure for coal mines was just over 5,500.

Coal production was dominated by output from Crawford and Cherokee counties, with the field centered around the town of Pittsburg. During the late nineteenth and early twentieth century migrants from Italy, Austria, Yugoslavia, Germany, France, Belgium, and Great Britain had moved to southeast Kansas to provide half the underground mining labor force.[10] However, since reaching a peak in 1918, output had declined considerably, with serious consequences for employment and the fortunes of the local economy. In 1918 Kansas miners worked, on average, 234 days to produce 7.6 million tons of coal. A decade later output had fallen to 3.5 million tons. During the whole of 1929, Crawford County deep mines employed 3,185 men who worked, on average, only 122 days during the year to produce 1.5 million tons of coal.[11] In Crawford and Cherokee counties many mine operators found strip mining, where output per man per day was four times greater than in deep mines, an attractive means of reducing costs in a competitive industry.[12] Unfortunately for labor, the increase in the number of power shovels contributed to the shaft mine unemployment and underemployment that became endemic. A further disadvantage was that once stripped, the land was unsuitable for agriculture, and its low value had adverse implications for

8. Between 1920 and 1930 the population of Dodge City doubled. This was the most dramatic increase of all Kansas cities.

9. U.S. Department of Commerce, *Mineral Resources of the United States 1930*, Part II, *Non Metals*, 799–800.

10. William E. Powell, "European Settlement in the Cherokee-Crawford Coalfield of Southeastern Kansas," 150. For some interesting background information see the paper by the same author, "Former Mining Communities of the Cherokee-Crawford Coalfield of South-eastern Kansas," 187–99.

11. Kansas Department of Labor and Industry, "Report of Coal Mine Inspection Department for 1929," 9.

12. C. A. Herbert and C. W. Owings, "Methods of Mining and Preparation of Coal," 9–11, and F. G. Tryon, "Production, Distribution, and Use," 13–19. Both papers in U.S. Department of Commerce, *Analyses of Kansas Coals*. R. H. Sherwood, "The Development of Strip Mining," 31.

county tax revenue.[13] Moreover, economic difficulties exacerbated tensions in an industry that had a long history of serious labor unrest. Output and employment were frequently disrupted by strikes and lockouts.[14] Cherokee County also had deposits of lead and zinc, which provided employment for miners and smelters, but zinc prices had begun to weaken in 1927.[15] With all these disadvantages, the economic future for southeast Kansas looked bleak even before the depression began to bite. Moreover, the steady decline in Kansas coal production resulted in less freight for the railroad companies that transported bulky fuel. And the decision by railroad companies to convert to oil-powered locomotives contributed to the depressed coal market, as did the switch to natural gas by many urban households and leading industries.

Between 1919 and 1929, manufacturing employment in Kansas also fell by more than 22 percent. Although this seems a massive contraction, it was one shared by virtually all states in the New England, Mid-Atlantic and Mountain regions.[16] However, the *Census of Manufactures* (1929) shows that Kansas shared in the nationwide boom of the late 1920s. Between 1927 and 1929 the number of wage earners in manufacturing rose by more than 4 percent, the sector's wage bill increased by nearly 6 percent, and the number of businesses expanded by 8 percent. In 1929 the state's manufacturing enterprises employed 9,968 salaried staff and 47,373 wage earners. The Kansas City, Kansas, industrial area provided jobs for nearly 30 percent of the total, Sedgwick County almost 13 percent, Shawnee County 8 percent, and Montgomery County 7 percent. The dominant industries, measured by the number of wage earners, were meat packing (9,068), railroad repair shops (8,810), petroleum refining (3,113), foundry and machine shop products (2,513), and flour milling (2,401).[17] However, despite this surge in growth in the late 1920s, the performance of the manufacturing sector over the entire decade was disappointing, and the proportion of the nation's wage earners living in the state declined by nearly 20 percent.[18] Although Kansas was not a leading national cen-

13. Fred N. Howell, "Some Phases of the Industrial History of Pittsburg, Kansas," 276–77.

14. William E. Powell, "The Cherokee-Crawford Coal Field of South-eastern Kansas: A Study in Sequent Occupance," 119–21.

15. M. D. Orten, "The Present Economic Condition of The Tri-State Zinc District," 417–28.

16. Harold D. Kube and Ralph D. Danhof, *Changes in Distribution of Manufacturing Wage Earners, 1899–1939*, Table 6, 29.

17. U.S. Bureau of the Census, *Fifteenth Census of the United States, 1930: Manufactures: 1929*, Vol. 3, Reports By States, Tables 1, 2, 12.

18. Zickefoose, *Kansas Income Payments*, 31–37; Kube and Danhof, *Changes in Distribution of Manufacturing Wage Earners*, Table 2, 25.

ter for manufacturing, employment levels were such that a major downturn in activity could still cause misery for many urban families.

Most Kansans entering employment had a relatively good educational background. School attendance in both rural and urban areas was better than the national average, as were the participation rates for high school and college.[19] It is reasonable to deduce that, for the state as a whole, the labor force possessed reasonably high skill levels, which should have been particularly advantageous during a period of economic crisis.

Prosperity in Kansas depended very heavily on the performance of the state's 166,042 farms, half of which carried a mortgage debt.[20] About 90 percent of total available land area was in farms, and Texas was the only state that had more acres under cultivation than Kansas. In 1930, when 37 percent of the state's population lived on farms, the volume and value of agricultural output was ranked fourth in the nation, and for the production of wheat Kansas ranked first.[21] The description "meat and wheat state" is apt for Kansas. Between 1924 and 1929, 57 percent of the cash returns that farmers received from marketing their output came from livestock and livestock products; the remainder came from marketing crops.[22] However, further analysis shows that beef cattle accounted for 44 percent of returns from livestock and hogs 19 percent, while wheat was the dominant cash crop, accounting for 74 percent of cash marketings.[23]

The striking change in Kansas agriculture during the first three decades of the twentieth century was the rise to national prominence of hard winter wheat cultivation. Under the stimulus of wartime demand the acreage devoted to wheat increased dramatically after 1914, and the plow-up of the prairie continued after the shock of the severe depression of 1920–21 had been absorbed. Wheat cultivation expanded into the west-central counties, but especially into southwest Kansas where, between 1921 and 1930, one million acres of buffalo grass was plowed up. In other words, wheat cultivation spread into the most arid part of the state. In the past, cycles of drought in this part of the state had spelled disaster for farmers, and each year a considerable percentage of the seeded acreage was abandoned prior to harvest. The decade of the 1920s was, however, unusually moist, and increasingly optimistic operators convinced themselves that

19. Francis W. Schruben, *Kansas in Turmoil, 1930–1936*, 13.

20. U.S. Bureau of the Census, *Fifteenth Census of the United States, 1930: Agriculture*, Vol. II, Part 1, Kansas, Table 1, 1290; Table XI, 1368.

21. In 1920, 42 percent of the population lived on farms. Bureau of the Census, *Fifteenth Census of the United States, 1930: Agriculture*, Vol. II, Part 1, Kansas, Table 1, 1290.

22. Kansas State Board of Agriculture (KSBA), "Cash Receipts from Marketings, 1924–1952," *38th Annual Report, 1953–54*, 407.

23. KSBA, *Price Patterns: Prices Received by Kansas Farmers, 1910–55*, 16.

the big plow-up was responsible for permanently changing the weather.[24] Cultivators were encouraged to maximize wheat acreage because the returns from the crop more than justified the costs of breaking the sod, the market being buoyed by a growing demand from commercial bakeries for the high-protein wheat that Kansas produced. Moreover, the use of tractors enabled farmers to plant a greater acreage than had been possible using their horse-drawn teams. Kansas farmers also took the lead in the purchase of combine harvesters, which, crucially, reduced their reliance upon costly, casual harvest labor. Motor trucks then speedily transported the grain to the nearest elevator. This rapid move to mechanized farming raised labor productivity, lowered costs, and—provided that rain came at the right time—delivered profits to the farmer.[25] It seemed rational for operators to borrow in order to acquire land and then go further into debt when they purchased expensive machinery on credit. It also seemed logical to maximize wheat acreage in the sure knowledge that even if this year's crop failed, next year's would easily make up the loss.

Unfortunately, national consumer tastes in food were changing. Purchases of fruit, fresh vegetables, and dairy produce were on the rise, but the consumption of grains had for some time been declining. Although Kansas farm prices began a significant recovery in 1924, even by 1929 the purchasing power of farm products was 12 percent less than the average prevailing between the years 1910–14.[26] In view of the numbers of autos, trucks, and expensive farm machinery that were purchased, no one could claim that the farm sector was in penury.[27] Farmers, however, were bitterly disappointed that their economic strength had failed to return to the levels of 1910–14, which they regarded as normal.

Among the aims of the Federal Reserve System, which had been established in 1913, were the prevention of financial panics and bank failures and, of course, the provision of credit to farmers and businesses. However, only a minority of banks had joined the Fed by 1929. While all national banks received their charters from the federal government and were obliged to become members of the Federal Reserve, state-chartered banks

24. Leo M. Hoover, "Kansas Agriculture After 100 Years," 7–9.

25. Peter Fearon, "Mechanisation and Risk: Kansas Wheat Growers, 1915–1930," 229–50; W. E. Grimes, "The Effect of the Combined Harvester-Thresher on Farming in a Wheat Growing Region," 773–82; S. C. Salmon and R. I. Throckmorton, "Wheat Production in Kansas," 7–11, 59–66; Edwin A. Hunger, "Kansas Outstanding Leader in Use of Combine," 187–95.

26. KSBA, *Price Patterns*, 8–9.

27. In 1930 Kansas was the third most motorized state, with 3.16 inhabitants per motor vehicle. *Facts and Figures of the Automobile Industry* (New York: National Automobile Chamber of Commerce, 1931): 15.

were merely encouraged to become members; few did. A major obstacle was that state banks were usually far too small to satisfy the minimum capital requirements for membership. In addition, many state bankers wished to avoid the examination and regulation that were a necessary part of the federal system. National banks were normally located in urban centers, and they were far less likely to fail than smaller institutions. During the period 1922–31, for example, the failure rate for national banks in Kansas was a modest 7 percent; the figure for state banks was 21 percent.

Kansans viewed banking as more than the means of lubricating the wheels of commerce and agriculture. In spite of national pressure in favor of branch banking, the state's bankers and legislators were fierce in their defense of unit banking. At its annual meeting in 1925, for example, the Kansas Bankers Association placed on record its disapproval of branch banking, believing it to be "un-American in spirit and conducted for the sole purpose of earning dividends rather than service to the community."[28] In 1933, W. W. Bowman, executive vice-president of the association, saw extensive branch banking as "more suited for a monarchical form of government" leading to an unhealthy concentration of banking power by absentee owners while offering depositors no additional stability. He supported locally organized, owned, managed, and capitalized unit banks that owed their existence to neither the state nor the federal government.[29] This idealized view of banking as a service to the community rather than a business was equally popular with the vast majority of the state's decision makers, and at the very end of the decade Kansas was one of the twenty-two states that prohibited branch banking.[30]

Why were Kansas banks so vulnerable during the 1920s? Was there a serious deficiency in the banking structure or, as the supporters of the status quo maintained, a problem with the economy? Kansas had an extraordinary number of banks, many of them very small and under-resourced.[31] In 1931, for example, the state had 5.2 banks per ten thousand residents; the national figure was 1.6. By the late 1920s, only in the Dakotas and in Nebraska could one find banks with a smaller average equity

28. *Topeka Capital,* May 29, 1925.

29. W. W. Bowman, "Rural Banks and Banking," 22–29. Another distinguished Kansas banker, Roy L. Bone, believed that it would be impossible to thoroughly inspect and regulate branch banks. See his paper, "Could Branch Banking Be Properly Regulated?" 130, 184.

30. *Federal Reserve Bulletin* (Washington, D.C.: Board of Governors Federal Reserve System, April 1930): 258.

31. The comments in this paragraph are based on the *Report of the Committee on Economic Policies of the Kansas Bankers Association* (Topeka, February 1933): 3–28.

than those in Kansas. The result was wasteful competition. Banks encouraged depositors to open and maintain small accounts, reduced credit standards to the minimum, and offered expensive services in an attempt to secure business. These under-capitalized banks depended heavily upon the economic strength of their immediate locality. Every banker could see the advantages of a diversified loan portfolio, but small rural banks found diversity impossible to attain. Moreover, the large number of banks placed an impossible strain on the available managerial talent. Individuals with no training or evident expertise in banking operated many institutions, loans were often poorly judged, and there was a disturbing tendency to borrow short from depositors and lend long, especially on real estate. When land values fell steeply, both borrowers and lenders could not avoid a major financial readjustment. "Over banking" was the main problem: there were too many marginal banks for good times and far too many to withstand a major economic crisis.[32]

The Curse of Plenty: The Economic Collapse, 1929–32

The changing fortunes of wheat producers provide an excellent example of the enveloping misery of the Great Depression. Between 1924 and 1927 the average price received by farmers for a bushel of wheat was $1.27. In both 1928 and 1929 the price had declined to 99 cents per bushel, but, because harvests were good, the value of sales was sufficient to keep producers content.[33] The disadvantage of plenty was that at the beginning of 1929 Kansas had the largest reserves of wheat, and also of corn, since 1920, to which the 1930 bountiful wheat harvest added. As Kansas farmers received only 63 cents for each bushel sold in 1930, the value of total sales had fallen by more than 30 percent. The immediate reaction of many producers to growing adversity was to plow the sod and plant more wheat.[34] Between 1929 and 1931 an additional 1.2 million acres of grassland was cleared and seeded, with the southwest region leading the way with an extra 700,000 acres. Favorable weather for the 1931 harvest led to high yields and the largest ever wheat crop to date, further depressing surpluses. A local politician wrote to Governor Woodring, "[T]his is the

32. Mary Scott Rowland, "Kansas Farming and Banking in the 1920s," 193–99; David C. Wheelock, "Regulation and Bank Failures: New Evidence from the Agricultural Collapse of the 1920s," 806–22.

33. Figures from KSBA, *38th Biennial Report,* 40.

34. Details of the acreage planted and harvested for both wheat and corn in each county are available in KSBA *Biennial Reports.*

first time I have ever seen a bumper crop year leave farmers more discouraged than if they had a complete failure."[35] To their alarm, producers received only 33 cents for each bushel they sold in both 1931 and 1932. The total value to farmers of wheat sales fell catastrophically from $153.5 million in 1928 to a paltry $29 million in 1932. Land values, too, followed a swift downward course. Farmers who had property or machinery mortgages, taken out in more favorable times, struggled with repayments, as they did with their tax demands.

Corn prices also collapsed. Farmers had received 73 cents for a bushel of corn in 1929, but in 1932 the price was only 27 cents, the lowest since the late 1890s. As most corn was fed to hogs, livestock producers could see some benefit from the cheaper feedstuffs now available. Indeed, between 1930 and 1932 the quantity of wheat fed to livestock dramatically increased as farmers sought a use for their surplus crop. Inevitably, however, livestock values also declined. Hogs fetched $12.80 per head in 1929 but only $5.40 in 1932 and $3.80 a year later. Cattle prices during the same period fell from $52.40 per head to $22.00 and, in 1933, to $17.20. As serious as the position of livestock producers became, they were not as badly affected as cash grain farmers. In fact, the stimulus of cheap feed led to an increase in the numbers of hogs in 1932 and 1933 and of cattle from 1929–34.

A general decline in all prices was a telling feature of the depression, but it is clear that farm prices fell more steeply than the prices of the goods that farm families had to buy. By 1932 the buying power of farm prices had fallen to 49 percent of the 1910–14 average, farm real estate values had declined by more than 20 percent since 1929, and farm foreclosures were becoming common.[36] Farm families were forced to make the most draconian economies. Only the most vital purchases were made; taxes and other debts were often left unpaid. Non-farm workers, especially those employed in auto sales or construction, where business depended on the willingness of consumers to take on additional debts, soon felt the adverse effects of this reduction in consumer demand. Because of the abundance of price data, it is easier to judge the impact of the depression on the agricultural sector than it is to assess its effect on non-farm workers and their families. Statistics on unemployment, under-employment, and wage movements were not systematically recorded, though with each year of the depression data collection improved. As late as Novem-

35. Rep W. A. Doerschlag to Woodring, July 31, 1932, Papers of Harry Hines Woodring, Kansas State Historical Society, Topeka, Box 4 (hereafter "Woodring Papers").

36. KSBA, *Price Patterns*, 8; USDA, *Farm Real Estate Situation*, 1939–42, 4.

ber 1931, however, the estimate of unemployment in Kansas given by state officials to a representative of the President's Organization on Unemployment Relief (POUR) was an imprecise 20,000–40,000 persons. It is hardly surprising that the national picture often lacked clarity.[37]

The Kansas Department of Labor and Industry began collecting monthly data on employment and payrolls in 1931. The University of Kansas Bureau of Business and Research was already gathering similar information for Kansas City, as was the local Chamber of Commerce in Wichita. A number of Kansas companies were also cooperating with the U.S. Department of Labor as part of a statistical sample aimed at constructing a nationwide estimate. All these sources were brought together to produce an index of employment and payrolls, which is reproduced as Table 2. The base of the index, April 1930, was chosen deliberately to coincide with an attempt by the Bureau of the Census to collect information on national unemployment.[38] Participation by Kansas companies was not universal, and even in 1932 only 1,100 out of 1,900 establishments provided information. Nevertheless, for all its imperfections this index was a distinct improvement on the barren period before 1930.

The index measures changes in eight industrial sectors and in the state as a whole. It shows that employment declined by just over 30 percent between 1930 and 1933, while payrolls shrank by just over 50 percent. The payroll index fell further than that for employment because it measures not only shorter hours worked by the employed but also wage cuts, which became common as the economic crisis worsened. In Kansas, workers with part-time jobs, even if only for a few hours each week, were classified as employed. Fluctuations in the payroll index, therefore, provide essential information on income decline. Both indexes moved in unison until the middle of 1931, but from that point the decline in payrolls was much more pronounced.

How did the Kansas experience compare with the national average? John Joseph Wallis has provided estimates for the changes in three different types of employment for every state during the 1930s, using August

---

37. *Kansas. Preliminary Report of Visit by Field Representative* (Nov. 1–5, 1931) POUR Office of Assistant Director, State Files Misc. (Kansas) 2, Records Group 73, National Archives, Washington, D.C. (hereafter, National Archive holdings will be identified as "NA," preceded by Records Group [RG] number and additional file information). An excellent account of the attempts made to calculate unemployment and the difficulties that the estimators faced can be found in Udo Sautter, *Three Cheers for the Unemployed: Government and Unemployment before the New Deal*, esp. chap. 4.

38. State Commission of Labor and Industry, *Annual Report 1932*, 32–46, and *Annual Report 1934*, 24–27. U.S. Bureau of the Census, *Fifteenth Census of the United States, 1930: Unemployment*, Vol. 1, *Kansas*, 373–87.

Table 2. Index Numbers of Employment and Payrolls in Kansas
(April 1930 = 100)

Year	All industries		Food & Allied Products		Mineral & Mineral Products		Metal and Wood Products, construction materials		Flour milling		Public utilities & public service		Service industries		Trade & finance		Misc. manufacturing	
	A	B	A	B	A	B	A	B	A	B	A	B	A	B	A	B	A	B
1930	100.4	98.4	95.7	97.2	99.2	101.0	98.0	95.1	97.6	110.3	103.4	101.6	95.7	95.8	98.2	94.8	98.6	99.7
1931	86.4	79.9	79.6	91.1	93.6	101.7	67.0	58.1	86.5	91.5	90.6	89.1	81.5	72.7	88.0	80.3	85.8	86.9
1932	72.0	54.2	73.5	59.8	87.1	74.6	49.0	36.1	69.5	53.6	67.7	58.2	65.4	55.2	75.3	56.7	71.0	61.1
1933	69.3	46.6	71.3	57.2	87.9	70.4	50.5	32.4	68.3	48.5	60.5	57.7	50.3	39.1	72.3	48.3	73.3	52.4
1934	72.8	52.4	86.4	75.8	86.7	79.1	55.4	41.2	71.1	50.1	63.5	53.5	54.1	44.1	79.1	52.2	80.3	57.9

A = Employment
B = Payroll
Source: Kansas Commission of Labor and Industry, *Report of Labor Department* (various).

1929 as the base. His three categories are total employment, manufacturing employment, and non-manufacturing employment. His calculations show that in 1932 the Kansas figure for total employment had declined to 87.5, a fall less steep than the national figure of 78.3. However, only in 1937 and 1938 did the state's index of general employment exceed the 1929 base. In 1932, Wallis's manufacturing employment index for Kansas reached 65.5, very close to the national figure of 64.8. The trough for manufacturing employment in Kansas, 63.4, was reached in 1933, but the subsequent recovery was weak, and the index had reached only 74.4 in 1940. Finally, the index for non-manufacturing employment showed a modest fall to 92.0 in 1932, while nationally that category fell to 82.2.[39] Non-manufacturing employment was more resilient than manufacturing across the country, and in 1937 the Kansas index had reached 119.1, far better than the national figure of 99.9. It would seem that the Kansas employment experience during these troubled years was close to, or better than, that of the country as a whole.

It is important to remember that the figures quoted above measure employment, not unemployment. An accurate measure of the unemployed as a percentage of the work force would be of extraordinary value, but difficulties in computing the size of the labor force make this a hazardous exercise.[40] Instead, the Kansas Index of Employment can be used as a valuable guide to social and economic change, though its messages need careful interpretation. One key problem is that the index base, April 1930, assumes that conditions were identical at that time in all the employment sectors identified; this, however, was far from the truth. Take, for example, the data on mineral and mineral products, which would appear to indicate that employment and payrolls in the industries that comprised this sector—coal, lead, zinc, salt, gas, and oil—declined relatively modestly. However, economic conditions in the coal, lead, and zinc industries were already extremely poor on the eve of the slump, and short-time working was commonplace. The Federal Unemployment Census, taken in April 1930, indicated that 3.2 percent of all the state's gainful workers were out

39. John Joseph Wallis, "Employment in the Great Depression: New Data and Hypothesis," 45–72.

40. For example, estimates prepared for the Social Security Board indicate that Kansas, with an average of 21 percent of its gainful workers unemployed between 1930–33, was below the national average of 25.8 percent. The figure for the neighboring state of Missouri was 24.2 percent. *Social Security in America: The Factual Background of the Social Security Act as Summarized from Staff Reports to the Committee on Economic Security*, 58–59. Unfortunately this table gives no indication of the minimum age for labor force participation.

of a job, but for coal mining the figure was 20.8 percent.[41] In already seriously depressed industries the scope for further major employment contraction was limited. It would be a mistake to conclude that employment and wages in this sector were relatively buoyant in 1932, and it is clear, therefore, that to take the index always at its face value can be misleading. This observation does not invalidate the index; it merely calls for thoughtful interpretation.

The depression-induced problem in agriculture was not unemployment; it was the serious decline in farm income. This affected the rest of the state through a reduction in the ability and the willingness of operators to purchase goods and services. The suppliers of those goods and services were forced to respond to a relentless reduction in their incomes by restricting spending, adding to a vicious downward economic spiral. Unemployment was almost exclusively an urban phenomenon, though in 1934 the advent of serious drought reduced employment opportunities for farm laborers and even some farmers. But unemployment, short-time working, and wage cuts inevitably squeezed the income and the confidence of thousands of consumers. Although substantial price falls presented the public with many potential bargains, financial prudence became the norm. After all, why buy now, particularly as goods were likely to be even cheaper in the future? Moreover, it was clearly sensible not only to stick to the purchase of essentials when economic misfortune might be lurking just around the corner but also to avoid incurring debts.

The general atmosphere of gloom was deepened by bank failures. Between September 1930 and 1932, eighty-seven failures and sixty mergers reduced the number of state banks.[42] There were two main problems. First, the fall in farm prices had led to both a marked reduction in the income of operators and a disturbing decline in land values. Those in debt found repayment difficult or impossible; the desperate in need of credit found that the banks were now very reluctant lenders. The second and related difficulty was the sharp decline in bank deposits. Many people faced with escalating financial problems withdrew their savings, as did the anxious who, fearing bank closure, felt that their money would be safer at home. Worried bank presidents wanted to hold the maximum amount of cash so that depositors could be paid promptly. To do this they cut down on loans and put pressure on borrowers to repay, even if this meant selling the family farm or business in a falling market.

41. Bureau of the Census, *Fifteenth Census of the United States, 1930: Unemployment*, Vol. 1., Kansas, Tables 1, 6. Census enumerators asked about unemployment on the day preceding their call. No information was gathered on unemployment over the past year, and part-time workers were excluded from the count.
42. Kansas Bank Commissioner, *21st Biennial Report*, September 1, 1932.

A widespread economic decline of such magnitude inevitably created much social distress. How were Kansans who struggled to cope with misfortune cared for? Could the state's welfare system adapt to the mounting costs of the greatest depression in its history?

Care for the Destitute: The Pre-Depression Model

Kansas pioneers, who introduced legislation in 1862 establishing the poor law, would have had no difficulty in recognizing the welfare system that operated during the 1920s. Although there was public sympathy for the "deserving poor," a group that included the blind, the elderly, the mentally and physically sick, widows with dependent children, and orphans, assistance for the able-bodied destitute had always aroused concern.[43] The traditional view was that an able-bodied male should be able to secure work and provide for himself and his family. A failure to do so might indicate a less-than-diligent search for employment. To avoid dependency, assistance had to be minimal and given under such harsh conditions that even the most undesirable employment would be preferable. Many supplicants were expected to perform menial tasks—like leaf raking, snow clearing, or wood chopping—to qualify for a small amount of cash or grocery orders. The able-bodied in receipt of relief were designated paupers, a description that carried with it, as it was intended to, public shame and humiliation.

The administration of the poor law was based on two important principles that emphasized local delegation. First, responsibility for assisting the poor was given to the county in which they had settlement. Second, settlement could be gained by residence in a county for a minimum of six months, and lost either by a deliberate absence of six months or by settlement elsewhere. Supplicants without settlement could be given emergency assistance before being returned to their legitimate place of residence. This model was very similar to that of other states, although Kansas was one of only a few that did not recognize family responsibility. Parents were not obliged to support their children once they reached majority, and children were under no legal obligation to support their parents, even if

43. Mary Scott Rowland, "Social Services in Kansas, 1916–30," 212. In 1885 destitute Union veterans and their immediate families were accorded special "deserving" status. They were to be given outdoor relief rather than committed to an institution, and counties were obliged to provide funds to prevent burial in a pauper's grave. Honorably discharged veterans of subsequent wars were later granted these privileges.

they could afford to do so.[44] Local responsibility was considered an important way of targeting relief to the deserving and of safeguarding against excessive expenditure. To this end, the board of county commissioners was given financial responsibility for care of the poor, while trustees of the townships and the mayors and the councils of incorporated cities were nominated as overseers of the poor. The county commissioners had the power to levy a property tax, within limits that had been set by the state legislature, to finance both institutional and outdoor relief. It seemed sensible to assume that local people would know who was and, most important, who was not entitled to relief; moreover, as taxpayers themselves, officials would be anxious to keep relief expenditure to a minimum.

The original idea was to grant relief in either a poor house, or in a poor farm that could be self-financing. By 1912, ninety-five counties had an institution that could care for the indigent. However, it became clear that certain categories of needy should not be forced into institutional care. For example, the poor house was considered an unnecessarily harsh regime for the elderly, widows with children, and even the temporarily unemployed. As a result of these compromises, in the early years of the century expenditure on outdoor relief eventually overtook spending on institutions, many of which had fallen into decay by the late 1920s.

Expenditure on poor relief rose noticeably across the nation during the 1920s.[45] Relief spending in Kansas followed this upward trend. In each of the four years from 1927 to 1930, five counties levied more for poor relief than the permitted legal maximum. In 1927, thirty-three counties had reached the legal maximum, a position that sixty-four counties held by 1931.[46] Table 3 not only charts rising expenditures that became increasingly burdensome even before the onset of the depression, but also illustrates the importance of private charitable agencies to the state's relief effort. In 1924 the counties dedicated $614,000, or 47 percent, of their total relief expenditures, to direct relief. By 1929 this figure had risen to $861,000, which as a proportion of total relief expenditure was the same as in 1924. Spending on poor farms absorbed $256,000 in 1924 and $346,000 in 1929. The remainder of the relief budget was absorbed by the funding demands of non–poor farm institutions like hospitals, pensions, and mother's aid.[47]

44. Grace A. Browning, *The Development of Poor Relief Legislation in Kansas,* 19, 94.
45. Anne E. Geddes, *Trends in Relief Expenditures,* 6–15.
46. Carroll D. Clark, "Public Poor Relief in Kansas," 117.
47. *KERC Bulletin* No. 127, December 1, 1934, "Public Welfare Service in Kansas: A Ten-Year Report, 1924–1934." This source provides annual data on relief spending

Table 3. Kansas Relief Expenditures from County,
Private and City Funds ($)

Year	Counties	Private agencies	Cities	Total
1924	1,297,142	372,647	15,403	1,685,192
1925	1,382,520	394,208	14,878	1,791,606
1926	1,493,228	411,537	17,597	1,922,362
1927	1,540,856	439,062	20,122	2,000,040
1928	1,682,762	479,255	18,912	2,180,929
1929	1,809,075	541,914	13,757	2,364,746
1930	1,965,164	597,645	41,340	2,604,149
1931	2,333,841	737,814	121,966	3,193,621
1932	2,878,972	1,043,017	211,653	4,133,642
1933	3,090,508	827,896	127,829	4,064,233

Source: "Public Welfare Service in Kansas: A Ten Year Report, 1924–33,"
KERC Bulletin 127, December 1934, 46–48.

Private charities played a crucial role at this time. Community Chests, which accounted for just over 40 percent of private relief spending in 1924 and just less than that figure in 1929, were the most significant agencies, whether measured by caseload or expenditure. Following them, ranked in order of expenditure, were Associated Charities, religious organizations, Fraternal Clubs, and the Red Cross. If the work of the private charities is measured by caseload per year, between 1924 and 1929 the rise was from roughly 30,000 to just over 45,000. Comparison with the public sector is difficult, partly because the private charities offered assistance to out-of-state relief applicants who could not expect much sympathy from the counties. However, the major problem with these figures, both public and private, is that they were not always collected or coordinated in a systematic manner. Consequently. they should be used with care.[48]

from 1924 to 1933. The figures do not fully reflect the sums raised by private charities since administrative costs are not included. Moreover, the possibility of duplication cannot be ruled out, as record keeping was not systematic. The figures for county and city funding do not include the road improvement schemes used to provide work relief but paid for from the highway budget.

48. For the national picture, see Sydnor H. Walker, "Privately Supported Social Work," in *Report of the President's Research Committee on Social Trends, Recent Social Trends in the United States,* Vol. 2, 1168–1222.

There was a surprising lack of uniformity in the way in which public relief was administered during the 1920s. Unfortunately, this diversity was usually the result of historical accident rather than a diligent search for best practice. In most counties the county commissioners, or the county clerk, or the mayors of second-class cities administered the poor fund. However, county commissioners differed in the way in which they handled their responsibilities. Some divided the county and shared the burden equally, but in others a single individual took on most of the work. In rural counties the county clerk usually assumed the role of administrator, and the names of potential relief cases were sometimes published in a local newspaper so that residents could have the opportunity to lodge objections.

Thirty-five counties with a population greater than twenty-two thousand were entitled to appoint a salaried commissioner of the poor, but by 1929 only seventeen had chosen to do so. The board of commissioners would normally select the paid commissioner, and one would expect patronage to play a role in the appointment. Of the counties that refused to take up the option of having a salaried commissioner, nine used the board of county commissioners to distribute relief, four used township trustees, and the others used a Red Cross employee, a Salvation Army officer, or a county clerk.

A few counties chose to have all their relief handled by the Red Cross or another private organization; yet another variation was to employ trained social workers from the Red Cross or from Family Welfare societies, who would work in partnership with county commissioners. In one county, a Red Cross social worker was employed as overseer of the poor, probation officer, and truant officer. She developed a close working relationship with the board of county commissioners, who were required to approve all relief expenditure. Unfortunately, only five counties had developed a partnership with professionally qualified staff by 1929.[49]

Poor houses and poor farms also had a bewildering variety of administrative models. On the eve of the depression, fifty-seven counties used salaried superintendents to manage institutional relief. However, seventeen counties were apparently satisfied with other arrangements. These included paying the manager a fee to board the inmates while the county paid for clothing and medical care. Another model required the superintendent to operate the poor farm and take full care of the inmates in exchange for a monthly capitation payment; farm produce that was not

49. Vivien S. Harris, "The Program of the American Red Cross in Outdoor Relief," 143–48; Carroll D. Clark, "Public Poor Relief in Kansas," 119–22.

consumed by residents could be sold for profit by the management. Three counties paid a salary to the superintendent, which was topped up with a sum for each inmate. There was little effective monitoring of these institutions, and there was no attempt to appoint managers with the appropriate social work training or to provide training for those in the post. The main criterion was to keep the cost of running each institution to a minimum rather than to provide a high standard of care. However, an investigation of poor farms showed most were not only badly run, but very expensive because of their high costs per inmate. Institutional care, which in the mid–nineteenth century was seen as an essential part of the provision of relief, had fallen from grace by the eve of the depression.[50]

Whether we consider indoor or outdoor relief, or public or private welfare, the picture is one of depressing administrative confusion.[51] Individuals who for the most part had no experience or training for the role they were trying to discharge were appointed to posts of great responsibility. Political and personal patronage was to the fore in making appointments. Ostensibly there was a great concern with giving the taxpayer value for money, yet while relief expenditure was increasing, there was no appreciation of the fact that inefficient management is always costly. Both public and private bodies were grossly deficient in record keeping and in coordinating their activities, and they followed no set standards for the delivery of care. Instead, there was a misplaced trust that local people could always identify those who deserved to receive relief and make a decision on what they should receive. This relief system depended heavily on the efforts of amateurs who struggled to provide care even before the economic crisis that was to come. They certainly would not be able to do so if the burden on them materially increased.

A New Challenge: Help in Hard Times

The depression was slow to bite in Kansas; the rise in relief expenditure from both public and private charitable sources in 1930 followed increases during the prosperous years that preceded the national economic decline. In November 1930, Republican Governor Clyde M. Reed's response to a request for information from the President's Emergency Committee for

50. *Kansas Emergency Relief Committee Bulletin* No. 307, "A Study of Kansas Poor Farms," October 1935, 8–9, 37–43; Peter Fearon, "Kansas Poor Relief: The Influence of the Great Depression," 144, 150–51.

51. Kansas was not unique. See Michael B. Katz, *In the Shadow of the Poorhouse: A Social History of Welfare in America*, 208–10.

Employment (PECE) was that, although the economic situation was worsening, Kansas could manage and did not require external assistance.[52] However, there were signs of depression-induced activity. During that same month, the State Chamber of Commerce, responding to PECE encouragement, gave its support to a circular from State Commissioner of Labor C. J. Beckman urging the mayors of all small cities to take the lead in creating employment agencies. The function of these agencies was to persuade householders to create work by employing builders, decorators, and other tradesmen; to encourage employers not to dismiss workers; to promote public works; and to act as a clearinghouse for information on available work. The agencies would also liaise with charities and make them aware of emergency relief needs. The PECE also suggested a campaign for women, who, that organization believed, had a special role to play in holding back the tide of depression. The Committee urged women: "[D]on't wear old clothes. Buy new ones for yourself and your children. Recommend that the other adults in your family do likewise, thus helping to create jobs."[53] If one wanted an indication that PECE had failed to grasp the realities of the depression, this advice would suffice.

Heartened by the news that the state had embarked on the largest road program in its history, senior PECE officials believed that the only significant new problem facing Kansas at the end of 1930 was unemployment in railroad repair shops and among train crews. Governor Reed was urged to request the railroad companies to repatriate unemployed Mexicans, who might be competitors for construction work, in as considerate a manner as was possible.[54] The PECE wrote directly to all Kansas mayors during December, and although it was clear that unemployment had increased in urban centers such as Wichita, Topeka, and Coffeyville, there was no reason to suppose that this growing problem was not under control. Indeed, these cities had already set up committees designed to survey and register their unemployed and to create some relief work for them.[55] The PECE was sticking to its remit, which limited its role to en-

52. Reed to Col. Arthur Woods, November 6, 1930, State Files Misc. (Kansas), Box 82, File 620.1, Central Files, PECE, RG73, NA.
53. J. F. Lucy to Beckman, November 21, 1930; "Relief Plan for Unemployment in Kansas," circular from Beckman to all Kansas Mayors, n.d., File 620, Kansas State Committee, Central Files, PECE, RG73, NA (hereafter, "PECE").
54. Lorraine Edmonds (signed for Beckman), November 15, 1930; Lucey to Reed, November 16, 1930; Lucey to Woods, November 19, 1930, PECE.
55. The mayoral responses are in PECE.

couraging states to take care of their own disadvantaged, but not intervening in the resolution of local problems.[56]

On January 10, 1931, Reed, in what was virtually his last gubernatorial act, established a Governor's Committee for Employment and chose Harry Darby as its chairman.[57] This action followed a request from PECE to all states urging them to set up such bodies, primarily to act as a channel of communication. Reed's committee of twelve men was inherited and retained by his successor, Democrat Harry Hines Woodring.[58] The committee, which saw its role as a gatherer and disseminator of information so that local organizations would be fully informed of good practice and better able to attack unemployment, held its first meeting on January 12.[59] The task of the local committees was to try to find, or to create, work for the fit unemployed, but not to dispense relief, though close working relationships with charitable organizations would be established.[60] The ideas discussed and agreed to by the committee at its inaugural meeting were identical to those suggested by the PECE. Employers would be urged to cut hours rather than jobs and consumers exhorted to create work by hiring men to undertake a variety of domestic tasks. The committee also urged Kansas employers to only hire Kansans, and it was hoped that all residents would purchase Kansas coal rather than out-of-state fuel.[61]

By the middle of 1931 some progress had been made in generating a grass-roots response.[62] By October, twenty-three cities had agencies and fourteen communities had committees dedicated to finding work for the

56. Albert. U. Romasco, *The Poverty of Abundance: Hoover, the Nation, the Depression,* 144–49.

57. Lucey to Reed, January 5, 1931; Lucey to Beckman, January 5, 1931, PECE. Harry Darby, Jr., was president of the Darby Corporation, manufacturers of boilers in Kansas City, Kansas.

58. Woodring defeated his Republican opponent, Frank Haucke, by the narrow margin of 251 votes in a poll of over 600,000. The campaign was complicated by the campaign of a "write-in" candidate, Dr. John R. Brinkley, who had gained national publicity by his advocacy of "goat gland" transplants as the Viagra of its day. Keith D. McFarland, "Secretary of War Harry Woodring: Early Career in Kansas," 210–12; Homer E. Socolofsky, *Kansas Governors,* 166–67.

59. Beckman to Lucey, January 23, 1931.

60. "The Governor's Committee for Employment" and "Plans for the Organization for Employment Committees in Kansas," Labor Conference-Governor's Employment Committee, Oct. to Dec. 1931, Folder 1, Box 11, Woodring Papers.

61. "Emergency Employment Activities," January 10, 1931, Records of State Labor Department, Kansas State Historical Society, Governor's Committee Meetings Folder, Box 58 (hereafter "Records of State Labor Department").

62. For a full account of economic problems in Kansas and the provision of relief, see Peter Fearon, "From Self-Help to Federal Aid: Unemployment and Relief in Kansas, 1929–1932," 107–22.

jobless. However, in at least seventeen cities a single organization combined employment and relief activities, tasks that the Governor's Committee wished to keep separate.[63] This may well have been a recognition that so little work could be provided for the unemployed that they were ultimately forced to approach private charities in order to supplement their pay. The second meeting of the committee was held in Topeka on June 11, and members restated their opposition to wage cuts, their support for the use of only local labor on all work relief projects, the need to avoid charity, and the importance of returning transients to their place of residence. At Woodring's suggestion, the membership of the committee was increased from its original dozen to include a representative from cities with more than five thousand inhabitants. The committee also accepted an estimate of fifty thousand unemployed for the state, about three thousand of whom were miners, though there is no indication of how this calculation was made. Representatives of both organized labor and business in Crawford and Cherokee counties had written to the committee in April, stressing the misery experienced by deep shaft coal miners and their families. The market for coal had collapsed, leading to financial hardship that had eroded the tax base of these counties and made it very difficult for them to maintain schools. The petitioners wanted the state to compel industry and the railroads to use only Kansas coal and to exclude fuel that had crossed the state line. The committee felt that more information was needed and agreed to implement a survey of these troubled counties. This was the first sign of a depression crisis moving out of local control, but the committee clung to the view that unemployment was a local problem best solved by those close at hand.[64]

However, the social and economic trauma resulting from the collapse of an already depressed coal industry illustrates the inability of localities to effectively tackle the costs of a major industrial dislocation. The following example shows both this and the inevitable frustration of those who tried to protect the affected. Inmates at the state penitentiary at Lansing operated a deep shaft mine to raise coal for prison use and for distribution to a number of other state institutions. Not surprisingly, Crawford County labor unions regarded this as unfair competition and asked the

63. "Relief Activities in Kansas Have Started," *Kansas Labor and Industrial Bulletin* 1 (October 1931): 3; "The Unemployment Program and Charitable Relief," *Kansas Labor and Industrial Bulletin* 1 (January 1932): 3.

64. "Kansas Committee for Employment," June 1931, Records of State Labor Department, Governor's Committee Meetings Folder, Box 58; Businessmen of Arma to Woodring, April 16, and Ira Hall to Woodring, April 29, both 1931, Records of State Labor Department, Coal Industry Folder, Box 59.

state commissioner of labor to close the mine for a year, or at least restrict its output to prison use. The response from Topeka was swift. The mine was valuable state property and closure for a year might do it irreparable damage. Moreover, maintenance of the prison was costly, and if the revenue from the mine were reduced, the legislature would have to allocate scarce resources to it from other sources. Finally, if the prison did not have its own coal it would be obliged by state law to purchase from the lowest bidder, which would be strip-mined, not deep-mined coal.[65]

The commissioner also sent a detailed memo to Woodring that offered no easy solutions to the coal problem. Beckman pointed out that the main competitor for Kansas coal was oil and gas, not the prison or out-of-state mines. Domestic and industrial consumers, including the railroads, had converted to oil and gas because those fuels were so cheap. Furthermore, the railroads had suffered a serious loss of freight revenue and jobs from the spread of oil and gas pipelines. Although the depression had dramatically reduced oil and gas prices, Beckman felt that it might be possible to persuade some state institutions to use high-quality southeast Kansas coal, but his principal recommendation was a major publicity campaign to make all segments of Kansas society aware of the benefits of buying coal from their own state's mines.[66] By November 1931, if not before, Beckman had no doubt that the worst conditions in Kansas were to be found in the coal, zinc, and lead-mining industries in Cherokee and Crawford counties.[67]

In the summer of 1931 a minor panic gripped officials in Lawrence, Salina, and Topeka. The fear was that a small number of Mexican families, whose principal wage earners had been discharged by the railroads, might become an illegitimate charge on the communities where they resided. Help was sought from the U.S. Immigration Service, and a representative visited Salina, only to report that none of the families interviewed could be deported as aliens since they had resided in the country far too long. Moreover, none of them had been a public charge and none had criminal records.[68] In Lawrence there was deep concern that the rail-

65. Harry Burr (Secretary, Kansas State Federation of Labor) to C. J. Beckman, June 24, 1931; Beckman to Burr, July 3, 1931, Records of State Labor Department, Coal Industry Folder, Box 59.

66. Beckman to Woodring, April 27, 1931, Records of State Labor Department, Coal Industry Folder, Box 59.

67. Beckman to J. F. Lucey (President's Committee on Unemployment Relief), November 16, 1931, Records of State Labor Department, Coal Industry Folder, Box 59.

68. C. H. Bien (Secretary, Salina Chamber of Commerce) to U.S. Immigration Service, July 13, 1931; Bien to C. J. Beckman, June 22, Records of State Labor Department, Governor's Committee for Employment, File spring–summer 1931, Box 59; Beckman to Woodring, July 3, 1931, Commission of Labor and Industry File, Box 10, Woodring Papers.

roads might try to avoid their responsibility of caring for the people whom they had brought to Kansas because they had a vested interest in maintaining a supply of cheap labor close at hand.[69] By "caring for" the correspondents meant removing. Alerted to this problem, Woodring reminded F. A. Lehman, general manager of the AT&SF Railroad, that the state had the authority to require rail companies to provide free transportation of indigenous Mexicans back to their own country. However, by September the problem had disappeared and the correspondents no longer felt that actions against Mexicans were necessary. Some of them had left of their own accord, some had found work, and the AT&SF agreed to provide free transport to those who wished to return to Mexico.[70]

In August, Woodring called more than forty labor representatives to a Conference on Unemployment, the purpose of which was to discuss plans for job creation during the coming winter.[71] The ideas advanced by organized labor were far more radical than any considered by the Governor's Committee. Unionists believed that it was the state's duty to take a positive role in the provision of both employment and of relief. However, they considered that the tax burden was unfair and must be shifted away from farmers and workers and skewed, by the introduction of income tax, more toward those who could afford to pay. Reliance on charities compounded inequities since the poor gave relatively more generously than the rich. Given the problems, an increase in tax revenue was essential, and labor proposed raising the state tax on gasoline from three to five cents per gallon, so that a public works program could be adequately funded. The proposers called for a special session of the legislature to implement the tax hike and also to deal with other initiatives, which included the introduction of a compulsory five-day week and six-hour day for state and municipal employees, and for all other workers too, with no loss of pay. Cities and counties should be permitted to issue three-year bonds to fund relief for citizens with at least two years' residence. If that could not be done immediately, the state should also consider raising funds by issuing scrip, which could be redeemed from future sales of bonds.

Woodring did not receive these proposals with great enthusiasm, and his promise to have them considered by the Governor's Committee was accompanied by comments that emphasized his discomfort. All politi-

69. Alta Marti to Beckman, August 22, 1931; Mrs. Carey to Beckman, July 5, 1931, Records of State Labor Department, Coal Industry Folder, Box 59.
70. Woodring to Leman, August 6; Lehman to Beckman, September 6, both 1931, Commission of Labor and Industry File, Box 10, Woodring Papers.
71. Conference on Unemployment, August 31, 1931. A full transcript of this conference is in the Library of the Kansas State Historical Society, Topeka.

cians were aware that campaigns to reduce taxes were gaining in popularity, and the governor was wary of offending voters. He did point out
that an emergency appropriation by Congress in September 1930 had provided Kansas with funds for highway work, and he successfully urged
the meeting to give its support for further Congressional funding. The
condemnation of married women working in offices when there were unemployed male white-collar workers gained universal approval at a meeting where no women appeared to be present. B. L. Marchant and G. B.
Winston, two African Americans from Wichita, spoke about the particular disadvantages facing black workers.[72] They claimed that racial discrimination had hit the black community disproportionately hard and
that, as a result, many families were heavily dependent upon the earnings
of women. The protests from white union leaders that their movement
would under no circumstances tolerate racial discrimination does not dis-
pel the notion that practice in hiring and firing often differed from aspiration. Moreover, disproportionately high black unemployment was an
unfortunate national phenomenon. As one study showed, by 1931 white
women in Wichita and Topeka had begun to displace blacks from their
traditional jobs as domestics and waiters.[73]

In October, a subgroup of the Governor's Committee produced a response to the initiatives proposed by organized labor that was, not surprisingly, steeped in economic orthodoxy. The people of Kansas, not the
state, had the responsibility of providing work for the unemployed, and
labor's departure from this maxim was viewed as a revolutionary proposal for a "semi-dole" system. Public works could only be provided
when funds were available, and heavily burdened taxpayers would not
tolerate a departure from fiscal rectitude. Raising revenue by increasing
the gasoline tax was superficially attractive, but it was a move that would
penalize both consumers and businesses, ultimately leading to a reduction in the federal funds, which matched part of the gasoline revenue. As
one would expect, the group added that it was impossible to reduce the
length of the working week without a pro rata reduction in pay. And fi-

72. Marchant had complained to Woodring that there were no black representatives
on the governor's original list of participants at this meeting. Woodring extended an
invitation to African Americans. Marchant to Woodring, August 27; Woodring to
Marchant, August 28, both 1931, File Governor's Employment Committee, Box 10,
Woodring Papers.

73. *Unemployment Status of Negroes: A Compilation of Facts and Figures Respecting Unemployment Amongst Negroes in One Hundred and Six Cities*, 20–21. There were also complaints that blacks were excluded from state highway work in Sedgwick County.
Marchant and Winston to Woodring, September 15, 1931, File Governor's Employment Committee, Box 10, Woodring Papers.

nally, in a particularly disingenuous statement, they opined that there was no need to issue scrip, as the county commissioners were obliged by law to take care of the destitute.[74] Thus the proposals put up by organized labor were systematically demolished, though it is interesting to note that while budgetary problems were seen as a formidable barrier to additional state expenditure, Woodring was prepared to call for further congressional spending at a time when the federal budget was moving into deficit.

The Governor's Committee that met on October 7 stressed the need to make the public aware that charity and employment creation were distinct and separate activities.[75] However, some members of the group also recognized that they might have to consider assuming a charitable role in a few communities if local effort was insufficient to combat real suffering. The committee heard an ominous warning from Beckman that the attitude of the unemployed was changing. They were now restless and becoming organized, and their distress was making them sympathetic to the siren calls of communist agitators. The specter of communism appeared frequently in meetings such as this, though no concrete information on the reality of the threat was ever provided. Beckman also conceded that it was "impossible to make an accurate survey of unemployment in Kansas," though information on the numbers seeking work was improving. Much of the discussion traveled over old territory; Kansas jobs to be reserved for Kansas residents and the need for a reduction in hours to spread employment were popular themes. However, trades unionists, while accepting the inevitability of pro rata decreases in pay as hours declined, voiced their opposition to a reduction in wage rates and made the valid point that many families could not survive on three-day wages.

One of the purposes of this meeting was to agree to a new and effective organizational structure that would be in place before the trials posed by the approaching winter materialized. The committee adopted a plan, proposed by Jay M. Besore, which called for the formal establishment of local employment committees. Mayors were given the task of appointing a suitable person who would act as chairman of an executive committee, which would normally include representatives of business, labor, and the professions. Members of the executive would chair one of a number of

74. "Consideration of Proposals by Organized Labor," n.d., Records of State Labor Department, Coal Industry Folder, Box 58. See also "Answer to Labor Proposal," n.d., Papers of Frank T. Stockton, Spencer Research Library, University of Kansas, File Governor's Committee on Employment, Box 28 (hereafter "Stockton Papers").

75. "Minutes of a Meeting of the Governor's Committee for Employment," October 7, 1931, Records of State Labor Department, Governor's Committee Meetings Folder, Box 58.

subcommittees dealing with registration, employment, and finance, and detailed instructions were sent to all mayors on how this model was to operate.[76] Each local committee was responsible for providing work for all unemployed bona fide residents, though the financial needs of applicants were supposed to be taken into account when allocating work. The aim was to obtain a full register of all those seeking employment; from that a calculation could be made of the costs of providing work for them. The finance subcommittee could then explore the ways in which the community could raise the funds required to put the unemployed to work. The employment committees were instructed to establish good working relationships with the county commissioners and the officers of charitable organizations. However, it was made clear that the registration desk of an employment committee must never be in the offices of a charitable organization. It was also stressed that payment for relief work should be in cash, not in kind, as grocery or fuel orders put the recipient on the path to charitable dependency. The function of local committees was to carry out placement and planning activities related to work, not to devise means of charitable relief.

The tasks given to these committees were formidable. They were supposed to plan, help fund, and implement public work projects; ensure that there was no decline in private employment; ensure that work was spread among the available workers; and try to ensure that local wage rates were maintained. That was not all. Other obligations included investigating some applicants to discover if a remedial loan was a solution to their problems, and taking steps to deport aliens, or to return transients to their place of settlement after an investigation of their circumstances by a member of the committee. Some communities, presumably the most urbanized, were encouraged to establish a subcommittee to thoroughly investigate the financial background of applicants for assistance, giving priority to the most needy. Add to this the chore of registering the unemployed and the time-consuming fundraising, all undertaken by volunteers with no training in social investigation, and one can see how difficult this scheme was to implement and what stresses it placed on participants as the depression dragged on.[77] Recognizing the difficulties these

76. "Plans for the Organization of Employment Committees in Kansas," Circular from Jay M. Besore, State Director for Kansas, U.S. Employment Service, n.d., File Labor Conference, Governor's Employment Committee, Oct. 1–Dec 1931, Box 11, Woodring Papers.

77. These tasks are taken from "The Governor's Committee for Employment," Report of Sub-Committee on Policy and Procedure, n.d., File Governor's Committee on Employment, Box 28, Stockton Papers.

amateurs faced, and the fact that no training was provided for them, the Governor's Committee circulated to all local committees a short bibliography of reading materials, which, it claimed, would provide details on the planning of community employment programs.[78] How easy these works were to acquire, or whether they were ever consulted, is not recorded.

A few communities had already taken steps to deal with hardship. For example, the Governor's Committee had embraced the Besore plan after it had heard that a similar operation seemed to be working effectively in place in Kansas City, Kansas.[79] However, the majority of the committee was hostile to the suggestion that its role should embrace charitable relief. It was agreed, for example, that a special group be appointed to consider the difficulties in southeast Kansas, but with reference only to employment. It is not surprising that Harry Darby's proposal of an Executive Committee was accepted without objection. There can be no doubt that decision making would be more effective in a smaller group, aided by recommendations from its own subcommittees, than within the unwieldy body that he had created. This would become especially important as sustained economic recovery remained elusive.

Woodring was in a particularly difficult position, for the festering resentment of taxpayers to their burden was becoming apparent. As prices fell, the real value of each tax dollar demanded increased, and when income and property values tumbled, the ability to pay taxes was affected. As early as 1930, fifty-three counties had budget deficits caused by declining property value; as a result, they were forced to reduce spending. The proportion of farm income demanded for taxes rose from 7 percent in 1928 to nearly 14 percent of a much-reduced income in 1932. More than three-quarters of local government finance came from property taxes, but property values were down at the very time when there was a strong social case for extra spending.[80] By mid-summer 1931, many counties were

78. "Circular No. 1. The Governor's Committee For Employment," November 16, 1931, File Governor's Committee on Employment, Box 28, Stockton Papers. Local committees were advised to consult Joanna C. Colcord, *Community Planning in Unemployment Emergencies: Recommendations Growing Out of Experience*, a number of booklets published by the Family Welfare Association, materials produced by the PECE, and, finally, a publication issued by the U.S. Chamber of Commerce.

79. The Citizens Employment Committee of Topeka had an Executive Committee of fifteen and seven subcommittees. In order to provide employment for needy citizens the committee anticipated it would need to raise more than $60,000 during the winter of 1931–32. G. L. Jordan (Chairman, Finance Committee) to Woodring, November 27, 1931, File Labor Conference, Box 11, Woodring Papers; *Topeka Journal*, November 24, 1931.

80. Harold Howe, *Local Government Finance in Kansas*, 1–17.

obliged to exercise leniency and suspend the time limit on tax payments; by 1933, nearly one-third of all farm land was tax delinquent.[81] As taxpayers had been forced to reduce their consumer spending, they expected all branches of government to be similarly parsimonious. There was growing support for the idea that by reducing the number of counties from 105 to 30 or 40, great savings could be made. Surely, it was argued, automobiles, paved roads, and telephones had made possible a more efficient and cheaper local government structure.[82] Republican Congressman-elect Harold McGugin struck a chord in the fall of 1931 when he advocated cutting by a quarter the salaries of all federal, state, and county employees. After all, as he pointed out, the pay of a county schoolteacher, who worked for only nine months during the year, was now the equivalent of thirty-four hundred bushels of wheat.[83]

Woodring was determined to stand for re-election in 1932 as a governor who cut taxes.[84] In this he was successful, but reducing wages and cutting the jobs of public sector workers served to further lower the demand for goods and services, thus adversely affecting employment and, ultimately, putting a strain on welfare services. In the short term, Woodring had little room to maneuver. In addition to taxpayer militancy, he faced a further obstacle, as borrowing by the state for general purposes, which included relief, was legally restricted. The Kansas constitution stipulated that the state could go into debt only with the approval of the legislature, and even then, borrowing outside general debt limits must not exceed $1 million.[85] However, the legislature would not convene until January 1933, so additional borrowing could not be considered until then, unless a special session was called. The counties and cities also had their taxing powers for relief proscribed by law, yet the demands on local government for assistance were remorselessly increasing. Attempts to raise additional revenue and make the tax burden more equitable by the introduction of a state income tax were pressing issues, but neither could be resolved quickly.[86] The state's fiscal structure was not designed to cope with a deep and lengthy depression.

81. Farm tax delinquency was a problem even in relatively prosperous times. In 1928 the figure for delinquent farm taxes stood at $2 million; by 1932 it had risen to $4.8 million. The problem was most acute in western Kansas. Harold Howe, "Tax Delinquency on Farm Real Estate in Kansas, 1928 To 1933," 1–3.

82. *New York Times*, September 27, 1931; Arthur Capper, "What Kansas Farmers Think," 54.

83. *New York Times*, September 13, 1931.

84. *Message of Governor Woodring to the Legislature of 1931* (Topeka, 1931): 4.

85. Earle K. Shawe, "An Analysis of the Legal Limitations on the Borrowing Powers of State Governments," 121–23, 126–27.

86. Kansas State Tax Commission, *Report of the Tax Commission to the Legislature, 1931*

In August 1931, PECE was replaced by POUR, and Walter S. Gifford, a committed believer in the efficacy of local effort, was appointed its director. The philosophies of POUR and PECE were identical. The aim was still to help states, counties, and communities cope with their own difficulties, and never to directly intervene, no matter how serious the problem.[87] In September, a POUR official wrote to the mayors of forty-five Kansas cities asking for details on the efforts being made to combat the effects of the depression. The twenty-four replies gave a picture of successful concerted effort and no indication that the problems were beyond local solution. Committees in Wichita, Topeka, and Coffeyville, for example, were busy registering their unemployed and raising funds to provide relief work for them.[88] It is hardly surprising that Washington believed that, with the possible exception of Crawford and Cherokee counties, conditions in Kansas did not give rise to concern.

In November 1931 a Kansas Coal for Kansans Committee was founded and a train hired to tour the state promoting local coal at the expense of out-of-state fuels.[89] At roughly the same time, members of the Governor's Committee visited Crawford and Cherokee counties, as, on a separate mission, did a representative of PECE, at the urging of William Allen White, the distinguished editor of the *Emporia Gazette*.[90] Governor's Committee representatives found that unemployment and short-time working were so serious in Cherokee County that merchants had cut off credit, forcing many of the destitute to live on bread and water. Children could not attend school because their parents could not provide footwear or clothing. The county's poor fund was in deficit, and the nearly two hundred families on relief could be given only $1.50 each week. Beckman, however, judged the situation in Crawford and Cherokee counties as serious but not critical, and he considered it manageable if the county and city commissioners functioned with greater efficiency.[91]

The PECE investigator also produced a report that described wide-

(Topeka, 1930): 5–9; Kansas Legislative Council, "Summary History of Kansas Finance," Research Report no. 60 (Topeka, October 1937): 28–30.

87. Romasco, *The Poverty of Abundance*, 162–66.

88. Circular from Conrad H. Mann, September 3, 1931, Office of Assistant Director, State Files Misc., Box 245, POUR, RG73, NA (hereafter "POUR"); Replies from cities in Files on City Unemployment Relief Committees, Box 248, POUR.

89. "Kansas Coal Train," *Kansas Labor and Industrial Bulletin* 1 (January 1932): 2.

90. White to Woodring, November 24, 1931, File Governor's Committee, Box 11, Woodring Papers. William Allen White (1868–1944), whose newspaper had supported the election of Herbert Hoover, was appointed by the president as the Kansas representative on the PECE Committee.

91. "Report of C. J. Beckham following four days survey on unemployment condi-

spread poverty and suffering. Visits to various parts of Crawford County confirmed that children were wrapped in newspapers during the winter months as their clothing was so inadequate. Men who had secured a little work took home food given to them by their workmates. Parent Teachers Associations provided school lunches, the Lions Club donated milk, the Elks paid for shoes, bakers gave one hundred loaves each day for distribution to the needy, and packing houses donated meat. The "liquor traffic has very evidently been the means of keeping most of these families alive. Positive evidence of this was available in many parts" and "farmers cannot leave home without their chickens and food being stolen" are quotations from the report which illustrate levels of suffering as acute as any experienced in the nation. The Crawford County poor budget was drastically overspent, and there was no trained social worker on whom private or public charities could call.

In Cherokee County, the Eagle-Picker Company had pumped water out of some abandoned lead mines so that men could dig out ore and sell it. The work was hazardous but, by the standards of the locality, financially worthwhile. Even at an early stage in the depression, many men had been out of work for three years and "suffering is severe. There is little evidence of care for those outside the villages." It seems clear from this account that neither the destitute nor the relief providers in Crawford or Cherokee counties could manage on their own meager resources. Indeed, William Allen White wired PECE headquarters asking for advice, as he was convinced that the acute problems confronting the poor in these counties was not confined to southeast Kansas.[92] However, in December Darby, Beckman, and Besore assured PECE representatives that Crawford County did not need outside assistance, as officials would soon be able to provide three days' work each week for the needy at $2.50 per day. According to Beckman, this sum would certainly keep rural families in a "very fine condition." Beckman believed that influential residents anxious to reduce taxes had put pressure on the county commissioners, who then became reluctant to petition the Tax Commission for the authority to issue warrants in order to raise more revenue. The situation changed once the commissioners agreed to take this step, from which point they became convinced that Crawford County had the resources to meet the relief demands placed on it.[93] In December, too, Woodring refused to sign a na-

tions in Crawford and Cherokee Counties," November 2, 1931, Coal Industry Committee Folder, Box 58, Records of State Labor Department.

92. Preliminary Report of Visit by Field Representative, (Nov. 1–5); White to Gifford, November 19, 1931, Box 245, POUR.

93. Report of Field Trip, December 11–19, 1931, Box 245, POUR.

tional petition organized by Governor Pinchot of Pennsylvania that called for Red Cross aid for soft coal districts. Woodring's view was that calling for Red Cross assistance would exaggerate the situation in southeast Kansas and hinder the work of the Governor's Committee, which was now receiving local cooperation. In any case, he added, "I am told that there will be no real suffering" in the region.[94]

A PECE field agent visiting Emporia, Newton, Wichita, McPherson, Salina, and Kansas City in November 1931 encountered contrasting views. Bankers, mayors, and those in secure employment expressed optimism. The unemployed, on the other hand, were depressed and sometimes rebellious. Urban communities were better organized to assist the unemployed, but judging the success of these efforts was difficult. In Emporia, for example, there was no agreement on the numbers unemployed, but in any case, of the either 310 or 360 who were registered, only 80 had secured relief work. Practically all the employed people in the city were donating one day's pay each month toward assisting the unemployed. Rural work relief presented particular difficulties. A road construction project organized in Ellsworth County gave work to about two hundred men, who could earn between $10-$12 each week, weather permitting. However, after deductions of $7.50 for board and travel the laborers had little left for their efforts. In all the cities surveyed, single men had so little chance of obtaining any relief work that they did not bother to register as unemployed. Many were sleeping rough and experiencing great hardship.[95]

Further meetings of the Governor's Committee took place on December 21, 1931 (Kansas City), February 3, 1932 (Wichita), March 5, 1932 (Topeka), and March 9, 1932 (Lawrence), but unfortunately the minutes do not seem to have survived. By this time, however, the executive and its subcommittees were doing much of the work.[96] On April 1, 1932, Woodring called a mass meeting at which twenty-five others joined the nineteen regular members of his committee. The account of this meeting provides an interesting insight into how Kansas communities were coping after three years of depression and how they would manage if the crisis continued.[97]

94. Woodring to Pinchot, December 2, 1931, File Governor's Committee, Box 11, Woodring Papers.

95. A. E. Howell, "Special Report on Unemployment Situation in Certain Cities Visited," November 20 and 21, 1931, Box 245, POUR.

96. Some subcommittee minutes can be found in File, Governor's Committee on Employment, Box 28, Stockton Papers.

97. "Meeting of the Governor's Committee for Employment," April 1, 1932, Statewide Committee Meeting Folder, Box 58, Records of the State Labor Department.

The heads of eight thousand families were out of work in Kansas City, Kansas, but only a few had been allocated work by a well-organized local employment committee. Nevertheless, the message was that the city could cope with its difficulties without external assistance. In Topeka, too, the Citizens Employment Committee registered the unemployed and organized relief work, but it could give men with dependents only two days' work each week at a daily rate of $3.20. The employed had responded to the call for funds to assist the less fortunate, and the committee paid men in cash to avoid the stigma of charity. However, in both Kansas City and Topeka, funds were running low and doubts being expressed whether it would be possible for local committees to finance their activities through another winter. The unemployed in Parsons, which had been hit badly by cuts in railroad jobs, made use of a soup kitchen. The city also established a committee of five men, whose identities were kept secret, to decide who would be chosen for the limited amount of work relief available.

Asa Messenger reported that the failure of banks and savings and loan institutions had made raising funds to assist the needy in Pittsburg especially difficult. A survey of the unemployed that had been undertaken, using mail carriers to collect the information, produced a total of 597 jobless, though given the method of collection not even Messenger was fully confident in its accuracy. Messenger was obsessed with the idea that claimants not entitled to relief might cheat their way to payments, or that the city would be flooded with transients who would try to claim assistance that should be for locals only, or that those entitled to relief might become dependent upon public assistance. Thus, not only were the names of the committee established to distribute relief kept secret, so were its objectives, as "we did not want to advertise and get everyone coming into our town." In order to avoid duplication and to test applicants' seriousness, a questionnaire was devised that "covered nearly every question you could think of and it was a pretty good size sheet of paper printed on both sides." Messenger was delighted that only 365 questionnaires were completed. Each applicant was then individually investigated to test the validity of his or her claim, and the investigator then made recommendations to another secret committee, which decided on the entitlement to relief. This process was designed to eradicate all but the most persistent, desperate, and educated. Those who were successful were paid in groceries and never in cash. The groceries were acquired by a Purchasing Committee, and "very few in town know who [*sic*] that purchasing committee is." Transients were compelled to chop wood before they got any assistance.

Asa Messenger also dismissed the unemployed in Girard as led by "a bunch of communists . . . who are going to ask for immediate cash relief."

"So far as Girard is concerned" he added, "I am not worried." However, Mrs. Minnie C. True, the Crawford County Red Cross representative, in revealing that her bankrupt local organization relied on monthly dona- tions of $1,000 from the national body so that her colleagues could assist the destitute in Arma, Frontenac, Arcadia, and Mulberry, provided the meeting with a clear indication that local effort was falling short of needs. Red Cross assistance was mostly for the provision of seed, allowing the needy to grow their own food.[98] W. B. Hayes of Atchison displayed the economic xenophobia that became all-too-common in the depression. To his fury, some out-of-state workers were recruited to construct a hospital in Leavenworth, leading him to call for "the elimination of foreign la- bor. . . . Are we going to let these foreigners, as we might term them, take this money back to Missouri with them?"

It was clear that efforts to combat the depression had absorbed a lot of volunteer hours. For example, charity football games and concerts were held, soup kitchens were organized, many employed gave up one day each month of their wages to help the less fortunate, and the police and fire departments in some cities adopted unemployed families.[99] The American Legion, the Kiwanis, the Elks, and the churches were heavily involved in fundraising and charity work. For example, in Iola the Elks Lodge supplied milk for school children and even provided shoes and clothing where teachers identified a need. However, in spite of all these efforts, unemployed heads of families could only be given a little work at pay so low that it had to be supplemented by charities. Much of it was no more than "make work"—menial wood chopping, street cleaning, or snow clearing. Moreover, there were real fears that some communities could not fund these efforts through another winter, as donors were un- willing, or unable, to keep up their contributions.[100] Many speakers ex- pressed fear of the dole, but there was also a fear of mob violence if more was not done.

A few key speakers articulated views they might have dismissed as heretical a year previously. Dean Frank T. Stockton asked how Kansas could sell its produce to other states if it refused to buy from them. He

98. In July 1932 the Salvation Army in Pittsburg reported that its 1931 drive fell short of what was needed, but since then the situation had worsened and the organization was unable to meet pledges it had made. Captain J. Davis to Minnie C. True, July 9, 1932, File Labor Conference, Box 11, Woodring Papers.

99. "Adoption of School Children Advocated by Mayor Cottman," *Wichita Eagle*, September 8, 1932.

100. In early 1932, a drive by Topeka's Citizens Employment Committee raised $26,000, 80 percent of which came from small-salaried people or wage earners. "Tope- ka Aids the Unemployed," *Kansas Labor and Industrial Bulletin*, 1 (February 1932): 3.

added his voice to commentators who had come to the conclusion that reliance upon charitable giving placed a disproportionate strain on lower income groups. The time had come to link fundraising with the ability to pay. Stockton also deflated the simplistic notions that many still held a means of defeating the depression. He explained that unemployment could not be eradicated by persuading each employer to add a few workers to the payroll, or by reducing everyone's hours of work. His solution was education for the unemployed to improve their skills, though a critic wanted to know how this would help the long-service railroad man who had just lost his job. Stockton also pointed out that although the Governor's Committee had tried to separate work relief from what it called charity, this was always an unrealistic distinction, since there was never sufficient created work to keep the needy away from relief offices. It was an additional misfortune that the provision of relief was so poorly organized. Samuel Wilson, manager of the State Chamber of Commerce, reminded his listeners that not all government expenditure was wasteful and that there was an unhealthy concern with balanced budgets. Governor Woodring noted that help offered to railroad companies by the Reconstruction Finance Corporation (RFC) was not called dole, so why should federal help for the unemployed carry that stigma? The loss of faith in traditional practice was not complete, but it was now extending beyond the confines of organized labor; there would be more departures from orthodoxy when the hardships of the third depression winter struck.

William Allen White gave the discouraging message that none of his colleagues in POUR expected an amelioration in the economy for at least another year. Unfortunately, desperate people would continue to rely on both public and private relief agencies, which were forced to cope with an increasingly unmanageable workload. At the conclusion of the meeting it was clear that few present were confident that their communities could raise the funds to cope with another winter. They had learned that the provision of work relief was costly, and that if the outcome was to benefit the public the projects must be carefully planned. Moreover, in spite of their efforts, many unemployed were dependent upon charitable relief, or the dreaded dole. The one positive idea to emerge from the meeting was that all the jobless should be encouraged to manage a relief garden, which would occupy them and provide food for the summer, and possibly the winter too.

An analysis of relief organization in Wyandotte County, the most urbanized in the state, illustrates the way in which the distributors and the recipients of relief struggled to come to terms with an unprecedented problem. Until the fall of 1932 three separate but uncoordinated agencies

provided relief in Wyandotte. The county played a significant role, as did the sixteen private agencies that made up the Community Chest, while the city spent only a small sum, principally on nurses and welfare officers. In 1932, the public welfare activities of the county were denounced as "an uncoordinated group of politico-welfare functions" that provided "often meager and inadequate" relief.[101] Part of the problem was that those appointing Poor Commissioners did not take into account the particular difficulties generated by the depression. The poor commissioner, who had neither experience nor training in social work practices, gave out fuel and grocery orders but did not try to determine the need for relief. Record keeping ranged from the inadequate to the nonexistent, but officials were given no clerical assistance.[102] Frequent changes in personnel appear to have been politically inspired rather than motivated by a search for the ideal officeholder. When, periodically, the commissioner ran out of funds, the relief office closed without notice, to the consternation of many applicants. Deficiencies in record keeping and a failure to liaise effectively with private charities led to a duplication of relief which resourceful mendicants could exploit to secure assistance from several sources. Alternatively, payments could even be made to the undeserving. In 1931, for example, a small number of monthly allowances for the disabled were never collected, perhaps because they were not needed.

County officials rightly complained that legal restrictions on the amount that could be raised for relief funding, combined with the fall in property values which had eroded the tax base, made their tasks especially difficult. By fiscal 1931, the county had levied to the full what was legally possible for the care of the destitute, and it was at the limit of its bonded indebtedness; however, as a result of pressure from the Tax Payers League, during the following year funding was reduced.[103] Like other counties, Wyandotte was forced to use funds that had been raised for bridge and roadwork maintenance to provide work relief. Any deficiency on the part of the county in caring for the destitute placed an extra burden on the private charities to which the unfortunate then turned. This

101. Bureau of Government Research, "Welfare (Poor Relief) Activities of Wyandotte County, Kansas"; *KERC Bulletin* 127, 571–75.

102. Bureau of Government Research, "Welfare (Poor Relief) Activities," 8–9; Report of Field Representative, January 16 and 24, 1932, Confidential report to Wyandotte County Commissioners, Office of Assistant Director, State Files Misc. (Kansas), RG73, NA.

103. Blake A. Williamson, County Counselor, Wyandotte Co., to Hon Clarence Waring, Chairman, Wyandotte Federal Relief Committee, Sept. 14, 1932, RFC Records Relating to the Emergency Relief to States, Kansas Loan 5 (Part 2), RG234, NA; Report of Field Representative, Nov. 1–5, 1931, Box 245, POUR.

was especially true for single applicants as county direct relief was targeted specifically toward families. The county's Employment Stabilization Committee had done what it could to provide work for the unemployed, but by 1932 the resources of public and private welfare providers were stretched to breaking point.

In 1932, private charities contributed just over 40 percent of Wyandotte County's total relief spending. The figure for both Sedgwick and Shawnee counties was similar.[104] In Wichita and Topeka, energetic campaigns effectively raised funds, and employment committees put (mostly) men to work. Sadly, the problem was too severe and too persistent for local generosity and concern to combat.[105] Organized private charities were generally to be found in the most urbanized counties; rural dwellers had scant support from this source.[106]

Washington Lends a Hand

Anticipating federal intervention, Woodring wired the mayors of eighty-eight cities on July 21, 1932, requesting information on the numbers of unemployed, how they would be cared for during the coming winter, and the funding that would be needed to provide work relief for them.[107] The governor received sixty-three responses. The mayors of Anthony, Belleville, Beloit, Kinsley, Marion, and Salina maintained that they were able to take care of their unemployed and did not request financial assistance. However, the vast majority believed that they needed help, though their responses were far from systematic. Some mayors provided no supporting evidence for their claims, others gave a not always precise estimate of the numbers unemployed, and another group concentrated on dependents, or families in need. Even though nine unhelpful respondents asked for an "indefinite" amount of aid, the total requested came to just over one million dollars, a sum that was almost identical to the amount spent by all private welfare agencies during 1932.[108]

On July 21, President Hoover signed the Emergency Relief and Con-

104. *KERC Bulletin* 127, 481–85, 491–95.

105. Peter Fearon, "Kansas Poor Relief," 157–59.

106. For an interesting account of problems in Finney County, see Pamela Riney-Kehrberg, "Hard Times, Hungry Years: Failure of the Poor Relief in Southwestern Kansas," 154–67.

107. *Under the Statehouse Dome. Our State Government. Radio Speeches of Governor Harry H. Woodring*, 7.

108. Labor Conference-Governor's Employment Committee, Federal Unemployment Relief Committee Folder, July 12–23, Box 11, Woodring Papers.

struction Act. In doing so he extended the scope of the RFC, which had been established earlier in the year to grant loans to railroads, banks, and other financial institutions. The new legislation provided $300 million, a not very generous amount, which could be loaned to the states for direct relief, and a sum of $1.5 billion to finance self-liquidating public works. In addition, a regional agricultural credit corporation was established in each of the twelve Federal Land Bank Districts to extend credit to farmers so that they would not be forced to sell their produce on a falling market.

A Self-Liquidating Division was created to oversee the funding of major public works projects, such as roads and bridges, which could recoup their costs by charging a toll. Unfortunately, the RFC created so many obstacles for potential borrowers, mainly because of its fear of potential default, that very few projects had got under way by the end of Hoover's presidency in March 1933.[109] It is interesting to note that the successor of the Self-Liquidating Division, the New Deal's Public Works Administration (PWA), was subject to the same criticism because of its failure to get its program operational quickly.

The Emergency Relief Division, which was to oversee the distribution of $300 million, was of much greater significance to Kansas. It was clear from the outset that as the claims would exceed the sum available, some system of rationing was needed, even though Congress had stipulated that no state should receive more than 15 percent of the total available. The rules under which the Emergency Relief Division operated were designed to ensure that federal aid would be a supplement to state effort, not a replacement for it: the responsibility for helping those in distress still remained with the states and the localities, not the federal government. National government had passed emergency legislation to supplement the state's private and public funds, but only where this was necessary. Indeed, need, not population numbers, was to be the criterion for distribution; public money could be used to put people to work, but on the basis of need, not merely of unemployment. The RFC advised states to propose worthwhile projects that would not otherwise have been undertaken but forbade the purchase of construction materials with federal money. Borrowers were constantly reminded that federal funds were loans and that repayment, with interest at 3 percent per annum, was scheduled to begin in fiscal 1935 as deductions from federal allotments for highway construction. The rules stipulated that state governors should make applications to the Emergency Relief Division, and each had to show that all

109. James Stuart Olson, *Herbert Hoover and the Reconstruction Finance Corporation, 1931–1933,* 77–79.

sources of revenue, including private charitable contributions, had been fully exploited in the fight to combat the depression and that these sources were now completely exhausted.[110] Only when that point had been reached could the plea for a federal loan be entertained.

On July 23, Woodring established the Kansas Federal Relief Committee (KFRC), with a membership of twelve. Dean E. Ackers, general manager of Kansas Power and Light Company, was appointed chairman, and John G. Stutz, who was loaned to the KFRC by the League of Kansas Municipalities for a charge of $100 per week, became executive secretary.[111] The committee's purpose was to administer, under the direction of the governor, funds received from the RFC for aid to the needy and the destitute. In order to create a new and effective administrative structure, the state was divided into eleven districts and one district each was assigned to a member of the KFRC. The KFRC appointed a County Federal Relief Committee (CFRC), with a minimum of three and a maximum of ten members, in each of the 105 counties. Each CFRC's role was to make applications to the governor for federal relief funds for its county and to administer the distribution of any funds granted. In addition, each was instructed to assist the regularly established poor relief agencies in the county.

The KFRC fully supported the philosophy of the RFC, which emphasized work relief rather than dole, had a commitment to relate relief to means-tested need, and also firmly adhered to the view that local communities should never shed their relief responsibilities.[112] Kansas retained a strong belief in self-help and wished to create a relief system that would help recipients support themselves as rapidly as possible. Soon after its formation, the State Committee concluded that local funds and private charitable contributions would be sufficient to take care of all the state's direct relief cases, and therefore that federal money would, except

110. *An Interpretation of the Relief Provisions of the Relief and Construction Acts of 1932. An Address Delivered by Hon. Atlee Pomerene*, 1–8.

111. Ackers graduated from the University of Kansas with a degree in engineering in 1917 before leaving for military service in France. His war service was recognized by the award of the Distinguished Service Cross and the Croix de Guerre. He later served on the Topeka Citizens' Employment Committee. Apart from Ackers and Stutz, the KFRC (later called the KERC) comprised Harry Darby, Jr., Homer Bastian (merchant and mayor, Atwood), Lee E. Goodrich (labor lawyer, Parsons), C. H. Humphreys (president, Barton Salt Company, Hutchinson), Walter P. Innes (merchant and president, Chamber of Commerce, Wichita), R. J. Laubengayer (publisher, *Salina Journal*, Salina), H. B. Mize (secretary, Blish, Mize & Spillman Hardware Co., Atchison), Clarence Nevins (merchant, Dodge City), E. L. Jenkins, (secretary of the Topeka Federation of Labor), and Ralph Snyder (president, State Farm Bureau, Manhattan), who resigned from the committee soon after it was formed.

112. *Topeka Capital*, July 30, 1932.

in very rare cases, only be used to fund work relief. Moreover, RFC money would never be used to cover administrative costs.

All County Committees were sent a copy of the detailed RFC instructions for making relief applications. These called for each CFRC to make a survey of the need for both direct and work relief and to record the information in a systematic manner. Each applicant for relief was to be subject to a full investigation by a properly trained or informed investigator, and this information was to be used to calculate the amount needed, from all sources, for direct and work relief for the remaining months of 1932. CFRCs would have access to information from all public and private relief agencies with details of the caseload and the amount spent each month on relief, as well as administration, since the beginning of 1931. Details of the poor fund levy and an estimate of all the funds that could be raised from public and private sources were demanded, as was information on any emergency actions contemplated before the end of 1931. This was a praiseworthy attempt to create a much-needed uniform system of record keeping and also to integrate the activities of many diverse public and private relief activities. However, the proposed schedule was too demanding for the recently formed CFRCs, especially as they had to act with great speed to enable Woodring to submit the state's application to the RFC in September. As a result of the need for urgency, a few counties, usually the most urbanized, provided their own registration forms for relief applicants, but the majority used different forms provided by the state Department of Labor. Moreover, the Red Cross, the Salvation Army, and volunteers from various citizens committees who were called on to help register applicants for relief failed to employ identical criteria.[113] This registration drive was an improvement on past practice, but it did not involve casework assessment and was limited to a rough count of numbers.

By September 15, completed applications for the period September 1 to December 31 had been dispatched by County Committees to the KFRC (Rice County alone failed to send a submission). They provide a fascinating snapshot of the depression's impact across the state.[114] Brown County was struggling with unemployment in Hiawatha and Horton caused by layoffs at the Rock Island Line workshops. In Greenwood County, low oil prices, bank failures, and bankruptcies among cattlemen had caused acute distress, as had low potato prices in Douglas County and general crop failure, together with delinquent taxes, in Decatur County. Hard

---

113. *KERC Bulletin* 127, 11; *Coffeyville Daily Journal,* November 2, 1932.
114. RFC, Records Relating to Emergency Relief to States, Kansas Loan File #5, Boxes 33–34, RG234, NA.

times in Dodge City, which had doubled its population during the 1920s, resulted in the construction of only one new dwelling in 1931. Many counties stressed tax-raising problems, unemployment seemed to be endemic wherever there were railroad repair shops, and drought appeared to be having an adverse impact on farms in some counties. The Johnson County application indicated that during the first four months of 1932, about one hundred men had been given two or three days' work in a county rock quarry. However, from early May, county funds were so badly depleted that their daily pay was reduced from $1.50 to just $1.00. The county had close to a thousand men in need of employment, and also many distressed farmers, but the levy for the poor fund was inadequate; in any case, the fund was already heavily overdrawn. Sedgwick County entered 1932 with a considerable deficit on its poor fund and the further handicap that additional revenue obtained under special statutes had been exhausted; as a result, the county was unable to care for the twenty-one hundred families who were calling for aid. Counties stressed the valiant efforts that citizens' groups, private charities, and public relief officials had made to care for their neighbors during these gloomy times, but the demands for assistance had grown and were still mounting while the means of delivering help could no longer be sustained.

The KFRC meticulously scrutinized the county submissions, a crucial examination as total claims were close to $4.3 million, far in excess of the $2.75 million that the state anticipated it would receive. It soon became clear that some CFRCs had either misunderstood the instructions that had been sent to them, or, possibly, their officials believed that a fanciful figure might be accepted, given the speed with which the operation was being conducted. The KFRC rigorously pruned most submissions. Cherokee County's application for $691,233 was reduced to $70,390, and that of Crawford County from $357,000 to $43,163. Meanwhile, Comanche, Ellsworth, Franklin, Graham, Jackson, McPherson, Nemaha, Stafford, Sumner, and Wabaunsee counties were judged to have sufficient resources to manage without RFC assistance. The committee, however, was prepared to raise bids if it seemed justified; Lincoln County, for example, had its modest application increased from $3,600 to $6,118. Shawnee, Sedgwick, and Wyandotte counties were allocated the sums they requested—$99,480 for the first named, and $100,000 for the others. The mistake most CFRCs made was to cost any work that could be done in their locality with relief labor and use that information to form their submission.[115] What the RFC required, however, was for relief to be restricted to those who were

115. Mindful of its failure to secure funds, Stafford County officials agreed that for

not merely unemployed but also in need, and then for the relief to be given according to the circumstances of each individual applicant. To conform to that request, each CFRC would have needed first-class information and a great deal of skill in using it. It is not surprising that the most professional submissions came from highly urbanized counties where the administration of relief was most sophisticated, and it is unlikely that more than a few CFRCs had been able to fully investigate all applicants for relief in the way suggested by the RFC, given the shortness of time and the shortage of personnel to undertake the task.

Kansas's application requesting $1,369,752 as supplemental emergency relief funds for ninety-four counties during the months of October, November, and December was mailed to the RFC on September 24. It included supporting details giving the relief requirements of every county, together with an assessment of the ability of each to meet the demands on it. The application also contained a description of the new administrative structure that had been created to gather information, and which would also be used to distribute its share of the RFC loan. Woodring's cover letter stressed that Kansas would employ federal funds for work relief on projects carefully selected to give the greatest public benefits. He also pointed out that the KFRC he had established was nonpolitical, though it had, in fact, a Democrat majority, as did the county committees whose members had to be approved by the KFRC itself. Kansas, Woodring went on, suffered from drought-induced crop failures in the west and unemployment in the east, greatly reducing the people's ability to continue supporting private charities and to pay their taxes. Information on the legal impediments that restricted the ability of the state and the counties to increase revenue for relief purposes, at least in the short term, was also included. The application sought relief for 46,039 families and 7,719 single persons, and only assistance from the RFC, the governor concluded, could keep many Kansans from "actual starvation and destitution."[116]

The RFC had to be satisfied that states had followed their published rules before a loan could be granted. The RFC directors received, from their staff members, an analysis of the Kansas submission which assessed the state's new relief administration, commented on economic conditions, and probed the constitutional provisions regarding tax and debt limita-

future investigations the word *unemployed* would be changed to *needy and destitute*. *Stafford County Courier,* October 29, 1932. Wyandotte County made its assessment on the basis of need, not on the cost of work relief. *Kansas City Kansan,* September 13, 1932.

116. Woodring to Directors of RFC, September 24, 1932, Records Relating to Emergency Relief to States, Box 33, RG234, NA.

tions.[117] The head of the Emergency Relief Division, Fred C. Croxton, also wired Roland Boynton, the Kansas attorney general, asking for confirmation that there were no funds that could be allocated for work relief in the State Treasury, and that none would become available during the next three months. Boynton gave the assurance that the RFC required.[118] The need for states to provide accurate and relevant data, and the determination of RFC staff to question it, opened up a new dimension in national welfare provision.

The RFC awarded Kansas $450,000 for the period October 1 to November 15. This sum financed 185,000 days of work relief on 450 projects, with single men receiving one day each week and those with dependents two or three days.[119] The RFC refused to lend for the full three months for which Kansas had budgeted, as it had no confidence in any state's ability to forecast its needs over such a long period. Moreover, lending over a shorter timescale would prevent complacency from replacing a firm commitment to relief effort at the local level, enable states to respond quickly to changing circumstances, and empower the RFC to retain greater control over the distribution of its resources. Indeed, when the RFC decided to loan Kansas a further $686,206 to cover the period from November 16 until the end of the year, the sum was advanced in two equal payments, the first immediately and the second on December 15. The November tranche included an allocation for five counties—Ellsworth, Graham, McPherson, Stafford, and Sumner—which had been excluded from the original submission but now, after a change of heart on the part of the KFRC and a favorable assessment by RFC officials, were considered deserving cases. Two other excluded counties, Franklin and Nemaha, had been received into the fold in early November. The RFC congratulated the KFRC on the manner in which it proposed to distribute federal funds.[120]

Kansas received $233,546 less than it requested for the last three months of 1932 even though, as the RFC conceded, the state's application was based on a minimum allocation for each recipient. A further disadvantage

117. Berth Nienberg to Directors, Re Application of Honorable Harry Hines Woodring, n.d.; R.M. Anderson to Directors, Constitutional Provisions Regarding Taxation and Debt Limitations of the State of Kansas, October 24, 1932, Records Relating to Emergency Relief to States, Box 33, RG234, NA.

118. Boynton to Croxton, October 1, 1932, RFC Record relating to the Emergency Relief to States (Kansas), Box 32, Approved State Loan Corresp., File July 18, 1932–March 31, 1933, Part 1, RG234, NA.

119. Croxton to the Directors, Recommendation, November 11, 1932, Approved State Loan Correspondence, File July 18, 1932–March 31, 1933, Part 1, RG234, NA.

120. J. H. Jones to Stutz, October 20, 1932, Approved State Loan Correspondence, File July 18, 1932–March 31, 1933, Part 1, RG234, NA; *KERC Bulletin* 127, 10–12.

was that $311,000 had been deducted by the Kansas Emergency Relief Committee (KERC) from its original submission to take account of a federal highway grant that would be used to support relief work on roads.[121] Unfortunately, by November the weather was so severe that roadwork was virtually impossible, and the favorable impact of this award could not be fully exploited. It is legitimate to complain that the congressional allocation for emergency relief was miserly, that the states had to accumulate debts in order to access the funds, that the RFC was more concerned with borrowers' ability to repay what they borrowed than with the implementation of good social work practice, and that the commitment to local relief was disingenuous.[122] If, however, the glass is considered as half full rather than half empty, it is reasonable to concentrate on the fact that during a crucial three-month period, more than one million dollars flowed from Washington to Kansas. This not inconsiderable sum was virtually identical to the amount distributed by the state's private charities during the whole of 1932.

The KFRC responded positively to the stimulus provided by the RFC. CFRCs were encouraged to sponsor work projects, and they were given details of what was expected from approved work relief schemes. The general advice was that projects should be located close to the homes of those employed on them and that expenditure on materials should be kept to a minimum. All work relief proposals had to be fully described to the KFRC and required an affidavit from the sponsor, who would assume full responsibility for the project. Details concerning the hours worked and a signed receipt acknowledging payment had to be submitted to the KFRC.[123] The imposition of administrative uniformity and a commitment to work relief became increasingly evident. In Kansas, RFC loans were used exclusively to pay work relief wages; work on projects for any individual was limited to no more than thirty hours in any week. Unemployables remained the responsibility of the counties, as did the needy who were fit for work but unable to secure a place on an RFC-funded project. The counties also supplemented the wages of men on work relief projects if they were still unable to support their families.

Spearheading the drive toward administrative efficiency was the executive secretary of the KFRC, John Godfrey Stutz, who played a leading

---

121. All these figures are taken from RFC files, but they differ slightly from those presented in *KERC Bulletin* 127, 10–11. In this publication an aggregate of $1,149,830 is reported compared to the RFC figure of $1,392,523. In addition, the KERC account lists 96 counties in receipt of aid; the RFC figure is 101 by the end of 1932.

122. See, for example, Edith Abbott, "The Failure of Local Relief," 348–50.

123. *KFRC Bulletin* No. 3A, October 1932.

role creating a first-class welfare service in Kansas. Stutz was born in 1893 in a dugout sod house in Ness County, about five miles from Utica. He attended the Common School in the county of his birth, graduating from the eighth grade in 1909. Stutz then secured his high school diploma from Kansas State Agricultural College in Manhattan before entering the University of Kansas in 1916. However, his studies were soon interrupted by service in the U.S. Army, where he reached the rank of first lieutenant. On resigning his commission, Stutz resumed his studies but switched to the University of Chicago, graduating in political science and sociology in 1920. During the following year he married fellow graduate Gertrude Edith Griffin. Their marriage was a long and happy one. John Stutz died in December 1996 at the age of 102; Gertrude died a few weeks later, aged 97 years.

Immediately after graduation the former Kansas farm boy became executive director of the League of Kansas Municipalities and editor of the *Kansas Government Journal.* In 1924 Stutz convened a meeting, held in Lawrence, with nine other state league directors to explore the means by which they could keep each other informed about best practice in municipal government. This meeting led to the foundation of the American Municipal Association, and Stutz served as the organization's executive secretary between 1924 and 1931. During the following year, the AMA moved to permanent headquarters in Chicago and hired its first full-time executive secretary. In 1964 the AMA became the National League of Cities. Between 1922 and 1929 Stutz also acted as the executive director of the International City Managers Association and editor of the organization's journal, *Public Management.* Stutz even found time in what must have been a hectic schedule to teach municipal government and administration at the University of Kansas.

During the first decade of his professional life Stutz's talents became widely recognized, and he built a national reputation among fellow professionals in city management. It is no surprise that he was also heavily involved in local politics, becoming, in 1932, a member of the executive council of the Douglas County Republican Committee. Although Stutz maintained that he ceased to play an active political role after the elections of 1932, local and national Democrats were never confident that his allegiance to the Party of Lincoln was fully subdued.

Unusual for American municipal managers, John Stutz considered international links of great value. In 1925 he traveled to Paris as the American representative to the Third International Congress of Cities. He was the U.S. representative at the Fourth International Congress held in Seville, Spain, in 1929 and at the Fifth held in London in 1932. His com-

mitment to these meetings continued throughout the 1930s. John Stutz was clearly a highly intelligent man of great energy, wide vision, and a commitment to excellence in public service. As a young man he quickly built up a national and international reputation in his professional field. Unfortunately, although the Stutz Papers deposited at the Spencer Research Library at the University of Kansas contain valuable information on the administration of relief during the depression, they contain virtually no personal information. Much of Stutz's character becomes evident through the observations of contemporaries, but an intimate portrait of the man who played such a vital role in building up one of the most respected relief administrations in the nation is not possible. Perhaps this is appropriate for an individual who saw himself as a civil servant, an administrator whose job it was to provide first-class advice and rigorously implement rules, rather than occupy the center stage.[124]

In August 1932, Dean Ackers wrote to Stutz saying that they must emphasize to all CFRCs that Kansas would only receive federal money if it was clear that the state, and its local political subdivisions, had done their jobs effectively.[125] This was a perceptive comment, but Stutz needed no prompting. His intelligence, training, and determination to impose high professional standards for relief administration on Kansas had already begun. He recognized that if, as was intended, all applicants for relief were to be interviewed and questioned about their income; the extent of their property ownership; their employment history; their previous record of relief; the details of any assistance from churches, lodges, relief agencies, or relatives; the amount of food the family had conserved for the winter; and the numbers of chickens and livestock kept, then the appointment of experienced investigators must be a priority. He also saw a pressing need to provide training, which would enable some of the state's enthusiastic welfare helpers to become skilled in the arts and science of social work. Persistent pressure on the counties was vital to compel them to deliver the high relief standards that Kansas had set as quickly as possible. To bring about this revolution, fundamental changes in the administration of the state's antiquated poor relief system was inescapable, and a catalyst for that would soon be provided with the publication, in January 1933, of the highly critical *Report of the Public Welfare Temporary Commission.*

In November 1932, Woodring faced the electorate. He had effected far-reaching economies by eliminating public jobs, reducing salaries, and cut-

124. Randy Arndt, "NLC Founder, John Stutz, Passes Century Mark," 20–21.
125. Ackers to Stutz, August 12, 1932, RH 327:1:1, Papers of John G. Stutz, Kansas Collection, Spencer Research Library, University of Kansas (hereafter "Stutz Papers").

ting back on the funding of state institutions and construction projects.[126] Indeed, he claimed that the only way to reduce taxes was to reduce expenditure, and his proud boast was that he was the only governor of Kansas who had spent less than the amount appropriated by the legislature.[127] Woodring's parsimony with public money won him support, but, unfortunately, his retrenchment also increased unemployment and lowered the demand for goods and services in Kansas. If the provision of leadership in the fight against the ravages of the depression was the key to gubernatorial distinction, Woodring's efforts must be dismissed as feeble. When addressing meetings of the Governor's Committee for Employment he was quick to concede that he had no plan for dealing with the emergency, and he certainly never supported ideas that might compromise his tax-reduction drive. On the other hand, he actively pursued the possibility of attracting federal money. Woodring always agreed wholeheartedly with correspondents who believed that dismissing women, "who did not need jobs," would somehow resolve the male unemployment problem.[128] Unfortunately many men and women, too, who were attracted to simple solutions seized on this false notion.

However, Woodring's economy drive was not sufficiently attractive to the electorate for him to retain the Governor's Mansion. In an election complicated by the strong performance of a bizarre Independent candidate, John R. Brinkley, the Republican Alfred Mossman Landon emerged victorious.[129] A rival tax cutter and staunch critic of state spending, Landon triumphed at a time when the Republicans, from Hoover downward, were feeling the electorate's wrath. In Topeka, a Republican governor would have to strike up a working relationship with a new national Democrat regime, but not until Franklin Delano Roosevelt took the presidential oath of office in March 1933.

126. The budget balancing was made possible without further reductions in expenditure by the grant of an additional $1.25 million in federal highway funding to create work for the unemployed. In total the federal government made $4.5 million available to Kansas for spending on highways, and the state was no longer obliged to find matching funding. *Kansas State Budget for the Biennium, 1934–1935,* Transmitted to the Legislature of 1933 by Harry H. Woodring, Governor (Topeka, 1933); Clarence J. Hein and James T. McDonald, *Federal Grants-In-Aid In Kansas.*

127. James T. Patterson, *The New Deal and the States: Federalism in Transition,* 39; Keith D. McFarland, *Harry H. Woodring: A Political Biography of F. D. R.'s Controversial Secretary of War,* 39–41, 54–5, 71; *Topeka Journal,* September 22, 1932.

128. Woodring to Fred Schmidt, July 22, 1931; Mr. Darr to Woodring, June 23, 1931. Darr urged the governor to help get the "DAMN PARASITIC WOMEN out of business." File Commission of Labor and Industry, June 1–December 31, 1931, Box 10, Woodring Papers.

129. Socolofsky, *Kansas Governors,* 172–74.

2

Kansas Republicans Welcome New Deal Funding

When Topeka's Alf Landon toasted his gubernatorial victory on November 8, 1932, Kansas was already struggling to create a welfare system that on the one hand could cope with continuing deprivation and on the other would also enable the state to capitalize on the federal funding that had just become available. Prior to his inauguration as governor, Landon wired Fred C. Croxton at the RFC informing him that he intended to retain in full the KFRC appointed by his Democrat predecessor. Landon's retention of a committee with a Democrat majority was later to prove a powerful weapon that was effectively used in deflecting the criticisms of his political opponents. There is, however, no evidence that Landon was pursuing a subtle, long-term political objective, and it is much more likely that he believed that it would be convenient for the newly appointed body to continue, unless there was firm evidence that it could not function effectively. The governor also stated that he would urge the state legislature, due to convene in early January 1933, to find some means of raising additional revenue for relief purposes.[1]

The provision of adequate relief was posing a serious problem as the country endured the fourth winter of the depression. Topeka's Citizens Employment Committee announced that its coffers were so depleted that married men with children could be given only four days' work relief every three weeks, at a daily wage of $2.50. RFC funds were close to exhaustion, and the committee implored fellow residents to contribute to a

1. Landon to Croxton, December 28, 1932, RFC Records, Kansas Correspondence/ Loan File #5 (part 1), RG234, NA.

drive that aimed to raise $75,000 to support the nearly 4,000 men and 1,300 women who had registered for work. However, attracting donations was a struggle, and after a month's strenuous effort the drive was still $25,000 short of its target. According to the *Topeka Daily Capital*, "relief of the poor is one of the most pressing problems confronting the present session of the Legislature." Most of the state's cities and counties had exhausted their poor funds, and many bills were now pending to enable some counties to issue bonds to cover indebtedness incurred in extending help to the needy and the unemployed.[2]

The Legislature at Work

In his lengthy message to the legislature, Landon emphasized the need for economy in government, and in doing so he reflected the views of his Kansas electorate. Hard-pressed taxpayers wanted restraint from their representatives, not expensive panaceas. There was strong support for the view that the public sector should not be protected from the forces that had assaulted the rest of the nation. Anticipating President Roosevelt's early economy drive, the new governor made it clear that pay cuts, including his own salary, and job rationalization among state employees were priorities for his administration. Landon also stressed the need for the state's fiscal burden, heavily dependent upon the taxation of property, to be both lightened and made more equitable. Like many governors, he could not fail to emphasize the seriousness of farm mortgage debt and the mounting threat of foreclosure. Nor could he ignore the parilous situation of some Kansas banks, which were closely tied to the fortunes of beleaguered farm communities. Landon gave the legislature, which had a small Republican majority in both houses, not only a clear account of the difficulties ahead but also suggestions for a way forward. He advocated the adoption of a state income tax, which the electorate had just approved, an emergency relief tax, the introduction of a uniform accounting system, and, through his support for a "cash basis" law, balanced budgets for all spending units.[3] However, during his election campaign Landon had been careful to reassure the needy that all citizens who were entitled to relief would receive it.[4]

When the legislature rose on March 24, Landon was satisfied with the

---

2. *Topeka Daily Capital*, January 3, 19, 20, 29, 1933; February 5, 10, 1933.

3. *Message of Governor Alf M. Landon to the Legislature of 1933* (Topeka, 1933): 4–5; *Message of Alf M. Landon, Governor of Kansas, to the Special Session of the Legislature of 1933* (Topeka, 1933): 1, 4–6.

4. *Kansas City Times*, September 27, 1932.

outcome. A state income tax, which progressively took between 1 and 4 percent of net personal income and 2 percent of net corporate income, had become law and would begin contributing to the budget in 1934. With the adoption of income tax, the state's tax base could be further diversified while ensuring a much closer link with an ability to pay. The introduction of an income tax also signaled a marked shift away from the traditional reliance on property tax, a move which was assisted by revenue from the motor carriers (ton) mileage tax, the cigarette tax, and the more conscientious collection of the gasoline tax.[5] As a result, the general property tax, which had contributed 72 percent of state revenue between 1920 and 1929, made a contribution of only 54 percent between 1930 and 1937.[6] Local government, however, still remained heavily reliant on the property tax.

Landon recognized the need for federal funds to supplement local relief efforts, and he advised that for a two-year period, counties should be able to levy an Emergency Relief Tax if the county commissioners could persuade the State Tax Commission that there was a need for it. These funds could be used for relief work only. Landon believed that without this additional revenue, the state would not be entitled to its full share of federal funds.[7] The governor also urged that the *Budget Law*, which the legislature had adopted in 1931, be strengthened. This required cities and a number of other taxing units to prepare their budgets so that the source of funding and the planned spending was transparent. After the publication of the budget, taxpayers were able to challenge officials at a public meeting. Landon wanted this practice extended to all spending units as he was convinced that the discipline it imposed would reduce public expenditure. Landon also attacked the legal limitations designed to restrict tax levies on the grounds that they were far too high and encouraged officials to tax to the maximum. By passing the Tax Limitation Act, the legislature enabled the state to set an example of restraint to other taxing units.

Continuing his drive to reduce expenditure, Landon confronted taxing units that consistently overspent their budgets, or used tax funds that had been raised for one purpose but were later dedicated to an entirely different activity. The governor was determined to restrict spending, moderate

5. Glenn W. Fisher, *The Worst Tax? A History of the Property Tax in America,* 148–49, 159–60.

6. For changes in state tax policies see Harold Howe, "Local Government Finance in Kansas"; *Summary History of Kansas Finance* (Topeka: Research Report Publication No. 60, Kansas Legislative Council, October 1937); Peter Fearon, "Taxation, Spending, and Budgets: Public Finance in Kansas during the Great Depression," 233–37.

7. *Message of the Governor,* 10–11.

the creation of debt, and control financial flexibility for every taxing unit. At his urging the legislature passed the Cash Basis Law, which forced county commissioners and all other taxing units to limit their spending to no more than the funds that were available during the current financial year. This was the crucial piece of legislation in Landon's fight for the control of public spending, and after its adoption it became virtually impossible for taxing units to exceed their budgets.[8] Public officers were aware that if the provisions of the Cash Basis Law were violated they could be removed from office. By enhancing the ability to increase revenue and by strictly controlling spending throughout the state, Landon laid the foundations for his reputation as a budget balancer.[9] However, some local taxing units, still heavily dependent on property taxes for revenue, found that the imposition of the Cash Basis Law compromised their ability to adequately fund relief. Although Landon is closely associated with the Cash Basis Law, which was soon adopted by other states, the architect of the legislation and one of its most powerful advocates was John Stutz.[10]

The legislature also extended the Kansas Moratorium Law. For six months after March 4, 1933, the foreclosure of mortgages was forbidden, and the governor was given the authority to extend the restriction for a further six months if the situation had not materially improved.[11] This action gave distressed farmers an important breathing space while supportive national programs could be introduced. It was also significant in helping to keep farmers on their land and off the relief rolls.

Landon's determination to cut state and local payrolls gained public support, but unfortunately where expenditure cuts involved job losses, the number of those searching—often fruitlessly—for scarce jobs or for relief increased. The legislature had, however, radically changed the financial parameters within which all taxing units operated. Cities and other governmental units were forbidden to create indebtedness, unless unencumbered money was available in the appropriate fund to discharge the debt. All local taxing units were required to publish their budget plans and to live within them. Early in his office as governor, Landon had set out his stall as a fiscal modernizer and a budget balancer.[12]

---

8. Alfred M. Landon, *America at the Crossroads*, 61–63.
9. Morton Taylor, "Budget-Balancer Landon," 272–74.
10. Randy Arndt, "NCL Founder, John Stutz, Passes Century Mark," 21.
11. Francis W. Schruben, *Kansas in Turmoil, 1930–1936*, 107.
12. *New York Times*, July 7, 1935.

Banks in Crisis

While the legislators were in session, a dramatic banking crisis developed. State Bank Commissioner H. W. Koenke advised Landon that if Kansas was to avoid declaring a bank holiday, which many other governors had been forced to introduce, legislation was urgently needed to limit depositors' withdrawals. His suggestion of a 5 percent limit did not receive the immediate support of the directors of the State Banking Association. However, on receiving news of an impending bank closure in Kansas City, Missouri, Kansas bankers quickly shifted direction. They threw their weight behind Koenke's proposal and rushed emergency legislation through the legislature limiting depositor withdrawals to 5 percent.[13] On March 4, all Kansas banks created new accounts for their depositors in which they placed 5 percent of each old account, the new limit for withdrawals. New deposits were not bound by this restrictive ruling and could be paid in full on demand.[14]

No sooner had limitations on deposit withdrawal been introduced than Landon received an urgent message from the comptroller of the currency requesting that he close all Kansas banks as part of a national bank holiday. Landon complied, and on March 6 Roosevelt signed the proclamation that declared a moratorium on all banking operations in the U.S. Kansas banks, along with those in the rest of the nation, shut their doors until March 13, when twenty-eight Kansas institutions opened for business as part of the first stage of a phased reopening of all sound banks in the country. It was a tribute to the faith that depositors had in their new president that, after a considerable period without recourse to their funds, on the first day that they were open for business Topeka bankers reported lines of customers making very heavy deposits and only a few making light withdrawals. Indeed, customers making even the most modest withdrawals felt the need to offer profuse apologies to the tellers who gave them their cash. Many reacted almost as if they feared the accusation that their actions were disloyal and therefore contrary to the national interest.[15] It was clear, however, that the fear of bank failure had dissipated and confidence in banks in Kansas and, indeed, those across the nation had returned.

One reason depositors renewed their trust in the banking sector was the assurance given to them during the bank holiday that only those institu-

13. Donald R. McCoy, *Landon of Kansas*, 125–26.
14. *Topeka Capital*, March 4, 1933.
15. *Topeka Capital* and *Topeka Journal*, both March 14, 1933.

tions that had satisfied the scrutiny of experienced examiners would be permitted to reopen. Following the national bank holiday, sixteen Kansas banks remained closed pending the completion of a reorganization of their liabilities, and twenty-five were obliged to retain strict limits on withdrawals. Of these forty-one institutions, fifteen could not be saved and were eventually liquidated, seven were merged with other banks, and eighteen were reorganized and reopened. Depositors in the failed institutions waited anxiously as the liquidation process ran its course. The majority of them would only receive a return of somewhere between 30 to 90 cents on each dollar deposited.[16]

After March 1933 Kansas banking was relatively stable.[17] Once the fear of mass withdrawals had subsided, the key issue facing Kansas bankers and politicians was the concern that national legislation might promote branch banking and penalize the system of unit banks to which Kansas was fully committed. A significant feature of the Banking Act of 1933 was the creation of the Federal Deposit Insurance Corporation (FDIC), which was designed to give protection to depositors and thus to prevent the panic withdrawals that had been so demoralizing during the worst years of the depression. Although there was support in Kansas for a deposit insurance scheme, there was also great unease that membership of the FDIC would only be open to banks that were sufficiently large to join the Federal Reserve System.[18] Informed Kansas opinion remained steadfastly loyal to small, independent banks, which were viewed as an essential part of thriving rural communities and sympathetic to the needs of farmers. There was rejoicing among the state's bankers when this rule was eventually abandoned in 1939.

The Attachment to Self-Help

During the winter of 1932–33, as the nation waited for Hoover to quit the White House and the newly elected president to move in, Governor Landon encouraged the search for self-help initiatives begun under his predecessor. A paper destined for presentation to the governor's Com-

16. Letter of Transmittal from State Bank Commissioner, September 1, 1934, *22nd Biennial Report of Bank Commissioner*, 3.

17. Board of Governors of the Federal Reserve System, *Banking and Monetary Statistics, 1914–41*, Tables 8, 72, 80, 81, 82.

18. Many members of the Roosevelt administration and the managers of large banks did not support the introduction of deposit insurance. Charles W. Calomiris and Eugene N. White, "The Origins of Federal Deposit Insurance," 145–78.

mittee on Self-Help Enterprises analyzed the current relationship between agriculture and industry in Kansas. Its authors concluded that it would be folly to recommend a "back to the land" policy as a permanent solution to the nation's unemployment ills for those who lacked experience as farm operators. However, the cultivation of planned gardens as a means of agricultural rehabilitation by the unemployed had considerable appeal. A half-acre garden could be managed without the use of power machinery and would supply a family of five with basic foodstuffs for a year, if they had been instructed in canning skills. Larger holdings would enable families to keep poultry, some hogs, and perhaps even a cow. The paper urged that vacant lots in urban areas should be assigned to gardeners who would be advised on suitable techniques by county agents and extension workers. The committee, which accepted this suggestion, observed that as approximately half of Topeka's unemployed had farm experience, many urban jobless men possessed agricultural skills that could be beneficially harnessed.

A much bolder suggestion was that a number of families not currently engaged in farming should be placed on small tracts of land so that they could eventually achieve economic independence. The notion of small-tract or part-time farming won support because it was viewed as a means of lessening risk for the economically vulnerable by encouraging the diversification of employment. A flexible mix between agriculture and industry seemed suited to the new economic uncertainty facing many Americans, whose recent experience had led to the conclusion that full-time non-farm employment, though desirable, was an unrealistic goal. However, those moving on to small tracts would require assistance to meet start-up costs, which were calculated in the order of $1,000–1,500, as well as long-term practical support and advice. Recognizing that a commitment to small-tract farming at a time of agricultural surpluses might arouse opposition, the proposers made it clear that their aim was to encourage farming as a supplementary activity in order to help families who were unable to cope with urban crises. The tracts would be located close to urban centers that, hopefully, would provide some non-farm work, and as the holdings would be small there should be no surplus for the family to market. In the longer run, when these resettled families achieved their economic independence, they would be removed from the relief rolls and their extra spending power would benefit the whole farm sector.

Another popular element in the self-help equation was barter. A shortage of cash and credit had encouraged the adoption of barter in various parts of the state. Farmers with surplus butter, eggs, or cream would exchange these goods for groceries or services, although unsuccessful at-

tempts had been made to organize barter transaction in the cities of Fredonia and Topeka. Enthusiastic members of the Committee on Self-Help projects advocated the creation of local bodies and clearing houses to promote barter, as well as the use of newspaper "swap columns" to provide fuller information to potential participants. A related plan to promote the regional exchanges of farm commodities caught Kansans' imagination for a short while.[19]

With the exception of relief gardens, none of the proposals eagerly embraced by the Committee on Self-Help had a lasting impact in the form in which they were suggested. Some of the initiatives—for example, the emphasis on the benefits to the unemployed from the settlement of families on tracts of land—were either taken over by the New Deal or the potential beneficiaries were never as enthusiastic as the original proponents had expected. New Deal initiatives also injected sufficient cash into the state's economy to render irrelevant the notion that the creation of a barter-based society had a useful future. Nevertheless, it is interesting to see that some of these local initiatives anticipated national developments, and, as became apparent, the local early start usually provided a firm foundation for quick progress once national programs were inaugurated.

On the other hand, the promotion of relief gardens figured largely in the state's relief efforts. By the end of 1933 more than twelve thousand garden plots had been developed in backyards or on vacant land, a number that would increase to more than fifteen thousand a year later. Relief clients had their budgets increased so that they could receive free garden seeds, but only after the family head had filed a subsistence garden project that had been approved by the county agricultural agent. All participating relief families were expected to involve themselves in educational programs offering instruction on cultivation and the techniques of canning and preserving food. The relief administration believed that the gardens would not only enable families to provide food for themselves, but also improve morale and encourage thrift. Boards of county commissioners cooperated with county agricultural agents to promote the advantages of domestic cultivation.[20]

19. The information on self-help comes from the papers of Frank T. Stockton who was, in 1933, dean of the School of Business at the University of Kansas and heavily involved in a number of state committees. "The Relation of Kansas Agriculture to the Unemployment Situation," n.d.; "Small Tract Farming as a Possible Means of Self-Help," n.d.; Committee on Self-Help Projects in Kansas, Minutes of Meeting, June 17, 1933; Meeting June 24, 1933; Stockton, Grimes and Wilson to Landon, July 5, 1933; Stockton to John Stutz, August 30, 1933; Sub Committee on Barter Exchange, Reports 2, 3, Box 28, File Kansas Self-Help, Stockton Papers.
20. *KERC Bulletin* 127, 28–31; *KERC Bulletin* 289, 753–54.

The Legislature and Welfare Reform

State legislators were aware that if Kansas were to continue receiving all the federal relief funds to which it was entitled, significant changes in the poor laws would be necessary. The need to draw up accurate applications for federal assistance had exposed serious deficiencies in many relief administrations. The most pressing problem in Kansas, however, was how to generate additional public funding to help the growing number of relief applicants whose resources were totally depleted. In January 1933, the total state caseload reached 63,547 resident families, 6,081 single individuals, and 9,666 transients. This represented a disturbing seven-fold increase over a six-month period.[21]

The legislature directly addressed the welfare issue during its regular session, but lawmakers dealt with some unfinished business during a special session in October and November. In a detailed letter to Fred C. Croxton at the RFC in February 1933, Landon stressed the significance of the proposed welfare changes then before the legislators. They would, he wrote, authorize the counties to make an emergency levy for poor relief, which would enable each to generate up to three times the amount previously thought sufficient to deal with the crisis. Moreover, the counties would also be able to issue poor relief bonds up to the same amount authorized for the tax increases. Over the three-year period that this emergency legislation would be in force, Landon envisaged that an additional $3 million would be added to the $1.7 million currently raised for poor relief. Another aim of the legislation was to strengthen the powers of boards of county commissioners and also to employ only qualified officials in the administration of relief throughout the state.[22] A crucial point was that the proposed legal changes would enable state and local government to take full advantage of federal relief programs and to address the administrative deficiencies that made the delivery of a modern welfare service virtually impossible.

The legislation to which Landon referred transformed the administration of poor relief in Kansas. The new law retained the county as the unit of responsibility for the administration of relief but stipulated that every county had to employ a "properly qualified" poor commissioner. Poor commissioners would have to demonstrate their knowledge of the principles and practices widely accepted by social workers as being the key

21. *KERC Bulletin* 127, 12.
22. Landon to Croxton, February 15, 1933, RFC Records, Kansas Correspondence/Loan File #5, RG234, NA. This letter accompanied the state's request for additional RFC funds.

elements in modern welfare administration. The maximum annual pay for poor commissioners was set at $1,500, and for the first time they were permitted to employ assistants who could be paid up to $50 per month. However, the salary limitations imposed on poor commissioners and their assistants by a suspicious legislature were too low and seriously limited the possibility of attracting top-quality candidates. It is indeed curious that the new salary maximum was less than the $2,100 established for poor commissioners under the old legislation. Generous local funding, and the willingness of the KFRC to supplement pay, was necessary to make Kansas salaries competitive.

Each poor commissioner was required to operate within a more centralized system. The KFRC prescribed standard forms for registering relief applicants, recording financial information, relief budgeting, and entering information on the amount of relief given. All public agencies in receipt of taxpayers' money and giving a poor relief service were obliged to register with the poor commissioner and to provide information at regular intervals on official cards. The aim was to impose the best administrative practice upon counties and in so doing to avoid duplication in the granting of relief. It is important to stress that Kansas had seized the initiative for welfare reform and administrative reorganization before the Federal Emergency Relief Administration (FERA) sought to impose minimum standards upon the states. At an early stage, state administrators had seen the advantage of a uniform system of poor relief. They also knew that the insistence upon relevant qualifications and experience for officials administering it was an important prerequisite in the creation of a modern service.

Any Kansas legislators who believed that the system of poor relief that existed prior to 1933 had considerable merit received a sharp jolt to their complacency when the *Report of the Public Welfare Temporary Commission* was published in January. This Report was a vigorous spur to reform. The Public Welfare Temporary Commission, which had been established by the legislature in January 1931 to undertake an analysis of welfare provisions, produced a devastating critique based on a detailed examination of ten counties. What emerged was a sorry tale of inadequate record keeping, unprofessional behavior on the part of officials, and the inevitable duplication of relief. Record keeping had been so slipshod that the commission found it impossible to calculate accurately the total quantity of aid provided by the numerous private agencies. Indeed, records that had been retained by officials consisted for the most part of receipts for items of expenditure. Duplication was a persistent problem, with many clients receiving help from two or more sources. It was obvious that relief had

been extended to individuals not entitled to it and that social investigation into family circumstances was almost entirely absent. On the other hand, counties under great pressure often gave temporary assistance to keep utter destitution at bay. Their actions could be described as "hit and miss," but it is important to recognize that the "hits" were of tremendous significance to some of the state's poorest citizens. The commission concluded that "the relief program of the average Kansas county is an unbelievably haphazard one, in which the county, city and private agencies are engaged in a frantic, uncoordinated effort to stem the tide of need swept in by the depression. Their methods have been almost entirely stop-gap,—the giving of temporary material relief in amounts just sufficient to stave off destitution." An especially telling criticism was that the lack of a constructive welfare service beyond material aid had a pauperizing effect.[23] The commission believed that in many counties the key deficiency was not a shortage of funds but an absence of trained social workers to dispense relief in a proper professional manner. Local effort, however well intentioned, was insufficient in good times and sadly deficient during a period of severe hardship. There was no excuse for state legislators being unaware of the serious deficiencies in the public welfare system.

The governor told those attending the special session of the legislature held during October and November that $7 million was needed to fund the state's relief obligations up to June 30, 1934. Landon believed that the FERA would contribute $2.8 million toward this total, and the counties had the ability to add a further $2 million. He urged that the $2.2 million shortfall be met by giving the counties additional bond-raising powers, but any money raised would be available for spending on relief work only. Without this additional source of revenue Landon knew that federal funds would be at risk.[24] The special session also made the settlement laws more restrictive. Before November 1933, it was possible to gain settlement in Kansas by residing continuously in a county for six months, and to lose it by an absence of six months. The new law, which was consistent with the federal government's definition of inter-state transients, required continuous residence for one year to gain settlement. However, settlement could be lost by an absence of only six months. A further piece of legislation was necessary to enable the counties to participate in public works schemes where the costs were not fully covered by federal funds. In such circumstances, cities and counties were allowed to issue bonds to

23. *Report of the Public Welfare Temporary Commission, State of Kansas,* 175–96. The quotation is from page 178.

24. *Message of Governor Alf M. Landon to the Special Session of the Kansas Legislature of 1933* (Topeka, 1933): 2–3.

cover payments for supervision, engineering inspection, and materials. By these measures Kansas hoped to secure the maximum benefit from federal work relief initiatives, especially where federal funding was conditional upon a contribution from the state or its subdivisions.

Federal Field Officers and the Encouragement of Best Practice

The highly critical report by the Public Welfare Temporary Commission made defense of the existing system impossible and provided critics with firm evidence on which to base their commitment to reform. Most importantly, as the Kansas reformers moved into positions of authority, they were influenced by experienced RFC officials who acted as liaisons between Washington and the states. These seasoned advisors not only helped to interpret national legislation, they also fulfilled an important role in encouraging local relief administrations to escape from the darkness of poor practice. Field officers frequently visited the states for which they had been given responsibility, debated with the key relief officials, and gave informed comment and advice that would be foolish to ignore. Their detailed reports to their Washington superiors provided the background for crucial decision making. Field officers had been previously employed as information gatherers by such Washington-based agencies as the President's Emergency Committee for Employment and the President's Organization on Unemployment Relief, but by early 1933 their influence on policy implementation was growing. They participated in what William R. Brock has described as a system of "parallel government."[25]

For example, field officer Sherrard Ewing spent January 29, 30, and February 1, 1933, visiting Kansas and meeting, among others, Governor Landon, Dean Ackers, and John Stutz. He reported to his Washington superiors that although Kansas had "done an outstanding job in developing 600 or more work projects," there was some cause for concern. So much emphasis was placed on work relief that it seemed the state had an employment rather than a relief policy. In other words, Kansas counties encouraged applications from the jobless but could not provide the proper social investigation that was essential to determine whether they were genuinely in need. The end result was a fixed amount of work relief for all the unemployed, though because it was spread over a large number of people, the amount of work available was often so small as to be valueless. The example he cited was Kansas City, Kansas, where there were nine

25. William R. Brock, *Welfare, Democracy, and The New Deal*, esp. 171–203.

thousand relief cases but sufficient work relief to provide only two days each month to five thousand of them. Moreover, he believed that there were no safeguards against favoritism in placing men on relief payrolls, and no unequivocal state instructions to determine which applicants should be accepted onto the relief rolls and which should stay on them. Nor was there any means of shifting surplus funds from one county to another where they were desperately needed. He was horrified to learn that Dean Ackers, the KFRC chairman, regarded most relief applicants as "loafers who don't want to work." Ewing recommended that in future all RFC applications from the state should be scrutinized to ensure that the needs of those entitled to relief could be met. Furthermore, he urged RFC officials to put pressure on Ackers so that the KFRC would retreat from its fixation with work relief.[26]

Invited by Ackers, Sherrard Ewing also attended a meeting of the KFRC Executive Committee in February 1933 where he played a leading role in the discussions.[27] First, he complimented the state on the development of its work-relief projects, but then he advised that steps should be taken to ensure that only those eligible for relief were employed on the project. He explained that an assessment of eligibility required an investigation by properly trained welfare officials and should include a home visit, repeated every thirty days, without which a relief budget could not be constructed. Ewing was very cautious in his response to questions relating to the welfare reforms then being debated by the Kansas legislature; instead, he emphasized the need for employing properly trained caseworkers in every county. He also indicated that the KFRC should take a more active role in informing the CFRCs, all of which were beginning to construct subsistence budgets for their clients, of the average amount that each family on relief should receive.[28]

Ewing's role in this debate is particularly interesting. By engaging in constructive criticism he wanted to convince the committee that good social work practices were essential if relief was to reach the people who needed it most. The RFC had not emphasized the administration of relief, concerning itself, primarily, with the justification for financial assistance that each state submitted and its ability to repay the loan. Ewing's promi-

---

26. "Report on Working Relations with Governor, Chairman Ackers and Sec. Stutz." S. Ewing, January 29, 30, 1933; February 1, 1933. RFC Records Relating to Emergency Relief to States, 1932, Kansas Approved Correspondence/Loan File, RG234, NA.

27. Ackers to Croxton, January 27, 1933, Kansas Correspondence/Loan File #5, Part 1, RG234.

28. Minutes of the KFRC, February 13, 1933, 327:1:30, Stutz Papers. Ewing's region covered Kansas, Nebraska, the Dakotas, Minnesota, and Iowa.

nence is the first indication of a pattern that would become common under the FERA—intrusion, usually quite justified, by federal field agents in the state management of relief. Agents like Ewing were able to comment on relief activities from a position of considerable strength. In the first place, they were highly experienced professionals while state committees were composed mostly of local worthies without experience of relief administration. Moreover, their close association with developments in Washington and their professional relationships with officials in several states kept field staff informed on a wide range of developments. In the states that comprised their territory, they got to know the principal relief officers and supporting staff intimately and became aware of their strengths and weaknesses. As they became more widely known and respected, agents were given information on both an unofficial and official basis, allowing them to provide answers to complex questions quickly. Indeed, queries and complaints from leading national and local politicians were often sent, via senior officials, to field agents for draft responses. Field agents did not make policy, but they built up influence, especially under the FERA, both in the states and in Washington. It is not surprising, therefore, that Washington bureaucrats came to rely heavily on field staff to keep them fully informed about developments in the states.[29]

In mid-February, Ewing wrote again to Croxton reiterating his view that an excessive reliance on work relief in Kansas was poor practice and a cause for concern. He claimed that funds that could have been properly used to support direct relief had been diverted to work relief, even though some counties had failed to fully utilize their RFC allocation. Mismanagement of relief had already led to serious problems in Kansas City, Kansas, he claimed, and it would not be surprising if similar difficulties surfaced in Topeka and Wichita.[30] As field agents reported to the most senior RFC officials, there is no doubt that key decision makers were fully informed about the background in each state as they reached their conclusions.

On February 20, 1933, Croxton reported to his fellow RFC Directors that the governor of Kansas had applied for a $642,634 loan to cover the months March and April and would be allocated $641,868. In justifying this decision, Croxton made full use of Landon's letter dated February 15, quoting sections in full and noting with approval that Kansas counties would soon be able to raise more funds for relief purposes. The gover-

29. Josephine Chapin Brown, *Public Relief, 1929–1939*, 192–93, 199–200.
30. Ewing to Croxton, February 16, 1933, RFC Records relating to the Emergency Relief to States, RG234, NA.

nor's pledge that poor relief organization was to be changed so that a more thorough investigation of the budgeting of relief cases would take place was welcomed as an acceptance of good practice. RFC funds, Croxton reminded the directors, had to target those in need, and the amount given to each applicant had to be determined on the basis of need. A full investigation of all cases was therefore essential. RFC loans gave additional support to twenty-five Kansas counties for March and fifty-one for April. The remainder were either judged capable of providing assistance from their own resources, or they had sufficient unspent RFC balances that could be used to meet relief needs.[31]

In mid-March Ewing expressed his delight that an experienced Red Cross official had been loaned to Kansas for one month in order to undertake fieldwork for the State Relief Committee. The field agent was confident that the influence of a trained social worker was essential if the inadequacies of the Kansas relief system were to be eradicated. He wrote, "[T]he investigations and the adjustment of relief to need are on the low side in Kansas." The need to appoint trained staff was acute, but Ewing wondered if it would be possible to make the appointments required, given the low annual salary cap of $1,500 for poor commissioners.[32]

The Significance of the RFC

Between October 1932 and June 1933 Kansas borrowed $2,592,934 from the RFC. Notably, however, there was no single month during this period when all 105 counties were in receipt of federal funds. A peak was reached in March 1933 when 102 counties were using RFC loans, but usually six or seven counties each month were judged capable of coping entirely with their own resources.[33] However, by early summer the $300 million that Congress had allocated to the RFC was close to exhaustion, and a decision had to be made whether to make another allocation to the RFC or to provide a different means of channeling much-needed relief funds to the states. The final monthly RFC allocation to Kansas came in June 1933, by which time the program was being phased out to make way for its successor, the FERA.

RFC loans made a major difference to the funding of relief in Kansas, as

31. Croxton to the Directors, February 20, 1933, Kansas Correspondence/Loan File #5, Part 1, RG234, NA.

32. Ewing to Croxton, March 16, 1933, RFC Records relating to the Emergency Relief to States, Kansas Correspondence/Loan File, Part 1, Box 32, RG234, NA.

33. *KERC Bulletin* 127, 11–12.

we can see by comparing the amount which that agency provided over a nine-month period with other spending. For example, relief expenditure financed from county funds rose remorselessly throughout the depression. In 1930 the counties spent an estimated $2 million; in 1931, $2.3 million; in 1932, $2.9 million; and in 1933, $3 million. However, although expenditure increased greatly, it could not keep pace with the rising demands for assistance. The estimates of the unduplicated county caseload for the four years from 1930 inclusive were: 21,551; rising to 31,229 in 1931; to 49,689 in 1932; and on to 55,947 in 1933.[34] Private expenditure on relief also rose. In 1930, private agencies contributed $597,000 toward assisting the needy; in 1931, the figure was $738,000; a year later it had risen to just over $1 million, only to fall in 1933 to $828,000; the private-sector caseload increased from 56,538 in 1930 to 93,207 in 1932. The strain on private charities became so intense that many were unable to continue caring for their clients who were transferred to county relief rolls. The RFC, therefore, provided a considerable injection of additional funding at a crucial time. When the economic situation was at its bleakest, the RFC was able to match the total relief expenditure of Kansas counties. Furthermore, because states were forced to apply for RFC loans, for the first time information about the needy was sought, gathered, and presented in a systematic manner, although not yet in all counties. Moreover, the Statistical Division of the RFC analyzed Kansas finances, paying particular attention to tax receipts, the state's debt, and its credit standing.[35] The governor's claim that all available resources to assist the poor were being fully utilized was tested, and the RFC had to be assured that the loan would be repaid. It would be a little while before the data on the numbers of relief recipients and the amount spent on them could be regarded with full confidence, but the RFC set in motion a long overdue statistical gathering exercise. Spurred on by federal initiatives, Kansas grasped the opportunity to radically reform its relief administration and, as a result, the state was well positioned to enjoy the benefits of New Deal largesse.

Nevertheless, such was the pressure on resources that the sums avail-

34. The figures for county and for private relief expenditure are taken from *KERC Bulletin* 127, 46–49. The unduplicated caseload represents the total number of families and single individuals who have received any kind of aid in a given period. Unduplicated caseload figures are only available from counties. Unfortunately, the caseload data for private relief expenditure contain unavoidable duplication. Because of the inadequacies of record keeping, the expenditure figures for both counties and private agencies have to be regarded as estimates.

35. "Financial Condition of Kansas," RFC Statistical Division, October 26, 1932, Records relating to the Emergency Relief for States, Kansas Correspondence/Loan File, RG234, NA.

able for distribution to the needy were very modest, and there was an understandable determination in both county and private agencies to keep
case costs to a minimum. Between 1924 and 1930 the average monthly
case cost for each resident family on direct relief and reliant on county
funds was $6.22. In 1931, this fell to $5.78; in 1932 to $4.74; and in 1933 to
$4.70. Some clients on direct relief received payments in both cash and
kind, but most relied entirely on kind. The monthly case cost for those on
county-funded work relief schemes was a mere $2.99 in 1931 and $2.51 a
year later.[36] Although the purchasing power of the dollar had risen considerably during this period of deflation, it is clear that the destitute were
being cared for in a very cost-conscious fashion.

The FERA, the PWA, and the Culture of Work Relief

The new Democrat-dominated Congress knew that there was widespread support for public works rather than the dole as a means of com-
bating the depression.[37] Political leaders and the mass of their con-
stituents believed that federally funded public works would stimulate the
economy, while at the same time providing morale-boosting employment
for the army of unemployed. Moreover, the public would benefit from the
completion of carefully chosen projects, and even the most hardened of
fiscal conservatives would not object to programs that emphasized the
necessity of self-liquidating investment. In the first one hundred days of
his administration, Roosevelt presented to the American people a bold
plan to combat the effects of the Great Depression. How effectively would
these initiatives attack the serious social ills that were the inevitable outcome of nearly four years of economic decline in Kansas?

The PWA was set up in June 1933 under Title 11 of the National Industrial Recovery Act, and Harold L. Ickes was named as its administrator. A
major task of the PWA was to re-energize heavy industry through a comprehensive program of major public works and to provide employment
directly through projects, and indirectly through the purchase of large
quantities of materials. It offered states and local government a combination of grants and loans. Grants, however, were not to exceed 30 percent

36. The estimates for work relief do not include the employment of the jobless on
projects funded by county road and bridge funds, nor is federally funded work relief
included.

37. For the background to public works see Udo Sautter, *Three Cheers for the Unemployed: Government and Unemployment before the New Deal*, esp. 268–318.

of the total cost of any project (raised to 45 percent in 1935), and the balance of the cost was to be covered by loans. The PWA organization was devolved and PWA committees were established at both the state and the local levels. Unlike other agencies, the PWA could bypass state governments and make its funds directly available to local units. It was also empowered to grant funds to federal government departments and even to grant loans to private corporations for the purpose of capital expenditure.

Applications made to the PWA in Washington gave details of all projects; the applications were then subjected to a searching analysis that explored their engineering, legal, and financial rationale. For example, the PWA had to be satisfied that the proposals would lead to the creation of extra jobs and that the information provided was accurate. This process was not only extremely lengthy, but the information required was also so detailed that many applications were judged inadequate and therefore rejected. Unfortunately, most states did not have meticulously planned major work projects on hand that they could immediately forward to the PWA. It took many months to draw up plans for large-scale projects, and even longer to purchase the land on which the construction would take place. Nor did all states have the professional staff—engineers being in especially short supply—to quickly produce project plans that would satisfy the challenging standards laid down by the PWA. Kansas, further advanced than most in its commitment to worthwhile relief work, faced a different problem. Ickes was determined to ensure that all borrowers could repay their debts. Borrowers usually funded their 70 percent of project expenses either by bond issues purchased by the PWA, private borrowing, or a combination of the two. The PWA legal team was very conservative in its assessment of the ability of states and their political subdivisions to borrow, since constitutional limitations could severely limit their freedom of action. If there was a doubt about the financial security of the application it was, after a time-consuming investigation, rejected.[38] Sometimes there were considerable delays, as PWA approval could not be granted until the electorate had approved bond issues. This provided many states, Kansas included, with the incentive to change the financially restricting clauses in their constitutions, but the process took a while.

By January 1, 1934, the PWA had spent only $110 million and had provided employment directly to a mere 280,000 men.[39] Indeed, in the early stages of the PWA's operation, loans to federal government departments

38. Henry J. Bitterman, *State and Federal Grants-In-Aid*, 316–22.
39. Corrington Gill, *Wasted Manpower: The Challenge of Unemployment*, 209.

were far more significant than those to states or municipalities. Large federal agencies could easily produce carefully crafted plans for major projects, and there were no legal complications over borrowing. Commentators who had anticipated that the PWA would vigorously press ahead with its mission and make deep inroads into the massed ranks of the unemployed were deeply disappointed. The PWA's failure was one of the reasons why the Civil Works Administration (CWA) was hurriedly introduced to care for the unemployed during the winter of 1933–34.

Although the PWA can be seen as an attack on unemployment through work creation schemes, its thrust differed from that of the Federal Emergency Relief Administration (FERA). One important difference was that PWA employees did not have to be certified as needing relief in order to work on projects. The sort of major projects that came to dominate PWA employment—for example, the Grand Coulee Dam—required the recruitment of many skilled workers who could not be found on the relief rolls. Moreover, large-scale projects required lengthy planning and a relatively heavy expenditure on materials, and they could not always be located close to centers of unemployment. Unlike the FERA, PWA wages were determined either by trades union bargaining or by paying the local prevailing wage. The PWA was not a work relief agency, nor was it equipped to provide a speedy solution to the unemployment crisis. Indeed, by the mid-1930s, 70 percent of PWA expenditure was spent on materials and the remainder on wages. However, major projects did have a positive secondary effect on unemployment, as jobs were created in transportation, manufacturing, quarrying, and other sectors of the economy.

In May 1933, the FERA replaced the RFC as the principal relief agency, though the two bodies shared some similarities.[40] Like the RFC, all FERA applications were made through the governor, who requested the amount needed, gave detailed information on the use to which the funds would be put, provided full information on the resources available within the state, and had the added responsibility of assessing the quality of the state's relief administration. As with the RFC, federal funds were not expected to replace but to supplement local effort. FERA director Harry Hopkins was determined that states should make the maximum contribution to the care of their needy and undertake a rigorous social investigation for all relief applicants. Indeed, he believed that relief expenditure would be reduced if competent social investigation was widely adopt-

40. For a meticulous account of the background and development of the FERA and CWA, see Doris Carothers, *Chronology of the Federal Emergency Relief Administration May 12, 1933, to December 31, 1935.*

ed.[41] Nevertheless, it was significant that FERA awarded grants in aid to the states, not loans, and the loan policy of the RFC was discontinued. In June 1934 the requirement that RFC loans be repaid was waived. Advised by his staff, Harry Hopkins determined the amount of funds to be given, distributed them to individual states, and created a regulatory framework to control their use.

Initially Congress provided the FERA with $500 million, sufficient, the legislators judged, to underwrite relief needs for six months. The amount allocated was divided into two equal parts. The first tranche of $250 million was available for distribution to every state on a matching basis. One dollar of federal money could be secured for every three dollars spent on unemployment relief over the previous three months, though the operation of each state's relief administration had to be consistent with the standards laid down by the FERA. This was an attempt to ensure each state made a fair contribution to the care of its own destitute citizens, and the majority of grants during the first few months of operation were awarded on a matching basis, with the result that this fund was close to exhaustion by late 1933.

The second tranche of $250 million was given to the administrator to allocate on a discretionary basis. Thus Harry Hopkins was accorded quite extraordinary powers to oversee the allocation of federal relief funding, and the states in making applications to the FERA accepted the situation. Furthermore, when Congress added to its financial support for the FERA, and ultimately the agency received a total of $3,100 million, these funds came under the heading of discretionary rather than matching awards. The nation's lawmakers realized that the most poverty-stricken states were unable to participate in a program that required them to spend three dollars for every one received from the federal government. The varying impact of the depression and the marked differences in the capacity of individual states to cope with the relief problems that the economic collapse had caused rendered impossible the imposition of a national formula to guide the distribution of federal grants. The FERA, therefore, was given the authority to decide what contribution should be expected from each state in the fight to help the destitute.

The responsibility that Hopkins accepted was great, but the task he was given was far from easy. He had to ensure that taxpayers' money was spent honestly and to maximum effect, when the temptation for states was to persuade the federal government to take over as much of their

41. George McJimsey, *Harry Hopkins: Ally of the Poor and Defender of Democracy,* 53–54.

burden as possible and the temptation for him was to pursue political advantage. Hopkins was also determined to impose an administrative structure that would ensure minimum professional standards for relief delivery in states where provision was most deficient. He wanted the states to develop imaginative work relief projects and abandon the work tests, such as leaf raking or wood chopping, that destroyed rather than elevated morale. The administrator was also committed to the principle that all states should contribute financially to relief costs according to their ability.

How did Hopkins decide what was a reasonable request, and how were requests to be verified? Verification was a concern for both matching and discretionary grants. FERA officials favored cash payments to clients, but many cities and counties had no experience in administering cash-based relief.[42] Moreover, although a number of congressional hearings had provided evidence that local relief was often inadequate and more assistance would have to be provided, detailed knowledge of the relief problems in many states was lacking. This deficiency had to be remedied quickly, as genuine pleas for assistance were pressing urgently. The states were instructed to collect a wide range of statistical and qualitative information and send it to the FERA as part of a carefully structured monthly report. Details of the numbers receiving relief, the case load and case load costs, the nature of relief operations in the state, the influence of seasonal factors, and general administration policy were called for. To these were added information on economic conditions, taxation, current and future debt, and the possibility of raising additional tax revenue. In all, the FERA demanded a wide variety of supporting data collected in a systematic manner from the states.[43] Indeed, the FERA was eventually able to produce a comprehensive picture of relief conditions across the nation from the monthly reports submitted to it.[44] The information sought by the FERA was far more wide-ranging than that asked for by the RFC, which was almost exclusively limited to financial matters. The FERA also required an auditing of accounts by the state auditor.

Staff in the FERA's newly created Division of Research, Statistics and Finance, under the leadership of an assistant administrator, analyzed this information from the states, and forwarded their comments and recommendations to Hopkins. In the early stages the returns were obviously incomplete, or inaccurately compiled, because some state ERAs had never previously gathered the details that the FERA needed. These deficiencies

42. Joanna C. Colcord, *Cash Relief,* 35–36.
43. M. Riggs McCormick, *Federal Emergency Relief Administration Grants,* 7–16.
44. Edith Abbott, *Public Assistance,* Vol. 1, *American Principles and Policies,* 795–99.

forced the FERA to rely heavily on the information provided by field officers and on their assessment of conditions in the states for which they had responsibility. Indeed the input of the field staff into the FERA's decision making process was crucial, especially in the early period when the data from the states were far less than robust.[45]

Welfare Excellence Achieved

After a short transition period lasting until August 1, private agencies were excluded from the administration of FERA funds, which in the future could be handled only by a recognized public agency. Each state had to create a central body, known as the State Emergency Relief Administration (SERA), which would distribute FERA grants, and appointments to it had to be approved by the administrator. To conform to this ruling the KFRC became the KERC and the CFRCs were renamed CERCs— County Emergency Relief Committees. Kansas was fortunate in that the radical welfare reforms that had been adopted in early 1933 for the most part met the minimum FERA requirements. It seemed that the state was in a position to deliver the modern welfare system that the New Deal regime was trying to encourage.

It is important to see the FERA as a state- and local-run initiative that functioned because of federal cooperation rather than federal ownership. Relief applicants did not receive their work relief wages, or their grocery orders, from FERA officials, but from local relief agencies, with the amount allocated being determined by the budgetary deficiency principle. No one would dispute that Washington's guiding hand was more noticeable than it had been under the RFC, but in Kansas the touch was never oppressive. FERA officials became fully aware of deficiencies in many relief administrations and tried to impose minimum standards on all by advising on matters such as eligibility and methods of social investigation, as well as hours of work and the rates of pay on work relief projects.

The FERA was a child of crisis. Congress saw the need for rapid action so that the destitute could be assisted immediately, and in a more generous manner than they had been under the RFC. However, it was emergency legislation, and the nation's lawmakers did not envisage a permanent federal presence in welfare provision. Congress and the public hoped for a rapid economic recovery, as had occurred after the serious depression of 1920–21, and with it a rise in farm income and an expansion

45. Brown, *Public Relief,* 203.

in urban jobs. Because the social costs of both rural and urban unemployment were seen as a deeply complex problem requiring a variety of solutions, four new emergency relief initiatives were begun and located within the FERA program. The Emergency Education, College Student Aid, Rural Rehabilitation, and Transient programs were created soon after the FERA began to operate. In addition, separate federal agencies were created to tackle specific problems or to assist identified groups. The Civilian Conservation Corps (CCC) was established in April, the Federal Surplus Relief Corporation (FSRC) in October, and the CWA in November. All will be analyzed later. Together with the FERA and the PWA they led the attack on the social costs of the depression, though many of their policies were also designed to stimulate the economy.

In May 1933 Ackers and Stutz traveled to Washington, D.C., to attend a meeting addressed by Hopkins, where the new administrator made a powerful impression on both men. Stutz reported to Landon that although Hopkins had congratulated Kansas on its work relief programs, "we have very few credits, however, for the manner in which we have administered the relief from the point of view of good social work."[46] Writing some months later, Ackers conceded that he had always opposed the advice given by Sherrard Ewing to spend more on administration, because Ackers believed that administrative costs should be kept to a minimum in order to maximize the sums available for work relief. But Hopkins had argued with conviction that money spent on administration that successfully targeted those who were eligible for relief paid for itself many times over. The Hopkins plan called for a poor commissioner and a case worker (or workers) in each of the 105 counties. Ackers was happy to note that the Kansas legislature had anticipated this structure earlier in the year. However, although he was not entirely convinced by Hopkins's emphasis on administration, as a practical man he concluded that "we have had the alternative of either complying with their rules and regulations or endangering our future allotment of federal funds."[47]

From the summer of 1933, Kansas's welfare administration underwent a profound transformation. In May, F. H. Marvin was recruited from Louisville, Kentucky, as a professionally qualified superintendent of relief. Over the next few months the appointment of four trained state case supervisors, each assigned to a district, provided a senior management team that could assist the counties in the reorganization of their relief administrations, allowing them to meet both federal and state laws. Private

46. Stutz to Landon, June 14, 1933, Stutz Papers, 327:1:3,.
47. Ackers to Landon, Nov 13, 1933, Stutz Papers, 327:1:3.

welfare agencies also helped with the reorganization. In some counties the Red Cross, occasionally with the support of other agencies, assisted in paying or supplementing the salaries of trained social workers. Sometimes cities gave similar financial aid as well as providing much-needed office space. This was an important means of circumventing the unreasonable restrictions imposed by the legislature on salary and on the numbers of assistants that a poor commissioner might appoint. Within a short while welfare was administered across the state on a more uniform basis, with all citizens who had had a claim on public assistance, in theory, being treated equally. A marked improvement in record keeping enabled the KERC to monitor the case load and the amount spent on a monthly basis.

The FERA organized a relief census during October 1933. The results showed that if all direct and work relief cases financed by both county and federal funds were added together, Kansas had a total of 42,953 resident families and 4,918 resident singles on relief.[48] The county with the highest number of cases was Wyandotte (5,322), followed by Sedgwick (4,981), Shawnee (4,046), Crawford (2,459), Montgomery (1,700), and Cherokee (1,294). It is interesting to note that the October total of 47,871 relief cases was considerably lower than the March peak of 75,940. Part of the difference between these two figures can be explained by a better recording of the data, which reduced the number of duplications. However, a significant fact was also the more meticulous investigation of all relief applicants, in some counties for the first time, which removed cases on the grounds of ineligibility. The figures present only a very rough estimate of the division between direct and work relief because some counties did not supply the information. It appears that at least 10,500 families and 1,800 individuals were in receipt of direct relief in October, while a minimum of 35,000 families and 2,500 singles were on work relief.[49] In November the total caseload rose from its October trough to 52,202, but large numbers of unemployed were about to be removed from the relief rolls by the creation of a new agency, the CWA.[50]

Conscious of the urgent need to appoint more qualified staff members at a time when the competition for them was great, Kansas organized its own imaginative training program. From September 25–29 the first School of Public Administration was held in Wichita. It attracted 181 participants, comprising poor commissioners and case supervisors and oth-

48. FERA, *Unemployment Relief Census, October 1933. United States Summary*, 6, 79, 116, 142.

49. "Families and Single Persons Receiving Direct and Work Relief, September and October, 1933," Stutz Papers, 327:5:9.

50. All figures are taken from *KERC Bulletin* 127, 18–19.

er relief administrators. A formidably experienced instructional staff addressed relief officials from 94 counties on a wide range of relevant issues.[51] One distinguished participant, Professor A. Wayne McMillen from the Graduate School of Administration at the University of Chicago and a leading professional in the field, wrote to both Landon and Ewing to praise the exercise.[52] Kansas constantly stressed the value of in-house training as a means of upgrading the skills of partially qualified personnel. Training sessions were very important in building confidence among welfare staff and making them aware that they were part of a team that had a commitment to career development and high professional standards.

These improvements in relief administration did not escape the attention of FERA field agents. In April Ewing was convinced that the only distinguishing feature of poor relief in Kansas was an over-emphasis on work relief and a dependence upon county commissioners. By July, however, his tone had changed. He enthusiastically approved the appointments of Marvin and the new state case supervisors, and he noted that Stutz was "bearing down almost too hard on counties in regard to qualified personnel." A few months later Ewing urged Hopkins to support Ackers and Stutz in an overly strict interpretation of the qualifications needed for social workers employed in the most heavily urbanized Kansas counties. On the strength of this advice Hopkins responded to a critic of Stutz that the executive "is a good man and . . . thoroughly competent." In October Ewing told Hopkins that Kansas had "one of the best administrative set-ups" that he had encountered. At the end of 1933, Ewing assessed Stutz's office as "well managed" and a "strong and smooth running organization." Another field agent, T. J. Edmonds, was so impressed with Stutz's managerial skills that he placed on record his view that the Kansas central relief organization was "the best that I have seen"; the office was "cluttered with MAs and BAs and technical experts but of course you would expect an efficient organization from a League of Municipalities man." These agents had used their considerable authority to help bring about this improvement, and the minutes of the Executive Committee of the KERC provide a telling example. In September the committee was told that Ewing insisted that federal funds should be withdrawn from Leavenworth County unless an acceptable relief administration had been appointed within two weeks.[53] The committee was left in no doubt that this was not a matter for debate.

51. *KERC Bulletin* 127, 15–18.
52. McMillen to Landon, McMillen to Ewing, both October 5, 1933, FERA State File, 1933–36 (406 Field Report File), RG69, NA.
53. Report by Ewing, April 1933, FERA State Files, 1933–36, RG69, NA; Report by

For its part, the KERC believed that in 1933 a national shortage of personnel with the appropriate skills and experience was so serious that the state was compelled to make some appointments that fell below the professional standards to which it aspired.[54] The alternative, which was making no appointments at all, was judged impractical. An attempt to control the excessive burden that many relief staff carried, by imposing upper casework limits of 125 urban families and 75 rural families per month, was impossible to implement throughout the state, as it was not possible to hire the extra staff required. The additional administrative burden imposed by the CWA, introduced in November, was a further impediment to raising the quality of public welfare staff. Nevertheless, John Stutz and his senior colleagues were entitled to feel pleased with the progress that had been made during the last half of 1933. The state had moved away from its heavily criticized fixation with work relief to a stance that, while still emphasizing work for all fit to undertake it, was consistent with a professionally delivered welfare policy and, of course, with FERA standards.

Kansas quickly secured its matching FERA funding, but an anxious debate took place as state officials tried to estimate what discretionary funds would be forthcoming. On October 11, Hopkins informed Landon that, following a report by Sherrard Ewing, the FERA was prepared to grant Kansas 40 percent of the monies needed each month to meet relief for the needy. Hopkins could, of course, alter this ratio whenever he judged circumstances had changed. The FERA administrator did not accept Landon's estimate that Kansas relief costs over the next nine months would reach $7 million because he was unconvinced that robust predictions could be made over such a long period. Landon was told that the FERA could not even guarantee a specific grant each month. Instead the agency would examine the relief needs in Kansas on a month-by-month basis and use that information to calculate the sum to which the state was entitled.[55] In other words, Kansas was to be regularly "means tested," as it had been by the RFC, and its relief allocation adjusted accordingly.

At a meeting of the KERC Executive Committee held in August, Stutz had stressed the importance of raising more local public money to fund relief activities in order to satisfy the federal government that Kansas was making an adequate contribution to the war against deprivation. In Oc-

---

Ewing, July 23, 1933, ibid.; Hopkins to the Hon. Harllee Branch, October 9, 1933, ibid.; Ewing to Hopkins, October 6, 1933, ibid.; Ewing, Report on Kansas, December 5–6, 1933, ibid.; Edmonds to Betters, December 5, 1933; Edmonds to Hopkins, Report February 2–3, 1934, ibid.; *Minutes of the Executive Committee of the KERC*, September 30, 1933, Stutz Papers, 327:1:30.

54. *KERC Bulletin* 289, November 1, 1935, "Public Welfare Service in Kansas, 1934," 19.
55. Hopkins to Landon, October 1, 1933, Stutz Papers, 327:1:4.

tober another meeting was informed of Harry Hopkins's decision to provide discretionary funding on a 60/40 basis from November 1. However, when an anxious Stutz mailed Hopkins asking for a stay of execution on the implementation of the 60/40 rule because the Special Session of the Legislature was taking longer than he had expected to reach agreement on fiscal matters, the request was refused. FERA staff analyzed the legislation being considered by the Special Session, and they came to the conclusion that the increase in county borrowing powers for relief purposes was welcome, but the change was not as radical as the lawmakers believed. There was some concern that the plan to divert about a third of the highway budget for work relief was not an entirely satisfactory way for Kansas to make up its 60 percent contribution. Nevertheless, in spite of some misgivings, FERA officials considered the legislation broadly acceptable.[56] In fact, Stutz worried unnecessarily. Hopkins became much more generous in assisting relief in Kansas than these early exchanges indicated, and the federal contribution soon rose to nearly 70 percent of the total rather than forty percent.

Although the federal government expected the state to contribute as much to relief expenditure as it could, there was total freedom to vary contributions and to distribute the funding among the counties. In September 1933 nine counties were allocated no, or virtually no, federal money, but for some others FERA funds were judged crucial in the struggle to provide basic assistance to the needy. The contribution from Cherokee, Crawford, and Leavenworth counties, for example, was less than 1 percent of the total federal grant. For the major urban counties the local contributions were as follows: Sedgwick, 32 percent; Shawnee, 47 percent; and Wyandotte, 37 percent.[57] There were fluctuations in the balance between federal and local funds each month, but it is clear that some counties became heavily dependent upon FERA grants and that marked deviations from the mean were acceptable to Washington.

Federal grants to the states, which had a long history, were used extensively for the New Deal's relief programs. Grants in aid accounted for only 3 percent of federal expenditure in 1929, but this figure had risen to 32 percent by 1939. Grants grouped under the heading "social welfare, health and security" accounted for 85 percent of total grant expenditure

56. Stutz to Hopkins, November 4, 1933; Edmonds comment November 6, 1933; J. R. Blough to Bookman re House Bill No. 49, November 6, 1933, FERA State Files, Kansas May/December 1933, RG69, NA.

57. September 1933. Map of Local and Federal Funds, Stutz Papers, 325:5:8. The nine counties were Doniphan, Ellsworth, Greeley, Jewell, Leavenworth, Pratt, Rice, Stanton, and Wallace.

in 1937.[58] However, while Washington had rightly concluded that grants rather than loans were the means by which the current crisis should be tackled, there was a growing concern that the dynamism that had marked the "first 100 days" of the administration had not been maintained. A new and bold initiative was sorely needed.

Washington's New Role: The Civil Works Administration

By the fall of 1933, sluggish economic performance across the country had given rise to anxiety that a new recession might be on the way during the difficult winter months. Full recovery, which the New Dealers had believed would follow rapidly on the creation of many new government agencies, remained elusive. The need for a new and vigorous federal initiative to kick-start the economy and to provide millions of new jobs was becoming ever more pressing. On November 8, the CWA was established with the purpose of generating, by December 8, four million jobs for people currently unemployed yet fit for work. It was anticipated that two million men and women who were on work relief would be swiftly transferred to the new agency and that a further two million would be recruited through local re-employment agencies designated by the United States Employment Service (USES).

The CWA was a radical initiative that departed from the means-tested relief to which Americans had seemed totally committed.[59] New Dealers aimed to eliminate dole payments and provide a wide variety of work at "fair wages" for all the unemployed, not just those in need. The anticipated result was a massive boost to the economy as the newly waged spent their earnings and businesses hired more staff. This exercise would need considerable administrative skill at the local level to meet these ambitious employment targets in the short timescale envisaged by Washington. The need for speed was not the only requirement. State relief administrations were also instructed to ensure that all work projects were socially and economically worthy.

Although all CWA workers became federal employees and the program was federally administered, Washington identified a key role for the existing local emergency relief administrations. In Kansas, the KERC was designated the State CWA; all county ERCs, with the addition of two

58. James. A. Maxwell, *Federal Grants and the Business Cycle*, 3–6, 14.
59. Jeff Singleton, *The American Dole: Unemployment Relief and the Welfare State in the Great Depression*, 132–33.

members chosen from the board of county commissioners, became local CWAs; and the county poor commissioners served as local civil works administrators. John Stutz was automatically appointed state civil works administrator.

At the commencement of the program, Kansas received a CWA quota of 45,000 positions, 1,297 less than the number of cases receiving direct and work relief during October 1933. On November 25, the first CWA payday, 32,000 employees shared the sum of $267,000. By way of contrast, the final work relief payroll in November had been a modest $53,000. The recruitment drive continued apace so that on December 7, 45,000 men and women were at work, 90 percent of whom had been transferred to the CWA from the relief rolls. There was no time for a relaxation in recruitment as the state's quota was progressively increased, until it peaked in January 1934 at 64,500, with the final tranche of 4,500 being specifically targeted at the southwestern drought counties where lack of rain was leading to increasing hardship. The KERC distributed the quota among the counties in much the same manner in which the state's total had been derived. Three-quarters of the weighting was based on population size, and one-quarter on the proportion of the population on relief. However, if a county was unable to employ its quota, the numbers were transferred to where the need was greater.[60]

The CWA was innovative because it targeted the unemployed whether they were eligible for relief or not. Up to December 6, the relief rolls provided the CWA with virtually all its workers, but after that date recruitment was carried out by re-employment offices or by union locals, if the project sponsors had specifically requested the employment of trades unionists. In a letter to John Stutz, Harry Hopkins made it quite clear that he saw CWA workers as employees and not relief cases, even to the extent that any of them could be dismissed from their CWA jobs for good cause in the same way as private-sector employees.[61] However, in spite of the efforts the CWA made to cut the link between the provision of work for the unemployed and the culture of relief, there is no doubt that a strong relationship remained. For example, it was calculated that just over 80 percent of the Kansas CWA workforce had at some time received either

60. Much of the information on the CWA is taken from *KERC Bulletin* 127, 581–84, and *KERC Bulletin* 289, 15–16, 79–80. See also the two-volume typescript, "Review of Civil Works Administration," Stutz Papers, 327:4:1. This is a draft for the CWA report in *Bulletin* 289, but it contains additional information. It is cited as hereafter as "Typescript."

61. Hopkins to Stutz, November 24, 1933, CWA Administrative Correspondence, Kansas Box 17, RG69, NA.

work or direct relief. In Crawford County and in Kansas City, Kansas, the army of unemployed on relief was so great that the number of CWA positions available was not sufficient to accommodate them all, and the remainder became a charge on the county.[62] There can be no doubt that many clients viewed the CWA as yet another relief agency, especially when they encountered the same staff who cared for them under the FERA. The links between relief and CWA employment in Kansas remained strong.

John Stutz was later convinced that the implementation of the CWA program in Kansas proved a remarkable success, primarily because the state had been in an excellent position to exploit the opportunities that were made available by the federal government. The state had appointed experienced and qualified social workers, and although the need to implement the CWA program imposed a serious and unforeseen administrative burden on all relief staff, the fact that the restructuring exercise had already begun was of great benefit. Furthermore, because the allocation of relief in Kansas had always emphasized work, with no one who was physically capable of labor being given direct relief, except in an emergency, a number of worthwhile projects were under way that could immediately be transferred to the CWA. Others were at such an advanced stage of preparation that they could follow the same route without difficulty. Federal Field Representative T. J. Edmonds formed a positive view of the CWA program when he visited Kansas during April 1934, concluding that work relief was extremely cost effective because of the close supervision of projects by trained social workers.[63] Inevitably, however, the need to respond rapidly to federal prompting led to misjudgments, and in the early stages of the CWA some projects created work but could not be defended as sound investments. Nevertheless, the state's administrators were unshaken in their belief that the most appropriate way of remedying this deficiency was to leave, as far as it was possible, the choice and operation of projects to counties, cities, and school boards. Local ownership, it was felt, was the key to the adoption of work projects that would be highly valued by communities.[64]

Widespread unemployment had some advantages. In a lax labor market, it was possible to hire the experienced and highly trained personnel, including county and city graduate engineers, who were needed to organize and manage construction work. A serious attempt was made to fit the

62. *KERC Bulletin* 289, 16.

63. Note from Edmonds attached to letter from Stutz to Hopkins, April 13, 1934, FERA State Files, 1933–36, Kansas, 40–420, RG69, NA.

64. *KERC Bulletin* 289, 41–43.

projects to the hours for which the workers were available so that continuous operation could be achieved. Deficiencies in key skill areas were addressed with vigor and imagination. For example, because it was evident that the additional administrative demands of the CWA would stretch the available accounting resources beyond the breaking point, a systematic search took place to locate the state's unemployed accountants. From more than one thousand, 10 percent were selected to act as certifying officers, a post that became one of considerable significance, guaranteeing the prompt payment of CWA workers and also ensuring the proper monitoring of financial procedures. Stutz was justified in feeling proud of the speed with which Kansas put its full CWA quota to work and correct in identifying the relief structure recently put in place as the determining factor in this success.[65]

Several federal field representatives, in the course of their regular reports to Harry Hopkins, affirmed confirmation of the improving professionalism of relief in Kansas. Sherrard Ewing, writing in early October 1933, commented, "[W]e have in Kansas one of the best State Relief Administration set ups." His admiration for Stutz's judgment seemed boundless. T. J. Edmonds wrote in January 1934 "[T]his is a strong and smoothly running organization." He detected a weak spot in the relationship of the central administration with the re-employment service, but he singled out for praise the appointment of a properly qualified certifying officer in each county.[66] Thus at an early stage in the CWA's life its organization in Kansas was being held up as a model of best practice by experts who had a detailed knowledge of operations in other states.

Throughout this program—that is, from November 17, 1933, to the end of March 1934—CWA workers in Kansas earned $11 million, all of which came as cash payments. Wages for both December and January exceeded $3 million. In all, the federal government channeled $12.2 million into the state, to which we can add the contributions of local sponsors who spent $2.4 million on tools, materials, and engineering supervision.[67] Counties absorbed the administrative costs, as they had under the FERA. Clearly the CWA initiative resulted in a large injection of funding, mostly in the form of cash wages, at a crucial time in the depression, and CWA pay far exceeded the sums previously handled by any poor commissioner's of-

65. "Typescript," Vol. 1, 24.

66. Ewing to Hopkins, October 6, 1933; Edmonds to Hopkins, January 6, 7, 1934, Papers of Harry L. Hopkins Papers, Box 57, Franklin D. Roosevelt Library, Hyde Park, N.Y. (hereafter "Hopkins Papers").

67. Works Progress Administration, *Analysis of Civil Works Program Statistics*, 18, 24, 25, 28, 30.

fice. It is not surprising that the recipients were keen for the program to continue as long as possible.

The expansion of the state highway system and the development of local connecting roads dominated CWA work, resulting in an investment of considerable benefit, as counties and townships that had exhausted their funds had neglected secondary roads for years. Approximately 70 percent of Kansas's projects were road oriented and provided much work for the unskilled who dominated the relief rolls. Fortunately, in November 1933 many road construction schemes were already under way and could easily be transferred to the CWA. These projects quickly created jobs for the unskilled, either directly in road construction, or indirectly by employment in quarrying and transport. Other projects included the repair of city streets; the construction and improvement of public buildings, like schools and hospitals; the upgrading of parks and cemeteries; and work on drainage and flood prevention. The emphasis on construction explains why three-quarters of Kansas CWA jobs were graded as unskilled, though it is probable that some of the men working on these projects had skills that were neither recognized nor utilized. The opportunities for skilled CWA employment were limited. Workers like bricklayers, carpenters, electricians, masons, plumbers, seamstresses, and welders made up less than 5 percent of the state quota, while clerical positions contributed just over 6 percent.

Relief Work for Women

An inevitable and unfortunate result of the concentration on construction work was an inadequate provision of employment for women and, indeed, for the white-collar unemployed of either sex. To address this deficiency, a Civil Works Service (CWS) program was established to provide a range of jobs that would not rely primarily on physical strength; most of its efforts were targeted at women. The CWS was administratively linked to the CWA but differed from it in at least three significant respects. First, while women employed on CWA projects were chosen on the basis of their qualifications for the job, all CWS employees had to show that they were not merely unemployed but also in need of relief. However, to reduce the amount of time a full-scale social investigation to assess need would take, professional organizations like the Red Cross were allowed to decide on eligibility. Second, SERAs administered all CWS projects, and workers on them were paid from local, state, or federal relief funds, not from the CWA budget. This financial separation was mirrored in the de-

cision not to assign separate quotas for CWS jobs. Exactly how many positions would be surrendered from their CWA quota to accommodate service workers was often a difficult decision, and one that was left to individual states. Finally, the county poor commissioners, acting on the recommendation of county case supervisors, selected CWS employees, and there was no role here for the re-employment service.

There is no doubt that the CWA initiative broke new ground nationally and locally. For the first time in the history of Kansas, employment was offered to women who were on relief, laying the foundations for the imaginative women's projects later launched by the county relief administrations. During the first three months of 1934, CWA/CWS projects employed a total of 4,195 females, whose pay for CWS work averaged $10.75 for a thirty-hour week. Women who were fortunate enough to work on CWA projects, however, received $11.20 per week for the same number of hours. The difference in pay is partly explained by the fact that CWA wage scales were set for men and therefore relatively high, and partly because CWS scales were driven by local prevailing wage rates, which were usually lower than CWA rates. As there were approximately 12,000 unemployed women in the state at this time, more than one-third of that number enjoyed a cash income, albeit for a short while.[68]

In November 1933, Stutz received a letter from Mary Dewson, director of the Women's Division of the Democratic National Committee, unambiguously giving her support to individuals for the position of director of women's work. She wrote: "Mr. Hopkins agreed with me that if any woman had given her time and energy to elect the President, and who is *thoroughly available for this position,* she should receive it in preference to some woman who had either not worked for the election of President Roosevelt or who had opposed it." Dewson suggested that Mrs. E. R. Corey of Lawrence, Mrs. Lina Tullcross of Emporia, and Mrs. Mary P. Hogue of Topeka should be seriously considered for the post.[69] It was, however, State Supervisor Miss Lou E. Hume who took charge of the Kansas CWS program.[70] It was her idea that each county case supervisor should seize the initiative and establish a committee of representative fe-

68. Information on Women's Programs is taken from *KERC Bulletin* 127, 584, and *KERC Bulletin* 289, 16, 52–59.

69. Dewson to Stutz November 16, 1933, KERC Correspondence, September 8, 1932–November 5, 1936, Stutz Papers, 327:6:26. The emphasis is Dewson's.

70. Lou E. Hume was awarded a bachelor's degree by Albion College, Michigan, and began her career as a social worker in Detroit in 1918. She held a variety of welfare appointments in Michigan, Illinois, and California before taking up the post of executive secretary, Royal Oak Township Branch of the Detroit Community Union in 1930. In September 1933, she was appointed state case supervisor by the KERC.

males who would liaise with her and ensure that no part of the state was neglected. With the assistance of local professional groups and the re-employment offices, counties were able to locate suitable premises and begin the process of employment selection. However, in some counties where men on relief had absorbed the entire CWA quota, there was a con-siderable reluctance to organize women's projects, especially if to do so would require the removal of men from the CWA payroll. Occasionally women's projects could not get under way until some men had complet-ed their projects and left CWA employment.[71] In some rural counties, so few of the women available for work were on relief that it was not con-sidered worthwhile to organize projects for them. On the other hand, women with appropriate skills could be hired immediately for office work, and many CWA/CWS programs created an instant demand for clerical and technical staff. Similarly, hard-pressed poor commissioners and case supervisors needed additional clerical support, and, once the funding was in place, they could also readily find employment for women who could provide bedside nursing or assist home demonstration agents. However, most women in need did not have relatively sophisticated skills, and the large numbers who had not been in regular employment for some time perhaps lacked the confidence to contemplate positions at the edge of their capabilities.

Of the 2,069 women at work on CWS projects in Kansas during the week February 16–22, the majority—that is, 1,318—were employed on sewing-room projects. The next most significant employment groups were clerical (204), nursing (149), education (134), and janitorial services (96). The women who participated in the sewing-room projects not only learned or honed a skill, they also became familiar with the discipline of work, were able to socialize in the work place, and produced clothing for relief families throughout the state. Moreover, most of the women em-ployed were widows or "young girls" from homes with large numbers of dependents.[72] CWA and CWS sewing rooms operated in fifty-three coun-ties and employed between 1,500 and 2,000 women each week. Another CWA initiative provided employment for 105 nurses, who gave much needed home assistance to, among others, relief families. These, and oth-er projects, boosted morale and signaled the arrival of a much more sym-pathetic and constructive attitude toward women. Most importantly, women's projects were continued after March 31 under the aegis of coun-

71. Hume to Mrs. Ellen S. Woodward, Director of Women's Work, January 6, 1934, FERA State Files, Kansas, 1933–36, Kansas File, Director of Women's Work, RG69, NA.
72. Hume to Woodward, March 8, 1934, ibid.

ty relief schemes. Although placement on these was limited to women who had been certified for relief and who also lacked the support of an able-bodied wage earner, nevertheless, on December 31, 1934, 6,302 women were employed on relief and administration projects.

Relief Wages and Hours

As with all work relief projects, the construction of a comprehensive wage and hours model posed problems. The administration, and Harry Hopkins in particular, wanted to pay CWA workers a wage that would be viewed as a fair reward for the job rather than, as with the FERA, a relief payment based on individual or family needs. Furthermore, a commitment to high wages was at the core of Washington's industrial recovery strategy, and no New Dealer could defend CWA payments that might have a depressing effect on private-sector wages. On the other hand, it was always the view of Roosevelt and his advisors that when private jobs became available, those on work relief should have every incentive to take them. Work relief projects should not hoard labor by paying too generously.

Because CWA funding came via the Public Works Administration, Hopkins's first inclination was to use the PWA as a model, which meant dividing the country into three broad geographic zones and establishing minimum hourly wage rates in each for both the skilled and the unskilled. CWA rates for the Central Region, which included Kansas, were $1.10 for skilled workers and 45 cents for the unskilled. The CWA also imposed limits on hours of work. Except for executive, administrative, supervisory, or clerical positions, no individual was permitted to work more than thirty hours each week. Clerical employees, who can serve as an example of groups not bound by this rule, could be engaged for up to thirty-nine hours. The vast bulk of CWA workers fell into the thirty hours category.

In practice the simplicity of the wage structure outlined above had to be compromised. The PWA set only skilled and manual wage rates, but the CWA employed a more diverse work force, many of whom were semi-skilled. A pay grade for CWA workers was established between the skilled and the unskilled rate, after taking local pay levels into account. This was a practical although not very scientific approach to wage determination, but it was no more open to criticism than the crude averaging used to calculate the skilled and unskilled rates. There was a further complication. Men working on CWA road and street projects had to accept wage rates imposed by each state highway department, which were set in accordance

with the prescriptions of the National Industrial Recovery Act. This was a source of conflict when unskilled workers on highway and road projects received the minimum rate of 40 cents per hour while similar grade labor employed on city streets was paid the CWA minimum of 45 cents. This county/city differential caused considerable resentment when the two groups worked close to each other and became more aware of the differences in their rewards. For clerical and white-collar workers the CWA instruction was that wage rates should be identical with the prevailing wage in each community, but in the Central Region it must never be less than $15.00 per week.

Relatively generous wages and long hours resulted in a very expensive program that could not be sustained, especially as the president was a firm believer in a balanced federal budget.[73] In January 1934 a serious funding shortfall made changes in the wage/hours model inevitable. Weekly employment for those working in rural areas (that is, in settlements of less than 2,500 inhabitants) was cut to 15 hours, while their counterparts in urban centers, or in counties judged predominantly urban, faced a reduction to twenty-four hours. The hours of clerical workers declined from thirty-nine to thirty. Hourly wage rates were unchanged, but given the reduction in hours worked, take-home pay plummeted, making CWA jobs less attractive. Indeed, the average monthly pay for CWA work, which was about $50 before hours were reduced, declined to half of that figure afterward.

The Legacy of the CWA

In fact, this bold experiment was near its end. During February, all states were instructed to begin a cull of their CWA/CWS employees, with those least in need being laid off first. In an attempt to ensure equality, states were also asked to ensure that during this period of contraction no discrimination occurred against needy women. Most social workers opposed the decision to terminate the CWA, giving professional support to the establishment of a permanent program that would provide assistance to all the unemployed, not merely those who were in need. They disagreed strongly with Harry Hopkins's view that the CWA was no longer

73. The president had also become disenchanted with some states' failure to develop work relief projects that did not rely on leaf raking and wood chopping or other make-work tasks. Harold L. Ickes, *The Secret Diary of Harold L. Ickes: The First Thousand Days, 1933–1936*, 256, 293.

required.[74] The unemployed, too, were strong supporters, provided that CWA wage rates were linked to a thirty-hour working week. Governor Landon also added his voice to those who urged the administration to continue with the CWA. In a letter to Roosevelt he was unambiguous in his opinion that "this Civil Works program is one of the soundest, most constructive policies of your administration, and I can not urge too strongly its continuance."[75] It is, however, difficult to reconcile Landon's support for a balanced budget with the continuation of such a costly program.

During February and March 1934, the administration put into effect a rapid end to the CWA and turned its attention to three separate groups that had been identified as deserving special attention. The first of these groups, distressed families in rural areas, were assisted so that they could support themselves on the land. The second group, "stranded populations," defined as communities dependent on a single failed industry, needed help from a number of federal agencies whether they decided to move to a new location or decided to stay. Finally, the government offered hope to the needy unemployed in the cities through a flexible system of public works that provided employment for all groups, whatever their skill level. Direct relief was not seen as a solution; the continuing belief was that the needy jobless should contribute something of value to the community in exchange for the assistance they received.

Meanwhile, desirable ongoing CWA/CWS projects would be transferred to a new Emergency Work Relief Program for the unemployed, but only for those who could demonstrate that they were in need. Moreover, the zonal influence on wage determination that the CWA had copied from the PWA was abandoned, and the budgetary deficiency system to determine the level of earnings was reimposed. Under the Emergency Work Relief Program, employment was limited to a maximum of twenty-four hours each week. Hourly wage rates were based on an assessment of local prevailing wages, which were to be determined by Wage Rate Committees, made up of one representative from organized labor, one from the business community, and one from the local relief administration. The only constraint they faced was the national imposition of a minimum hourly rate of 30 cents. Any household head requiring more to support the family than could be earned in twenty-four hours would have the balance of his or her weekly budget made up from direct relief. On the other hand, if budgetary need was estimated to require less than three days'

74. Jacob Fisher, *The Response of Social Work to the Depression*, 49–55.
75. Landon to Roosevelt, January 16, 1934, FERA State Files, Kansas, 1933–35, Kansas File, Jan.–May 1934, RG69, NA.

work per week, or fifty-four hours per month, direct relief alone was recommended.[76] It is a tribute to their efficiency that Kansas county poor
commissioners and county case supervisors were able to place 75 percent
of their caseload in work under the new system by May 1934, despite the
need for rigorous investigation and budgeting.[77]

The CWA period in Kansas was one of industrial tranquility. There were
a few labor disputes, usually relating to wage issues, but they were re-
solved fairly quickly.[78] It is not surprising that confusion arose with the
imposition of uniform wages across a state that, like all others, had considerable local wage variations. One result was that the lowest CWA wage
rate was not only higher than the prevailing unskilled rate in many
Kansas counties, it was actually higher than the skilled rate in some. One
can understand why farmers, who were eligible for CWA work if they participated in New Deal agricultural schemes, were keen to obtain such employment and then hire men at lower wage rates to take care of their
farms.[79] It is also understandable that farmers who could not secure CWA
positions complained bitterly about the increasing cost of hired labor. Before the dramatic reduction in hours, which was introduced in January, it
was possible for men to earn at least as much working for thirty hours
with the CWA as they had previously with a longer working week.

In general, trades unions are more interested in the well being of their
employed members than in that of the unemployed. Organized labor welcomed the CWA, but it had as its priorities the preservation of skilled jobs,
the recruitment of union members to CWA positions, and the maintenance of existing wage rates. Some union locals strove to preserve all
skilled CWA jobs for their members, and they were also quick to challenge
the grading of tasks on projects, in case skilled work was downgraded. In
a dozen counties, union locals directly requisitioned labor for CWA
work.[80] Such was the union concern over wage rates that the significant
reduction in hours of work elicited little reaction: a reduction in wage
rates, however, would have resulted in vigorous protest.[81]

76. *KERC Bulletin* 44, March 26, 1934.

77. Ibid. 289, 17.

78. In this respect, Kansas seems to have conformed to the national pattern. Bonnie
Fox Schwartz, *The Civil Works Administration, 1933–1934: The Business of Emergency Employment in the New Deal,* 125.

79. *KERC Bulletin* 289, 779.

80. The counties are Atchison, Bourbon, Butler, Crawford, Labette, Leavenworth,
Lyon, Reno, Riley, Sabine, Shawnee, and Wyandotte. A total of 820 workers were recruited, of whom 359 were from Crawford and 135 from Wyandotte. *KERC Bulletin*
289, 780.

81. Schwartz, *Civil Works Administration,* 119–20.

While the CWA/CWS program was in operation, counties still had to discharge their obligations to relief applicants after a proper casework investigation to determine needs.[82] The most numerous group in this category were unemployables, but there were also a number of employables who were unable to obtain CWA/CWS jobs because the quotas were full. Wherever possible, locally funded relief work was arranged for those physically capable of labor. However, it is clear that in spite of the ambitious aims of this costly CWA program, inadequately funded county work relief or dole was unavoidable for some of the able-bodied. Moreover, locally funded relief could be crucial even to those in CWA employment. It was sometimes the case that large families could not manage even on a CWA wage; this was especially true once hours had been reduced. For these clients, supplementation of their budgets by the county was necessary. No family living at the edge of its resources could cope with a medical crisis, and here again the counties were obliged to provide assistance, though the appropriate amount of work relief to help cover costs was often required. Other initiatives included the Plan for Relief in Education, where qualified teachers eligible for relief were employed, though the charge did not fall on the counties as special FERA funding was available.[83] The same funding source financed the College Student Employment Project, which provided part-time employment for college students.[84]

What did Kansas gain from the CWA/CWS? There can be no doubt that extra money enabled many people to spend more freely and to pay off some of their debts, which was of considerable benefit to shopkeepers and other small businesses. The threat of a serious winter recession did not materialize, but the cash injection from the CWA was not sufficient to play more than a marginal role in the performance of the whole economy. The plight of unemployed women had been recognized at last, and many had acquired new skills and more confidence. All over the state citizens could see that physical improvements had taken place in just a few months. Many roads, schools, hospitals, airfields, and leisure facilities had been, or were in the process of being, transformed. Yet if these gains were to be more than transitory, projects still had to be completed and new ones begun. New road systems and other major construction projects are not built in a few months; the key to CWA/CWS success would lie in the continu-

82. *KERC Bulletin* 5, December 28, 1933.
83. Ibid. 11, January 11, 1934.
84. Ibid. 25, February 8, 1934.

ation of projects for most if not all the unemployed. The CWA/CWS did remove considerable numbers of employables from the relief rolls but only temporarily, as is evident from the following figures. At the beginning of 1934, 64,500 men and women were employed on CWA projects, and approximately 21,000 received assistance from county relief funds. At the end of 1934, a total of 82,000 individuals in Kansas were receiving work or direct relief.[85]

Welfare professionals described the transfer from the CWA to the Emergency Work Relief Program as a unique challenge to social workers. As work relief was now based on family need rather than solely on unemployment, social workers had to be aware that clients might exaggerate need. Moreover, although minimum wages and hours had been established for the new FERA program, this was in the context of a meticulously calculated budget that, previous experience had shown, was unlikely to be fully funded. The expectation was that many families would receive less than was needed because of inevitable funding shortages.[86] There was also a feeling among welfare professionals that the CWA had fundamentally altered attitudes toward relief, especially toward work relief. The stigma so long associated with an application for assistance had diminished, so that in the future people would request or demand help, even if not destitute. Many of these more demanding applicants would not understand that the help available for them was now only available on a much more restrictive basis. Social workers believed that the unemployed who were judged not to be in need would become angry and aggressive once it was clear that they no longer qualified for government jobs. Apprehensive observers believed that the CWA had given the unemployed a group cohesion that could be exploited by malcontents in the future, and that a sense of solidarity formed under the CWA banner would make possible the formation of vociferous pressure groups that would vent their spleen on local relief workers and committees. The lower rates of pay introduced under the new Emergency Work Relief Program provided a possible flashpoint in parts of the state where the jobless were most numerous and best organized.

Stutz articulated this fear very clearly and frankly in a letter to Harry Hopkins. "The temperament of the unemployed or ex-CWA employees may be reported as anxious and expectant," he wrote, adding, "[W]e are experiencing some difficulty in the transition from Civil Works to Work

85. Ibid. 289, 11.
86. Ibid. 47, April 1934.

Relief because the relief clients have had much more income under Civil Works than will be possible under work relief." Unfortunately Stutz's optimistic forecast that "no violence is anticipated" was soon exposed as grossly inaccurate, especially by the Wichita riot in May 1934.[87]

In April 1934 applications for relief, which had averaged between 6,000 and 7,000 in the first few months of the year, rose to 41,542, overwhelming the social workers who had to interview all applicants. The causes of this increase can be found primarily in the closure of the CWA program and the inability of the economy to provide sufficient private sector jobs for those who needed them. In addition, numbers were swelled by applicants who had previously refused to apply for direct relief because of the stigma attached to it; now, inspired by the CWA, they were prepared to explore the possibilities of work relief. The caseload was further increased at the end of April when drought in central and western Kansas became so serious that farmers in the region had to be placed on relief. Moreover, as had been anticipated, insufficient federal funding for family budgets led to the further expense of county supplementation.[88] In order to manage the increase in relief applications, Kansas appointed additional social workers so that the average individual caseload declined from its peak of 274 in April and May to 155 at the end of the year. To attain this improvement staffing increased fourfold during 1934.[89] The post-CWA budgeting procedures called for more detailed casework investigation; indeed, those who had doubted the merit of hiring trained and experienced social workers at last began to see their value.

At the close of the CWA program Governor Landon had the presence of mind to write to Harry Hopkins asking for a statement that could be released to local newspapers concerning the FERA and the Kansas relief administration. Hopkins felt that he personally could not make such a declaration, and the responsibility for preparing it was delegated to T. J. Edmonds. Landon must have found it difficult to contain his delight when a paean from Washington arrived in April 1934. Among many praiseworthy statements, Edmonds noted that "the organization plan of the relief and Civil Works developed in Kansas is one of the best in the country" and made possible "one of the most prompt and effective executions of the relief and Civil Works of any state in the union." Furthermore, the work of John Stutz was "unexcelled in any state," and the department

87. Stutz to Hopkins, April 4, 1934, Stutz Papers, 327:1:4.

88. Stutz to Corrington Gill, July 6, 1934, FERA State Files, Kansas File, June–Sept 1934, RG69, NA.

89. *KERC Bulletin* 289, 17–18, 23–24.

heads Messrs Marvin, Morrison, Marsh, and Ford were also singled out for praise. Apart from raising morale throughout the state, this was a significant vote of confidence for a Republican administration from the heart of the New Deal. It is not surprising that the letter was reproduced in full in the *Kansas Relief News-Bulletin.*[90]

& KS is praised for its program

90. Edmonds to Landon, April 25, 1934, Papers of Alfred Mossman Landon, Kansas State Historical Society, Topeka, Folder 3, Box 12 (hereafter "Landon Papers"). See also Folder 1, Box 13; *Kansas Relief News-Bulletin*, No. 5, May 21, 1934, 3–4.

3

Unemployment, Riots, and the Emergency Work Relief Program

After the closure of the Civil Works Administration program, some Kansas communities experienced tensions that led to demonstrations and even riots. Many applicants for assistance resented the intrusive investigations of their personal circumstances that the Emergency Work Relief program demanded to determine their eligibility for relief. Detailed inquiries into family finances, including one home visit by a case worker every thirty days to assess any change in circumstances, would have been more tolerable if the results had always matched the expectations of prospective clients.[1] When unavoidable delays developed as social workers struggled to deal with a large influx of applicants, frustrations built up. Resentment increased when, after investigation, some unemployed applicants were rejected on the grounds that although jobless, they were not in need. In addition, many clients who were classified as in need developed a sense of grievance when it became evident that federal funding was insufficient to deliver their meticulously calculated budgets in full. It is not, therefore, surprising that discontents crowding the relief offices often lashed out at officials. Poor commissioners, case supervisors, and, of course, John Stutz, were popular targets.

1. Home visits were reduced to one every six weeks in October 1935. *KERC Bulletin* 282, October 12, 1935.

Relief: The Kansas Model

It is important to understand the relief structure in which state and federal officials had such confidence and explain why, in spite of its outstanding qualities in Kansas, the allocation of relief periodically aroused the wrath of the unemployed. At the peak of the organizational pyramid was the KERC, the state's supervisory and policy forming body, whose members the governor appointed. Each month the FERA made a grant in aid to the state, and it was the responsibility of the KERC to allocate federal funds and surplus commodities to the counties so that they could be distributed to the needy. The KERC also appointed the members and monitored the progress of each CERC, as well as approving the appointment of all county relief officers. John Stutz was the executive director of the KERC, and a line of responsibility ran directly from him to Harry Hopkins, the federal relief administrator. Stutz had overall responsibility for the administration and distribution of all federal relief in Kansas, whether it came in dollars or in kind. The role of the CERCs was purely advisory, but members were able to express their views to the county commissioners on a variety of important issues, including the appointment of staff and the administration of relief funds. Poor commissioners convened meetings of CERCs on a regular basis and also acted as secretary to the groups. The views of the CERCs thus had some force, as they possessed a direct line of communication to the KERC.

In the Kansas system, counties were fully responsible for the distribution of federal funds and the surplus commodities allocated to them. The KERC drew up clear lines of demarcation and responsibility for all individuals engaged in relief administration and provided full job descriptions so that the possibility of overlapping responsibilities, as might occur between poor commissioners and county case supervisors, could be eliminated. The result was a clear administrative structure with each board of county commissioners accountable to the KERC for the provision of an effective relief service. The county commissioners had the responsibility of appointing and paying staff but could do so only after the approval of the KERC had been secured. Indeed, all county commissioners were obliged to conduct policy and practice within a framework set by the KERC, which in turn was circumscribed by FERA regulations. The commissioners appointed the three key officials who were to manage relief, namely the poor commissioner, the county case supervisor, and the supervisor of the relief program. In addition, a certifying officer appointed and funded by the KERC, whose role was principally that of an auditor, was attached to each county.

The poor commissioner was the principal administrator for all relief matters in the county, including federal grants in aid.[2] This was a position of major significance. The poor commissioner focused on the selection, training, and development of staff; in addition, he or she carried the responsibility of overseeing the finances of the county relief program. From October 1934, all holders of this office had to have, as a minimum qualification, administrative experience with some practical knowledge of relief and the principles of social work. In addition, three hours of college credit in each of two courses chosen from political science, economics, sociology, biology, or psychology were essential. Although poor commissioners were particularly concerned with the administration of direct and work relief, they never became involved in the investigation of individual cases, which was the task of the county case supervisor. Poor commissioners managed the administration of relief under the direction of the board of county commissioners, with whom he or she had frequent meetings. Other key responsibilities included the assignment to the supervisor of work program of men budgeted for relief, the daily accounting of relief expenditures, and the provision of regular reports to both the county commissioners and the KERC. As we will see, the poor commissioner was also closely involved with the county case supervisor in constructing monthly budgets.

The primary duty of the county case supervisor was to investigate thoroughly—using interviews, home visits, and other techniques—all individuals who applied for relief, whether the source of funding was federal or local. After the assessment was complete, a decision was taken on the needs, or the budget, of any client whose application for relief had been judged successful. This decision ultimately determined the amount of assistance in the form of work relief, direct relief orders, or surplus commodities that would be allocated. It was the county case supervisor who initially authorized all relief expenditures, but these orders also required the signature of the poor commissioner before they could be actioned. County case supervisors were expected to encourage client families and individuals to become self-sufficient so that they could be removed from the relief rolls, to liaise with other welfare agencies, and to be constantly aware of resources available in the community that could be used for relief. County case supervisors working in the most populated and demanding counties were required to hold a college degree, have three years' case working experience in a recognized case working agency, and

2. All relief job descriptions are fully recorded in *KERC Bulletin* 289, November 1, 1935, 18–26, 34–40.

possess some administrative and supervisory experience. Those seeking an appointment in counties where the relief load was not overwhelming needed a college degree and one year's case working experience. Men and women without college degrees but with two years' experience in a recognized case working agency could be considered for employment in what were described as Group 11 counties. The post of county case supervisor was a demanding one, and the KERC believed that the training undertaken by the county case supervisor with a recognized social agency was equivalent to the internship of a medical doctor.

The third post, supervisor of work program, only became part of the relief management structure when the CWA reached the end of its life and was replaced by the Emergency Work Relief Program. Each supervisor was required to be a qualified engineer and to possess additional training experience in construction projects. The approval of the KERC's own engineering department had to be secured before the appointment could be confirmed. The rationale for this position was to provide expertise, which would ensure that the appropriate number of laborers, tools, and foremen were employed on projects, giving validity to the projects themselves.

Relief officials had to operate within closely defined but periodically changing FERA rules, though sometimes a degree of local flexibility was permitted, especially in budget setting. In April 1934, for example, the FERA stipulated that no person on its funded projects could be employed for more than eight or less than six hours per day. However, if the calculated relief budget deficiency resulted in less than eighteen hours of work relief per month, the client was instead to receive direct relief.[3] This eminently sensible policy was designed to reduce the managerial problem of absorbing into projects large numbers of clients who would require work for just a few hours. The FERA set maximum hours (twenty-four per week), while wage rates were based upon estimates of those prevailing locally after investigation by a Wage Rate Committee. However, the calculated deficiency budget determined weekly income, and in setting it social workers had to have considerable freedom. Although the FERA gave states detailed advice on the methodology required to undertake the intricate investigations necessary to set a relief budget, this was only guidance on procedure. As the cost of living varied considerably, not just between but within states, the amount of relief required to enable each client to maintain the minimum standard of living necessary to prevent physical suffering had to be determined individually at the county level.

Once an application for relief had been filed and the client's legal set-

3. *KERC Bulletin* 51, April 14, 1934.

tlement established, social workers had to draw up a budget that assessed need against income. This was a "minimum need budget," and it was constructed after discussions with every client. The starting point was an analysis of essential items in family expenditure, including food, shelter, fuel, clothing, household necessities, transportation, insurance payments, and allowances for health care, education, and recreation. In proceeding with an examination of each of these items, the caseworker relied on guidelines provided by the KERC.[4] For example, the most important item in the list was food, and the advice given was that between 40 to 45 percent of the total minimum budget should be allowed for food, though monthly revisions to reflect changing prices could be necessary. The calculation of food allowances for the family was sophisticated. Account was taken of the age and gender composition of the household and of any special circumstances, such as the presence of a pregnant or nursing mother. When a family member performed an arduous physical work relief task, a compelling case could be made for a higher food allowance. Transportation allowances included the cost of essential trips to and from work, school, or market, if the distance was too great to walk. The accompanying advice to the caseworker was that discussions with the family should provide information on the most cost-effective way of making these journeys, and allowances in the budget should reflect minimum expenditure. Just taking into account variations in the cost of living between urban and rural Kansans, it is easy to see why families of identical size could have very different minimum need budgets depending on where they lived. An important additional instruction to social workers was that the full minimum needs of the family should always be considered in constructing the budget, even if it was clear that these needs eventually could not be met by the funds available.

After drawing up the minimum need budget, the next step was assessing the client's income, which included every item of cash, goods, or wages coming to the family. Information on farm products consumed and sold; CCC and AAA allotment payments; earnings from lodgers; gifts from churches, relatives, or private relief agencies; wages from all but the most irregular odd jobs; and any income from property, investment, or pensions was supposed to be gathered meticulously. In addition, the family's resources, which included the value of saleable or mortgageable property, cash savings, stocks and bonds, and stored food, were also ascertained and considered in the determination of net income.

4. Ibid. 174, February 20, 1935, has full instructions on "Eligibility and Budgeting." See also ibid. 70, July 5, 1934, for "Suggestions for Determining the Clothing Minimum Budgets of Families on Relief," and Mary A. Nicol, *Family Relief Budgets,* 140–65.

With all this information it was possible to construct for each client a budget deficiency—that is, the difference between the minimum need budget and the income plus the available resources at the client's disposal. The "deficiency budget," as it was known, helped to determine the number of hours of work relief which those who were assigned to FERA projects could be allocated. However, it is important to recognize that the deficiency budget was used as a guide rather than a rigid formula in determining both eligibility for relief and also the amount of local relief recommended. Each county case supervisor had regular conferences with the poor commissioner to reach an agreement on the total amount required by the county to finance clients' budgets and also to relate that sum to total funds available. Every month the poor commissioner would prepare for the county commissioners an estimate of the number of cases that had a legitimate claim on local funds, and a similar calculation was forwarded to the KERC so that an assessment could be made as to how much work relief could be financed from federal funds. The county relief budget would be further discussed with the board of county commissioners. A clear idea of the gap between needs and resources was crucial, because when the county had insufficient funds to meet all its relief obligations, the amount of relief recommended for most clients had to be reduced. Indeed, only in rare instances were counties able to fund the deficiency budget in full.[5] Each month the poor commissioner had to deduct unavoidable expenditures—for example, on administration—from the county's budget. Once that had been done the percentage relationship between the amount available for relief and the total required to meet budget deficiencies could be calculated. It was in each county's interests to maximize the amount of federal aid to relieve the poor, as any shortfall had to be filled from local funds. All counties operated within the constraints of the Cash Basis Law.

The problem of managing any deficiency is clearly illustrated by the hypothetical example used in the guide *Instructions on Eligibility and Budgeting*, which was issued to all poor commissioners and county case supervisors. Readers were asked to consider a situation where the amount available for relief was only 67 percent of the total sum calculated as necessary to cover budget deficiencies.[6] As a result, the poor commissioner had to ensure that each minimum need budget was reduced to 67 percent of the original, and that this sum was deducted from the client's relief income. These calculations, together with the budget deficiencies, were re-

5. *KERC Bulletin* 289, 79.
6. *KERC Bulletin* 174, 7. Presumably, a shortfall of 33 percent was a realistic figure.

turned to the county caseworker who, with the assistance of aides, assessed each case individually. A decision was then made as to which clients would suffer excessively if the full reduction were implemented. Some cases were judged so problematic that no reduction was possible, but as the caseworker had to operate within a fixed budget, something had to give. The result was that less urgent cases experienced either a major cut or, indeed, a total cut in relief. In the real as opposed to the hypothetical world, each month social workers had the difficult task of reconciling the limited amount of relief funding available with the needs of their clients. The final deficiency budget calculation determined the hours of work relief that would be given to those judged fit for employment and fortunate enough to get it, or the quantity of direct relief that would be available to the remainder. Caseworkers were also responsible for the distribution of surplus commodities that came to the states from the Federal Surplus Commodities Corporation (FSCC).

The need for sensitive, trained, and experienced social workers to implement the budgetary procedures is obvious. It is also clear why the poor commissioners and case workers were vulnerable to criticism; they had to make very difficult decisions that could lead to unanticipated reductions in relief for many hard-pressed clients. For example, the unemployed who were not assigned to federal work relief programs, which always paid cash wages, had to rely on county relief where the sums available to them were not only considerably less but also usually in kind. We can see this clearly by looking at a few examples. In 1934 Sedgwick County received fractionally over $1 million from the federal government for relief, virtually all of which was used as cash wages for work projects. The county also spent $634,000 on relief, but only $55,000 of this sum was available in cash; the remainder, $579,000, was distributed in kind. The situation in Wyandotte County was similar. The federal government advanced $1.3 million, virtually all of which ended up in the wage packets of relief workers. The county raised $261,000, but only $8,000 of this sum was distributed in cash.[7] County work relief programs were modest, and they did not always pay a cash wage.

A further problem arose with the manner in which federal funding was allocated. States received their allocations monthly, following an application to Harry Hopkins that FERA staff evaluated. There was inevitably an uncertainty about the level of the grant, which in any case, always lagged behind rapid and adverse changes of circumstance. One can sympathize

7. See *KERC Bulletin* 289, Table IV, "Analysis of Payments in Cash or In Kind for all Relief Granted," 620, 730.

with the determination of the FERA to ensure that demands on the tax-payer were supported with the most up-to-date information. However, when, as was frequently the case, states received less than they had requested, their relief budgets had to be instantly pared. Little wonder that men and women existing on the very edge of acceptable living standards should resent their already meager relief being cut, often at short notice, and that they would blame local officials for inflicting this misery.

Despair, Protest, and Occupation

Relief in Kansas was devolved to the counties, but unfortunately, where acute need coincided with an inability to raise more than modest amounts to supplement federal funding, the limited sums available for distribution led to serious deprivation. Furthermore, the Cash Basis Law incorporated by the state required counties to have funds in hand and available for use before expenditure could be undertaken. Especially deprived counties, like Cherokee and Crawford, exposed a major weakness in the Kansas model, as neither was sufficiently financially robust to assume full care of their relief cases. As a result, both counties experienced serious hardship. Inadequate federal and county funding combined to create pockets of unrest that periodically erupted into conflict between the unemployed, who increasingly organized themselves into unions, and those whom they believed responsible for their distress. Although in 1935 the KERC could report friendly relations between itself and unemployed organizations and labor unions, violent protests became a worrying feature for relief administrators and politicians.[8]

As early as the fall of 1933, Olaf Larsen, founder and president of the Topeka-based Worker's Educational and Protective League of Kansas, had begun recruiting the city's direct and work relief clients to his organization. A self-appointed champion of the unemployed, he had gained publicity by leading a relief demonstration to Topeka's courthouse on October 30, 1933.[9] Larsen was a compulsive letter writer, especially to prominent political figures, and the president, Mrs. Roosevelt, Harry Hopkins, Frances Perkins, and Governor Landon were among the recipients of Larsen's florid prose.[10] On April 2, 1934, the very day that the FERA re-

8. *Work Relief in Kansas* 2, April 1934–June 1935, 77, Stutz Papers, 327:4:5.
9. Lyle O. Armel, Poor Commissioner Shawnee County to S. M. Brewster, U.S. District Attorney, November 1, 1933; Armel to Stutz, January 10, 1934. Both in Stutz Papers, 327:2:25.
10. Larsen to President Roosevelt, November 27, 1934; to Mrs. Roosevelt, December

placed the CWA, 1,500 of the unemployed followed Larsen's call and held a meeting in Topeka's auditorium. According to the *Topeka Journal,* which reported the event in full, this was the largest meeting of its kind. At it the CWA was roundly denounced, with speakers demanding the removal of both Shawnee County Poor Commissioner Lyle O. Armel and John Stutz.[11] The demonstrators, who included women and children, marched peacefully though Topeka flanked by two motorcycle policemen. A relieved Mayor Omar Ketchum congratulated the marchers on their commitment to orderly assembly. Governor Landon also addressed the crowd, assuring listeners that the Special Session of the Legislature, scheduled for October, would address many of their pressing relief issues. Landon also spoke for about two hours with representatives of the unemployed, whom he saw in his private office. This incident shows how a large group of unemployed, most of whom had time to spare, could be effectively mobilized. Once gathered they became a threat; politicians had to take them seriously. Curiously, much of the protest was directed against the CWA, which had attracted a great deal of support earlier in the year and which, in any case, had just closed operations.

Although peace reigned in Topeka, it did not in Crawford County. On April 24 approximately 150 people, angered by a reduction in the work relief program, marched on the relief offices in Pittsburg. About twenty men, undeterred by the tear gas released to repel them, attacked and hospitalized one of the county commissioners, William A. Beasley.[12] All federal aid to the county was immediately cut off, and the county relief office was closed. This was a serious matter, as without federal funds the entire relief burden fell on the county. Stutz delivered a very clear message that relief work would not resume until he had received assurances from the county attorney, the sheriff, and the chief of police at Pittsburg that there would be no further interference with the program. Beasley later claimed that mob rule prevailed in Pittsburg and that elected officials were prevented from administering relief effectively. He requested police protection for himself and the county case supervisor, Miss Marie Youngberg, who was under great strain.[13] The demonstrators were led by Alexander Howat, a

---

18, 1934; to Hopkins, December 2, 15, 1934; to Perkins, November 28, 1934; to Landon, December 11, 1934, all in CWA Admin. Correspondence, Kansas Box 17, RG 69, NA. In his letter to her, Larsen enrolled Frances Perkins as Honorary Member #1,000 of his organization.

11. *Topeka Journal,* April 2, 1934.

12. Beasley was struck over the back with a chair. Stutz to Edmonds, September 18, 1934, FERA State Files, 1933–36, Kansas Field Reports, RG69, NA; *Kansas City Star,* April 29, 1934; *Wichita Beacon,* April 24, 1934.

13. Beasley to Landon, May 12, 1934, Box 13, Folder 1, Landon Papers.

former president of the United Mine Workers of America for the district of Kansas, who, together with his supporters, had been expelled from the union in 1922 by John L. Lewis.[14] The volatile Howat, who even Lewis could not control, was now prominent in the Worker-Farmers Legion of Crawford County, a union specifically for the unemployed.[15] John Stutz complained bitterly that Crawford County officials had gone to a great deal of trouble to appoint Beasley and Youngberg. Both were well quali-fied and capable of exercising independent judgment, qualities he felt were certainly lacking in Alexander Howat.[16] Some weeks later, Howat asked Landon to dismiss Stutz, only to receive a typically apposite and brusque rebuff. Stutz, Howat was informed, had been appointed by a Democrat governor and also enjoyed the full confidence of Harry Hopkins, who re-garded him as one of the best relief administrators in the country.[17]

While the violence orchestrated by the Worker-Farmers Legion was un-justified, the poor of Crawford County did have sound reasons for dis-content and protest. Bryan Dobson, a union official and Pittsburg resident, provided an insight into the deplorable conditions that provoked the un-rest when he wrote to American Federation of Labor chief William Green, imploring him to contact President Roosevelt. Dobson expressed fears that there would be bloodshed and serious rioting as the quality of life ex-perienced by the unemployed and their families was so dire. "Little chil-dren and women [were] suffering from want of food," he wrote, adding that urgent attention to addressing their plight was needed.[18]

The Wichita Riot, May 1934

Events in Pittsburg were minor compared with the riot that occurred in Wichita on May 9, 1934. Wichita had no previous history of mob violence,

14. People with trades union experience and single men were most likely to display aggression toward relief officials. Gabriel Almond and Harold D. Lasswell, "Aggres-sive Behavior by Clients toward Public Relief Administrators: A Configurative Analy-sis," 650–54; Samuel A. Stouffer and Paul E. Lazarsfeld, *Research Memorandum on the Family and the Depression,* 62–63.

15. *Pittsburg Sun,* May 11, 1934. For many years after his expulsion, Howat would leap onto the platform at the annual mine workers convention and denounce Lewis before being unceremoniously removed. Saul Alinsky, *John L. Lewis: An Unauthorized Biography,* 44, 51, 52, 54, 56–57.

16. Stutz to Edmonds, September 18, 1934, Stutz Papers, 327:1:4.

17. Howat to Landon, July 30; Landon to Howatt, July 31, 1934, Box 13, Folder 1, Landon Papers.

18. Dobson, Local Union No. 312, to Green, April 27, 1934, FERA State Files, Kansas File, January–May 1934, RG69, NA.

and this disturbance so alarmed Mayor Schuyler Crawford and City Manager Bert Wells that they sent a frantic appeal to Governor Landon requesting that he dispatch Kansas National Guard troops to the city. The riot was a climax to a series of increasingly bitter confrontations between groups of unemployed men and women protesting inadequate and poorly administered relief and the city's police, who attempted to contain them. The reaction of the authorities was to arrest twenty-six people, including two women, and arraign them on the serious charge of criminal syndicalism.[19]

On April 20, more than two thousand angry unemployed demonstrators met relief officials at the Forum, Wichita's largest civil auditorium. The demands of the meeting, articulated by the leader of the protesters, James "Whitey" MacLean, included twenty-four hours of relief work each week for all unemployed at 40 cents per hour, and the dismissal of both Poor Commissioner B. E. "Gene" George and County Physician Cyril Black. During the following day protesters entered the relief headquarters, and although there was no violence, staff felt intimidated by their presence. Stutz immediately suspended federal relief. Groups of the unemployed also marched on North Broadway demanding, sometimes forcefully, that those fortunate enough to be engaged on work relief should drop tools and join the protesters. Panic-stricken relief officials responded by promising some additional temporary help, but MacLean made it very clear that his followers would not be satisfied until a permanent and acceptable solution to meet their demands was found.[20]

On the morning of Tuesday, April 24, the county commissioners met with six representatives of Wichita's unemployed and gave them the opportunity to air their grievances. The men complained that the investigations undertaken by social workers to determine eligibility for relief and the construction of relief budgets were "insulting" and felt it was not surprising that social workers has been physically threatened by their clients. The men also claimed that relief work was not distributed fairly and that wages were inadequate. They were especially critical of Poor Commissioner George, whom they accused of insensitivity, and they castigated the provision of medical care for the jobless. They demanded relief work for all the unemployed, not just for those in need. As one of the group put it, "[T]here is a bunch of people that haven't got any work and they are demanding it. . . . [I]f part of them can be put to work, they reason that the rest can be put to work, and better the rest be cut down and the remain-

---

19. For a full account of the riot see, Peter Fearon, "Riot in Wichita, 1934," 266–79.
20. *Wichita Beacon*, May 21, 22, 23, 1934.

der of the people put to work, and treat them all the same." The men were also angry at Stutz's decision to close down all relief work that was disrupted by strikes or demonstrations.[21] The commissioners, anxious to restore a peace that would ensure the restoration of federal relief, tried to buy off the protesters. They accepted the concept of including as many of the unemployed as possible in distributing relief and believed that by using county funds to supplement federal grants they could support a relatively generous work relief program. However, in doing so the commissioners conceded that they would "have to spread it [relief] out pretty thin. Just so much butter will cover so much bread." They not only increased the number of work relief jobs, but they also introduced a new high-wage scale similar to the rates that had operated under the CWA. Work relief was offered on a sliding scale, which gave single men $3.20 each week and the heads of large families $12.80. This was based on an eight-hour day and a wage rate of 40 cents per hour. In fact, although the protesters accepted the deal offered to them, they really wanted the restoration of the CWA rule that the wages paid and the hours worked should be the same for all workers and should not be related to need. Unfortunately, the commissioners had only sufficient funds to finance this scheme for two weeks, and if at the end of that period additional funding had not been raised they would be in a very difficult situation. However, at least the commissioners could breathe a sigh of relief when federal aid was restored on April 28.[22]

Why did the commissioners take this gamble? After all, they knew that both federal regulations and state law required a thorough investigation of relief applicants, and that the relief given would be based on the budgetary deficiency principle. Moreover, the hourly work relief wage would depend upon the findings of a Wage Rate Committee. Stutz's view was that as one of them, Thurman Hill, was a Democratic candidate for the gubernatorial nomination and another was up for re-election, they were prepared to take a risk and pander to the demands of the protesters.[23] Federal Official T. J. Edmonds gave his broad support for this view. He reported that in order to provide immediate relief on CWA scales, the commissioners had diverted local money that should have been kept in re-

21. Minutes of Meeting between Board of Sedgwick County Commissioners, County Attorney John W. Wood, and a Committee of the Unemployed in Wichita, April 24, 1934, Stutz Papers, 327:2:29.

22. *Wichita Beacon*, April 28, 1934.

23. Stutz telephone conversation with Jacob Baker, May 10, 1934, FERA State Files, 1933–36, Kansas File, Wichita Strike, May 1934, RG69, NA (hereafter "Wichita Strike File").

serve to meet small, unforeseen financial difficulties that would occur throughout the year. After two weeks, however, the funds ran out and the new relatively generous relief payments had to be reduced to "pretty small" levels compared to the CWA.[24]

On May 4, using the title President of the Unemployed of Sedgwick County, MacLean sent a petition to Landon that contained a veiled threat. The work relief program, he claimed, provided insufficient payment to allow unemployed citizens to live and feed their families to the standard he felt appropriate, even though, as he acknowledged, officials had done all that was possible within the existing laws of Kansas. However, his message adopted a sinister tone when he added that although the unemployed did not seek conflict, the protestors could not be responsible for any violence that might occur if additional assistance was not granted.[25]

A walkout of Wichita's 4,200 relief workers was threatened on May 5 if the new lower pay scales, which the commissioners had been compelled to introduce, were not increased. On May 8 approximately 3,000 unemployed met at Payne's pasture, an athletic field on Wichita's west side. The crowd's mood favored a strike, and MacLean advised anyone present who had employment on a work relief project not to return to work until the grievances of all potential relief recipients were settled. On the following day 1,500 demonstrators returned to Payne's pasture, where they listened to an address by MacLean before moving toward the city with the aim of persuading fellow reliefers working on projects to join their strike. Once in Wichita, the marchers came into conflict with the police and a series of clashes took place, but apart from one police officer, Lieutenant C. D. Murrell, who was stabbed in the back, the injuries were superficial, being caused by fist, stick, and stone. The crowd dispersed before the evening, but during the following day groups of protesters returned to Payne's pasture only to be confronted by four units of the National Guard who—together with police, sheriff's, and marshal's forces—used tear gas to disperse them. Arrests quickly followed. Approximately eighty people were taken into custody, and the eight ringleaders, having been charged with criminal syndicalism, a serious misdemeanor carrying a five- to ten-year prison sentence, were sent to the State Industrial Reformatory in Hutchinson. Eighteen others, including two women, were also charged with criminal syndicalism, though these charges were soon dropped, and sixteen protesters were charged with disturbing the peace. The others

24. Edmonds to Hopkins, May 17, 1934, Wichita Strike file.
25. Petition to Landon from James C. MacLean, President of the Unemployed of Sedgwick County, May 4, 1934, Box 13, Folder 1, Landon Papers.

who had been detained were released after questioning. There was a suspicion that the mob had been inflamed by outside agitators, but investigation showed that the marchers seem to have been entirely local, and many were heads of families. Ironically, CWA labor had remodeled the city's old fire station, converting it into a police headquarters and the jail to which the some of the rioters were sent.

The events in Wichita had caught Stutz by surprise. He and his second in command, F. H. Marvin, held Commissioner George in high regard, and although both were aware of mounting discontent in the city, they believed that he would be able to skillfully handle the growing difficulties in Wichita. This was a serious miscalculation on the part of Stutz, who later wrote that this affair "turned out to be one of the most difficult assignments of my 40 years of political service."[26] However, federal officials soon intervened, taking matters rapidly out of Stutz's hands. The level of federal involvement in the immediate aftermath of the riot is instructive, not just because of its swiftness, but also for the meticulous concern with detail and the seniority of the Washington figures involved, whose influence in deciding the appropriate punishment for the perpetrators of violence and the restoration of tranquil work relations was immense.

On May 10, Jacob Baker, acting specifically on the instructions of Harry Hopkins, telephoned Stutz for a firsthand account of the situation. While letters between Washington and Topeka were always formal, this telephone conversation was relaxed, and the easy use of first names illustrates the close relationship that had grown up between those responsible for the administration of relief at the federal and the state level. Baker suggested that in view of the seriousness of the situation all federally funded work relief should be immediately halted. Stutz demurred, but not because he felt that closure was a step too far; indeed, he had employed this weapon on a number of occasions himself. His concern was that once the flow of federal money was cut off, the direct relief burden, which would need to be met entirely from county resources, would be substantial. Moreover, meager local relief might exacerbate an already volatile situation. Baker suggested using federal money for direct relief, but Kansas was determined to employ federal funding only for work relief. Nevertheless, Baker asked Stutz to explore this option with some urgency, and meantime he kept his boss, Harry Hopkins, fully informed.[27]

---

26. Marvin to Edmonds, November 9, 1933, FERA State Files, Kansas File, May/Dec. 1933, RG69; *Wichita Beacon,* May 1, 1934; Stutz, handwritten note, October 18, 1980, Stutz Papers, 327:2:29.

27. Baker, telephone conversation with Stutz, May 10, 1934; Baker to Hopkins, May 10, 1934, Wichita Strike File.

By the following day Baker's instructions to Stutz had become firmer. He was now adamant that work relief should not continue under the protection of the National Guard, and he expressed firmly his view that the indictments for criminal syndicalism, of which he had just become aware, were Draconian and should be withdrawn. Stutz was urged to travel to Wichita as a matter of urgency, where he could meet up with a T. J. Edmonds.[28]

The level of concern in Washington reached such heights that Hopkins himself called Stutz the next day. As this extract from their phone conversation shows, he unequivocally instructed Stutz to halt all federal work relief:

> **Hopkins**: Well the impression is that we have a work program and the men go on a strike and we have to call out the militia to keep the people working. The public impression is that these men don't need work or they wouldn't strike.
> **Stutz**: If I stop it, then they accuse me of starving people.
> **Hopkins**: I wouldn't worry about that. It makes us look ridiculous to have strikes on relief jobs.[29]

Stutz agreed to withdraw federal relief as long as the National Guard was needed for the imposition of order, and he left for Wichita immediately. On Saturday, May 12, he, together with Edmonds and another federal official, William Nunn, began a long series of meetings with public officials, including the commander of the National Guard, the chief of police, and delegations of the unemployed.[30]

Both Edmonds and Nunn submitted detailed reports of their time in Wichita to their Washington superiors. Unlike local officials, who had been shaken by the riot and were determined to secure speedy and severe punishment to act as a powerful deterrent, they took a more detached view and accepted that periodically there would be serious employer-employee conflicts on relief projects. However, they suspected that clumsily imposed miserly relief payments in Wichita, together with the absence of any organized recreation in the city, played a significant role in this disturbance. Both men put relentless pressure on City Manager Bert Wells, Chief of Police O. W. Wilson, and County Attorney John Wood to abandon the criminal syndicalism charges, which in Edmond's view were both outrageous and unsustainable. Indeed, he believed that it would be

28. Baker to Stutz, May 11, 1934, Wichita Strike File.
29. Hopkins, telephone conversation with Stutz, May 11, 1934, Wichita Strike File.
30. Nunn to Baker, May 13, 1934, Stutz Papers, 327:2:29.

impossible to secure a conviction if the charges were not reduced.[31] Eventually the more serious charges were dropped; the male defendants pled guilty to the lesser offense of misdemeanor and received thirty days in prison. The women were paroled and released immediately; the National Guard left the city on May 13. As soon as order was restored, federal funds were made available for work relief wages, and Stutz made it clear that in future a Wage Rate Committee would deal with any complaints concerning wages. His unambiguous message was that federal rules and Kansas laws relating to the administration of relief would be meticulously followed.

In an added twist to this story, Edmonds and Nunn became suspicious that MacLean and his fellow riot leaders were "stool pigeons." An examination of the payment for work relief that eight of the men had received prior to the riot seemed to indicate that the sums they received were greater than their deficiency budgets allowed. Moreover, Nunn believed that although money changed hands, no work was actually done.[32] Was the principal rioters' role more complex that it would appear? Conspiracy theorists might believe that suspicion is the equivalent of evidence, but the archives contain no support to substantiate Nunn's intriguing supposition.

As the dust settled, Stutz promised to keep a representative, Jay M. Besore, in Wichita for several days in order to thoroughly investigate the complaints of the unemployed. In a positive move designed to improve the quality of life for the jobless, an educational and recreational program was introduced. Nunn, who praised Stutz in his report, hoped that all the strikers would soon return to their projects, but his view was that federal funds should be withdrawn immediately if there were any further disturbances. On May 19, Edmonds informed Stutz that Harry Hopkins seemed to be entirely satisfied with the part that the Kansas man had played in the Wichita debacle. However, Hopkins recommended that Besore remain in Wichita for a while with an authority superior to that of the local relief administration.[33]

Unfortunately for Stutz, a rigorous investigation into the organization of relief in Sedgwick County demonstrated that his faith in Poor Commissioner B. E. George and his subordinates had been misplaced. A small committee headed by Besore and Marvin conducted a series of wide-ranging interviews on June 13 and 14, which culminated in the produc-

31. Ibid.; Edmonds to Hopkins, June 21, May 17, 1934, Wichita Strike File.
32. Edmonds to Hopkins, June 21, Wichita Strike File.
33. Edmonds to Stutz, May 19, 1934, FERA State Files, Kansas File, June–May 1934, RG69, NA.

Wichita
commissioners
found to be
incompetent

tion of twenty-five affidavits detailing both illegality and gross professional misconduct. Gene George was accused of intoxication at work, serious mismanagement, and of spending part of the working day locked in his office with his secretary. Eual Snodgrass, who was responsible for the distribution of commodities, was accused of drinking in the workplace, approaching female colleagues "for immoral purposes," and dishonesty in the distribution of commodities. Other employees in the relief office also contributed to a widespread culture of dishonesty, incompetence, gross unprofessional behavior, and the abuse of power, especially toward women.

The testimony of four female relief workers, all employed as clerks in the relief office, presents a picture of an administration not effectively managed by the poor commissioner. Mrs. Bowers witnessed lots of drinking, with liquor provided by the "official bootlegger" to the relief office. She took a drink with Snodgrass, "thinking it would help hold my job," but after rejecting a sexual advance he "treated me like a dog." Mrs. Holloway stated: "[P]eople [were] given commodities that weren't entitled to them. Larger amount given to some people. Special friends. We were notified to keep still about that which we did. That was our job." Mrs. Kennedy told the committee that when Snodgrass asked her opinion about which women to employ, "I knew what he wanted. He wanted someone who was a 'good sport', someone to keep their mouth shut." Indeed, there was much to keep quiet about, as all the women knew of the distribution of clothing, blankets, and other commodities to those not entitled to receive them, including full-time employees in the relief office. These women, assured of confidentiality by the committee, were frank in their denunciation, but at work things had been different. Mrs. Collins was reluctant to speak out. "We were afraid that we would lose our jobs. I questioned his [Snodgrass's] motive several times in giving these commodities when it was hard for other people to get them as they had to go through the Case Worker. Usually it takes three days, sometimes a week. His friends came in the front door and came to my desk and got them."

These women had been CWA employees but had lost their jobs when the agency was run down, and they were delighted to be taken on under the FERA as clerical employees, even for a few hours each week. They were in a very weak position and highly vulnerable. When, according to Miss Cantwell, George's assistant disbursment officer insisted that on payday "each girl [had to] smile sweetly before she can have her check," this must have been a humiliating experience. But the same man also "unsnaps snaps, unties bows etc." and was able to interfere with the clothing of female workers without fear of objection. The women knew that if they ceased to be "good sports," their jobs would be forfeited.

In his evidence, Mr. Rasure, a full-time relief officer, confirmed the harassment described above and agreed that the women had to put up with it or quit. He also stated that relief checks were issued to men who had never worked, that an official who was drunk made illegal cash payments to relief workers, and that record keeping was very poor. Rasure also put forward an interesting explanation for the riot. He maintained that CWA employment had been reduced in an arbitrary or improper manner. The reduction was supposed to take into account the needs of each individual worker, but in Wichita, George allowed single men and favorites to be kept on the payroll while family heads were discharged. This enraged many relief clients and made them ready for a riot. However, others who investigated the causes of the riot did not substantiate this interesting thesis.[34]

At the close of the investigation, the *Wichita Sunday Beacon* was given all the gory details, and its front-page headline, "Graft, Booze, Attacks on Women Charged in 25 Wichita Affidavits," no doubt helped to sell many extra copies of that issue.[35] The newspaper reported that surplus goods had been sold and the money pocketed by relief officials, that attempts had been made to extort money from grocers who dealt with county relief orders, and that women who repulsed sexual advances were fired. In a particularly horrifying account, the thirteen-year-old daughter of a relief worker was fortunate to escape the attentions of a sexual predator while visiting her mother. Details also emerged of the "revolting conditions and neglectful treatment" of the sick in the county hospital, with "ants and roaches crawling over patients." The serious point here is that the investigation had revealed that the charges made by the unemployed relating to the dereliction of professional duties on the part of relief officials had considerable validity.

Stutz wired Hopkins, "[T]here must be a cellar to garret house cleansing [of the] local relief administration, including the removal of the County Poor Commissioner and all department heads."[36] There can be no doubt that George was aware of the serious irregularities that took place in the Wichita relief office. He had delegated a great deal of authority to subordinates, especially to Snodgrass and to Donald Potter, his assistant

34. The only material in the public domain relating to this investigation are the notes on interviews with Mrs. Bowers, Mrs. Collins, Mrs. Holloway, Mrs. Kennedy, Mr. Rasure, and Miss Campbell, June 14, 1934, Stutz Papers, 327:2:29. See also notes on an interview with Eual Snodgrass, June 13, 1934. Snodgrass, who was in charge of commodities and clothing at the Central Applications Bureau, denied all wrongdoing. Stutz Papers, 327:2:30.

35. *Wichita Sunday Beacon*, June 17, 1934; Edmonds to Hopkins, June 20, 1934, Wichita Strike File.

36. Stutz to Hopkins, June 21, 1934, Wichita Strike File.

county disbursing officer, but he had failed to appropriately supervise their activities and those of others for whom he was responsible. According to Stutz, George was disqualified by the KERC as a poor commissioner and summarily dismissed from office by the Board of County Commissioners. Raub Snyder, a resident of Meade County and a member of the Executive Council of the KERC, became acting poor commissioner until a permanent replacement could be hired. Dr. J. C. Montgomery, a former secretary of the State Board of Health, was appointed to undertake a complete reorganization of the medical services offered to those on relief as the complaints concerning the quality of the existing provision were accepted. The proposed appointment of two assistants to the case supervisor and twelve additional caseworkers was a much-needed attempt to significantly lessen the burden on hard-pressed staff and make possible better professional relationships with those on relief.[37]

An improvement in the quality of care offered to clients was essential. Unfortunately we hear little from the men and women who felt compelled to apply for relief about the service they were forced to accept. However, consider the case of Mrs. Anna E. MacAlexander, a widow living in Wichita, who was trying to repay debts that she had incurred following her husband's death a year previously. In early 1934, after the loss of her CWA job, Alexander saw a social worker and explained her financial situation. She was told that a man and his wife would be moved into her accommodation and that half her rent would be paid as compensation. As the man had served a prison sentence for killing his son-in-law, MacAlexander refused to accept the arrangement. As a result, all her relief was cut off. In desperation she appealed to one of the county commissioners, and after his intervention she was given a grocery order. She was then assigned work at the County Home washing walls and ceilings prior to painting. As she explained, this was arduous and physically demanding work:

> The washing of the ceilings in particular was difficult for women to perform, due to the fact that we were required to reach over our heads, which resulted in the dirty water running down our arms and soaking our clothes. While performing this work I contracted a severe cold, and was barely able to talk for about a week. . . . We were not provided with overalls or other suitable working apparel, but from necessity were forced to wear house dresses or other ordinary apparel as is worn by women. This fact proved very embarrassing, due to the fact that we were compelled to work on ladders, while men were in the room below us, from time to time.

37. Nunn to Stutz, June 8, 1934; Stutz to Nunn, June 30, 1934, Wichita Strike File.

MacAlexander also told how long it took her to secure grocery and clothing orders at the relief office. Having arrived at the relief office at 8:30 A.M. one Friday morning, she spent the whole day either waiting in line or walking between various buildings. She had to return early the next day, and her business was not fully completed until noon.[38] Relief clients like Anna MacAlexander, and others in her situation, needed trained and experienced social workers to give sympathetic advice and to ensure that the appropriate work was allocated to them. In addition, a well-run relief office would reduce the frustration of a lengthy wait for commodities. Fortunately, there was a rapid improvement in the provision of relief for the needy in Sedgwick County. In September, Edmonds commented that Wichita was peaceful and that the new county relief administration seemed highly efficient.[39] The relief load in the county continued to be relatively high, with nearly 20 percent of the population on relief in December 1934.[40]

The revelations concerning George proved particularly embarrassing for Landon, who, on Stutz's advice, had publicly praised the poor commissioner at an early stage in the Wichita debacle. In an extraordinary memo to Harry Hopkins and Aubrey Williams, T. J. Edmonds explained how he had devised a solution that would enable Stutz to save face and take the heat off Landon. His suggestion would at the same time counter what he regarded as the totally unjustified accusations made by Kansas Democrats, led by Congressman Fitzwilliams, that Landon and Stutz were playing politics with relief. Edmonds advised that Landon issue a press statement which would say that although he disagreed with Stutz in his opinion of George, there was nothing that he could do about the poor commissioner's removal from office, as he had no control over the state relief administration. Stutz would respond by saying that he disagreed with the governor, but that the decision to discharge George was his alone and Landon never intervened in matters relating to personnel or in any way with the conduct of relief administration. That Edmonds could explain to Hopkins and Williams how he was assisting Kansas Republicans to counter attacks by local Democrats speaks volumes for the confident nonpolitical stance taken by field representatives and for the freedom of expression given to them.[41]

---

38. *Affidavit. Mrs Anna E. MacAlexander, subscribed and sworn on May 26, 1934,* Stutz Papers, 327:2:29.

39. Edmonds to Hopkins, September 25, 1934, FERA State Files, Kansas Field Report No. 2, RG69, NA.

40. *KERC Bulletin* 289, 617.

41. Edmonds to Hopkins and Williams, June 27, 1934, Wichita Strike File.

Curiously, B. E George did not withdraw from public service. In July he was appointed superintendent of the Lake Wabaunsee Transient Camp at Eskridge, a move that aroused strong opposition from Elizabeth Wickenden at the Transient Bureau in Washington, D.C. Noting George's less-than-perfect past, she vehemently expressed the view that the appointment could not possibly be confirmed by her office. The response from Stutz and his colleagues came a few weeks later. The appointment of George, they maintained, was consistent with the Kansas policy of removing people from jobs that were too demanding and reallocating them to more suitable roles. According to Stutz, George had not been dishonest in his previous post, he was simply incapable of discharging the responsibilities that he had been given. His new position, however, was more suited to his talents, and there was no doubt that he would be able to function effectively in it. This was a very generous assessment of George's culpabilities, and it showed that Stutz was prepared to overlook the telling criticism of the former poor commissioner that had surfaced during the post-riot enquiry. However vigorously one might question the decision, T. J. Edmonds supported Stutz. In a letter to Wickenden he wrote that since the Kansan's judgment was near flawless, the appointment of George should stand.[42] However, the *Wichita Evening Eagle* suggested that George was favored because he was a Republican and that Stutz had also forced the Sedgwick County commissioners to accept Edgar M. Leach, another Republican, as poor commissioner.[43] It would be unwise to dismiss the strength of the political connection in both cases.

After Wichita, Stutz was determined to keep himself much better informed about potential unrest amongst the unemployed, and in August 1933 he sent an investigator, Harold M. Slater, to Emporia, Wichita, Newton, Hutchinson, and Salina to conduct an "undercover" operation. He was instructed to report, while maintaining anonymity, the presence of any outside agitators, possibly communists, working in these communities who might be scheming to create unrest among the unemployed being cared for by the KERC. After questioning a number of the jobless and some police officers in all five cities, Slater reported that there was no evidence of either outside agitators or of possible unrest.[44] Stutz, now chas-

42. Wickenden to Gerard Price, State Transient Director, July 31, 1934, FERA State Files, Kansas File, June–Sept. 1934, RG69, NA; Wickenden to Edmonds, August 6, 1934, Stutz Papers, 327:1:4; Nunn to Wickenden, September 14, 1934, Wichita Strike File; Edmonds to Wickenden, August 8, 1934, Stutz Papers.

43. *Wichita Evening Eagle,* July 24, 1936.

44. Slater to Stutz and Marvin re: Labor Conditions, September 1, 1934, Stutz Papers, 327:2:27.

tened after his Wichita experience, also ensured that a representative of his spied on meetings of unemployed groups in Topeka and had a report sent to him promptly. Starting in April 1934, all gatherings of the Worker's Educational and Protective League and a rival organization, the Unemployed Association, were subject to infiltration. Before these two organizations merged to form the Worker's Protective League in November 1934 and after Larsen fell from grace, reports, some of them substantial, were produced for Stutz on thirty meetings. A further seventeen reports were filed before records ceased in May 1936.[45] In January 1936, Stutz's principal informant, Harry B. Johnstone, actually claimed to have been elected president of the Kansas Allied Workers (KAW), a newly formed union of the unemployed.[46] Stutz and his close colleagues were instantly and fully aware of the aims and ambitions of Topeka's organized unemployed, though a reading of the reports suggests that talk was usually far stronger than action.

It is difficult to be sure how many organizations of the unemployed were formed in Kansas during the depression. An assiduous compiler, Ernest F. McNutt, lists eight founded in 1933, twenty-six in 1934, and nineteen in 1935, but his count is deficient because it includes only those groups that took out state charters.[47] Several of these organizations chose not to register with the state, and of those that did, some were short lived, while others either split or merged and reformed with a new title. On June 7 and 8, 1935, after meeting at Emporia, twenty-five of these unemployed organizations agreed to form a statewide body entitled Kansas Allied Workers.[48] In general, the most active of these groups functioned in urban areas, where there was an established tradition of unionism. However, the relationship of unemployed organizations with organized labor, which strongly supported the New Deal and usually opposed strikes against the government, was often uneasy.

Many relief officials and state politicians had to deal with relief protest, which frequently involved strike action and was sometimes intimidating. Stutz's usual response to strike action was to stop all federal work relief

45. The reports can be found in the Stutz Papers, 327:2:36. Larsen was accused of taking money to campaign for Omar Ketchum but deserting the Democrat cause to campaign for Landon. Johnstone to Stutz, November 2, 1934, Stutz Papers, 327:2:36.
46. Johnstone to Stutz, January 16, 1936, Stutz Papers, 327:2:36. There is, however, no mention of Johnstone in Ernest F. McNutt, comp. "Kansas Unemployed Organizations, Their Programs and Activities," 68.
47. McNutt, "Kansas Unemployed," 68.
48. For the national picture, see: William H. and Kathryn Coe Cordell, "Unions among the Unemployed," 498–510; Frances Fox Piven and Richard A. Clowerd, *Poor People's Movements: Why They Succeed, How They Fail,* 73–86.

immediately. Thus in June 1935, when relief workers in Lyon County went on strike protesting the wages paid to them, Stutz closed down operations and the strikers resumed work after four days. Stutz had reacted in exactly the same way in March when strikes halted work on projects in Crawford County, and thirty-five hundred men were denied work for a few days.[49]

A major source of friction concerned wage rates, even though New Dealers had assumed that the establishment of Wage Rate Committees would prevent, or at least significantly reduce, all disputes relating to pay. These committees were instructed to discover the prevailing wage rates for each city and the surrounding areas and forward their findings, together with the supporting evidence, to the KERC. Unfortunately, some Kansas committees forgot that their task was limited to the discovery of the existing rates. They assumed the responsibility of setting a new prevailing rate, which they thought more appropriate for people on relief.[50] As early as September 1934, Stutz complained that the minimum rate of pay for relief clients was greater than the actual wage rate for rural employees because a number of Wage Rate Committees had insisted on establishing rates in excess of the prevailing wage.[51] The dispute in Lyon County mentioned above came when Stutz challenged the local committee, as he was entitled to, to produce evidence for the very high prevailing wage they had just announced. When the evidence was not forthcoming Stutz declined to accept the proposed rate, much to the anger of those who were looking forward to receiving it.[52] Where Wage Rate Committees saw their role as self-appointed arbiters of social justice whose function was to increase low wages rather than report evidence, they rashly raised expectations and failed in their remit.

Workers involved in private sector labor disputes, however, were treated differently from those on work relief. During the summer of 1935 a bitter conflict broke out in the lead mines of Crawford County. An attempt by the established International Union of Mine, Mill and Smelter Workers to bargain collectively with their employers was rebuffed, and a strike was called. Some of the workers who refused to withdraw their labor formed a separate organization, the Tri-State Union, with which the operators ne-

49. *Topeka Daily Capital,* June 8; *Emporia Gazette,* June 13, 1935; *Topeka Daily Capital,* March 12, 1935.

50. *KERC Bulletin* 39, March 9, 1934; ibid. 130, December 14, 1934, "Establishing Wage Rate Committees and Wage and Salary Rates."

51. Records of Meeting of the KERC, September 25, 1934, FERA State Files, Kansas File, 1933–36, RG69, NA.

52. *Salina Journal,* June 10, 1934.

gotiated and the mines continued to work. Violent picketing, and the inevitable violent response to it, eventually resulted in the National Guard being sent to Crawford County on two separate occasions.[53] In response to letters from Kansas politicians, Nels Anderson and Aubrey Williams gave a firm assurance that there would be no discrimination against needy strikers, and that they would be considered for relief on exactly the same basis as other applicants. John Stutz confirmed in a response to Anderson that this was indeed the policy in Crawford County.[54]

On August 6, 1935, the anger of the jobless in Wyandotte County came to a head. More than one thousand relief workers joined the unemployed in a demonstration outside the county courthouse, protesting a cut in relief funds of 67 percent over the next five weeks. The hostile crowd occupied the building and vowed to remain until the county commissioners agreed to issue bonds in order to fund more relief. They called on men and women who were still at their relief jobs to drop tools and join the protest. The organizers of the action expressed their demands in an elaborate twelve-point manifesto that included a call for a 25 percent increase in relief budgets until WPA projects came on-line, a guarantee that families on relief would not be evicted for nonpayment of rent, and the right to organize unions on WPA projects that would be able to negotiate with officials over hours and pay. They called on the commissioners to provide food and beds for the group occupying the courthouse and proposed that the poor commissioner and other relief officials drawing monthly salaries of at least $100 should donate one month's pay to the relief fund. Less well paid officials should have 50 percent of their monthly salary deducted. About one hundred protesters spent the night occupying the courthouse.[55]

The chairman of the county commissioners, Fred Holcomb, tried to explain that the reduction in relief payments had been forced upon the county by a substantial cut in federal funding, and that as the county had just

53. *Independence Reporter,* June 8, 1935; *Kansas City Star,* June 28, 1935; *Topeka Capital,* June 30, 1935; *Pittsburg Sun,* July 11, 1935; *Topeka Journal,* August 20, 1935; State Commission of Labor and Industry, *Annual Report of the Commission of Labor and Industry,* December 31, 1935. For a full account of this dispute see George G. Suggs, Jr., *Union Busting in the Tri-State District: The Oklahoma, Kansas and Missouri Metal Workers Strike of 1935.*

54. Hon. E. W. Patterson to Hopkins, May 14, 1935; Williams to Patterson May 17, 1935; Anderson to Patterson, June 4, 1935; Capper to Hopkins, May 23, 1935; Anderson to Capper, June 4, 1935, FERA State Files, Kansas Official File, February–May 1935, RG69, NA.

55. *Kansas City Times,* August 7; *Kansas City Kansan,* August 7; *Iola Register,* August 6, 7, 1935.

sold a $175,000 bond issue, state officials would not permit another issue until at least January 1936. The commissioners made the customary plea to Washington for extra funding and attempted to placate the strikers by providing emergency grocery orders for those people on relief facing real hunger. In addition, ice and milk were made available for relief families with children, and office space was provided in the old county jail building for representatives from the committee of protesters. These gestures, together with Holcomb's explanation, were sufficient to persuade a number of the pickets to call off their action immediately.

Others were not so easily placated and the demonstration lasted until August 11, by which time the protesters had polarized into two groups. One group, which came to recognize the difficulties facing the commissioners, was content with a further concession from them to increase relief payments and appeared to have lost enthusiasm for continuing the struggle. There were, however, a number of hard-liners who wanted to hold out for a total victory. The protest eventually came to an end when the police arrested four ringleaders, followed by four more of the most voluble strikers who had led a march of about one hundred to police headquarters, in an attempt to free their colleagues. Four of those arrested were released, but three who were found guilty of vagrancy and forming a mob were fined $50 each. A fourth, who was said by police to have communist party literature in his home, was charged, in addition to vagrancy, with having no lawful occupation. Three of the four came from Missouri, and they were instructed, on release from custody, not to return to Kansas City, Kansas. Frank Paine, a leader of the protesters, had come to resent the way in which strident nonresidents had attempted to take over the movement. He called on demonstrators to disband as they had obtained all the concessions that they could reasonably expect from the commissioners.[56]

Help for the Most Needy

Crawford, which was considered by many social workers and political commentators to be the most volatile and deprived county in the state, deserves special mention. Its experience was one of continuing misery punctuated by periodic disasters that threatened to overwhelm the population. The county had been beset with serious structural problems for some time, but during 1934 its already depressed economy was further hit by

56. *Kansas City Kansan,* August 8, 11, 12, 1935.

drought, crop failure, the continuing retrenchment of railroad repair shops, and the closure of a clay products plant. In addition, the sudden closure of a number of deep coal mines in May led to job losses for twenty-two hundred miners, the overwhelming majority of whom had worked for only ninety-two days during the past year, and resulted in an appeal for federal assistance by the board of county commissioners directly to Harry Hopkins. The possibility of further violence alarmed Congressman McGugin, who, in a letter to Hopkins, highlighted the distress in the community. Stutz agreed that the crisis would lead to 1,000 extra families immediately joining the 1,536 already on relief, and a further 500 being added by the end of the month. He calculated that an additional $30,000 funding was required to cope with this problem, and he too asked the FERA for assistance.[57]

There is no record of Kansas receiving additional funding, and it is possible that a redistribution of federal money by the KERC in Crawford County's favor was all that was possible. In 1934 Crawford received $902,000 from the federal government for relief purposes, while the county raised only $102,000 itself. A comprehensive survey of relief in the county revealed that about half the families of the unemployed had received either federal relief or CWA employment during the twelve months ending on April 1, 1934. During this period, the total amount of federal relief received per family ranged from less than $25 to more than $300, with the average being a very modest $152.[58] It is important to remember that federal payments were cash, while county-funded direct relief was distributed largely in kind; its value to the average resident family was a mere $4.14 per month.[59] It is not surprising that even a few weeks of federal work relief was so highly prized, and—given the hardships that many had to endure—that riot and protest were attractive.

In general, how much relief did clients receive? Moving away from a single county to consider the entire state, the average amount of county-funded work relief available for resident families during each month of 1934 was $7.56; single people were awarded $5.04. The average direct relief monthly payments for both categories were $7.30 and $6.17 respec-

57. Ben Morgan and W. P. Johnson to Hopkins, May 1, 1934. Morgan and Johnson were two members of the board of county commissioners. The third, W. A. Beasley, was hospitalized following an assault by relief demonstrators; McGugin to Hopkins, May 2, 1934; Stutz to Aubrey Williams, May 9, 1934. All in FERA State Files, Kansas File, January–May 1934, RG69, NA.
58. Crawford County Survey, "A study of need for educational, social and vocational readjustment programs for the unemployed mining population. A summary" (Topeka: Progress Report for Kansas State Planning Board, September 1934), 166–68.
59. *KERC Bulletin* 289, 205–11.

tively. Small as they might seem, these sums were considerably more generous than payments in the immediately preceding years; during 1932 and 1933, for example, the average family had received $4.72.[60] However, caution is required when interpreting calculations of average value of relief, as deviations from the mean, heavily influenced by factors such as family size, were considerable.

In order to cope with the increase in caseload following the closure of the CWA, the number of senior relief staff was increased. An assistant superintendent of relief and a casework consultant now worked with a staff of six case supervisors. Of these eight social workers, seven were female. During 1934 there were some notable improvements in the efficiency of welfare provision. Perhaps the most significant was the result of a large increase in the numbers of caseworkers and case aides, a growth that was really only apparent after August. By December there were four times as many caseworkers employed as there had been at the very beginning of the year, and, as a result, there was a considerable decline in the average caseload per worker. Furthermore, the KERC, which had already agreed to supplement the salaries of poor commissioners and county case supervisors, extended this supplementation in October to include case aides. Salary supplementation was an important means of attracting and retaining high-quality staff in a competitive hiring environment. The improving staff to client ratio was more evident in urban than in rural counties and was still in excess of what was considered desirable, but, nevertheless, it did enable the KERC to push ahead with its commitment to a greater emphasis on casework, which had not been possible earlier in the year. For example, there was a significant rise in the number of home visits, especially in counties where the average caseload had fallen furthest. Increasing the number of staff so rapidly could have led to a compromise on quality, but these skill issues were tackled by the establishment of seven training centers for social workers, operated by county case supervisors and assistant case supervisors. A marked improvement in statistical services led to the more systematic collection of data so that by the close of 1934 all counties had accurate information on the identity of clients who had obtained relief from both federal and county sources.[61]

The KERC stated clearly that "merit was the only basis for the selection of personnel," and the feeling was that toward the end of 1934, with the adoption of more rigorous standards, the quality of staff in post had begun to improve. By late 1935, 472 of the 602 social workers employed in

60. "Average Relief Per Month," Stutz Papers, 327:5:4.
61. *KERC Bulletin* 289, 18–25.

Kansas (including poor commissioners, case supervisors, and case aides) had college degrees. Of the total number of graduates, 146 had undertaken some graduate work and 27 had been awarded master's degrees. The state relief administration continued to hold training schools and to develop the careers of those involved in local relief administration through the use of county training units. Nearly three hundred young men and women, mostly social science graduates, had served apprenticeships in well-staffed county departments, and a number had remained in Kansas on completion of their training. Young social workers were attracted to the state by the provision of scholarships and the promise of professional support. The provision of in-house training meant that by late 1935, approximately 80 percent of poor commissioners had been promoted through the ranks. The growth of qualified staff during 1935 resulted in the reduction of the average caseload per social worker from 136 in January to 109 in December.[62]

The KERC deserves praise too for its commitment to programs for women, which were continued after the Civil Works Administration/ Civil Works Service, and also for the introduction of a program for non-manual workers. By December 1934, 6,302 women were employed on relief and administrative tasks, a dramatic rise from the 750 working in March. Positions on sewing projects provided most opportunities (approximately 3,173 were at work each week in December) and many items of clothing were provided for relief clients. Classes were organized for females who lacked the necessary skills so that they could eventually find employment in sewing rooms. In addition, at the end of the year, nearly 1,500 women were working in KERC canning plants that processed surplus foodstuffs for distribution to the needy, and 150 busied themselves on library projects in thirty-three counties. The nonmanual initiative began in September, and by the end of 1934, 2,220 were working on sixty-seven projects.[63]

In December 1933 the FERA-funded Public Works Art Project was established, which aimed to provide work for unemployed artists. In June 1934 this project became the responsibility of the KERC, and Professor George M. Beal of the University of Kansas was selected as state supervisor. More than one hundred people who felt qualified to contribute to this initiative applied, but only twenty could be selected. Up to October 1934, when the program was substantially reduced, sixteen painters, three sculptors, and one photographer secured rewarding employment. One of

[handwritten margin note: Women's Jobs]

[handwritten margin note: Public Works Art Project for artists Dec 1933]

62. *KERC Bulletin* 355, July 1936, "Public Welfare Service in Kansas in 1935," 14–16.
63. Ibid., 55–69.

the most noteworthy contributions to Kansas cultural life to emanate from this project was the mural for the Natural History Museum at the University of Kansas.

In August 1934, the KERC appointed an experienced social worker, Louise T. Clarke, to advise on relief problems within the black community. The belief was that as an African American, Clarke was in an ideal position to establish an effective professional relationship with both black leaders and potential relief clients. The post had wide-ranging responsibilities. Clarke was expected to adjudicate on all queries and disputes concerning relief cases in which blacks were involved. She also had the authority to fully investigate individual, family, or community conditions where these were relevant to the provision of relief for African Americans.

Louise Clarke immediately saw the need for accurate information to measure the impact of the depression on black Kansans, and in September she was responsible for the implementation of the first state survey to identify the number of African Americans on relief in each county. The results of this investigation showed that a disproportionate number of black residents were on the relief rolls. The statistics collected indicated that 38.5 percent of the state's African Americans were receiving relief, compared to 13.1 percent of the population as a whole. Indeed, blacks, who composed only 3.5 percent of the state's population, accounted for 10.3 percent of all relief recipients. The vast majority of African American relief cases, more than 80 percent of them, were urban dwellers who resided in cities with more than five thousand inhabitants, and there was, inevitably, a concentration in the eastern part of the state. This investigation also revealed that 83 percent of the black caseload had been allocated work relief, which indicates that unemployment for this group had reached very high levels. African Americans were usually employed on canning, county roadwork, city street improvement, laundry work, and sewing projects. Most had previously worked as domestic servants, janitors, and unskilled laborers, though a significant number had craft or white-collar skills.

Another survey taken in December 1934 showed that the situation had worsened, and in counties where blacks were most numerous, social distress had reached disturbing proportions. In Wyandotte County, for example, 55 percent of the black population was on relief; in Shawnee County, the figure was 34 percent; in Sedgwick County, it was 38 percent; and in Leavenworth county, 21 percent.[64] The decision to statistically separate black and white relief cases was a significant development in the fight against black poverty, as was the appointment of Louise Clarke. Howev-

64. Ibid., 758–61.

er, identifying the plight of black Kansans would only be of material value if this information were used to alleviate distress.

During 1935, the county commissioners in the eight counties where the black caseload was heaviest appointed twenty-two African American case aides. The updating of statistical information continued with three further surveys in March, June, and October. The March survey identified 27,264 individuals, or 41 percent of the black population, who were on relief, compared to 17 percent of the total population falling into the same category. In the spring of 1935, blacks made up 8 percent of all relief cases, or 11 percent of the total caseload.[65] Black families benefited from the remittances of the 524 young men who had enrolled at the state's three segregated CCC camps and further from the leisure and education programs sponsored by fifteen counties and the jobs created by this initiative. However, the incidence of unemployment among blacks in Kansas was so serious that they, more so than whites, depended heavily upon an efficient and fairly run county relief administration.

A federal census taken in March 1935 to ascertain the occupational characteristics of the relief population provides further evidence of black misfortune. It is interesting to note that in Kansas, whereas women constituted 29 percent of the white cohort who were in receipt of relief, females accounted for 41 percent of the African American relief total. Of the sixty-four hundred black male relief recipients, 24 percent were classified as unskilled nonfarm laborers, and 16 percent as domestic or personal service workers. However, 23 percent of the total was, when employed, skilled or semiskilled workers. Sixty-three percent of the black women receiving relief were classified as domestic and personal service workers. Of these, just over 60 percent were described as normally working for private families as servants.[66] The occupational composition of black families on relief differed significantly from that of the white relief population. The concentration of African American women in personal service, a low-pay occupation offering little security in hard times, demonstrates the vulnerability of black Kansans to depression misery.

Local Politics, the New Deal and Federal Officials

The strong, mutually supportive relationship between Kansas administrators and federal field agents, which had been developing since the

65. Ibid., 292–93.
66. *Workers on Relief in the United States in March 1935: A Census of Usual Occupations*, 60–61.

RFC program began, continued to mature. These agents came to the defense of Stutz and his colleagues with utter dependability when local Democrat politicians challenged their competence or impartiality. For example, senior Washington officials told Rep. Randolph Carpenter, who objected to Republicans' running any part of the New Deal in Kansas, not only that local initiatives were an important part of the program, but also that the federal funds distributed to his state were administered fairly. Democrats in Greenwood County raged against the appointment of young female social workers who possessed a college degree but lacked the experience of life that age and masculinity had granted to their critics. C. M. Fitzwilliams, chairman of the Sedgwick County Democratic Central Committee, echoed this charge, adding that he also resented the appointment of young female college graduates who, he believed, were incapable of "imparting the true aims of the FERA." The basis of these complaints was the curb on patronage that prevented the county commissioners from exercising favoritism in making political or personal appointments unless, of course, their candidates were sufficiently qualified to satisfy the KERC. T. J. Edmonds, who was given the responsibility of responding to these complaints, wired John Stutz to quiz him on his political allegiance. Not for the first time, Stutz responded robustly that he was not a Republican precinct committeeman, held no political party office, was not campaigning for Landon, and did not favor Republicans in relief matters. Edmonds was convinced by his reply and praised Stutz for resisting political pressures in making appointments and for insisting upon minimum qualifications that would improve the quality of relief administrators.[67]

Congresswoman Kathryn O'Loughlan McCarthy launched a bitter personal attack on Stutz, whom she accused of constantly politicizing relief, and she also directed her wrath toward the Washington apparatchiks who, she believed, supported him at every turn. T. J. Edmonds was dismissive of her charges. He reminded Hopkins that seven of the twelve members of the KERC were Democrats and that all, including Stutz, had been appointed by Governor Harry Woodring, a Democrat, and were all retained by Landon. In a memo to his Washington colleagues on this issue he commented, "Stutz is above suspicion and a very efficient and honest administrator." He concluded, perhaps disingenuously, that it would

67. Carpenter to Hopkins, August 24; Carpenter to Bruce McClure, September 16, 1934; Tillie J. Stanhope, Vice Chairwoman Greenwood County Central Committee, to Nellie Taylor Ross, Democrat National Committee, September 8, 1934; Fitzwilliams to Hopkins, October 1, 1934, all in FERA State Files, Kansas File, General A–Z, RG 69, NA. Stutz to Edmonds, August 21, 1934, Stutz Papers, 327:1:4. Carpenter again raised the issue of Republican malpractice in December. *Topeka Daily Capital*, December 18, 1934.

be very difficult for Stutz to play partisan politics on behalf of this Republican governor, as Landon did not interfere in any aspect of relief management.[68] It is easy to understand the frustration of Kansas Democrats, who persistently lobbied their own people in Washington in an attempt to get rid of Stutz, only to find that the support for him among influential fellow administrators, to whom many of their complaints were directed, was so strong.

During the run-up to the 1934 elections, political tension became acute, as state Democrats struggled to prevent Landon's gaining political advantage from the New Deal programs. A *New York Times* journalist, giving an informed outsider's view, described the New Deal as a "grand slam" for Kansas Republicans. He cited in particular Republican control of the relief administration at the state and county level and also of the CCC, where, the journalist believed, Landon had placed his own men in key positions. Given the enormous patronage possible from the millions of relief and highway fund dollars that had flowed into Kansas, it seemed that Governor Landon was in a virtually impregnable position.[69] The views of this reporter are contrary to those of the field agents who always defended Landon and Stutz against charges of political chicanery. Although it is hard to believe that Kansas Republicans did not seek to press home the advantages that they had, if this had been done as crudely and extensively as claimed by the *New York Times*, federal field agents would have commented on it.

However, many Kansas Democrats fulminated against what they saw as the politicization of relief by their opponents, though this did not prevent State Chairman Clyde L. Short from asking the voters to return Omar Ketchum for governor on the grounds that the election of a Democrat would lead to a more generous allocation of relief funds from Washington.[70] Landon, of course, calmly claimed that he had cooperated fully with the national recovery and relief programs and that Kansas had benefited from his nonideological stance. Moreover, the support that he had extended to New Deal programs had been confirmed by congratulatory messages from luminaries like Harry Hopkins, Harold Ickes, Hugh Johnson, and Field Agent T. J. Edmonds.[71]

---

68. McCarthy to Williams, August 16 and 30, 1934; Edmonds to Hopkins, September 25, 1934; Edmonds to Lansdale and McClure, September 25, 1934, all in FERA State Files, Kansas File, June–September 1934, RG69, NA.

69. *New York Times*, October 21, 1934.

70. *El Dorado Times*, September 9, 1934; *Neodesha Sun*, September 12, 1934; *Cherryvale Republican*, September 26, 1934.

71. *Emporia Gazette*, September 22, 1934; *Kansas City Times*, October 11, 1934; *Topeka Daily Capital*, October 12, 1934.

After Landon's re-election in 1934, a resentful Randolph Carpenter charged that political manipulation had indeed played a crucial role in the governor's success.[72] He claimed that white-collar applicants for relief were favored because of their family backgrounds, while "hungry toilers" had their applications ignored. In other words, the influential, who presumably had strong Republican sympathies, flourished, but the more deserving lost out. This complaint was made to Harry Hopkins with such force that he felt compelled to set up an inquiry.[73] On January 15, 1935, two FERA special investigators, R. J. Bounds and Dudley Frank, interviewed John Stutz in his Topeka office. Although the transcript of this meeting does not indicate that the two investigators were acting on Hopkins's behalf, it is a safe assumption that they were.[74]

During this interview, Stutz admitted that he had been a member of the executive council of the Douglas County Republican Central Committee and had been elected precinct committeeman in August 1932, but that he had never held any public political office. A confident and assured Stutz claimed that his political functions in Douglas County ceased after the election in the fall of 1932, that he had resigned his position on the executive council in late 1933, and that his political activities had always been limited to his own locality. He was also questioned closely on the appointment of former Sedgwick County Poor Commissioner B. E. George as manager of the Lake Wabaunsee Transient Camp. Stutz skillfully defended the decision, pointing out that it was strongly supported by two senior colleagues, Gerard Price and F. H. Marvin, and that when difficulties arose over the confirmation of the appointment the matter was turned over to a federal official, T. J. Edmonds, for resolution. Other issues centered on problems that now seem relatively minor but at the time had clearly exercised the individuals concerned. For example, complaints that Stutz had been reluctant to meet "workers committees" when they came to the relief office, or concerns relating to the influence he might have had on county appointments do not indicate that the investigators were aware of any major offenses that were worthy of investigation. The report that Bounds and Frank would have submitted to Harry Hopkins was not archived, but given the nature of the questions, and the responses to them, it cannot have found Stutz guilty of improper political favoritism.

---

72. In 1934 Landon was the only incumbent Republican governor to be re-elected.
73. *Topeka Daily Capital*, December 11, 1934; *Winfield Courier*, December 19, 1934.
74. "Hearing of Mr. John G. Stutz, Executive Director, The Kansas Emergency Relief Committee, before Mr. R. J. Bounds and Mr. Dudley Frank, Special Investigators, The Federal Emergency Relief Administration," Stutz Papers, 327:1:25.

Relief and the Faltering Economy

At the close of the CWA in March 1934, only thirty-eight hundred of the thirty-six thousand men and women who had been discharged from this employment program had to be granted direct relief. As the season passed from spring to summer, it seemed as if the economy would recover with sufficient pace to absorb the unemployed, raise farm income, and consign the depression to bitter memory. Unfortunately, although there was a broadly based improvement in business conditions, it was not sufficiently robust to make substantial inroads into persistent unemployment or rural misfortune. One adverse factor was the continuation of drought, which became particularly serious during 1934 and added substantially to the relief rolls. Lack of rain and relentless sun devastated the corn crop, causing suffering to livestock and financial hardship to owners. However, although crop output declined, a rise in prices was sufficient, when added to the remuneration from New Deal agricultural programs, to push farmers' spending toward much higher levels than in the previous few years. The impact of the drought, and the New Deal's attempts to rescue the farm community from the grip of the depression, is fully analyzed in Chapter 4.

An examination of the nonfarm sector during 1934 reveals that although payrolls improved by 12 percent over the previous year, they stubbornly remained 47 percent lower than in 1930. Employment rose in food products, the service sector, and trade and financial services, but the experience overall did not sustain the hopes that had been present in the spring. Unemployment declined from February to July, but then rose briefly before falling again in September and October. However, that glimmer of hope was dashed as unemployment worsened during the last two months of the year. Indeed, the insecurity many urban dwellers felt can be seen in the continuing shift of population from urban to rural areas in spite of evident distress in the countryside. During 1934 the state's cities experienced a decline of approximately fifty thousand while the total population of Kansas increased very slightly.[75]

Long-term unemployment was a depressing characteristic of the depression throughout the United States. A detailed analysis of the jobless in Kansas was undertaken in late 1934 when the cases of 59,153 men and 11,650 women who registered at ten employment and re-employment offices were scrutinized. This was a substantial sample, as approximately 30 percent of the state's labor force lived in the ten counties included in the study. Of the males who were investigated, 58 percent had been unem-

75. *KERC Bulletin* 289, 785–89.

ployed for more than one year, and 27 percent for more than three years. Employers would consider many of these long-term unemployed as unemployable. The female long-term unemployment rate was only marginally better; 20 percent had been jobless for more than three years. Thirty-seven percent of the females in the sample were either widowed or divorced. More than three-quarters of the men studied had lived in Kansas for at least fifteen years, half of them were aged between twenty and forty years, and 88 percent of them were white as, indeed, were 84 percent of the women. The largest concentration of African Americans was found in Wyandotte County, where they comprised 26 percent of the unemployed men and 44 percent of the women. It comes as no surprise to learn that the higher the level of educational attainment, the lower the risk of unemployment. However, although the possession of skills reduced the risk of unemployment, it did not remove it. Nearly one-third of the males in this study were described as skilled or semiskilled.[76]

The federal census taken in March 1935 revealed the usual occupations of Kansans who were on the relief rolls. Of the 72,364 white males receiving relief during that month, 23 percent were described as farmers, 17 percent as farm laborers, another 17 percent were unskilled nonfarm workers, 16 percent were normally working in the building and construction industry, and 12 percent in manufacturing and related industries. The census count identified 27,098 females as receiving relief, of whom 25 percent were classified as domestic or personal service workers. An obvious economy measure for middle-class families in the depression was to dispense with domestic help, or reduce hours and pay. This was also an area where white women could successfully compete with black. Almost 55 percent of the females recorded were classified as "inexperienced workers," which meant that they were housekeepers working in their own homes but wanted paid work, or young women seeking their first job, or older people looking to return to the labor market. None of these women had undertaken waged employment during the preceding ten years.[77] Only 35 percent of black women on relief were placed in the "inexperienced" category, which shows that a relatively high proportion of African American females had always sought paid employment.

76. *Kansas Labor and Industrial Bulletin,* January and February, 1935, 15–24.

77. Works Progress Administration, *Workers on Relief in the United States in March 1935: A Census of Usual Occupations,* 3, 60–61. Only persons aged sixteen to sixty-four years who were members of households receiving general relief were enumerated. Transients, workers of households which only received assistance from the FERA Special Programs, Drought Relief, Rural Rehabilitation, or Surplus Commodities were excluded.

The national economic recovery failed to generate sufficient new jobs to materially reduce the numbers out of work. This deficiency, together with the growing impact of drought, is reflected in the persistently high number of work and direct relief cases. The unduplicated caseload in Kansas fell to a post-CWA trough of 49,195 in June 1934, but then rose steadily each month to reach 82,646 in December. In that month 70,478 cases were employed on work relief projects funded by the federal government, and a much smaller number, 1,085, worked on projects financed by local funds. Locally funded direct relief took responsibility for 24,033 cases. These figures, when added together, are substantially higher than the 82,646 total because of unavoidable duplication, which arose because locally funded work relief wages and direct relief allocations served several functions. Individuals unable to work were an important part of the welfare responsibility of each county. However, the counties also provided assistance to the able-bodied who could not secure a place on a federal project and also supplemented, usually in kind, the wages of clients with large families whose earnings on federal projects were judged inadequate. The costs of medical care and hospitalization were also a local responsibility, though some counties required a family member to work the appropriate number of hours to cover the expense.

There was a continuing decline in the significance of the private welfare agencies that once had such a significant relief function. In 1934 private agencies spent $537,000, which amounted to a monthly average expenditure of a mere $3.75 for each case they cared for. Clearly, these agencies were able to provide only peripheral assistance, often in the form of wage supplementation. A particular problem facing virtually all private agencies was an inability to raise sufficient funds from the public to enable them to continue in a leading role. Indeed, the progressive fall in the total funding that they were able to generate as the depression progressed is striking. During 1933 a total of $828,000 had been contributed to their coffers, a significant decline from the $1 million that had been raised in 1932. Donor fatigue and the persistent reduction in income for many individuals and businesses go some way toward explaining this decline in 1934. However, it could be that more and more people reached the conclusion that the provision of relief was a national problem and had rightly become the responsibility of the federal government rather than private individuals.[78]

The Kansas public welfare philosophy always emphasized work relief and, from the time federal funds first became available in October 1932,

78. *KERC Bulletin* 289, 80–82.

the state determined that this money would be spent only in this way. Kansas officials worked hard to ensure that work projects begun under the CWA would be seamlessly continued by the Emergency Work Relief Program. However, the continuity was not slavish, and soon the emphasis on roadwork, so prominent under the CWA, was reduced. About 65 percent of CWA projects had been oriented toward road and street improvements, but by late 1934 this proportion had declined to around 24 percent. A prominent new addition to the project portfolio was the production and distribution of goods specifically for the needy, which absorbed nearly 19 percent of projects. The output flowing from the state's sewing rooms, the canning of surplus foodstuffs, and the distribution of surplus commodities had achieved a new significance. Other valuable projects included the installation of pumping plants, the construction of garden and farm ponds, and the digging of some 700 new wells. Given the distress caused by the drought, water retention schemes were especially valuable, and all 105 counties sponsored water conservation projects. About 78 percent of the funding for the work relief program came from the federal government, while the rest was local. Of the federal input, 68 percent was for relief wages and salaries and nearly 13 percent for nonrelief wages—that is, payment to persons with particular skills who were not on relief but who were essential for the management and the successful completion of projects.

The total sum spent on relief in Kansas during 1934, excluding CWA expenditure, was $23 million. An analysis of the source of these funds shows that the most important contributor was the federal government, with $15.4 million, followed by the counties, whose total expenditure was $5.6 million; the cities contributed $956,000 and the state $331,000, while townships and school districts together raised a modest $178,000. We must add to these figures the $632,000 collected by private charities and $1.8 million, which represent the estimated value of the surplus commodities distributed to those in need. Anyone analyzing these figures would be immediately struck by the weight of federal contributions. The significance of Washington's economic role is even greater if the CWA injection of more than $12 million to the Kansas economy is included.[79]

Kansas voluntarily channeled all FERA funds into work relief, and the numbers engaged on federally funded projects reached 68,301 in December 1934 and climbed to a peak of 77,193 in February 1935, but by June they had declined to 60,794.[80] There were, however, significant monthly

79. KERC, "The Cost of Social Welfare Service in Kansas," 58, n.d., Stutz Papers, 327:3:59.

80. Theodore E. Whiting, *Final Statistical Report of the Federal Emergency Relief Administration, WPA,* Table IV, 155.

fluctuations in the sums allocated for federal work relief, which naturally affected the numbers that could be employed. For example, in December 1934, Kansas received $1.6 million from the FERA; in January 1935,
$1.9 million; in February, $1.7 million; and in May, $1.9 million.[81] As large
as these amounts seem, they were not sufficient to provide assistance for
all the able-bodied, needy unemployed.

On March 1, 1935, 71,130 family heads and 5,781 single men and women
were employed on a variety of work relief projects, drawing their wages
on a deficiency budget basis. However, it is important to note that at the
same time, approximately 135,000 men and 15,000 women were registered at the National Reemployment Service as actively seeking work.
These registrations included all those receiving work relief wages because
they were still classified as unemployed. If their numbers are subtracted
from the total, there were roughly 73,000 active work seekers who wanted, but could not get, either work relief or private sector employment.
Some of the men and women working in the private sector, or on work relief projects, were either underemployed or had skills that could not be
fully utilized. Moreover, this count underestimates the numbers out of
work by as much as 15 percent, as many white-collar workers did not
bother to register with the Reemployment Service.[82]

Between April 1934 and late 1935, when FERA grants were terminated,
federal funding for Emergency Work Relief projects in Kansas amounted
to $26.7 million. If this total is broken down, the federal contribution to
work on highways, roads, and streets was $11.2 million; to conservation
projects, $2.9 million; to parks and recreation improvements, $2.3 million;
and to the erection and improvement of public buildings, $1.8 million.
These were very significant sums. An examination of the source of public
funding for emergency relief during the period January 1933 to December 1935 reveals the crucial nature of federal finance. Approximately 72
percent of funding came from Washington, about 26 percent was provided by the counties, and a mere 2 percent by the state.[83] Nationally the proportion of federal funding varied widely. For example, many states in the
Deep South, where poverty was endemic, had more than 90 percent of
their relief expenditure provided by Washington. There were also marked
differences in the distribution of the internal funding burden between the
localities and states, and there are some examples where county contributions were proportionately higher even than those in Kansas. This was
true for Indiana (35 percent), Iowa (38 percent), Maine (40 percent), and

81. Ibid., Table V, 160.
82. Kansas State Planning Board, *Inventory of Public Works: A Study of Possibilities in Kansas*, 2–3.
83. Whiting, *Final Statistical Report*, Table XV111, 307.

Massachusetts (47 percent), all of which required relatively high county contributions.[84] These variations illustrate the latitude given to the states by the FERA and Harry Hopkins's authority to exercise his judgment when assessing the ability of states and the localities to contribute to the relief bill.

In Kansas, local effort was concentrated on general relief. Cases in this category had reached 54,466 in July 1934, rising to 80,281 in December. After a 1935 peak of 87,249 in March, case numbers fell to 71,838 in June, and in December, following the transfer of clients to the WPA, there were 35,377. Under the influence of the New Deal the payment of cash benefits became more common.[85] As a result, the average amount of relief given per case rose from the very low levels evident at the beginning of 1933, though there were marked variations in monthly awards. Thus in 1934, the range by case embraced $10.00 in February to $23.69 in November; in 1935 the value of the average monthly award was $25.23, but in September it was only $16.22.[86] However, average benefit figures always understate the sums which a family totally dependant on relief would receive, since the calculations include clients who were on the relief rolls for only part of the month and others who received small sums for supplementation. It should also be remembered that cash wages were paid to men and women working on federal programs, but county relief relied heavily on payments in kind.

FERA Special Programs

The FERA introduced four special emergency relief programs, each of which was designed to reach out to a particular identifiable group and give it targeted assistance. Rural rehabilitation was a major initiative and will be analyzed elsewhere. Two others, the Emergency Education and the College Student Aid programs, had a marginal impact on the alleviation of the depression in Kansas, if assessed by the numbers employed and the amount spent. However, since both were imaginative experiments that had a positive effect on the participants, they do deserve some comment. The Emergency Education Program targeted adult education teachers who were both unemployed and in need. As part of a national attack on

84. Edward Ainsworth Williams, *Federal Aid for Relief,* 217–18.
85. During the first six months of 1935 only four states distributed a higher proportion of their general relief benefits in cash than Kansas. Enid Baird, *Average General Relief Benefits, 1933–38,* 8.
86. Whiting, *Final Statistical Report,* Table V11, 169.

illiteracy, FERA funds were used to pay relief wages to teachers who could instruct adults in reading and writing. Employment on this program peaked at just over 380 during March and April 1934, but then declined; from June to December, virtually no instructors were hired. In the spring of 1935 the program was revived, and from April to October it provided jobs for roughly three hundred teachers. By March 1937, $265,000 had been spent on this modestly funded initiative.

College Student Aid aimed to provide an incentive for young men and women to commit themselves to an education from which they would gain personal benefits. An added advantage was that while they were in the classroom they would not compete for scarce jobs in a depressed labor market. Kansas University chancellor Ernest Hiram Lindley played a leading role in the creation of the College Student Aid program. He effectively lobbied both Harry Hopkins and the president, urging the provision of funding for a scheme that would enable needy university students to earn money by performing paid tasks on campus. Educational institutions that agreed to participate in this initiative were given quotas, initially 10 percent of enrollment, and FERA allocated funds to them so that they could employ needy students in a variety of jobs—for example, in the maintenance of buildings and grounds, in the library, or as clerks. Care had to be taken that student employment did not displace other workers. This imaginative initiative was limited to students who would have found it impossible to attend college without financial assistance from waged work. At the University of Kansas, students were limited to no more than thirty hours of employment each month and paid an hourly rate that ranged between 30 and 50 cents. During 1934 the university employed an average of 950 men and 611 women each month. Lindley was convinced that without the program, three-quarters of the students who received help would have not continued with their studies, and the remaining quarter would not have enrolled for their courses. The program, which was suspended during the summer vacation months, employed nearly fifteen hundred Kansas undergraduates between February and May 1934, and two thousand each month between September 1934 and May 1935.[87]

A fourth and significant special program was devoted to migrants. In July 1933, the FERA established a Transient Division and invited states to submit plans to manage a problem that many residents did not consider a priority. The FERA proposed to finance state programs that would ad-

87. Richard B. Sheridan, "The College Student Employment Project at the University of Kansas, 1934–1943," 208–10; *KERC Bulletin* 289, 775–76.

dress the relief of both interstate transients and intrastate migrants who had acquired settlement in the state but not in the county to which they had applied for assistance. Relief for transients, defined as people who had resided in a state continuously for less than one year, was a significant departure from previous practice. Many communities bitterly resented destitute outsiders who, they believed, were a drain on scarce local resources to which they had made no contribution. Moreover, residents feared that extending the hand of friendship to transients might mean that even more of them would materialize.[88] Nevertheless, Kansas submitted a plan in September 1933, and the FERA approved it shortly afterward.[89] The KERC was advised that the proposed program would be funded, initially with a monthly grant of $15,000; within a week Gerard F. Price was appointed state supervisor of the Transient Division of the KERC.[90]

Price established the new administrative structure that FERA had approved, which required the creation of two types of service centers and residential camps, all of which would form part of a national network. Reference centers were established in every county under the direction of the poor commissioner, and these were to be the first port of call for transients. After registration, the migrant received food and temporary lodging and a meeting was arranged with a social worker. The next step was referral to a treatment center, either for families, or for single males, where medical help and accommodation were available. The intention was to develop a plan with each client at the treatment center that would bring wandering to a halt.

Separate treatment centers were established for both families and single males; single females and boys younger than fourteen years were accommodated with families. In a laudable attempt to integrate them with their neighbors, transient families were lodged in private houses in various parts of the towns in which the centers were located. As the Transient Service was able to pay higher rents than those offered by county authorities, their clients could count on preferential treatment. Unattached males, however, were accommodated in single buildings close to places where railroads would discharge their nonpaying passengers and near where

88. Edmonds to Hopkins, Digest of Conversation between Gerard F. Price and Frances Moore, Field Supervisor, FERA, April 13, 1934, FERA Transient Files, Narrative Reports and Correspondence, State Files, Kansas File, RG69, NA.
89. Minutes of Executive Committee of KERC, August 31, 1933, Stutz Papers, 327: 1:30.
90. A more detailed account of the treatment of migrants can be found in Peter Fearon, "Relief for Wanderers: The Transient Service in Kansas, 1933–35."

they could find work. Both Kansas officials and the FERA stressed the importance of regular work for a return to a settled life, and they made great efforts to find continuous employment for all those fit for it. The first family treatment center was opened in Wichita in November 1933, and others in Kansas City and Topeka soon followed. Single males benefited from the opening of the Railroad YMCA building in Topeka, also in November, and another center at Fort Scott. By the end of 1934, there were nine treatment centers for men, of which four were work camps located at the Wabaunsee, Gardner, Howard, and Sedan Lake projects. When the program closed in September 1935, the three family treatment centers were part of a sixteen-center operation that included a hospital for transients in Topeka.[91]

The numbers cared for each month show marked fluctuations because of the influence of the weather and the onset of school vacations, which influenced family travel. In January 1934, the state Transient Service had assisted 310 families and 3,737 single men and women. These numbers rose in December to an annual peak of 1,436 families (of which 1,322 were helped by the three family treatment centers) and 11,523 unattached persons. During 1935, on average, 14,523 nonresidents were cared for each month.[92] However, these figures understate the number of travelers because they are limited to transients who registered at centers and obviously cannot include those who did not ask the Transient Division for assistance. Kansas received $2.1 million as its share of this national program.[93]

The treatment centers provided social workers with an opportunity to work closely with their clients and gave families, in particular, the opportunity to take advantage of a full range of medical services that many had never before encountered. Most migrant families came from Oklahoma, Texas, Missouri, and Arkansas, where relief was not as well organized as it was in Kansas. Each center had a small medical unit where tubercular or venereal cases could be isolated, and where acute illnesses received nursing care. All transients were administered typhoid jabs, and those under twelve received diphtheria toxin. Dental care gave relief from suffering, and the Transient Service also provided dentures, but only for younger men who were best placed in the job market; they received extra

91. KERC Transient Service, "History and Development of the Transient Service, 1933–35" (Topeka, August 1936). This informative and lengthy typescript can be found in the Stutz Papers, 327:3:29.
92. The 1934 figures are from *KERC Bulletin* 289, 743–45; for 1935 data, see *KERC Bulletin* 355, 18–20.
93. Whiting, *Final Statistical Report*, 71–73, 297, 310; *KERC Bulletin*, 743.

hours of work to help pay for their treatment.[94] The high quality of medical care was a great boon to a group in poor general health that had never previously been so carefully screened by medics.

Initially, transient families received only relief in kind. In return for the completion of various tasks, families had their rent and utility bills paid, clothing issued, and groceries purchased. From October 1934, however, willing and able men were allocated work relief on exactly the same budgetary deficiency basis used for resident cases in the counties. Females who headed households were also employed, if they had the appropriate skills and the time, in office work, sewing rooms, or as cleaners. The toys, dolls, and clothing produced were distributed to other transients, or became the property of their makers. Employment on work projects was viewed as an important part of the rehabilitative process as it gave transients the opportunity to appreciate the demands and the limitations of family budgeting. Families who were judged incapable of providing a worker continued to receive direct relief.[95]

Unattached men were treated differently than families, with the majority being accommodated in camps or living together in centers.[96] Because transients were seen as competitors for scarce jobs, local apprehension, or even hostility, was never far below the surface. Officials tried to assuage fears by, for example, inviting community leaders to the centers for social occasions, and they encouraged integration by arranging sports events where center teams competed with locals. However, the fear that transients, who had the advantage of being fed and housed, could displace other workers never disappeared. A major problem for migrants was that if they did no work they could be derided as scroungers, but if they did work they were denounced as competitors.

Men working on lake construction projects at the four transient camps were viewed as less threatening, distant as they were from urban centers. The cohesion of camp life enabled social workers to develop a comprehensive program of leisure activities for the men and also to put on classes that encouraged the use, or the acquisition, of employment-related skills. Within each camp was a full range of tasks to be performed, and the skills of all clients could be usefully employed. Moreover, both the camps and

94. KERC, Transient Division Monthly Report, January 1935, FERA State Files 1933–36, Kansas Transient Division, RG69, NA.

95. *KERC Bulletin* 289, 745.

96. The centers for single men were large. In early 1934, Fort Scott had accommodation for 300 but had registered 415 men; Hutchinson, with 300 registrations, was nearly full, while Topeka had registered 320 men but had accommodation for only 250. KERC Transient Division Monthly Report, January 1934, FERA State Files 1933–36, Kansas Transient Division, RG69, NA.

the centers had fully equipped workshops. Men were able to refurbish their accommodation and also produce high-quality office furniture that was used in a number of KERC offices. Some camps provided a public service in accepting parolees from the state penitentiary and the Boys Industrial School. For example, in February 1934, the Transient Service accepted sixteen men who had been paroled from Leavenworth prison, though this could be seen as indicating that the camps were a halfway house between incarceration and the real world rather than part of an integrated relief program.

The Kansas Transient Service became highly regarded. In 1934, FERA field supervisor T. J. Edmonds commented to Harry Hopkins, "[T]his Kansas set-up looks awfully good to me."[97] However, in 1935 the Works Progress Administration (WPA) replaced the FERA, and the funding of the transient program disappeared. From late 1935 on, able-bodied transients could, in theory, obtain WPA employment, while unemployables became the responsibility of the counties in which they had legal settlement. The prospect of taking care of transients who had gained settlement while living in centers or camps attracted a hostile reaction. The *Hutchinson News* reported that Ford, Reno, and Shawnee county commissioners had declared that they had "no intention of supporting the federal castoffs."[98] An extra effort was made to return clients who had a legal settlement outside Kansas, and during 1935, 364 families, 38 men, and 69 women and girls were removed. However, in October 1935, 278 families who had gained legal settlement by living in Kansas counties continuously for at least one year became the responsibility of their new county, which received a grant toward the cost of their care. During subsequent months families were transferred to the counties as they acquired settlement. The family treatment centers were closed in February 1936, and the Transient Service continued to fund the care of families until they acquired legal settlement, which all had done by September.[99]

Unattached men presented different problems. The unemployables, who were, by definition, not eligible for WPA work, eventually became county charges after the exhaustion of the final grant that accompanied them. All employables were transferred to camps, and work continued on water conservation and other related schemes. In November 1935, the

97. Edmonds to Hopkins, April 12, 1934, FERA State Files 1933–36, Kansas Transient Division, RG69, NA.

98. *Hutchinson News,* October 10, 1935. The local fear was that eight of the sixteen residents in the Hutchinson center would immediately become legal residents. See also *Norton Telegram,* October 10, 1935; *Dodge City Globe,* October 30, 1935.

99. *KERC Bulletin* 380, January 2, 1937, "Public Welfare Service in Kansas 1936," 26–28.

WPA approved the continuation of the three remaining projects at the Gardner, Howard, and Wabaunsee camps, thus enabling the men who worked there to prolong their employment.

It is difficult to assess the effectiveness of the transient program, especially as many families and unattached individuals firmly resisted plans to stabilize them. A report on the operation of ten of the twelve treatment centers between January 1 and December 21, 1934, which shows the average length of stay of transient families, is revealing. In the first place it is clear that there were significant variations in the average length of stay. In five of the centers the percentage of clients staying for less than two days was 58, 90, 67, 68, and 77. Even in treatment centers, a high proportion of transients were very short-term visitors and, therefore, not candidates for stabilization. The long-term residents were to be found at the Wabaunsee and Gardner camps, where 53 and 48 percent of clients, respectively, remained for longer than one month. In contrast, the family treatment centers had a very rapid turnover of clients, with only a small proportion remaining longer than four days.[100] For many transients their stay was too brief for the stabilization process to be effective, except where the service successfully persuaded them to permanently return to their place of legal settlement.

Kansas officials appreciated that the high-quality service they offered could be abused. The "gasoline group," for example, claimed to have no resources; they demanded gas and groceries but refused to cooperate in any stabilization plans.[101] A frustrated state director of the Transient Service wrote that an increasing number of clients believed that Kansas "is a land where the coffee tree grows and the sandwiches hang from the twigs."[102] He reported that men of all ages neglected to report to caseworkers and would only travel to treatment centers if the subsidized ride took them in the direction they wished to go. Even then they did not turn up at the centers. There was a suspicion that the program was encouraging government-sponsored panhandling, as migrants traveled to Kansas to enjoy better assistance then they could get at home.[103] In December 1934, an economy drive was instituted whereby clients who refused to return to their place of legal settlement were allocated no more than the

100. Ibid. 289, 745.

101. KERC Transient Division Monthly Report, July 1934, FERA State Files 1933–36, Kansas Transient Division, RG69, NA.

102. Price to William J. Plunkert, Acting Director Transient Activities, Washington, D.C., April 7, 1934, FERA Transient Division files, Narrative Reports, Kansas, RG69, NA.

103. KERC Transient Division Monthly Report, May 1934, FERA State Files, 1933–36, Kansas Transient Division, RG69, NA.

budget they would have received had they returned. The results were disappointing. Many families still preferred to stay in Kansas in the anticipation of eventually gaining settlement.[104]

Even for families who were prepared to work out a plan with caseworkers, stabilization posed formidable difficulties. Consider, for example, those clients who came from the backwoods of Arkansas and Missouri, where they had endured a miserable existence as tenant farmers. Perpetually in debt, even though every member of the family worked, now broken by drought and starvation levels of relief, they had no wish to return to their former communities. Kansas social workers felt that it would be cruel to send seriously disadvantaged people back to a depressing lifestyle, but they were also acutely aware that the transition to an unfamiliar urban existence would pose difficult problems as well.[105] Meticulous casework was essential with poor rural families, many of whom would have benefited more from subsistence homesteads than from urban work relief.

Before the liquidation of the Transient Service began in September 1935, the demand for its services was still buoyant in Kansas as the following figures demonstrate. During 1935, a monthly average of 1,743 families (comprising 6,106 individuals) and 8,730 unattached nonresidents received assistance; more than $219,000 was paid in cash wages, and the value of relief in kind exceeded $400,000. Some transients were actually able to start small savings accounts, which facilitated a move to private employment and personal budget management.[106] There can be no doubt that some migrants received valuable assistance at a time when economic misfortune acted as a catalyst for mobility. However, it is evident that a significant number of travelers, it is not possible to say how many, were prepared to use the Transient Service to help them on their way, rather than as a vehicle for stability. There is also some evidence that the quality of service offered in Kansas attracted the needy.

Youth Relief and the Environment: The Civilian Conservation Corps

In April 1933, Congress, acting on the instructions of the president, established the Emergency Conservation Work Program, designed to pro-

104. KERC Transient Division Monthly Report, December 1934, FERA State Files, 1933–36, Kansas Transient Division, RG69, NA.

105. KERC Transient Service, Monthly Reports, January and September 1934, FERA State Files, 1933–36, Kansas Transient Division, RG69, NA.

106. *KERC Bulletin* 355, 19–20.

vide young men with work relief that would specifically help to restore the nation's depleted natural resources. This environmental program soon became known as the CCC. The CCC targeted unmarried, unemployed males who were in good physical condition and, initially, between the ages of seventeen and twenty-three years. Young men who enrolled in the Corps had to be willing to join a camp, possibly in another state, and live in it for at least six months, unless a private sector job became available. Although priority was given to applicants from families eligible for relief, during the first two years men from economically marginal households could also be recruited. In 1935, new rules were introduced that restricted recruitment to those from relief families but extended the age range from eighteen to twenty-eight years inclusive.

Most CCC workers received a standard $30 minimum payment each month, of which a considerable proportion—in the case of Kansas Corps members, between $22 and $25—was sent by the War Department to their families. For a while there was public agitation in favor of a $50 payment, which was opposed by the Administration.[107] Washington officials pointed out that once in camp, clothing, food, shelter, and sustenance were provided by the federal government, as were educational benefits and medical care. Indeed, if the monthly cash allowance was added to these costs and other expenditures over the years 1933–40, the monthly average figure would fall within the range of $66 and $70.[108] This was a substantial amount compared to the per capita expenditure on other New Deal programs.

President Roosevelt himself initiated and was the driving force behind the CCC. He was motivated in part by a romantic attachment to the land, as well as by the satisfaction he had gained from conservation work on his Hyde Park estate. Roosevelt became such an enthusiastic supporter of the CCC that in 1935 he suggested that the camps become a permanent rather than an emergency feature.[109] Indeed, the prospect of young men, who would otherwise be idle, undertaking properly supervised practical work in healthy surroundings struck a national chord of approval. Both Governor Landon and Senator Arthur Capper admired the CCC; indeed, Landon promised that if elected in 1936 his administration would be firmly committed to the Corps.[110]

107. John A. Salmond, *The Civilian Conservation Corps, 1933–42: A New Deal Case Study,* 13–19.

108. Theodore E. Whiting and T. J. Woofter, Jr., *Summary of Relief and Federal Work Program Statistics, 1933–1940,* 10.

109. Franklin Delano Roosevelt, *Public Papers and Addresses of Franklin D. Roosevelt with a Special Introduction and Explanatory Notes by President Roosevelt,* Vol. 4, *The Court Disapproves, 1935,* 365.

110. Salmond, *Civilian Conservation Corps,* 68–69, 103.

In 1933 the KERC was designated the CCC Selection Agency for Kansas, and poor commissioners became registrars for selection. County relief offices scrutinized the relief rolls and compiled lists of potential CCC volunteers. These lists, together with information on comparative caseloads and relief needs, provided sufficient information to draw up quotas which the counties were permitted to fill. County case supervisors were instructed to conduct full interviews with each potential recruit, using casework procedure, in order to assess suitability for the CCC and to ensure that the challenge of camp life was fully understood. The recommendations of the county case supervisors acted as an essential guide for poor commissioners, who were ultimately responsible for certification and enrollment.

To construct and organize camps for more than 300,000 men at short notice was a massive task, and one that could only be undertaken by the army. The War Department supervised the erection of tents; the construction of a more permanent camp; the organization, feeding, physical examination, and payment of the men; and their leisure activities. During the working day experts recruited from the Departments of Agriculture and the Interior with appropriate skills in conservation, drought management, and forestry managed Corps members and directed their efforts, but the army provided the discipline within which the camps operated.[111]

In mid-1933, 3,693 young Kansans answered the first call for CCC places, a figure slightly below the state quota of 3,750. About 1,500 re-enrolled at the end of their six-month period of service when they were joined by new entrants, whose number ensured that the state had a total of 5,902 CCC workers at the very end of 1933. By then seventeen camps had been established in fourteen different counties, and early work concentrated on flood control and roadwork.[112] Soon, however, water conservation and attempts to combat soil erosion were the lead activities. There was also a valuable tree planting project in southeast Kansas, designed to reclaim land that had been devastated by strip mining for coal. In July 1934, as part of a national plan to assist states badly affected by drought, Kansas received an additional 800 CCC places but was only able to fill 735 of them.[113] The CCC was racially segregated, and of the twenty-two camps that existed in 1935, three had been established for African Americans. Of these one was located at Fort Riley, another at Fort Leavenworth, and one moved from Reading to Lawrence during the course of

111. Leslie Alexander Lacy, *The Soil Soldiers: The Civilian Conservation Corps in the Great Depression,* 72–73.
112. *KERC Bulletin* 127, 31–33.
113. Ibid. 289, 755–58.

the year. More than five hundred young black men were enrolled in these camps; almost one-third of them came from Wyandotte County. As the army was segregated at this time, doubtless officers were more comfortable with separation than integration, and there is no evidence that welfare professionals in Kansas felt uncomfortable with this policy.

Although the CCC was popular in Kansas and residents were profoundly grateful for improvements in water conservation techniques and the effective prevention of soil erosion, the KERC always emphasized the substantial savings on the relief budget that were the direct result of this program. The remittances of enrollees usually resulted in the removal of their families from the relief rolls, thus facilitating either a saving, or a reallocation of expenditure. The savings from this source were meticulously calculated for each county and regularly displayed in KERC Bulletins. In 1935, for example, 7,034 families comprising 33,474 individuals received allotments from the 7,424 CCC enrollees. As a result, 4,760 families were removed from the relief rolls, saving $98,799.[114] One of the reasons Kansas officials were anxious to recruit their full CCC quota, and minimize the numbers discharged other than honorably, was to maximize savings on the relief budget. They fretted that the family of each young man who abandoned his CCC camp was likely to return to the relief rolls because of the loss of his remittance. All recruiters were aware, however, that the CCC was a voluntary activity and county relief could not be withheld because of the refusal of a family member to join the Corps. A survey of the first CCC roll call in April 1933 showed that of the 3,693 young men recruited, approximately 35 percent either quit during the following six months or failed to re-enroll. Of this substantial group less than 20 percent had found work a few months later. The conclusion is that in 1933, camps offered a much better opportunity for employment than private industry.[115] However, it is also the case that a large number of young men must have found camp life too difficult to cope with in the long term.

There was little in the CCC for women, except indirectly as members of families who benefited from remittances, though the impact of this cash flow was considerable. However, the wider multiplier effects of New Deal agencies should not be ignored. In 1936, for example, the CCC provided employment for approximately twenty-four hundred nonenrolled persons. These included reserve officers who ran camps, technical experts who supervised the work programs, and numerous educational advisors and others who helped to manage the wide range of activities that had

114. Ibid. 355, 291.
115. Ibid. 127, 32.

been made available.[116] Local food suppliers also benefited. How many of these individuals would otherwise have been unemployed, or underemployed, is impossible to say, but it is clear that considerable benefits were generated beyond the confines of the camps.

By 1935 the energies of CCC workers were directed toward erosion control and the conservation of water through the construction of ponds and lakes, all priorities for a state struggling to cope with the impact of drought. The Soil Conservation Service supervised all CCC erosion work on private land and was able to demonstrate to farmers that fields terraced on the contour would hold water and check erosion. Cooperation with local farmer organizations, a feature of CCC operations, was a valuable way of spreading good practice. Lone Star Lake in Douglas County, a major CCC project, had both water conservation and significant recreational benefits. The CCC also planted trees and installed picnic tables and benches as part of their remit in improving state parks. For those young men—and most enrollees were below the age of twenty-one years—who did enjoy camp life, the CCC was a very attractive alternative to unemployment. Unlike the Special Programs, whose operations were halted in 1935, the CCC was so universally popular that it continued until the demands of war rendered it irrelevant.

The Kansas Model in Operation: A Case Study of Wyandotte County Relief Administration

By mid-1935, Kansas had developed a relief structure that had attracted many commendations from federal field agents, who were also loud in their praise for John Stutz and his senior colleagues. KERC bulletins lost no opportunity to extol the virtues of the Kansas model for relief, and there was a strong belief that the devolution of responsibility to the counties had not only resulted in economic prudence but had also delivered care of the highest quality. But if each county was to operate at the maximum level of professional excellence, highly effective performances on the part of both the poor commissioner and the county case supervisor was essential. This was only possible with the provision of a strongly supportive framework by the county commissioners. The experience in Wichita had demonstrated that when trust on the part of clients evaporated, the repercussions could be serious. Nor was this experience limited to Sedgwick County. There were many other examples of strikes and violent

116. Ibid. 380, 28.

action taken by frustrated groups of the unemployed. To discover how well the system worked, and at the same time assess how justified were the protests of those on relief, would require a critical analysis of several county relief administrations. Unfortunately, however, there is little surviving information on which to base a judgment.

An unnamed case supervisor made detailed notes on nineteen northwestern counties visited during May and early June 1935. The relief administration was found satisfactory in eleven counties, and less than that in the remainder. The main problem was the appointment of staff with the appropriate qualifications and the necessary drive. The case supervisor found that in several counties farmers and employers were unsympathetic to the relief program, usually because they believed that it would lead to a rise in wages. In railroad centers, such as Goodland and Phillipsburg, there was simmering resentment among relief clients toward transients who, they believed, received assistance with too much ease. Only Sherman County gave cause for concern because unemployment was high among former railroad workers, and those appointed to assist them were held to be of poor quality.[117]

Fortunately, State Case Supervisor Eleanor D. Myers subjected Wyandotte County to an inspection in early 1936, and the report has survived to provide the only detailed county scrutiny available to scholars. Though it cannot be regarded as representative, it does provide valuable insight into how the Kansas model actually worked at the grass roots. Moreover, the poor commissioner and the board of county commissioners had been in office since 1933. They had ample opportunity to mold the administration of relief to suit their standards of compassion and professionalism.

The Wyandotte County relief administration, the largest in Kansas, carried a caseload of 3,404 in February.[118] Four assistant case supervisors, twenty-seven case aides, and six clerical staff assisted the poor commissioner and county case supervisor. Myers relied on extensive interviews with staff and a limited examination of a number of both public and confidential case histories.[119] The investigation was more restricted than she

117. "Field reports on North-Western Counties," Stutz Papers, 327:2:16.
118. "Report of Wyandotte County Relief Administration February–March 1936," by Eleanor D. Myers, Supervisor, Division of Public Assistance, Stutz Papers, 327:5:45.
119. Eleanor D. Myers attended the University of Chicago and the Chicago School of Civics and Philanthropy. She began her career in 1916, working as an assistant director of employment in the Chicago Department of Public Welfare before moving to the U.S. Bureau of Labor Statistics and then to the Chicago Chapter of the Red Cross. After a short spell at the Child Welfare Board, Winona, Minnesota, she moved, in 1925, to become assistant director of the St. Louis Community Council, a post she held until 1932. In 1933 she was director of relief for the Louisiana Emergency Relief Admin-

desired because of the growing unease felt by senior staff, especially when significant procedural flaws and even departures from state law were uncovered. Poor Commissioner Lester A. Wickcliffe invited Eleanor Myers to assess the quality of the relief administration, to investigate the relationships that existed with other welfare agencies, to discover the amount of relief recommended and then actually given to clients, and to suggest improvements in the running of the department. The thirty-eight-page report is of immense value to our understanding of how a major Kansas relief administration actually functioned.

On the whole, Myers found that the administration of relief was not of a high standard. In her view, neither the poor commissioner, nor the county case supervisor, Eugenia B. Stogdale, had sufficient experience for the posts that they held. This is a puzzling observation since the poor commissioner had been in the post for at least three years, although Stogdale was a recent appointment. However, Wickliffe was variously described as an accountant, a businessman, or a politician who pandered to the views of a pressure group, the Citizens' Committee of Businessmen, on the grounds that they represented a significant proportion of the taxpayers in the county. As a result, it was evident to Myers that a "political atmosphere [was] felt throughout the organization." The poor commissioner's principal concern was a lack of funding so serious that he actually contemplated taking the extraordinary step of closing down the relief office. The Citizens' Committee was also concerned about the funding crisis and advocated a reduction in relief allowances, which Myers already thought "shockingly inadequate." It was clear to Myers that Wickliffe's primary goal was to administer poor relief in a way that would meet the approval of his financial masters rather than deliver satisfaction to clients.

Myers identified, and was disturbed by, a lack of leadership and managerial competence on the part of the county case supervisor. The result of this deficiency was inadequate record keeping by staff, poor investigation of applicants for relief, and no discernable attempt made to wean clients off relief once they had begun to receive it. The fact that applicants for relief were so readily accepted without sufficient evidence of need led Myers to conclude that if investigation were more thorough, the total county caseload could have been reduced by up to 25 percent, thus obviating the need for cuts in relief. Myers was also critical of bureaucratic procedures which placed an emphasis on form filling while at the same time paying too little attention to the development of case histories. In other

---

istration, and she joined the KERC in August 1934 as a state case supervisor. Myers was a highly experienced social worker.

words, an elaborate administrative structure had been created, but there was little evidence that the extensive paperwork resulted in good social work practice. Particularly worrying was Myers's judgment that the county case supervisor did not have the authority, or the strength of character, to counter the poor commissioner's inclination to ignore the needs of clients.

Moving from the general to the particular, the report found that budgeting procedures were seriously at odds with best practice. Relief was given on a sliding scale according to the numbers in each family and bore no relation to the client's budget. Furthermore, the relief given, which was in the form of food orders, seemed extraordinarily low. Myers was informed that the amount of relief had actually been raised by one-third in August 1935, possibly as a result of a vigorous protest by the unemployed, though this was not mentioned. Neither the poor commissioner nor the county case supervisor seemed overly concerned by the low level of relief payments. Both accepted them as an inevitable consequence of, on the one hand, insufficient funding to meet the legitimate claims of all clients, and on the other, pressure from the Citizen's Committee, which was seeking to impose a further reduction in relief.

Curiously, although relief was always given according to family size, social workers engaged in a laborious attempt to construct a budget for each individual or family. Even though this exercise involved the use of five different forms, the deficiencies in recording and updating the correct information were such that the results were imperfect. Myers concluded that families on relief were given less than the minimum food needs that had been calculated in their budgets. She illustrated her point with the example of a family comprising two adults and two children whose weekly food needs were assessed at $7.01. This family was given $3.38 in grocery orders and no further county relief. On the other hand, all single men were allocated either one day of work relief or $3.60 in grocery orders, regardless of their budgets. Sometimes sums were allocated to clients to cover fuel or transport costs without any justification for these awards. As case aides did not always make home visits, relief payments were often automatically continued because the crucial investigation required to monitor changed circumstances had not taken place. The district auditor, who in the course of an interview expressed a confidence in the paperwork that was clearly misplaced, was surprised to learn that the information so laboriously collected played no role in assessing relief needs.

Myers wondered why the low levels of relief did not result in acute physical suffering and could not understand how clients met unavoidable expenditures like rent and utility bills. She was forced to conclude that

some were receiving assistance from private agencies but that the sums were not being recorded, a distinct possibility given the inadequate record keeping she had uncovered. Charities, for example, the Salvation Army and the St. Vincent de Paul Society, periodically gave cash assistance to the needy. Parent Teachers Associations in various schools also helped, usually with clothing and food. There was, therefore, a strong possibility of duplication, as assistance by private charities was not systematically monitored. We cannot be certain, but it is possible that some of the poor in Wyandotte County were only able to survive because of some form of supplementation to their meager relief. However, such was the inadequacy of the paper work and the home investigations that it is also possible that some of the clients who were receiving relief did not actually need it.

Myers believed that the county commissioners displayed a lack of a properly developed sense of professional concern for the needy. The most common method of giving relief was to issue food orders, and in an attempt to spread business among grocery outlets, the commissioners decreed that there should be an upper limit of $300 on the value of orders that could be processed by an individual store. The result was that clients sometimes had to travel long distances, perhaps in inclement weather, to change their orders into goods when the store closest to them had reached its limit. When Myers raised this problem, the reaction of the poor commissioner and the county purchasing agent was decidedly unsympathetic. Both felt that the poor should be grateful for what they received and should not complain about an inconvenient journey. It was more important to these officials that "the grocers feel that the county is fair to them in distributing its business."

At no stage in this report did Myers comment on the provision of relief for blacks in need, even though cases were plentiful in Kansas City.[120] Indeed, when Kansas City, Kansas, applied to the Federal Emergency Administration of Public Works in September 1935 for funding to support a public housing project, the fact that 85 percent of the population living in the "negro slum district" was on relief and that tuberculosis was rampant was stressed.[121] The failure to assess the treatment of Wyandotte's African Americans is a surprising omission.

120. She does disclose that the county physician, Dr. Lawrence E. Growney, who took care of all white relief patients, was paid $150 per month. The monthly salary of the "colored physician," Dr. W. Clyde Allen, was $50. Although Dr. Growney performed most of the surgical procedures, this cannot explain all of the salary differential.

121. Application from Kansas City, Kansas, September 7, 1935, Public Housing Administration, Project Files 1933–37, File 8300, Box 392, RG196, NA. The application failed. A. R. Clas to Mayor D. C. McCombs, October 2, 1935, ibid.

Stogdale responded to the catalogue of criticisms by claiming that the social workers under her management were operating under considerable strain as they struggled to cope with staffing reductions following the transfer from the FERA to the WPA. As staff resigned, those who remained had to take over their caseload at short notice and were never able to come to grips with the problems presented by all cases. Because of high caseloads, case workers could not undertake the number of home visits that they should, and the pressure of work was a major contributory factor to imperfect record keeping. These excuses explain some but not all of the problems that were uncovered, especially as several of the deficiencies were long-standing. It is disconcerting to discover that an experienced and well-qualified poor commissioner in a major county relief administration could depart from the model of good practice laid down by the KERC. Nor does the conduct of the county commissioners shield them from criticism. Their neglect helped to create and to tolerate procedural imperfections in the Wyandotte relief administration that resulted in the devaluation of clients' interests. There was, therefore, a significant deviation between the best practice to which the KERC aspired and how the administration of relief actually operated in Wyandotte County.

Of course Wyandotte County could be an oddity, perhaps the only relief organization in the state to exhibit such serious imperfections. It might also be argued that Myers adopted a system of values that were too client-oriented and paid insufficient attention to political and financial realities. If Myers's report had been less rigorous, and Wyandotte an insignificant county for the provision of relief, then many of her criticisms could be dismissed. But Eleanor Myers was using as her yardstick the Kansas model of relief administration to which all counties were supposed to rigidly adhere, and it would be unfair to devalue her findings on the grounds that they were overly influenced by her concerns for the needy. The conclusion one must draw is that, in some counties, relief was not delivered according to the high standards set by the KERC and approved by FERA field officers. From that observation it follows that the complaints of striking relief workers were not always the result of fiery speeches by agitators determined to inflame idle hands, but were often a spontaneous reaction to miserly and poorly administered relief.

Kansas vested much authority in the poor commissioner, the county case supervisor, and the board of county commissioners, and the expectation was that they would all follow the letter and the spirit of the rules so carefully drawn up by the KERC. But, as we have seen, powerful commissioners could impose a culture of political intervention and cost cutting that could penalize clients. The Kansas model also placed a major fi-

nancial responsibility on the counties, but the poorest of them found it impossible to discharge their relief responsibilities in a way that guaranteed all of the needy appropriate assistance. Moreover, there is also evidence of a lack of understanding on the part of public officials of the rules of the New Deal game. When in early 1935 the *Kansas State Planning Board* asked counties which local PWA projects they would be prepared to fund, the quality of the responses was disappointing. Many counties, even though their representatives had considerable experience of what was required, failed to distinguish between public works and routine maintenance, or submitted poorly thought out plans that were no more than a transparent attempt to obtain federal money. Particularly disappointing was the lack of evidence of forward planning and the reluctance of most counties to commit themselves to financial support. A combination of difficulty in collecting taxes, high debt levels, and the Cash Basis Law, which required counties to have money in hand before embarking on projects, provided a strong disincentive to commit funding.[122] A significant weakness of the emphasis on county autonomy was that not all political units were in a financially robust position, and those that were not were unable to deliver a fully effective relief program.

The year 1935 saw dramatic changes to federal relief policies and programs. When Congress established the FERA in 1933, there was a clear national emergency. State and local relief organizations needed an injection of federal funds as a matter of urgency. By early 1935, however, it was evident that permanent as opposed to emergency legislation was necessary to create a welfare framework that would provide long-term security for all Americans. During the summer and fall of 1935 the FERA was gradually liquidated and a new Federal Works Program inaugurated.

[handwritten margin note: Summer + fall 1935 FERA out → new Fed. Works Program]

Given the difficulties that surrounded its implementation, the FERA was a remarkably successful agency. By 1934 the federal government was supporting roughly 70 percent of the nation's relief expenditure, an extraordinary contribution that had been reached in a very short time. The impact of federal funding of relief activities in Kansas has been analyzed in this chapter, and there is no doubt that without Washington's help, misery would have been far more acute. There was also a praiseworthy attempt by federal and local officials to force good administrative practices on the states and the localities. One should not underestimate the difficulty of changing long-held practices, which although deficient, had been

122. Kansas State Planning Board, *Inventory of Public Works*, 7–10. Governor Landon established the Kansas State Planning Board in late 1934, with the encouragement of the PWA. A bill to give the board permanence was narrowly rejected by the Senate in 1935. James W. Drury, *The Government Of Kansas*, 406–7.

rewarding to those who had exercised patronage. Fortunately, Kansas had anticipated the need for a sound administrative structure at an early stage, and even though practice at times deviated from its own ideal standards, the provision of relief in Kansas was extraordinarily efficient and effective compared to the experience in most other states.

4

Rural Kansas
Drought, Rehabilitation, and Relief

New Dealers accorded agriculture a high priority in the fight for economic recovery. As the farm sector had fallen so far, it seemed common sense to many observers that given some stimulus it could mount a vigorous upward surge and carry the rest of the economy with it. There was also a romantic attachment to the land, shared by Roosevelt and many leading decision makers, that translated into a resolve to save the family farm. As 25 percent of the nation's population lived on farms, the economic and political benefit from a transformation in this group's fortunes was a worthwhile prize. Considerable energy and ingenuity were employed, therefore, in creating a variety of measures designed to raise farm income from the depths to which it had sunk in 1932, and also to extend the helping hand of organized relief to rural communities that in the past had often been left to their own devices during times of economic crisis.

In Kansas, however, it was the weather, and especially the serious droughts of 1934 and 1936, that exercised the most powerful influence over farm output and income rather than New Deal regulation. Aridity reduced the surpluses that had caused price falls in the early 1930s; indeed, drought actually encouraged price rises and therefore provided a welcome boon to those farmers who had a crop to market. Their less favored brethren, however, more than matched these fortunates. A substantial number of Kansas farmers, especially if they lived in the western part of the state, were helpless and frustrated in the face of nature's onslaught.

While most, but not all, farmers were rural dwellers, many rural people did not live or work on farms. In 1930 the state's rural nonfarm population had reached nearly 24 percent of the total. Even in a predominantly rural county like Haskell, 40 percent of the workforce had non-agricultural occupations, and in Morton County, the figure was about 50 percent. Areas with low levels of urbanization could contain relatively large numbers of nonfarm workers, as in the western third of the state, where just over 12 percent of the population was classed as urban in 1930, yet nearly half of the workforce was engaged in nonagricultural pursuits. Nestling below the minimum level for inclusion in lists of urban places were eighty-five rural incorporated settlements with populations ranging from one thousand to twenty-five hundred inhabitants. These hamlets and villages were home to teachers, bankers, merchants, tradesmen, railroad workers, oil men, farm managers, laborers, and providers of services to the local community; they depended heavily on the spending power of farm families for their economic well-being.[1]

The number of farms in Kansas fluctuated during the 1930s. The 1930 *Census of Agriculture* recorded 166,042, but, in spite of increasing farm misery, the number had grown to 174,589 by 1935. This pattern was also evident in the rest of the nation, though it was most pronounced in the northeast, as urban Americans tried to escape from the tightening grip of depression by attempting to become self-sufficient on the land. In the first half of the decade the rise in the number of farms was noticeable in all parts of the state, but it was most prominent in the relatively urbanized east.[2] However, this "back to the land" movement was a short-lived phenomenon, and it was soon evident that subsistence farming on poor-quality land could not provide the long-term relief from the depression that its participants and early supporters had hoped.

Because of adverse circumstances, Kansas suffered a population loss of eighty thousand people during the 1930s. Many of those who left the state were young men who—faced with drought, dust storms, and grasshoppers—had become disillusioned with life on the farm. The older operators were inclined to remain and hope for better times. Rural dwellers also moved to the state's principal cities, but on a much reduced scale than that established during the previous decade. There was also some movement from small urban centers to the large.[3] As continuing adverse weather

1. John H. Kolb and Edmund de S. Brunner, *A Study of Rural Society*, 259–81.
2. Caroll D. Clark and Roy L. Roberts, *People Of Kansas: A Demographic and Sociological Study*, 160–61. Between 1930 and 1935 there was a general rise of 5 percent in the number of farms, but in the eastern third of the state the increase was just over 9 percent.
3. Emile B. Dade, "Migration of Kansas Population, 1930–1945," 8–17.

took its toll, many residents migrated from the open country to towns and villages so that they would be closer to both jobs and relief offices. As a result of this migration, the 1940 census recorded only 156,327 farms, and the average size of each holding increased from 283 acres in 1930 to 308 acres ten years later. The average value of Kansas's farms also fell victim to the depression, declining from $13,783 in 1930 to $9,092 on the eve of World War II.

In 1930, there were 57,151 full owners, 37,611 part owners, and 70,326 tenants operating farms in the state. Tenancy, seen as an indication of agricultural distress by those who believed that farm ownership was a sign of national strength, increased very slightly during the 1930s. By 1940, 45 percent of Kansas farms were rented. During the depression the ebb and flow of tenancy was influenced by a variety of factors. For example, a number of owners lost their farms because they were unable to meet their mortgage payments but continued to operate as tenants either on the same farm or on another. Some tenants were forced to remain as renters because they found it impossible or undesirable to make their expected transition to ownership once economic conditions deteriorated. On the other hand, other owners had leased their farms before the depression began to bite, but they were eventually forced to return to the land. There were also those who wanted to extend their farms but preferred to rent additional acreage rather than buy it, especially as times were so uncertain. There was little difference in status between tenants and owners, especially in central and western Kansas, and it is quite possible that some owners contemplating the burden of their debts envied renters, whose obligations were limited to livestock and machinery.[4] The proportion of tenant farmers in Kansas was not a cause for concern, though renters were more likely than owners to leave their farms during times of adversity and were found more frequently on the relief rolls. Moreover, many tenants were related to their landlords; indeed, in 1930 approximately 31 percent of them fell into this category.[5]

Because their farms could not generate enough income to support a family, many operators, or other household members, had to find additional employment for part of the year. For those living in the remote parts of the state far away from urban centers, nonfarm jobs were not easy to obtain, but even the more geographically favored found that economic decline had destroyed employment opportunities, forcing many operators to rely more than they wished on the output of their inadequate hold-

4. Clark and Roberts, *People of Kansas,* 191–92, 244–46.
5. W. E. Grimes, "Farm Tenancy in Kansas," 61–67; Clark and Roberts, *People of Kansas,* 191–93.

ings. In 1929, just over 30 percent of all operators spent some time working away from their farm; by 1934 this figure had risen to 35 percent, though by 1939 the percentage had declined to the pre-depression level. On the majority of the days worked at a distance from their homes, employment was on nonfarm jobs. It is important to remember how important work away from the farm was for the family, especially for the small marginal operator who found that drought had not only destroyed the crops he expected to market, but also those that were destined to feed his family and his livestock. Operators' sons also sought employment, sometimes as laborers on neighboring farms.[6] A contraction in outside employment opportunities during a period of low farm prices was potentially serious, even for the relatively secure, and often necessitated a visit to the relief office. Even then, the shortage of part-time opportunities made it difficult for family heads to supplement their inadequate relief budgets with work.

The depression brought pressure on the complex set of relationships that linked the price of farm products, their costs of production, indebtedness, land values, and bank stability. The prices that Kansas farmers had received for all their products had been remarkably stable between 1926 and 1929, but a sharp decline followed.[7] From its low point in 1932, the prices received index (1910–14 = 100) rose to 126 in 1937, but the recession that began in that year cut short recovery, and the index declined to 96 in 1938 and slumped even further to 93 a year later.

There are no separate calculations for fluctuations in the prices that Kansas farmers paid for the goods that they purchased, but it is possible to apply the national indices. This shows a growing disadvantage for farmers, as agricultural prices fell further than the cost of nonfarm products. Indeed, the relationship between prices farmers paid for nonfarm goods and the prices they received for farm products, the state parity ratio (1910–14 = 100), illustrates this disadvantage. The Kansas parity ratio stood at 88 in 1929, but it declined rapidly and steeply to 49 by 1932. From these depths Kansas farm prices staged a strong recovery, and the parity ratio rose to average 93 between 1935 and 1937, a better position, relatively, than in 1929. Unfortunately, the ensuing recession forced the parity ratio down to 77 during the two years 1938 and 1939. It is important to remember that relatively high prices do not necessarily guarantee good economic returns to all farmers. For example, cultivators in western

6. Tom Vasey and Josiah C. Folsom, *Survey of Agricultural Labor Conditions in Pawnee County, Kansas*, 2.

7. All price data are from Kansas State Board of Agriculture, *Price Patterns: Prices Received by Kansas Farmers, 1910–55*, 20.

Kansas, whose crops were wasted by drought during the 1930s, were not able to share in the benefits of high prices, as they sometimes had no crops or feedstuffs to harvest.

Deflation is a curse for borrowers because price falls increase the real burden of debt. In 1930, just over half of Kansas farms operated by owners were mortgaged, and the average amount of mortgage debt for each indebted farm was $4,460. During this period of declining income, many farmers faced a high level of fixed costs that had to be met. Most could not act like manufacturers and save money by dismissing some of their workforce, since they employed only their families. But they had to have cash to pay their mortgages, which usually had been agreed under more optimistic circumstances. Credit extended by local stores also had to be repaid, as did their taxes. A mortgage-free farm was not a guarantee of survival during these troubled times, but the payment of $200 or $300 in interest charges was, for some families, the difference between success and failure. In addition to their property mortgages, many wheat producers became heavily indebted to farm machinery suppliers, as a result of purchases of expensive equipment at a time when such investment seemed economically justified. Given the extent of the price falls, many more bushels of wheat or head of beef cattle had to be sold in order to repay each $100 of debt.[8]

One early effect of the depression's assault on the farm was that many indebted owners found it impossible to meet their mortgage payments, and for some, foreclosure was unavoidable. The rise in distress sales in Kansas reached a peak in 1933 at a higher level than the national figure. In general, farm mortgage distress during the 1930s was especially severe in parts of the U.S. that had been generally prosperous during the 1920s.[9] Were this generalization to be a universal truth, western Kansas in particular should have faced particular difficulties, but the state's farmers survived the mortgage crisis relatively well. If the Great Plains region is considered as a whole, between 1920 and 1940 western and central Kansas had fewer foreclosures than the northern and central parts of that region. Surprisingly, the highest mortgage foreclosure rates did not occur in counties that had the lowest wheat yields. In fact, the most seriously affected

8. Donald C. Horton, Harald C. Larsen, and Norman J. Wall, *Farm Mortgage Credit Facilities in the United States,* Table 64, 219.

9. Lawrence A. Jones and David Durand, *Mortgage Lending Experience in Agriculture,* 71–73. See also "The Land Price Situation With Special Reference to Trends and Their Causes" (Manhattan: Kansas Agricultural Experiment Station, Circular 246, January 1946): 8–10; Lee J. Alston, "Farm Foreclosures in the United States during the Interwar Period," 885–903.

counties had far fewer foreclosures than one would expect. This finding is supported by the research of Pamela Riney-Kehrberg, who has subjected southwestern Kansas during the dusty thirties to a searching analysis. The farmers in the five townships that she studied "experienced an amazingly low level of foreclosures and tax sales."[10] Riney-Kehrberg explains this seemingly curious phenomenon by pointing out that neither county officials nor mortgage lenders had a strong incentive to take over farms from dispossessed owners, as they would have been virtually impossible to sell. Moreover, the ownership of a farm could impose costly obligations on the operator. In particular, regulations obliged owners to take prompt action with tractor and plow in order to prevent their soil from drifting into neighboring farms during dust storms.[11]

It was preferable for the counties, many of which had in fact introduced unofficial moratoria on tax collections, and other creditors to let farmers stay on their land as tenants rather than become operators themselves. Other forces also further limited distress sales. These included state legislation making foreclosure more difficult and a range of New Deal initiatives, which included the debt extension services of the Farm Credit Administration (FCA). The FCA helped farmers refinance their debts, brought about temporary reductions in interest rates, and even introduced a temporary suspension in principal payments. At the same time, cash payments for participants in the wheat allotment and corn-hog schemes enabled some of the hardest pressed farmers to keep their creditors at bay.

Wherever they occurred, foreclosure sales caused great distress, and in a number of communities the reaction to them was so violent that both individual states and the federal government introduced protective legislation for mortgage holders. Faced with the need to assist farmers, the regular session of the legislature that met in January 1933 adopted a six-month mortgage moratorium, which Governor Landon later extended by proclamation, as he was empowered to do, for a further six months. Although this was popular legislation, district courts declared it unconstitutional on three occasions, so there were grave doubts about its permanence.[12] Kansas was one of a number of states that anxiously waited for a U.S. Supreme Court decision on the legality of the Minnesota moratorium law. In January 1934 a majority of five justices declared that the Minnesota law, which granted a limited moratorium on mortgage payments,

10. Pamela Riney-Kehrberg, *Rooted in Dust: Surviving Drought and Depression in Southwestern Kansas*, 152–53.

11. R. Douglas Hurt, "Agricultural Technology in the Dust Bowl, 1932–49," 141–44.

12. Archibald M. Woodruff, Jr., *Farm Mortgage Loans of Life Insurance Companies*, 106–7.

was constitutional. In reaching their decision the justices had been influenced by the extent of the emergency facing many farmers, which they believed was so severe that it justified extraordinary measures. In February a letter was mailed to every member of the Kansas legislature in advance of its special session, outlining the differences between the Minnesota and the Kansas moratorium laws. Landon's detailed message to the legislature urged the lawmakers to incorporate the basis of the Minnesota legislation so that Kansas home- and farm-owners could have reasonable protection during the current period of uncertainty.[13] The legislature complied with his request, and the bill became law in record time.[14]

In addition to state legislation, Landon, following the Frazier-Lemke Act, ensured that debt adjustment committees were appointed in every county.[15] The function of these committees, composed of unpaid volunteers, was to bring debtors and creditors together in order to persuade the latter to scale down the debt, so that farmers could carry on their activities. These committees were a valuable means of defusing potentially explosive situations, and they claimed credit for preventing more than three thousand foreclosures during a two-year period.[16] In general there was an absence of vigorous farm militancy in Kansas, and Milo Reno's Farmers' Holiday Association gained little active support, even when the going was particularly tough. In the fall of 1932 there was some sympathy for the Iowa farm strike, but it was not overwhelming and did not translate into vigorous action.[17] And when the firebrand farm leader visited Kansas in May 1934, he was unable to persuade those who listened to him that his direct action policies were what they needed.[18]

The Arrival of the New Deal

There was widespread acceptance of the need for federal intervention to bring about a rise in farm prices and to provide immediate coherent

---

13. *Message of Governor Alf M. Landon to the Special Session of the Kansas Legislature of 1934* (Topeka, 1934): 1–11.

14. *Kansas Union Farmer*, March 8, 1934.

15. The Frazier-Lemke Farm Indebtedness Act (June 1934) authorized the appointment of a conciliation commissioner in each county with more than five hundred farmers.

16. Wayne D. Rasmussen, *Taking the University to the People. Seventy-Five Years of Cooperative Extension*, 107; Gov. Alf M. Landon, "Farm Debt Adjustment," Kansas Agricultural Convention, *Report of the KSBA for Quarter Ending March 1934*, 69–70; *Kansas City Times*, August 21, 1935.

17. *Kansas Union Farmer*, September 29, 1932.

18. Francis W. Schruben, *Kansas in Turmoil, 1930–36*, 113–14.

support for indebted farmers. In late March 1933, the president issued an executive order creating the FCA and placing Henry Morganthau, Jr., at its head. The FCA was a single agency that took over the responsibilities for agricultural credit from a number of existing bodies, including the Federal Farm Board and the Federal Farm Loan Board. With the provision of credit now consolidated, the FCA could refinance farm mortgages and offer farmers direct assistance as they struggled to manage their debts.

The administration's Farm Bill was a broadly based attempt to accommodate the wishes of as many farm interest groups as possible. Its aim was to restore farm purchasing power to the relative position that it had occupied between 1910 and 1914. In other words, instead of being given guaranteed costs of production, the farm sector was told to look forward to 100 percent parity, a policy that the Farm Bureau had long advocated.[19]

The Farm Bill had three parts, or titles. Title 1 established the Agricultural Adjustment Administration (AAA), which was to play a major role in the fight to restore farm purchasing power by establishing a mechanism through which farmers would be persuaded to reduce the acreage that they dedicated to certain "basic" crops.[20] This was an attempt, similar to the economic philosophy at the heart of the National Recovery Act, to drive up prices by substituting scarcity for plenty. The original "basic" crops, all of them prone to surplus, were wheat, cotton, field corn, hogs, rice, tobacco, and milk and its products.[21] The scheme at this stage was entirely voluntary, although elements of compulsion were soon introduced for cotton and tobacco growers. However, although farmers were not compelled to participate, the powerful inducement of cash payments and entitlement to other benefits persuaded the vast majority to do so.[22] Farmers themselves had a role to play as local committees organized by

19. Christina McFadyen Campbell, *The Farm Bureau: A Study of the Making of National Farm Policy, 1933–40*, 55–57.

20. For the background to New Deal farm policy, see: William J. Barber, *Designs within Disorder: Franklin D. Roosevelt, the Economists, and the Shaping of American Economic Policy, 1933–45*; Mordecai Ezekiel and Louis H. Bean, *Economic Bases for the Agricultural Adjustment Act*; Peter Fearon, *War, Prosperity and Depression: The US Economy, 1917–45*; Gilbert C. Fite, *George N. Peek and the Fight for Farm Parity*; Richard S. Kirkendall, *Social Scientists and Farm Politics in the Age of Roosevelt*; V. L. Perkins, *Crisis in Agriculture: The Agricultural Adjustment Administration and the New Deal, 1933*; Theodore Saloutos, *The American Farmer and the New Deal*.

21. The Jones-Connally Act (April 1934) added rye, flax, barley, grain sorghums, cattle, and peanuts to the list of "basic" commodities. In May 1934 sugar beet and sugar cane joined the list, followed by potatoes in August 1935.

22. With the Bankhead Cotton Control Act (1934) and the Kerr-Smith Tobacco Control Act (1934) farmers who exceeded a set quota for either of these crops faced a punitive tax. However, neither cotton nor tobacco was a significant crop in Kansas.

the Extension Service administered the program and monitored its progress. Wheat producers who agreed to take part in the scheme were allocated an acreage that was determined for them and was influenced by an assessment of the domestic demand for the crop, the extent of stocks, the level of current prices, and the farmer's recent planting history. The aim was a planned reduction in output to a level consistent with domestic needs, plus a small surplus for export. This would be achieved by systematically cutting the acreage on which the crop was planted. Participating producers would gain quickly from the cash-adjustment payments to which they were entitled for agreeing to limit their wheat acreage for the 1934 and 1935 crops. Then, after a short lag, not only farmers but also the public at large should reap substantial benefits from the sustained growth in farm income and the concomitant stimulus to general economic recovery that would arise from higher wheat prices.[23]

The cash adjustment payments varied in accordance with the number of acres on which operators no longer cultivated "basic" crops, and were, of course, invariably related to the size of their farms. Those with large farms usually had the greatest wheat acreages and therefore received the largest payments. It was proposed to make the program self-financing by imposing a new tax on processing companies, like meatpackers, flour millers, producers of canned foods, and textile companies, rather than using general tax revenue. Naturally, the enterprises that had to pay the new processing tax were unhappy at its imposition.

Title II of this omnibus bill contained the Emergency Farm Mortgage Act, which recognized that private lenders were calling on thousands of destitute farmers to settle their mortgages and that private credit, so essential for farm operations, was becoming virtually impossible to obtain. This act provided funds for the land bank commissioner to refinance farm mortgages other than those held by federal land banks; in addition, interest rates on all land bank loans were reduced, and the payment of principal required on loans was extended. The Emergency Farm Mortgage Act, which confirmed the powers of the FCA, was of great significance not only to farmers but also to banks, insurance companies, and private lenders.[24] In June, the Farm Credit Act created a system of efficient, federally sponsored agricultural credit agencies that provided support for

[handwritten margin notes: Emerg. Farm Mortgage Act; June – Farm Credit Act]

23. An excellent account of the rationale of New Deal wheat programs and the reaction of Kansas farmers to them can be found in R. Douglas Hurt, "Prices, Payments and Production: Kansas Wheat Farmers and the Agricultural Adjustment Administration, 1933–39," 73–87.

24. Murray R. Benedict, *Farm Policies of the United States, 1790–1950: A Study of Their Origins and Development*, 280–83.

mortgage loans, production and marketing loans, and cooperative enterprises.

Thomas Amendment

Title III, the Thomas Amendment, gave the president wide powers to inflate the currency in order to bring about the price increases that many members of Congress felt were essential to stimulating farm recovery. There was a longstanding and widespread belief in the farm community, and beyond, that under the current deflationary circumstances, a vigorous expansionary manipulation of the currency leading to sustained inflation would quickly resolve the problem of low income for all the nation's farmers. Roosevelt himself was attracted by this reasoning and intellectually seduced by the simplistic analysis of two Cornell University economists, George F. Warren and Frank A. Pearson, who argued that if the price of gold rose then domestic prices would also rise, virtually simultaneously, and by the same amount. The gold standard was abandoned in April, and the RFC was instructed to purchase gold at relatively high prices, as the logic of this thesis dictated. By early 1934 the dollar had lost about 40 percent of its value in terms of gold, but it soon became clear that the desired inflation could not be stimulated by higher gold prices, and the president turned his attention to other schemes.[25]

May 12 1933 — Farm bill passes

The farm bill passed through Congress on May 12, and the president signed it into law on the same day. However, crop planting for the new season had already begun, and the estimates for cotton and tobacco output painted a bleak picture of price-sapping surpluses. In June, a plow-up of 25 percent of the growing cotton crop was ordered in a dramatic attempt to cut the excess supply, and tobacco growers also plowed under part of their crop. A similar plan to destroy growing wheat was discussed but dismissed on the grounds that drastic action was no longer necessary, as drought had significantly reduced output. Indeed, the United States, normally a major wheat exporter, became a substantial importer during 1934, 1935, and 1936. The main thrust of the federal government's policy to raise wheat prices emphasized production control, and the formal arrangements to achieve this were announced in the middle of June. Allotment contracts were offered to farmers based on the wheat seeded and the amount harvested during any or all of the base years 1930, 1931, and 1932. The contracts provided for adjustment payments on the 1933, 1934, and 1935 crops. Thirty-seven states participated in the program.

25. Kansas-born Pearson addressed the State Agricultural Convention in 1939 and conveyed the message that all the ills in the United States should be seen as a price problem. The paucity of questions following his paper suggests a bemused rather than a convinced audience. F. A. Pearson, "Money in Relation to Market Stabilization," 18–38. The devaluation of the dollar had little discernable effect on wheat prices. Joseph S. Davis, *Wheat and the AAA*, 329.

By late September, more than fifty-one thousand Kansas operators had signed wheat allotment contracts, more than in any other state.[26] By February 1934, 91 percent of the Kansas farmland seeded for wheat was covered by allotment contacts.[27] This gives a clear indication of the enthusiasm with which the state's wheat farmers were willing to sign up to the program. It was clear, however, that farmers who had a large proportion of their land in wheat during the base period signed up quickly, while those who were less committed took their time over the decision, or did not sign at all. Indeed, the significance of wheat cultivation during the base years was the key factor influencing farmers to join the program.[28] Initially it was hoped that the first payments could be made in the middle of September, but the program's logistics proved far more complicated than anticipated, especially in Kansas. Most farmers had to wait until the beginning of 1934 before they could enjoy this welcome cash injection, but Christmas came early to 9,145 cultivators who shared $1.3 million in December.[29]

The plan for transforming the depressed conditions facing corn and hog producers was especially complex, as two commodities were involved and there was no national organization of producers with which the Department of Agriculture could liaise.[30] As with wheat, the early thoughts of a corn plow-up were dismissed, as the crop had been so ravaged by drought. However, there was a surplus of hogs, and the decision to reduce numbers by a planned slaughter during the fall of 1933 aroused public anger, even though some of the consigned pork was available for distribution to the needy. This did not assuage the many Americans who were morally outraged at the wholesale destruction of food when large numbers of their fellow citizens were hungry. Others seemed to harbor a great deal of misplaced sympathy for cute piglets destined to perish before their time. Impoverished hog producers, on the other hand, benefited from the good prices paid for the livestock taken for slaughter. Nevertheless, when the cull was complete, the issue of how to ensure parity prices for corn and for hogs remained.

A corn-hog adjustment program for just one year was announced in Oc-

26. *Kansas Union Farmer,* September 21, 1933.

27. Sherman Johnson, *Wheat under the Agricultural Adjustment Act: Developments up to June 1934,* 57–58.

28. M. L. Robinson, "The Response of Kansas Farmers to the Wheat Adjustment Program," 359–62.

29. Henry A. Wallace to Capper, January 23, 1934, Farm Relief (22–1), Wheat Acreage Reduction, RG16, NA. *Kansas Union Farmer,* December 7, 1933.

30. For the background to this problem see Alonzo E. Taylor, *Corn and Hog Surplus of the Corn Belt.* See also Records of the Department of Agriculture, File no. 1, Corn-Hog, June 1, 1933–October 31, 1933, RG145, NA.

tober 1933, but the sign-up campaign did not get under way until the following January. Those participating agreed to reduce their corn acreage below the levels of 1932 and 1933 and also to cut the number of litters and the number of hogs produced for market. The rewards were proportionate cash payments for the corn that the participants would otherwise have grown, and a per capita payment for the reduced number of hogs they were now permitted to raise. In addition, the newly established Commodity Credit Corporation (CCCorp) made nonrecourse loans available, but only for participating producers. Very attractively pitched above the farm price for corn in the first year of operation, these nonrecourse loans went some way toward mollifying farm groups that had agitated in favor of a guaranteed fixed price for corn. However, while the initial support for the scheme was strong, enthusiasm quickly evaporated. In October 1934, when corn-hog producers were asked if they would support the continuation of the program for 1935, Kansas was the only state to record a negative vote, though by a narrow margin.[31] Nevertheless, in the next election, held a year later, a significant majority of Kansas producers indicated that they now favored the more liberal program that was put to them.

The national uproar that accompanied the hog slaughter was politically embarrassing and had created a public relations disaster for the administration that it could not ignore. New Dealers had been assailed in the most hostile manner, and all public figures supporting the program became easy targets for anyone who had not directly benefited from the cull. One way of dealing with the problem was the creation of a new agency that would systematically organize the distribution of surplus foodstuffs and raw materials to the needy. Though heavily criticized by social workers, who believed that food handouts were degrading, a plan to do just that was announced in September 1933, and during the following month, the FSRC was established.[32] Hastily concocted, the FSRC was initially seen as a short-run measure to deal with an immediate and pressing problem. However, this nonprofit organization, which acted as a link between the FERA and the Department of Agriculture until the FSCC replaced it in late 1935, did provide a means for diverting part of the depressing farm surpluses to many of the Americans who were on relief, in a way that gained the support of the public at large.

31. D. A. Fitzgerald, *Livestock under the AAA*, 158–59.
32. Janet Poppendieck, *Breadlines Knee-Deep in Wheat: Food Assistance in the Great Depression*, 111–31.

A Diversity of Experience

In a single state, in fact in a single county, the experience of many farmers can deviate significantly from the mean. Some farmers were simply more skillful than others, and those who knew and employed best-practice techniques were most likely to cope with the vagaries of the weather. In other words, the costs of production varied significantly between operators.[33] Farms with more fertile soil and operators who were fortunate with rainfall also had a survival edge. Some farms were too small, given the climate and the crop choice, to be more than marginal.[34] The persistent drought and searing heat inevitably led to low yields for many grain farmers, but for others, usually located in the western third of the state, adverse weather had an even more serious effect as they were left with literally no crop to harvest. This same relentless heat dried up streams, wells, and pastures, driving up the price of feedstuffs for beef and dairy farmers, as well as for the owners of other livestock. However, the misery was not total. Cultivators living in parts of the state least affected by drought could obtain excellent prices, in Kansas or nationally, for the feedstuffs they produced.

Nevertheless, the depression reality for many rural families was hardship, and this led to a reduction in spending, which had an adverse impact not only on businesses nationally but also on those small enterprises in the towns and villages that depended heavily on the farmer as a consumer. However, it is possible to demonstrate that adversity was present but never evenly distributed. For example, the 1940 *Census of Agriculture* notes that 88 percent of Kansas farms had an automobile in 1930, but by 1940 this figure had fallen to 83 percent. Even allowing for the increasing age of the stock of motor vehicles, this is not a dramatic change of circumstances. Moreover, at the same time, the number of farms having a truck rose from 19 percent of the total in 1930, to 25 percent ten years later. On the other hand, there is evidence of forced economies. For example, in 1930, 73 percent of Kansas farms possessed a telephone, but only 51 percent by 1940.[35] Farmers in the southwest region, the worst affected by drought, did not replace or even repair machinery, and the ageing stock

33. H. Craig Miner, *Harvesting the High Plains: John Kriss and the Business of Wheat Farming, 1920–50*, 70, 89

34. Michael Johnson Grant uses the term "Borderline Farmers" to describe these farmers in his *Down and Out on the Family Farm: Rural Rehabilitation in the Great Plains, 1929–45*, 12–35.

35. All the statistical information is from U.S. Bureau of the Census, *Sixteenth Census of the United States, 1940: Agriculture*, Vol. 1, State Reports, Part 2, Tables, 1, 5, 9, 11, 12, 19.

of rusting capital equipment was another symbol of farm communities struggling to live within their means. But elsewhere, farmers were more confident. The total number of tractors on Kansas farms rose from 49,798 in 1933 to 87,515 in 1940, and during the same period, the number of combine harvesters expanded from 24,197 to 41,572.[36] Another indication that the state escaped the worst of the agricultural depression can be seen by the fact that in the middle of 1935, only 8 percent of Kansas farm operators were receiving assistance in the form of relief or rehabilitation. This was marginally less than the national average of 9 percent, but considerably less than New Mexico (36 percent), South Dakota (33 percent), and North Dakota and Oklahoma (each with 27 percent).[37] No one could disagree that many rural Kansans suffered during these troubled years, but either through their own efforts, or by good fortune, or with the assistance of government, a significant number escaped the worst effects of the economic collapse.

A combination of very high temperatures and little rain when the crops needed it most led to low yields in many parts of the state, and even to crop failure in western Kansas. The year 1933 was not only exceptionally hot, it was also one of the driest years the state had experienced; the following year was even worse, as the average temperature broke all records, and only 1910 and 1917 had seen less rain. Those crops that could be harvested were often of poor quality, and dust storms were becoming increasingly severe. Corn, which was more susceptible than wheat to excessive heat and drought, failed virtually everywhere, with serious implications for hog producers. The few farms that raised a corn crop large enough to market took advantage of relatively high prices, but one can get an indication of the drought's savage, statewide impact by noting that the farm value of corn sales, which had hit $129.3 million as recently as 1928, struggled to reach a paltry $13 million in both 1934 and 1936. The principal sufferers were farmers who were forced to purchase feed at high prices because they were unable to provide their own. It is clear that events in 1934 had dashed the hopes of those who held to the old belief that if the wheat crop was lost the corn crop would be made.[38]

Table 4 vividly illustrates the Kansas drought problem. Rainfall decreased markedly from east to west, a meteorological phenomenon made worse by the fact that the western region is more elevated, experiences persistent wind, and has many hours of sunshine. Even when rain fell, it

36. See various *Biennial Reports* of the KSBA.
37. Berta Asch and A. R. Mangus, *Farmers on Relief and Rehabilitation*, 5–7.
38. *KERC Bulletin* 289, 785.

Table 4. Annual Precipitation in Kansas (Inches)

Year	N.W.	W.C.	S.W.	N.C.	C.	S.C.	N.E.	E.C.	S.E.	State Av.
1928	25.36	27.14	28.01	30.35	34.14	31.83	35.20	41.07	42.28	33.40
1929	20.10	18.27	19.10	25.48	30.56	28.08	34.41	36.32	39.09	27.96
1930	27.65	23.41	21.08	24.30	27.35	24.85	32.58	28.21	35.41	26.87
1931	17.07	16.32	14.49	25.16	22.55	25.78	41.43	36.01	34.09	25.90
1932	15.92	18.47	10.82	23.30	24.06	22.27	30.08	31.80	28.88	23.76
1933	19.65	19.46	15.99	18.65	18.89	18.44	25.23	28.92	33.32	22.18
1934	11.22	10.99	11.32	14.01	18.54	22.77	23.57	28.42	33.81	20.02
1935	15.88	17.04	13.47	27.92	25.11	27.43	36.27	41.44	45.27	28.47
1936	12.87	14.57	13.79	16.32	16.93	17.78	25.99	22.03	26.40	18.31
1937	15.12	12.67	10.95	19.06	20.51	22.69	22.77	27.46	35.17	20.88
1938	17.46	18.99	17.36	25.84	26.56	30.40	33.31	36.67	37.51	27.27
1939	14.56	13.79	11.37	21.04	20.75	20.14	28.83	24.85	27.54	20.08
1940	16.68	18.31	18.59	21.38	24.64	26.98	27.61	34.74	36.27	25.67

Source: *Kansas State Board of Agriculture 38th Biennial Report, 1951–52*, 409.

was quickly lost to runoff and rapid evaporation. However, the farmer is not merely interested in the total annual rainfall. Wheat growers needed adequate precipitation during the growing season from April to June, but not at harvest time, when too much rain spoiled the crop and made machine operations more difficult. Wheat is more tolerant of drought than corn, but when the mean annual rainfall is less than fifteen inches, it, too, becomes a victim. During the 1920s wheat growing expanded into the western part of the state, a region where yields were highly variable and where, even in this relatively moist decade, the crop sometimes did not repay the costs of harvesting. Wheat farmers in western Kansas tried to compensate for relatively low yields and high levels of crop abandonment by planting a large acreage, so that in years when the rains were favorable, the economic returns could be substantial.[39]

However, a marginal area in the best of times, western Kansas was devastated by a serious deficiency in rainfall during 1934 and 1936 especially.[40] Drought and intense heat scorched pastures and destroyed growing feedstuffs at a time when the numbers of dairy and beef cattle were rising steadily. The costs of hauling water and keeping herds fed became crippling for cattlemen, but the situation created excellent opportunities for some farmers in southeast Kansas, where the drought was moderate and high-price feedstuffs grew in abundance. Some opened their fields of growing wheat to cattle from other parts of the state so that they could graze on luxuriant pastures, a practice that had become more common during the 1920s and which, if practiced with skill, could improve the wheat yield.[41] But even in areas seemingly protected from the worst effects of this arid period, there were problems. During 1934, Crawford County farmers suffered from a rise in feed prices, a reduction in the quantities of vegetables available for home canning, and a shortage of cash as they had so little to market.[42] Living in a relatively moist region did not guarantee prosperity.

The year of 1936 was a disastrous one for Kansas agriculture. Blazing sun, continuing drought, dust storms, and plagues of grasshoppers ensured that wheat was the only crop that did not experience a major loss. Indeed, the value of the wheat crop in 1936 accounted for nearly two-thirds of the value of all crops. The difficulties for cattlemen continued,

39. Peter Fearon, "Mechanisation and Risk: Kansas Wheat Growers, 1915–30," 232–34; see also Paul Bonnifield, *The Dust Bowl: Men, Dirt and Depression*, 61–86.

40. The social costs of this devastating drought are covered admirably in Donald Worster, *Dust Bowl: The Southern Plains in the 1930s*.

41. KSBA, *29th Biennial Report*, 1933–34, 7–19.

42. Crawford County, Agricultural Extension Service Report, 1934.

while blowing dirt and heat created a miserable summer for many rural families. An apparent break in the drought during the fall of 1936 encouraged the largest planting of wheat in the state's history, and although abandonment of acreage was heavy in western Kansas where drought continued, the 1937 harvest was the most bountiful since 1931. Fortunately, drought-induced scarcity had ensured that wheat prices in 1937 were three times as high as they had been after the dismal harvests of 1931 and 1932. Better weather also helped improve corn yields, but as the acreage planted was only half that of the early 1930s, the total value of the crop was modest. Unfortunately, while moisture levels in 1938 led to an improvement in crop yields, the concomitant decline in farm prices was a bitter blow to growers, leaving them both deeply frustrated and despondent. Wheat prices remained depressed in 1939 and 1940 and did not begin a sustained upward movement until the following year. Farmers had so little confidence in corn that the acreage planted in both 1939 and 1940 was less than half of the annual average for the period 1929–36. Yields improved from the extraordinarily low levels to which they had sunk during the worst years of the drought, but prices remained stubbornly depressed. The decline in the number of hogs, cattle, horses, and mules eased, but it did not eradicate the pressure on feedstuff provision during difficult times.

The New Deal at Work: Rural Rehabilitation

At the close of the Civil Works Administration program in March 1934, there was widespread support for the view that programs for the rural needy must be positively linked with agriculture in a way that would enable them to become self-supporting. In this age of surpluses, no one sought to encourage an expansion of commercial agriculture. The thrust of the new self-support program was a commitment to assist the needy, first by helping them to improve their homes, and then by providing seed and stock for family consumption. The final part of this strategy was to ensure that there were opportunities for part-time, nonagricultural employment. Work relief, an essential part of the attack on urban unemployment, was not viewed as an integral component for the revitalization of rural communities. The central economic security for rural Americans would be rehabilitation through the generation of self-support activities, and the clear message from Washington was that the distinction between relief activities for normally employable people in rural areas and for those in the cities was so stark that they must be treated as entirely sepa-

rate problems. If families lived on land that was too infertile to provide the minimum returns for self-support, then the option of resettlement on better soil must be explored. The federal government would purchase the sub-marginal land and manage it in a way that would prevent soil erosion, or it could be converted to leisure use.

The rehabilitation program was restricted to those certified eligible for relief. Single people and families living in rural areas, or in towns of less than five thousand inhabitants, received assistance that was designed to ensure that the homestead they either owned or rented became self-sustaining. It was recognized that normal work relief disadvantaged some of the needy by forcing them to work away from their homes. However, if they remained in place and received both financial help and practical guidance, they could eventually become self-supporting. It seemed reasonable, therefore, that selected clients should be given the opportunity to work out their relief budgets by improving their own homesteads. The aim was to support needy people in the communities where they lived and where they would continue to reside when economic conditions returned to normal. In May 1934, Kansas was one of thirteen states that received the first FERA grants specifically earmarked for rural rehabilitation.[43] In October the Kansas Homestead Rehabilitation Corporation was established, and a few months later homestead rehabilitation was made a separate operating department of the KERC.[44]

A prerequisite for rehabilitation was that each client owned or rented land that could produce a subsistence living for the family, or have a family enterprise that could become productive. Initially, applications were not limited to farmers; they could include, for example, plumbers, plasterers, tailors, or seamstresses if they possessed tools and the essential equipment for their trade.[45] The federal government set out the broad objectives of the program but permitted each state to temper them to suit its needs. All applications for homestead subsistence aid had to be supported by a plan that demonstrated suitability for rehabilitation and provided evidence of the applicant's creditworthiness. After an initial scrutiny by the county relief administration, the plan was examined in turn by the county farm agent, the home demonstration agent, and the county rehabilitation committee. Each looked for evidence that the applicants had investigated the possibility of assistance from landlords, mortgagees, rela-

43. Asch and Mangus, *Farmers on Relief and Rehabilitation,* 15–22.

44. *KERC Bulletin* 355, 303. Raub Snyder was appointed the first superintendent of rehabilitation and manager of the Kansas Homestead Rehabilitation Corporation.

45. *Kansas Relief News-Bulletin* 7 (June 5, 1934): 1.

tives, and friends so that resources from a variety of groups could be mobilized in order to maximize the social and economic benefit to the family. For a realistic chance of success, applicants had to have farms large enough to become self-sustaining and the strength of character to persevere with their plan even if the initial optimism faded. Rehabilitation also stressed co-operative work. This could be undertaken with other needy families; with the agents of county, state, or federal institutions; or with others identified in the plan. Successful applicants for permanent homestead rehabilitation grants were assigned to a county home cooperative committee whose role was to engender a community spirit and also to emphasize local responsibility.[46] The KERC appointed a homestead rehabilitation advisor and a home economics advisor for each county, so that clients could be both supervised and instructed in best practice. Participants also received assistance with debt adjustment and, with the help of advisors, were able to develop a realistic financial program.

Once an applicant was accepted into the scheme, he or she would be paid budgeted work relief wages in cash for undertaking agreed capital improvements or production work on the homestead. This work was assigned a value calculated on the number of hours worked at the prevailing rate of relief wages. The prescribed capital improvements, or production work, when completed had to equal twice the amount of the client's deficiency budget. Relatives and others involved in the rehabilitation plan could help with the purchase of materials and tools up to the amount of relief wages paid, and mortgagees were encouraged to rescind part of the debt. In addition, the KERC created a material fund that advanced cash equal to 25 cents on each budgeted work relief dollar to assist with the purchase of materials. The creation and maintenance of subsistence gardens and the construction of farm ponds was seen as a crucial element in the rehabilitation program.[47] Clients who were accepted in the permanent rehabilitation program were expected to concentrate on managing and operating their farms. Farm wives also had an essential role to play in areas such as food preparation and preservation, household management, and clothing repair.[48] Tenants who wished to be involved in the program had to persuade their landlords either to make a contribution in cash or to donate materials for homestead improvements, or alternatively, to cancel some of the debt owed. Not surprisingly, landlords who had not re-

46. KERC, "The Homestead Rehabilitation Program for Families Eligible for Work Relief (Revised)," August 19, 1934, Stutz Papers, 327:2:50

47. *KERC Bulletin* 289, 77–78; 733; *Kansas Relief News-Bulletin* 7 (June 25, 1934): 1.

48. *KERC Bulletin* 355, 33.

ceived full rent payments for several years were often reluctant to make these commitments.

Federal field agents who visited in December praised the four-day training program for KERC staff involved in the rehabilitation program and the excellent monitoring procedures that had been introduced.[49] On January 1, 1935, the KERC claimed that about 600 permanent rural relief clients were receiving grants in aid under the first phase of the rural rehabilitation program, and many other applicants were also being considered. A temporary scheme gave small grants in aid to an additional 2,596 clients in return for work undertaken on garden projects and farm ponds. All those involved in the program were enthusiastic about its success to date, and it matched closely the views on self-help held by many Kansans.[50] Moreover, it was seen in a positive light by clients who did not consider rehabilitation as a relief program, "but rather as a specialized governmental program for people slightly hard up."[51]

The early rehabilitation efforts were part of an emergency program, but in January 1935 the FERA introduced a permanent policy for all rural relief clients, under which grants in aid were replaced by loans from the Kansas Homestead Rehabilitation Corporation, the body chosen to handle all the essential business transactions for this initiative. Repayment for the advances could be made in cash, in kind, or by work on approved projects. Eligibility for public assistance remained a prerequisite, and the program now dealt entirely with farm families who could expect help from a variety of sources as they improved their own farms. The services of trained specialists in farm management, finance, home economics, and social casework were available, as was assistance with debt adjustment. Where necessary, families were instructed in the maintenance of gardens, the art of canning, and how to keep pigs and poultry for their own use. The county welfare department was the responsible agency, and the federal government supplied specific funding for the administration of this program.

In late April, Washington decided that applicants for public assistance who were operating a farm as a commercial enterprise by selling some of their output would be directed toward the rehabilitation program. Now all families in this category had to borrow in order to secure food, cloth-

49. Visit to Kansas Relief Administration Office, December 7, 1934, Federal Relief Agency Papers, FERA-WPA Narrative Field Reports, Group 24, Box 57, Hopkins Papers.

50. *KERC Bulletin* 355, 303–7.

51. KERC, "Report of a Committee of the Relief Department on Homestead Rehabilitation," 1 (n.d., but must be late 1934), Stutz Papers, 327:3:14.

ing, seed, and other farm production expenses. This consistency of treatment removed the resentment that had been directed by those who had been forced to borrow to fund improvements toward more fortunate neighbors who had been able to secure work relief. However, common sense dictated that some flexibility should be shown toward farmers who were unable to work on their farms because of serious drought. As a concession, it was agreed that they could be allocated either work or direct relief until weather conditions improved. Starting in May, both owners and tenants applying for public aid for the first time had to submit a complete homestead rehabilitation plan, though in an emergency it was possible for loans to be advanced before the plan was approved. It was now clear to all operators that if it were possible to work on their farms and make them self-sustaining, they would not be eligible for work relief. However, rehabilitation was not suitable for the majority of rural people, including the operators of farms that were judged unsustainable, perhaps because of poor soil, or because they were too small, or because drought had made cultivation impossible. These marginal farmers hoped to secure places on federal work relief projects. Unfortunately, so did needy farm laborers, and so did the distressed who provided services for farm communities. The excessive numbers searching for places on federal work relief projects meant that many disappointed rural dwellers were forced to accept meager county relief.

In January 1935 Kansas county relief administrations had estimated that 28,000 families would be eligible for assistance under the rehabilitation umbrella. However, by June, it seems that only 7,244 households were receiving rural rehabilitation advances.[52] The KERC, for reasons that are not clear, calculated the number as close to 9,000, with more than 3,000 farm families having left the relief rolls because of a combination of rehabilitation help and improved crop conditions. Total advances by the Kansas Homestead Rehabilitation Corporation up to July 1, 1935, were almost $1 million, and the grants to both temporary and permanent clients totaled $98,000 in 1935 alone. Nearly 40 percent of the advances were for subsistence, and the next most important category (just over twenty percent) was for the provision of work animals.[53]

In response to encouragement from Washington, virtually all states created rural rehabilitation corporations, and this program expanded rapidly in the first half of 1935. But how realistic was the aim of raising desti-

52. Irene Link, *Relief and Rehabilitation in the Drought Area*, 8; Theodore E. Whiting, *Final Statistical Report of the Federal Emergency Relief Administration*, WPA, 66–70, 234.
53. *KERC Bulletin* 355, 306–7.

tute farm families to living standards that the majority of Americans would regard as adequate? Would families be able to repay the debts that they had assumed? For some the move to self-sustaining status would be a modest and achievable step. But for others, it would be a massive leap that would require the injection of considerable resources of a tangible and managerial nature if failure was not to be endemic.

An examination of the living standards of 719 Kansas families who submitted rehabilitation plans before May 15, 1935, is especially revealing in this context. Although one can assume that the standard of living of these early applicants was relatively high, since the clients judged to have the best prospects of repaying their loans were the first to be referred to the rehabilitation department, most were some distance from the comfort zone. Indeed, many of these families had poor health and lived in low-quality housing. Across the state variations in hardship were strongly influenced by the size of the family farm and local living conditions. The southeast region was the most disadvantaged. It had farms with the smallest average acreage, the highest proportion of homes rated poor, and land that was either too hilly or too prone to flooding to provide a satisfactory economic return. Unfortunately, misery was not contained within a narrow geographic area of the southeast; it was statewide, as can be seen from the following figures. Of all the homes in this survey, 91 percent had no running water, 97 percent had no electricity, 89 percent had no radio, and 29 percent did not even possess a sewing machine. Moreover, more than half the families had inadequate clothing, cooking utensils, household linens, and furniture. Just over 12 percent of family members required immediate medical attention, and 23 percent were in need of dental care. In comparison with other Kansas farm families that had become self-sufficient, and whose income in 1934 had averaged $762, the average annual income of these rural rehabilitation families would probably not exceed $601. Moreover, the debts of the latter and their average family size were relatively high.[54] Rehabilitation for a large proportion of the families in this study was not going to be an easy option. Ensuring some modest degree of success would require a significant improvement in farm performance from a disturbingly disadvantaged base. The obligatory investigations of applications for rehabilitation loans revealed examples of deficiencies in farm management technique and practice that had significantly contributed to the economic distress of many farmers. These findings help to explain why some cultivators fared much better than others,

54. KERC, "A Study of 719 Rural Rehabilitation Families Relative to their Standard of Living," Stutz Papers, 327:3:9 (September 3, 1935), 5.

even when adverse conditions were equally shared. Drought was responsible for much farm misery in Kansas, but inappropriate farming also played a major role.

It is not possible to discern the failure rate for rehabilitation applications across the state, but the experience of a single county can provide a reasonable guide. Of the eighty-two farm operators in Saline County who were receiving public assistance in June 1935, thirty-three had been accepted for the rehabilitation program, and forty-nine were to be found on the relief rolls. Relief officials expressed a hope that a quarter of their rehabilitation clients would soon become self-supporting, but even these would not be in a position to repay their loans.[55] It follows that a significant proportion of operators were compelled to accept general relief and that many rehabilitation clients would face a long, hard struggle to achieve the prized goal of self-support.

A growing awareness of rural poverty, the impact of drought, and the serious structural problems that affected farmers led to the establishment of the Resettlement Administration (RA) in April 1935. The RA was an independent agency, and its main responsibilities were farm debt adjustment, the retirement of sub-marginal land and its conversion to pasture or leisure use, the resettlement and rehabilitation of needy farm families on new land, and the continuation of the FERA rehabilitation program. In mid-1937 the Farm Security Administration (FSA) inherited the remit of the RA. Rehabilitation was a far more important commitment to Kansas farmers than resettlement.

The most significant contribution that the RA and the FSA made to assisting needy farmers who were judged capable of becoming self-sustaining was a standard rehabilitation loan. The borrowers were, however, subjected to close supervision to ensure that their approved plans could be implemented. Field staff advised on farming methods, inspected annual budgets, and reminded neglectful cultivators that they were required to plant subsistence gardens and that farm wives should attend classes on food preservation techniques, if they did not already possess the appropriate skills. Participants were supposed to be subject to similar levels of morale-boosting discipline that many New Dealers saw flowing from the work relief programs. However, while those on work relief received cash wages, farmers borrowed in an attempt to improve their holdings.

In addition to loans, small subsistence grants were advanced to needy

---

55. Hazle Bland, "Survey Of Current Changes in the Rural Relief Population, June 1935. Saline County, Kansas," Rural Relief Studies, Bureau of Agricultural Economics, RG83, NA.

farmers, some of whom might later be accepted as rehabilitation clients and others whose holdings fell below the threshold of self-sufficiency. These grants were considered vital by county relief administrations because they removed recipients from the relief rolls and ensured that operators remained on their farms. However, periodic funding shortages created panic at the local level when it seemed that a large number of farm families would suddenly have a claim on local resources. The chairman of Gray County's Board of County Commissioners explained this problem very clearly. The local resettlement supervisor had just announced that subsistence grants were to be discontinued forthwith and that no more applications for standard loans would be accepted. The county was not able to provide basic relief for additional farm families at such short notice and could certainly not support them in their efforts to continue farming. In April, the RA had issued 148 subsistence grant checks totalling $2,664. The RA calculated that during May this figure would be reduced because a number of families who had already been accepted for the standard resettlement loan would receive it, others would benefit from the receipt of wheat allotment money, and the welcome appearance of rain had improved the economic outlook for some more. As a result, the RA maintained that the county would need to care for only seventy-three families, though local calculations produced a figure closer to eighty-five. Whatever the total, the implications for local relief were alarming, especially as these families needed more than bare subsistence support. Farmers had to buy seed, repair machinery, and purchase fuel if they were to operate as cultivators. Without subsistence grants they could not till their fields.[56]

The problems facing rehabilitation clients in a drought region are further illustrated in a plea from the Wallace County Emergency Relief Committee in August 1935. The county's poor commissioner wrote that local farmers had borrowed during the summer in the expectation of harvesting a crop that had subsequently perished. They now had no funds to feed their livestock and meet other necessary expenditures through the winter. The county's poor fund could not withstand the additional strain of farm families in need of relief. Farmers and officials believed that work relief should be provided for men in these circumstances, as would be the case in urban settlements. It seemed that needy farm operators were not treated on the same basis as similarly disadvantaged city dwellers.[57] It is easy to sympathize with farmers who saw FERA and WPA clients receiving cash

56. Frank Renick, Chairman Board of County Commissioners, Gray County, and others to Landon, May 8, 1936, Box 13, Folder Relief Matters-Resettlement, Landon Papers.
57. Poor Commissioner Anna B. Enlow to Stutz, August 22, 1935, Box 12, Folder 15, Landon Papers.

wages while they had to borrow to ensure survival. However, property-owning farmers could not normally be assessed as "needy" and were, therefore, ineligible for work relief programs.

Sudden fluctuations in funding and changes in regulations to New Deal programs were a constant source of stress to both relief administrations and to those clients whose relief was reduced so that new cases could be accommodated. Periodically, farmers who had been selected for rehabilitation were smitten by calamity, drought being the most obvious cause, which undermined their plans. They relied on special drought-region programs, on wheat allotment payments, or CCCorp remittances to keep them from the descent into county relief. Marginal operators who relied upon grants remained a problem until war demands opened up employment opportunities off the farm. A survey of one hundred Ellis County families in receipt of grants, undertaken in 1939, revealed the economic shortcomings of this cohort. These families contained a high proportion of tenants, lived in poor-quality housing, and endured overcrowding and primitive sanitation. The grants they received, together with supplies of surplus commodities, made up the major part of household income. Many of their subsistence gardens had fallen victim to hail, drought, or grasshoppers, but a surprising 40 percent of families had not even attempted to raise a garden. Most of these households would never become self supporting.[58]

The County Experience

In October 1934 a state survey reported that there were 16,000 farm families on relief, of whom 59 percent were full-time tenant farmers and 41 percent were full-time farm owners.[59] It is possible to move from the general analysis in the previous section to the particular because that same year the Division of Farm Population and Rural Welfare of the Bureau of Agricultural Economics undertook a survey that provides valuable insight into relief problems in Hodgeman, Meade, and Sherman counties.[60] These counties were strongly rural, relied heavily on wheat as a cash crop, though cattle grazing was also significant, and had no important industries other than agriculture. At the time that the information was gathered, the FERA had just replaced the CWA, and drought had begun to make an impact on the farm sector but had not yet assumed the crisis levels that

58. Clair A. Bondurant, "A Study of One Hundred Farm Security Administration Grant Families in Ellis County, Kansas, 1939," 16–46.
59. *KERC Bulletin* 355, 304.
60. The region covered also included Colorado, Oklahoma, New Mexico, and Texas.

were to be evident in western Kansas over the next few years. Various New Deal initiatives were in place to assist the distressed farmer, and these investigations provided an early opportunity to assess their value.

In June 1934, 187 families, or 19 percent of the total number in Hodgeman County, were receiving relief.[61] June was normally a good month for employment, but only a few individuals had been able to secure harvest work. Very few of these families had been assisted before 1932, and the reason for the vast majority of relief cases was crop failure and the unemployment that accompanied it. In the summer of 1934 it was clear that the county's wheat crop was poor, that feed crops had failed, and that a shortage of rain had rendered fall and winter pastures inferior. Just to break even, Hodgeman County wheat farmers needed a yield of ten bushels per acre at a price of 70 cents per bushel, and aridity had ensured that for the previous two years the crop had been produced at a loss. Wheat harvested in 1934 sold for 82 cents per bushel, but as the yield was a dismal four bushels for each acre harvested, producers' losses continued.[62]

Many Hodgeman County farmers were in difficulty because they had purchased machinery on credit and were now unable to pay for it. In addition, persistent low prices had led to heavy borrowings on chattels, real estate, and life insurance policies at interest rates as high as 10 percent. About 65 percent of county farms were mortgaged, and the average debt for those farms was $4,382, a high figure in relation to the average valuation for each farm, which stood at $11,043. However, the overall assessment of the county's relief situation stressed concern rather than despair, and there was widespread agreement that once the drought broke, recovery would be rapid.[63]

The only cash income in Meade County came from wheat farming, but, since 1931, producers had not even been able to recover their costs of production.[64] Moreover, the current low output caused by drought had destroyed jobs for farm laborers; indeed, in all three counties, farm opera-

61. Hodgeman County had a population of 4,157, all of whom were rural and 72 percent of whom lived on farms. In 1935, 23 percent of the 790 farms were operated by owners, 32 percent by part owners, and 44 percent by tenants. *Agricultural Resources of Kansas* (Manhattan: Kansas State College Bulletin, October 1937): 96–98.

62. KSBA, *29th Biennial Report.*

63. K. H. McGill, Lawrence Vaplon, N. E. Woodard, Robert W. Crichton, Jr., and Katherine Wilson, "A Survey of Hodgeman County, Kansas," FERA, Survey of Rural Problem Areas Short Grass-Dry Farming Region, Bureau of Agricultural Economics, August 1, 1934, RG83, NA.

64. Meade County had a population of 6,858, all of whom were rural and 54 percent of whom lived on farms. The county had 883 farms in 1935, and 27 percent were operated by owners, 35 percent by part owners, and 37 percent by tenants. *Agricultural Resources of Kansas,* 133–35.

tors increasingly did work for each other in order to economize on hired help. Many Meade County laborers had migrated from the open countryside to towns or villages in order to be nearer relief offices and nonfarm work, where they were joined by tenant farmers who had lost their equipment and by older operators whose resilience in the face of adversity had been broken.[65] Drought was the principle cause of the increase in the relief load, though the rundown of the railroad repair shops in Goodland exacerbated the problem.[66]

In good years it had been the practice of Meade County farmers to buy more land rather than keep a cash reserve for lean times; however, since 1930, operators had received no income from wheat with which to pay either taxes or the interest on their debts; as a result, some farms had been foreclosed. Fortunately, since July 1933 the Federal Land Bank and the two National Farm Loan Associations operating in the county had advanced $736,000, mostly for refinancing private mortgages, thus reducing a potentially serious problem. Unfortunately, in the recent past overly optimistic operators had used credit to purchase expensive farm machinery, sometimes costing even more than their farm. Hard times meant that a 30 percent tax delinquency was anticipated during 1934, though this figure was less serious than had been expected because the recipients of all government loans were required to pay their taxes. Nevertheless, it was clear that the farm population was poised on the edge of an abyss, and unless plentiful rains came soon, the threat of bankruptcy loomed for many.

Lawrence Svobida has written the classic account of farming in the Dust Bowl in Kansas.[67] He arrived in Meade County in 1929 and remained there until 1938, by which time his formidable spirit had been broken by the disappointment of seven consecutive failed crops. Much of Meade County was marginal land whose light soils should never have been exposed to the sun and the wind, but the confident wheat farmers who broke the sod during the moist 1920s had discounted the possibility of serious drought. However, once regular rain gave way to persistent aridity, low yields, crop losses, and dust storms became perennial problems. Many farmers kept some hogs, dairy cattle, and chickens, often for domestic consumption rather than for market, and the difficulties of providing feed, water, and shelter even for these small numbers proved formidable. The natural response of the typical hard-pressed wheat farmer

65. "Open country" is defined as territory outside centers of at least fifty persons. Villages are rural centers with a population of not less than fifty or more than twenty-five hundred inhabitants.

66. K. H. McGill et al., "A Survey of Meade County, Kansas," August 11, 1934.

67. Lawrence Svobida, *Farming the Dust Bowl: A First-Hand Account from Kansas.*

was to work harder and plant more wheat. Svobida was an energetic, conscientious, and dedicated operator with a streak of independence that made him suspicious of some, but not all, aspects of government intervention. While he would have been happy to support an element of compulsion forcing farmers to adopt soil conservation practices, he was quick to emphasize his distaste for the petty bureaucracy that became part of the wheat allotment program, as well as the dishonesty of some participating farmers. He himself was a beneficiary of the wheat allotment program; indeed, 80 percent of the county's growers signed up to it. Without the substantial cash payments that flowed to the county, it would have been impossible for many farmers to purchase the tractor fuel and spare parts for their equipment, or the seed for planting.

Farm laborers and tenant farmers dominated the June 1934 relief rolls in Sherman County.[68] Although no farm owner was in receipt of relief, this group could not face the future with optimism as three-quarters were in debt and many of them faced bankruptcy. Many Sherman County farmers, like operators elsewhere, had purchased expensive power machinery on credit when the wheat economy had been buoyant. As a result of the deteriorating economic situation in Sherman County, approximately 25 percent of tax revenues could not be collected. Furthermore, school, county, and other bonded indebtedness amounted to $2 million, which resulted in a total debt load of $8 million imposed on a county with only seven thousand residents.

Each of these counties benefited from New Deal spending. Road construction and improvement dominated relief work, whether the origin of the funding was the PWA, CWA, FERA, or the county. Roadwork provided unskilled jobs immediately and was specifically organized to enable farmers who had not fully mechanized to use their teams. In addition, youths worked in CCC camps, and their earnings were a valuable source of support to their families, usually removing them from the relief rolls. Among their tasks, these young CCC men worked on the Federal Tree Planting or "shelter belt" program, which made possible extensive tree planting in counties to the south and the northwest of the great bend in the Arkansas River. These volunteers became part of an effective long-term strategy designed to combat the effects of rainfall deficiency and persistent wind. In Hodgeman County, for example, the Agricultural Extension Service assisted relief cases with the management of thirty-seven

68. O. S. Rayner, Verna McDowell, and Ralph M. Davidson, *A Survey of Sherman County Kansas* (FERA August, 1934), Bureau of Agricultural Economics, RG83, NA. In 1935 Sherman County had 839 farms, 19 percent of which were operated by their owners, 41 percent by part owners, and 39 percent by tenants. *Agricultural Resources of Kansas*, 196–98.

subsistence gardens and also provided advice on canning and dietary matters. Subsistence gardens and other attempts to grow food for family consumption, however, frequently fell victim to the sun, the wind, and the lack of rain. Fortunately, relief recipients were also entitled to surplus commodities that extended and improved their diet. Observers noted that some families economized by giving up newspapers, magazines, and even their radio and telephone.

There is no doubt that the most significant injection of much needed cash into all three counties went to farmers who participated in the AAA Wheat Allotment Program, which commenced in the early summer of 1933. Large-scale commercial farmers, who were most generously rewarded by this initiative, needed cash. They did not grow their own food, and their expensive machinery would lie idle if they could not purchase fuel and replacement parts. It is not surprising that the Allotment Program was extremely popular with Kansas growers, for the financial rewards were substantial and might be viewed as crop insurance, or even an essential relief payment, though the recipients certainly did not see them in that light. Nor did New Deal officials, and Secretary of Agriculture Henry A. Wallace himself was quick to stress that in no sense should the sums allocated to farmers under the corn-hog or wheat allotment programs be seen as the equivalent of dole; they simply constituted a payment for agreeing to comply with particular restrictions that had been introduced in order to reduce output and raise prices. However, there can be no doubt that the payments kept many farmers off the relief rolls and on their farms.[69]

In December 1933, participating farmers in Hodgeman County received $286,248 for their first wheat allotment payment, which enabled them not only to purchase food, fuel, feed, and seed, but also to pay their taxes. These farmers behaved in the same manner as others across the state. Responses to a statewide Extension Service questionnaire suggested that approximately 40 percent of the first adjustment payment was devoted to clearing debts; 26 percent was committed for home supplies, including food, clothing, and repairs to farm and home equipment; and 23 percent was earmarked for taxes.[70] The fact that the first wheat allotment payment was greater by $200,000 than all the relief payments in Hodge-

---

69. Wallace to Hon. Clifford R. Hope, April 12, 1934, Farm Relief (22–1), Wheat Acreage Reduction, RG16, NA. Allotment payments were not necessarily spent on the county to which they were sent. In 1935, for example, 30 percent of Haskell County farmers lived in another county. Earl H. Bell, *Culture of a Contemporary Rural Community: Sublette, Kansas*, 34.

70. Sherman Johnson, *Wheat under the Agricultural Adjustment Act: Developments up to June 1934*, 92–93.

man County from federal, state, and private sources between October 1932 and June 1934 gives an indication of the significance of this cash flow. Further assistance for farmers came from approximately $240,000 advanced to them as seed loans that would only be repaid after the crop was successfully harvested.

There are similar stories from the other two counties. The first wheat allotment payment for Meade County, $334,000, became available for farmers in January 1934, and a further payment of $135,000 was due in August. To these can be added $28,000 in corn-hog checks and $79,000 in payments under the drought cattle scheme. Some farmers who had signed contracts with the AAA for their own wheat actually rushed to rent additional land in order to plow and plant even more, as a compensation for the acreage they had willingly reduced. Their behavior not only helped to undermine the purpose of the scheme but also further diminished the valuable native grass area. To put these AAA payments into perspective, expenditure on all the principal federal relief initiatives in Meade County over the preceding three years amounted to $257,000.

Everywhere they were received in Kansas, wheat allotment payments had a dramatic effect on both the spending and the morale of farm families. Corn-hog payments were less significant in the three counties being considered here, but seed loans were of great benefit to farmers whose harvests had been so poor that they did not provide sufficient seed for the next planting. Nevertheless, this much-needed financial assistance does not entirely explain the resilience of drought-affected farm families. During her travels through Kansas in 1934, Harry Hopkins's special investigator, Lorena Hickok, reported on the extraordinary optimism and determination displayed by many of the people that she met in the drought area. While recognizing the value of many New Deal programs, they did not want to be resettled in a more favorable location, nor were they enthusiastic about rehabilitation—they just wanted rain. There was a firm belief that when the rains came, and that must be soon, everything would be restored to normal.[71] This mixture of stubbornness, optimism, and self-abnegation formed the character of people who were prepared to stick out the hard times and wait for the return of the good. However, a more critically inclined commentator than Hickok might have pointed out that it was such misplaced optimism that had led to the disastrous plow-up which preceded the "black blizzards" of the Dust Bowl and their attendant miseries.

It is interesting that the administration of relief in all three counties was

71. Richard Lowitt and Maurine Beasley, eds., *One-Third of a Nation: Lorena Hickok Reports on the Great Depression*, 335–41.

part of the remit of this survey. Although for the most part relief provision was judged satisfactory, social workers complained that their caseloads were too high to permit the appropriate number of home visits, and the rural rehabilitation program was slow in getting under way. Investigators also discovered how difficult it was to assess cases on the basis of a home visit. A good quality house might be inhabited by a family heavily in debt and with only a few days of feed left for their stock. In a general observation, relief staff reported that although residents had become more accepting of relief, only a small proportion actually demanded it.

In Sherman County the main problem was that after a relief budget for each client had been meticulously drawn up, the lack of funding from the KERC resulted in everyone receiving less than the sum to which they were theoretically entitled. In this county single persons were budgeted to receive between $10 and $15 per month, married couples between $20 and $30, and a few large families could be budgeted for between $56 and $60 per month. However, in common with other Kansas counties, all federal money was dedicated for work relief, and, given the wage rates used and the hours of work stipulated, no individual could earn more than $42 per month. This especially penalized the poor with large families, a particularly vulnerable group, and supplementation of their relief from county funds was necessary. In June 1934, for example, 143 relief cases were budgeted for $5,179, but as the county only received $3,317 from the KERC, many of the relief payments had to be reduced. One result of these monthly readjustments was a growing resentment on the part of relief clients, who usually had the relief administration in their sights when resentment turned to anger. This problem was not, of course, confined to Sherman County, but it was a frequent complaint from relief administrations and their clients across the state.

Relief in each of these three counties was given sensibly and seemingly rigid rules that were relaxed when the situation required it. For example, in an emergency brought on by a medical condition or resulting from a livestock feed crisis, help was provided quickly even at the cost of skimping the social investigation. In none of these counties did the investigators feel that there was a growing problem of dependency, as there seemed to be very few chronic relief cases. Surprisingly, there was a feeling of confidence that the vast majority of relief clients could be rehabilitated, but for this happy state of affairs to occur, plentiful rain and high farm prices were needed very quickly.

Although the cash payments from the wheat allotment and corn-hog programs were of great significance, they were only available for participating farmers, and the scheme favored the big producers over the small. What must be stressed is the development of an organized system of re-

lief distribution that transformed life for the poor in rural communities which had been previously neglected. Professionally qualified social workers gathered much-needed information on the hidden poor in the countryside and tried to assist them in a positive manner. For example, seriously deteriorating weather conditions in sparsely populated Greeley County, first apparent in 1932, made it one of the hardest hit in the state. Work relief and the CWA programs were of enormous benefit in 1933–34, but it was only in the latter year that the systematic compilation and filing of relief reports was implemented. By late 1934, accurate submissions were being made, and for the first time it was possible to deduce with certainty the sums spent on work relief, direct relief, Homestead Rehabilitation, and the distribution of surplus commodities by the FSRC. Nor should one lose sight of the fact that the county's residents also benefited from improvements to roads, public buildings, the drilling of two emergency wells, and the construction of eighty-three ponds, which formed the tangible gains from work relief.[72]

A permanent rather than an emergency relief program was needed because conditions continued to deteriorate in the county, as Case Supervisor Julia L. Miller reported in April 1935. At that time, there were 255 cases, representing 980 individuals out of a total population of 1,900, on the county relief rolls. According to Miss Miller, 22 families were living in one- or two-room grossly overcrowded sod houses, at least 12 of which had one corner caved in. Most of these houses had mud or cement plaster walls and cement floors; two families lived in bank houses with dirt floors. In the county seat, Tribune, it was very difficult to rent accommodation, possibly because of property ownership by suitcase farmers. The county had been ruined by successive years of drought that had destroyed crops, animal feed, and gardens. Every week dust storms added to the misery, and residents were forced to mortgage everything that they could. Their only income besides relief in 1933 and 1934 was $186,000 from the wheat allotment scheme, to which can be added $16,000 in corn-hog payments.[73] It is no surprise that these sums were very welcome, as was the total of $220,000 that was received as compensation under the same headings in 1935.

Morton County, in the extreme southwest, drought-affected corner of the state, also became heavily reliant on federal assistance. Of the total $70,420 spent on relief in 1934, 82 percent was provided by the federal

72. *KERC Bulletin* 127, 226–28; *KERC Bulletin* 289, 309–13.

73. Report for KERC by Miss Julia L. Miller, Case Supervisor, "Conditions in Greeley County, April 1935," Stutz Papers, 327:3:48

government and 13 percent by the county. In addition, the CWA contributed $52,325 during the months that it was in operation, the overwhelming amount coming from the federal government. During 1935, when on average 17 percent of the county's population was receiving relief, the federal government donated $73,300 to assist them. Work relief on road projects, especially for the victims of drought, was the most common form of assistance, but improvements to public buildings, children's playgrounds, and cemeteries were also valuable outcomes.[74] However, these figures seem puny when set alongside the sums received by participants in the wheat allotment scheme. In 1933 and 1934, $370,000 flooded into Morton County, and $249,000 was paid in 1935.[75]

Although one can question whether all the 105 county relief committees were functioning effectively, there can be little doubt that the overall level of performance was at least acceptable. This judgment was confirmed by the reports of two FERA field examiners who visited Kansas in January and April 1935. Louis T. Nein wrote that under the headings of commodity distribution, the transient program, and general administration, the Kansas organization was efficient and the personnel running it were of exceptionally high caliber. He did make the point, however, that the average relief extended to each case seemed high. A few months later, Martin Uhlman gave the relief administration a clean bill of health, and though never fulsome in his praise, it is clear that he was impressed by the efficiency that Stutz had imposed on his colleagues.[76] All relief clients gained from the considerable efforts made to professionalize the relief administration, especially in the recruitment and training of staff, and this is particularly true for rural clients who had the most to gain from a studied recognition of their misfortune.

The Impact of Drought

Drought is the key to understanding both the performance of the agricultural sector and the incidence of relief.[77] Distressed rural families, especially those residing in drought-stricken counties, were helped by a

74. *KERC Bulletin* 289, 483–88; ibid. 355, 182–83.
75. KSBA, *29th Biennial Report,* 617; *30th Biennial Report,* 585.
76. Louis T. Nein to Corrington Gill, January 22, 1935, "Report of Examination of State of Kansas," January 18/19; Martin Uhlman, Regional Director Emergency Relief Commission, "General Report on Kansas Relief Committee," April 29, 1935, FERA State Files, 1933–36, Kansas Field Examiner's Reports, RG69, NA.
77. For a full account of the impact of the drought see Michael W. Schuyler, "Fed-

number of New Deal and local initiatives that demonstrated a flexible response to worsening conditions. As late as July 1933, it seemed as though Kansas had committed sufficient resources to cope with the immediate needs of families living in the affected counties.[78] However, in September, and in response to urgent requests, the FERA advanced the first grants specifically for drought assistance to six states, one of which was Kansas. State Relief Administrations were permitted to liberalize their budgeting regulations so as to take into account the impact of drought-induced livestock feed shortages, and needy families who could not refinance their debts by means of loans from the Farm Credit Administration were supported locally as normal relief cases. The FERA also funded special road projects in the drought area, using relief labor, and these were taken over by the CWA after November. Farmers were informed that they could apply for CWA work on condition that they participated in AAA programs. Those who secured CWA jobs were relieved, and those who could not complained bitterly that CWA wages inflated the cost of farm labor. In addition, during the winter of 1933–34, the FSRC assisted drought relief families by providing up to thirty bushels of feed grains for subsistence livestock. From April 1934, the FERA Emergency Work Relief Program that succeeded the CWA was expanded in the drought counties, with a special emphasis on water conservation and roadwork. Relief families also benefited when their sons joined the CCC, as did the counties once these families were removed from the relief rolls.

In October 1933 the KERC had begun to operate a drought relief program that was initially confined to the eighteen southwest counties identified as the most seriously affected in the state.[79] The region's wheat crop had been an almost total failure, and there was a shortage of both seed and feed. Farmers in need of relief were allowed to earn their deficiency budgets on work relief projects, and the money earned helped to combat the impact of drought. Most of the men were employed on state highways, though some were engaged on county roads, and to assist farmers struggling to maintain their workhorses, a decision was made to use teams rather than trucks or tractors. Materials for this work, which represented 30 percent of the total project cost, were provided by a PWA fund dedicated to the drought area. The State Highway Commission sponsored the

eral Drought Relief Activities in Kansas" and the same author's *The Dread of Plenty: Agricultural Relief Activities of the Federal Government in the Middle West, 1933–39,* esp. chap. 4.

78. Ewing to Hopkins, June 24, 1933; Ewing to Hopkins, July 2, 1933, Federal Relief Agency Papers, Group 24, Box 57, Hopkins Papers.

79. *KERC Bulletin* 127, 27–31; 39, March 9, 1934, 1.

projects, and FERA funds were used for wages. As a result of this assistance, farmers were able to remain on their holdings and their children could attend school decently clothed and shod. An indication of the impact of the drought can be gauged in Haskell County in southwest Kansas, where wheat growing was the dominant farm activity. In 1934 it was estimated that 95 percent of the county's business was dependent upon wheat allotment payments and relief checks.[80]

The drought dominated relief and rehabilitation issues during 1934, the fifth in succession when measured rainfall was less than the previous year. After the CWA program was concluded in March 1934, relief administrators became convinced that Kansas could manage with fewer social workers, but these hopes were quickly dashed when the impact of drought led to a constant rise in the relief rolls from July. Heavy caseloads in rural counties presented special problems. It was difficult to attract highly qualified staff to work in more remote areas, and, for those in post, the distances that they had to travel to visit clients added an additional burden to an already considerable workload. In 1933, the federal government had confirmed the eighteen Kansas counties already locally identified as special drought counties.[81] By the end of 1934, however, the USDA had designated the entire state an emergency drought area. One advantage of this designation was that all farmers became eligible for the federal loans and special services that had previously been limited to residents of the original named drought counties

The KERC and various federal government agencies worked hard to lessen the immediate impact of drought and to lay down the foundations for a long-term solution to the problem. The KERC set in motion a work relief program focusing on water conservation. The drilling or digging of over six hundred community wells provided immediate work relief for those affected by drought, and care was taken to minimize the use of machinery in order to maximize the employment of hand labor. In addition, help was given to farmers so that they could more easily identify and solve their own water shortage problems. An energetic Governor Landon secured the loan of large pumping units from oil and gas companies so that temporary pumping plants could be established along the banks of streams, and more than 240 of these provided essential water supplies for livestock. Further emergency measures enabled more than 50 municipalities to maintain or increase their water supply, so that both households

---

80. *KERC Bulletin* 289, 339.
81. These counties were Barber, Comanche, Kiowa, Edwards, Hodgeman, Ford, Clark, Meade, Gray, Finney, Haskell, Seward, Stevens, Grant, Kearny, Hamilton, Stanton, and Morton.

and the fire service felt considerably more secure. Meanwhile, geologists scoured the state in an attempt to discover water sources that could be readily exploited.

For the longer term, rural rehabilitation clients constructed around eight hundred garden ponds on their own property, though needy neighbors were to be given access when a drought emergency was declared. Plans were declared for the construction of twenty-seven lakes, but it proved difficult to move from the idea to the reality, as all projects had to be completed by March 1935. By the end of 1934 municipal lakes had been approved for Howard, Paola, Sedan, Waterville, and Wellington only. Lake projects were always very popular with local people because they provided both a valuable source of water and much-needed leisure facilities.

The federal government became progressively more aware of the serious drought problem as 1934 wore on but, as it was impossible to predict the course of this national catastrophe, Washington's response was necessarily a reactive one. Funding came to Kansas, and the other affected states, in a piecemeal fashion, as hopes that rainfall would materialize at the right time, and in sufficient quantity to solve the problem, were regularly dashed. In May 1934, the heads of the FERA, the AAA, and the FCA reported to the president on conditions in the drought area. It was agreed that the FERA would develop a bold plan to purchase distressed cattle that were in danger of imminent death by starvation or thirst and that the AAA would relax its restrictions on farmers under contract so that they could grow summer forage crops.

On June 9, President Roosevelt asked Congress for an additional $525 million to finance a complex package of measures to fight the effects of drought. These included the purchase of herds, the provision of loans to provide emergency feed for livestock, a dedicated work relief program, the acquisition by the federal government of submarginal lands and the resettlement of affected families, and, finally, the creation of additional CCC places.

The Cattle Purchase Program

Partly because cattle raising had not been as seriously hit by the depression as other farm activities, producers had argued against the inclusion of cattle in the original AAA list of basic agricultural commodities. At the time, the majority of ranchers opposed the introduction of a cattle reduction program, and they were also resolutely united in opposition to

the new processing tax that they feared would shift the public away from beef consumption toward substitute foods. Cattle producers were convinced that the key to the resolution of their problems was the imposition of a tariff on fresh and processed meat to remove all foreign competition. However, as the situation facing cattlemen deteriorated, they began to agitate for government assistance, and in April 1934, the Jones-Connally Act added cattle to the list of basic commodities.[82] While negotiations over details with the AAA were progressing, it became clear that drought conditions had become so serious that they posed a major problem for livestock producers in a number of states.

Indeed, by the middle of 1934, it was evident that a major catastrophe was looming in Kansas, as not only was feed for cattle in short supply, but there was also an acute shortage of water. In June, Governor Landon informed the Federal Drought Relief Service that forty-two counties were now so badly affected that they would require immediate aid. The governor also lobbied for a reduction in freight rates so that both livestock and feedstuff could be moved to and from the drought areas. The railroad companies agreed to carry feed at two-thirds their normal rate, and they also permitted cattle to be shipped to new pastures at 85 percent of the old rate and be returned at 15 percent of the rate, thus effectively halving the cost of a round trip. Since the rail companies depended heavily on freight earnings from cattle and feed movements, they were, of course, serving their own interests in supporting policies to ensure the long-run survival of the livestock industry. Moreover, the federal government also exerted pressure on the rail companies to reduce rates. Vigorous efforts were made to try to coordinate the lists of available pasture with the needs of livestock farmers in the drought area. Unfortunately, the problem was far bigger than the proposed solution, and desperate livestock producers were soon trying to unload their beasts on a rapidly falling market, while still facing the problem of water scarcity. It was clear that further federal intervention was necessary.

The most significant of all the schemes that the president presented to Congress in June was the decision to give relief to livestock farmers by purchasing cattle from the most drought-stricken farms.[83] In Kansas, after the Drought Relief Service bought the cattle, they were donated to the FSRC and then passed on to the KERC. The KERC acted as an agent of the FSRC and was ultimately responsible for loading and shipping more than half a million head of cattle. On July 7, the first purchases were made in

82. Fitzgerald, *Livestock under the AAA*, 174–83.
83. R. Douglas Hurt, *The Dust Bowl: An Agricultural and Social History*, 103–19.

Meade County, and within a few days stockmen in Haskell, Kearny, and Finney counties were also enjoying the benefits of the scheme, which then spread statewide.[84] At this stage in the program, the purchasing quota for Kansas was set at one thousand head per day.

The scheme identified three classes of animals. Cattle whose condition had deteriorated so seriously that they were judged unfit for consumption were killed and then buried on farms. Nationally, 18 percent of all animals purchased were condemned, though in Oklahoma it was 40 percent and in Kansas less than 3 percent.[85] A second category was sent to packers to be canned and then distributed to relief clients, as part of the surplus commodities program. Thirdly, the best grade beasts were shipped to pastures, mainly out of state, and were either available for slaughter at a later date, or could be used as subsistence animals under the homestead rehabilitation program. In other words, a cull took place in which the worst quality stock was removed, thus lowering the pressure on feedstuffs while raising the general quality of herds. At the same time, the diet of selected relief clients could be supplemented with either fresh or canned beef. The price that the farmers received for each animal varied according to age and quality and was set, within guidelines established by the Federal Drought Relief Service, by committees operating in each county.

In the middle of July seven additional counties were added to the list of primary drought counties, but by August conditions had deteriorated to such an extent that all 105 counties were accorded this dubious distinction. By the end of the year, cattle purchases had been made in every county, with the exception of Allen. To select, value, purchase, transport, and slaughter tens of thousands of head of cattle presented a formidable logistical exercise; fortunately, many different groups rose to the challenge. The federal government showed admirable flexibility in dealing with the cattle purchase scheme. In the middle of August, the shipping quota for Kansas was raised to 6,000 head daily and raised again to 9,000 head at the end of the month. But the problem remained acute, and in early September the quota stood at 10,180 per day. Toward the end of September, federal funds allocated for cattle purchase were close to exhaustion, and the deadline set by Congress for the completion of the program

84. *KERC Bulletin* 289, "Purchases of Cattle under AAA Drought Relief Service Program," 761–68.

85. Fitzgerald, *Livestock under the AAA,* 207–8.

86. Charles L. Wood, *The Kansas Beef Industry,* 241; Fitzgerald, *Livestock under the AAA,* 376–77.

loomed. In recognition of the continuing problem, this deadline was progressively extended, as was funding. However, by early December, purchasing had virtually come to a halt, though it continued on a small scale until January 15, 1935. By the end of 1934, welcome rains had stimulated pastures in south and central Kansas, and cattlemen were confident that they could keep their reduced stock over the winter. Furthermore, a rise in livestock prices stimulated by the program helped producers, especially those in the eastern part of the state.

Over the period that the program operated in Kansas, 521,169 cattle were purchased and $7.5 million paid for them. The producers received an average of $14.40 a head for their cattle, which was above the national average of $13.50.[86] Allen was the only county that did not participate in the scheme, so the gains were widespread and the cash flow to some counties was substantial. Stockmen in Osborne County, for example, had 17,737 head of cattle purchased and received $250,000 for them; the figures for Lincoln County were 16,487 head and a payment of $249,000. We have seen how important AAA wheat allotment payments were to farmers in Hodgeman and Meade counties. Under this initiative livestock farmers, some of whom also qualified for wheat allotment payments, received $169,000 in the former county and $175,000 in the latter.[87]

Such was the pressure generated by the purchases that the FERA granted the KERC permission to establish a state canning program to take care of the 121,000 head of cattle that the commercial canning plants could not handle. The first plant began operations in Parsons on August 1, and was soon followed by eight others.[88] As Kansas had few commercial canning plants, the vociferous objections from commercial operators, which were evident in some other states, were not forthcoming.[89] By late October 1934, 6,628 men and 1,459 women, all relief clients, were working their relief budgets in these plants, and they produced thirteen million cans of beef during the period 1934–35 while the plants were in operation. As the normal rules of work relief had to be observed, none of the output was for sale; all of it was distributed to relief clients either as fresh or canned meat.

87. Details in *KERC Bulletin* 289, 765–66.
88. They were located at Kansas City, Wichita, Topeka, Leavenworth, Hutchinson, Coffeyville, Independence, and Chanute. *KERC Bulletin* 289, 768–72.
89. C. Roger Lambert, "The Drought Cattle Purchase, 1934–35: Problems and Complaints," 88–89.

Grass-Roots Problems

In June 1935 the Bureau of Agricultural Economics conducted another inquiry into the provision of rural relief, and as part of this exercise the agency surveyed thirteen Kansas counties. The timing of these investigations is interesting, coming as they did at the cusp of the transfer of national provision from the FERA to the WPA, which also had implications for the organization of relief at the county level. Moreover, these administrative changes required farmers who were eligible for rural rehabilitation loans to be removed from work relief lists by June 6, 1935. At this time all rural counties were suffering from the continuing effects of the drought, some more acutely than others, but the worst was yet to come.

Most of these counties shared a common theme, or at least a collective reaction to common problems.[90] Virtually all reported a recent migration from the open country to villages and towns. Among the causes of this population movement were the unprofitability of farming due to drought-induced crop failure, a reduction in renting because owners wanted to farm land themselves and claim the AAA allotment payments, and a desire by people who needed assistance to be near relief agencies. The overriding cause of misery was, however, drought. Tenants on marginal land—where farming could only be sustained when conditions were moist, prices high, and supplementary work readily available—had given up in despair. Indeed, the problems arising from farming marginal land are highlighted in several of these reports, and tenants were heavily represented on the relief rolls. In normal times, farmers had hired laborers to help with the preparation of the ground and for the planting of spring crops, harvesting wheat and oats in the early summer, haymaking, harvesting crops during the fall, and taking care of cattle during the winter. However, repeated crop failures had eradicated work for laborers, worsening an economic position that had already been significantly compromised by mechanization. Moreover, hard-pressed farmers continued to exchange work with their neighbors whenever they could in order to economize on paid labor.

In Saline County, young people moved from the open country and villages, where the prospects for employment were dismal, to towns, where work or a college place could be more easily secured. In Smith County, laborers had migrated to Colorado, Montana, and Idaho in search of sea-

90. The counties were Barber, Ford, Gove, Greenwood, Hamilton, Jefferson, Neosho, Pawnee, Russell, Saline, Seward, Smith, and Wabaunsee. The reports were submitted to the BAE between March and June 1936, and some contain observations on events after June 1935.

sonal work but had returned to their place of legal settlement to try to secure WPA jobs. In Wabaunsee County, farmers had no funds to replace worn-out machinery, and some had their tractors requisitioned by equipment companies because they had failed to meet purchase payments. Drought also affected local businesses as painters, carpenters, and plasterers could no longer find customers and were eventually forced to seek unaccustomed relief. Exactly the same situation was reported in Barber County, where tradesmen and workers laid off from a cement plant had been compelled to apply for relief, and some local businesses had been unable to avoid bankruptcy. The harvests of 1932, 1933, and 1934 had been almost total failures, precipitating a marked migration from the open countryside to villages. In Ford County, clerical workers and those whose small businesses had folded were to be found on the relief rolls.[91]

There was widespread support for the AAA allotment schemes that enabled farmers to pay their taxes; purchase seed, food, clothing, and gasoline; and also support local businesses. In Saline and Seward counties it was reported that wheat allotment payments and to a lesser extent payments from the corn-hog program were the only source of income for many farm families.[92] These payments were crucial in enabling farmers to stay on the land and off the relief rolls. In Russell and Neosho counties farmers were enraged at the Supreme Court's decision in January 1936 to declare the processing tax unconstitutional and thus strike down the 1933 AAA. Local businessmen, who supported farmers in a powerful plea for a permanent farm program, joined them in their protests. However, the supporters of farm subsidies conceded that the wheat acreage reduction that was supposed to follow from the 1933 AAA legislation had not taken place in a number of counties, as growers who chose not to participate in the program had actually increased their planting.

It is not surprising that there was strong support for the Soil Conservation and Domestic Allotment Act (SCDAA) that replaced the AAA in 1936. Although the KERC believed that the crop reduction program had con-

91. Hazle Bland, "Survey of Current Changes in the Rural Relief Population, June 1935. Saline County, Kansas"; Faye Worrel, "Survey of Current Changes in the Rural Relief Population, June 1935. Smith County, Kansas"; Elsie Flinner, "Survey of Current Changes in the Rural Relief Population, June 1935. Wabaunsee County, Kansas"; Miriam Peck, "Survey of Current Changes in the Rural Relief Population, June 1935. Barber County, Kansas"; Miriam Peck, "Survey of Current Changes in the Rural Relief Population, June 1935. Ford County, Kansas", all in Rural Problem Reports, Bureau of Agricultural Economics, RG83, NA.

92. Hazle Bland, "Survey of the Current Changes in the Rural Relief Population, June 1935, Saline County, Kansas." Also Seward County. Rural Problem Reports, Bureau of Agricultural Economics, RG83, NA

tributed to the increase in the rural relief load because it led to the with-drawal of land from production and encouraged a further growth in ab-sentee or suitcase farming, there is little evidence to support the centrali-ty of this claim.[93] In the first place, total wheat acreage was not reduced, and second, most farm hardship was caused by drought-induced crop failure. Farmers who were in debt and trying to cultivate marginal land, or who were fighting to preserve their livestock, faced an increasingly hopeless task, and many could not avoid a visit to the relief office. With farm prices stubbornly remaining below the costs of production, most cul-tivators were in difficulty. It was a lack of rain, sometimes combined with poor farming practices—like over-cultivation leading to a loss of soil fer-tility, as occurred in Jefferson County—that reduced farm output, not government schemes. In the counties covered by this survey, enthusiasm for the corn-hog program was more restrained than the commitment to the wheat allotment scheme, but by 1935 many early doubters had been won over.

Four of the counties analyzed offered the possibility of nonfarm em-ployment. Russell County's oil fields provided unskilled jobs suitable for farm laborers, and also gave many farmers an added source of income from leases as well as helping local business by boosting trade.[94] The pop-ulation of the county rose by 13 percent between 1930 and 1935, and the town of Russell experienced a remarkable population expansion of just over 50 percent during the same period. It is depressing to note that em-ployers in the oil industry were reluctant to take on relief clients when va-cancies arose, believing them to be inefficient. The availability of nonfarm employment helped prevent Russell County from meeting its CCC quo-ta, though another force acting against recruitment was the touching re-luctance of some mothers to see their sons flee the family nest.

As everywhere else, Russell County farmers suffered greatly from the effects of drought, which seriously affected key crops and also caused a big reduction in livestock between 1934 and 1935. In June 1935 the coun-ty carried 335 active relief cases, of which 263 received federal relief ex-clusively. Eighty percent of these cases were located on poor soil in the northern part of the county, remote from the oil fields. Local relief officials believed that the majority of the farm operators on relief could quickly be-come self-supporting, once a change in the weather enabled them to pro-duce an average crop. The officials did concede, however, that farmers in debt would require more than one good year to become solvent.

---

93. *KERC Bulletin* 289, 311.

94. Faye Worrel, "Survey of Current Changes . . . June 1935, Russell County, Kan-sas," Rural Problem Reports, Bureau of Agricultural Economics, RG83, NA.

In Greenwood County, the situation was less favorable, as the oil companies had stopped drilling and, since 1931, it had not been easy for oilmen to get work.[95] In addition, the county's livestock industry had been badly affected, leading to bankruptcies among the cattlemen. In 1933, Barber County had experienced a brief oil boom, which encouraged an inflow of population; unfortunately, when the boom subsided, even the skilled lost their jobs, and many of the families who had recently moved to the county stayed behind and had to be given public aid.

Conditions in Neosho County, which is located in southeast Kansas, provide a contrast to the drought region. The oil, gas, petroleum refining, railroad repair shops, and cement manufacturing industries gave employment to about 650 men. Because of its favored location in a relatively moist region, the impact of the drought was less serious in Neosho County than in the western part of the state. However, flooding meant that farmers were harder hit in 1935 than in any of the preceding five years. In June 1935, 13 farm owners, 55 tenants, and 167 laborers were among those receiving relief. The relief rolls had been materially reduced because 132 families had been removed from them on receipt of allotments from young men who had enrolled for work in CCC camps. Before the CCC was operational, these families had received, on average, $14.41 worth of relief each month.

By March 1936, WPA projects provided work relief for most of Neosho's unemployed, but 173 men who had been certified could not be assigned, as the county quota of 494 had been filled. The county dispensed grocery orders to the non-assigned, who had to earn the orders by working on old-fashioned, morale sapping projects such as woodcutting, leaf raking, and improvements to parks or cemeteries. During February 1936, an average of 112 men per week worked on the woodcutting project, and 29 were employed on the city project. Grocery orders averaged $2.30 each, and the men worked their orders out at 25 cents per hour. The WPA provided appropriate work for unskilled men, but there were few opportunities for stenographers, trained nurses, carpenters, mechanics, welders, and others with specialist skills on work projects. To add to the difficulties, the possibility of WPA employment in Chanute had lured migrants from the surrounding counties.

The major message from these surveys was the baleful influence of drought. Rain was needed to create jobs for laborers, to enable rehabilitation clients to repay their loans, to provide a growing income for farm operators that would create business opportunities for their nonfarm neighbors, to save relief gardens from failure, to reduce the relief rolls, and to

95. Miriam Peck, "Survey of Current Changes . . . Greenwood County," ibid.

give hope to rural people suffering from both psychological and physical hardships. However, drought made relief more acceptable to people who, in the past, would have felt too ashamed to visit the relief office. Optimists—and every farm community has them even in the bleakest periods—believed that one good crop would solve most difficulties; but levels of debt were too uncomfortably high to accept this simplistic notion.

In spite of the pressure on social workers and clients, the overall administration of relief was judged sound. Because there was national concern that relief would sap the spirit and lead to dependency, or that work relief would become more attractive than private sector jobs, each investigator explored these potential problems. They noted that in Saline, Seward, and Wabaunsee Counties, farmers complained that it was impossible to attract relief workers to their fields at harvest time because they could not offer competitive wages. But in general there was little evidence to support the view that relief workers refused private sector jobs when they became available, though farm labor, which was perceived as not only poorly paid but also requiring long hours, was an exception. It should be noted, however, that the harvest work offered by farmers was usually only for very short periods, and this added to the reluctance of relief workers, who feared that they could not easily be reemployed on the relief projects that they had just left.

In many of these counties, private charities like the Red Cross played a role that was small in terms of money spent but valuable if the aid given to the particularly distressed is considered dispassionately. Many large families could not manage adequately on the federal or county relief awarded, and private charities helped with supplementation, often in the form of fuel, grocery orders, and used clothing. Where the activities of the private charities were closely coordinated with the work of county relief administrations, they provided a valuable addition to welfare provision, though there were examples of undesirable duplication when well-intentioned intervention was not preceded by an adequate social examination of family circumstances.

Unfortunately it is not always possible to differentiate between farm, rural nonfarm, and urban Kansans in an analysis of the overall impact of the relief program. However, some legitimate observations relating to the social costs of the depression in the countryside can be made. Rural dwellers benefited substantially from the creation and development of a professional relief service based on casework investigation and operated at the county level. Previously, rural poverty had been ignored or neglected, record keeping had been seriously deficient, and the assistance available was both miserly and poorly administered. The imposition of

state and federal rules enabled those in need to be identified before receiving material help and valuable constructive advice. Of course one can argue, as for urban relief recipients, that payments were ungenerous and the administration was sometimes less than perfect, but, nevertheless, by mid-1935 relief provision for rural Kansans had materially improved.

It is difficult to disagree with Michael Grant's conclusions that in the short term rehabilitation assistance was an essential aid for many farm families during difficult times. Grants and loans kept them on their farms when there was no alternative employment. Pertinent advice brought about significant efficiencies in the way in which operators managed their enterprises during very challenging conditions. Advisors also effectively improved the way in which low-income households were managed.[96] However, it is important to recognize in a study of rural Kansas that there were large numbers of the needy who did not qualify for rehabilitation loans or grants. Operators of small farms, laborers, unemployed oil workers, railroad men, clerical workers, painters, decorators, teachers, and many other nonfarm rural workers looked to either the federal government or their counties for aid when they were in need.

It is apparent that where it existed rural misery was not evenly distributed across the state. Drought, for example, was much more severe in the west than in the rest of Kansas. The competence and the age of individual farmers, the size of their farms, the level of debt, variations in the quality of the soil, and whether sufficient rain fell at the right time all played a significant role in the determination of farm income. Owners did fare better than either tenants or laborers, and the latter groups were much more likely to be found on the relief rolls than the former. Non-owners and laborers were also most likely to migrate to villages or urban settlements in a desperate search for work or relief.

Above all else, there was a significant change in the role and presence of the federal government. Work relief paying cash wages was available under both the FERA and the CWA, and this could be supplemented from county or private charitable sources. Federal involvement was all invasive. The provision of surplus commodities for distribution to relief clients, CCC places, the FERA Special Programs, assistance with debts and mortgages, and the cattle purchase program is not an exhaustive list of Washington's new commitments to the struggle against rural poverty. The following figures demonstrate clearly how important federal money became as the principal means to alleviate a whole range of social problems.

In 1934, for example, $21.6 million was spent on the relief program in

96. Grant, *Down and Out on the Family Farm,* 156–60.

Kansas, and federal government grants in aid contributed $14 million to that total. In 1935, $24.9 million flowed from Washington to help finance the state's relief effort.[97] However, federal contributions to the relief effort seem puny when compared to the subsidies available from the two principal AAA programs. During 1933–34 farmers entitled to wheat allotment payments shared $37.8 million and a further $26.8 million in 1935. Those who signed up to the corn-hog scheme shared $8 million in 1934 and $13.8 million during the following year. In other words, these two programs led to the not-inconsiderable cash sum of $86.5 million flowing into Kansas over a two-year period, a far larger amount than was dedicated for relief. Moreover, these figures do not include the support given to livestock farmers by the Drought Cattle Purchase initiative or from a variety of other programs, including assistance with debts and loans from the FCA and the Federal Land Bank. Unfortunately the benefit payment scheme favored landlords over tenants and large landowners more than small. In January 1935 a number of tenant farmers from Elkhart, in Morton County, wrote to Secretary Henry A. Wallace protesting that in order to maximize allotment receipts, landlords were either dispossessing their tenants or raising rents to levels that erased the benefits of the payments to them.[98] This was not an isolated cry of frustration.

Neither the recipients nor New Dealers regarded AAA or FCA initiatives as relief. Indeed, the recipients were not assessed by social workers to determine how much they should receive. Rural people were also quick to point out that as industrialists and their workers enjoyed protection from tariffs, who could deny that they too were entitled to expect shelter when the storm was at its worst? There can be no doubt that the substantial cash flows and subsidized credit were instrumental in providing a lifeline for many farmers, enabling them to meet a number of their pressing obligations and also to remain on their farms. Appreciation of the allotment program was widespread. Senator Arthur Capper, who in the course of 1935 talked to the Republican county chairmen in fifty-nine counties, was told, "wheat benefits saved the lives of thousands of farmers." Although Capper believed that wheat allotment payments should continue only as an emergency measure, he publicly supported the program and had no doubts as to its overall popularity.[99] Between 1933 and 1935, Capper was so supportive of the Democrat administration's legislation that

97. Figures from *KERC Bulletin* 355, 41–45.
98. Schuyler, *Dread of Plenty,* 122.
99. Capper to C. A. Brewer, July 26, 1935; Capper to John J. Means, August 10, 1935; Kansas Farm Bureau to Capper, August 17, 1935, Box 16, File 12, all in Arthur Capper Papers, Kansas State Historical Society.

he has been described as a "Republican New Dealer."[100] In September 1935, the president sought the counsel and advice of the nation's clergy, asking them to write to him about conditions in their communities. Many of the Kansas preachers who responded identified wheat and corn-hog checks, the Civilian Conservation Corps, and banking legislation as the most praiseworthy of the New Deal's policies. On the other hand, they were distressed by the willful destruction of food, the persistent deficit in the federal budget, and, as one would expect, there were a variety of firmly held views on the ending of prohibition.[101] There was, however, widespread support for continuing federal help for distressed rural residents as there was from the public generally.

However, the Kansas problem was that there were too many farms and too many of them were marginal. The plow-up of the prairie during the 1920s contributed greatly to the crisis that the state and the nation faced during the Dust Bowl era. It would require a radical change in cultivation practices and the creation of many nonfarm jobs to generate prosperity in the countryside. Rehabilitation loans and other relief activities provided a lifeline for many farm families, but this assistance could only be temporary. Rural dwellers needed more than a return of the rains to escape from the need of relief and to build a prosperous life.

100. Homer E. Socolofsky, *Arthur Capper: Publisher, Politician, and Philanthropist*, 172–74.

101. Responses to letters sent to clergy in September 1935, Clergy Letters, Kansas, President's Personal File 21A, Franklin Delano Roosevelt Papers, FDR Presidential Library, Hyde Park, N.Y.; *The Public Papers and Addresses of Franklin D. Roosevelt*, Volume 4, *The Court Disapproves*, 370.

5

The WPA, the Dole, General Relief, and Politics

WPA

In the spring of 1935, national and local social policy was subjected to a radical overhaul. Congress passed the Emergency Relief Appropriations Act in April, and a new agency, the WPA, was established to oversee the federal government's new work relief program. The aim of the WPA was to give useful employment on locally sponsored work projects, at the appropriate level of skill, to those needy jobless who were fit for work. Some states used FERA grants to provide help for both employables and unemployables, but the president and his advisors concluded that responsibility for the latter should revert to individual states and local units. Jobless employables, it was felt, presented an entirely different problem. Unemployment was part of a national malaise, and therefore it was right that the federal government should commit sufficient resources to help individuals who were fit enough to work but were unable to find employment. In other words, direct relief was to be returned to the states and work relief was to be the responsibility of Washington.

1935 Social Security Act

Once the WPA commenced operations, the FERA Emergency Work Relief Program and the grants-in-aid to the states that it oversaw were quickly phased out. Another crucial part of the 1935 welfare revolution was the passage of the Social Security Act, which enabled the federal government to forge a new relationship with the states in order to provide assistance for certain categories of unemployable needy citizens. Federal grants became available for those states that established permanent approved support schemes for mothers with dependent children, and for the blind and the aged.

On January 4, 1935, in the course of his annual message to the Congress, Roosevelt firmly announced that "the Federal Government must and shall quit this business of relief."[1] In making this statement, the president had unequivocally reiterated his opposition to dole payments that, he believed, lowered morale and would inevitably lead to dependency. His plan for a national program of work relief for the three-and-a-half million citizens who were victims of the depression was viewed as both morally and economically sound, though it soon became clear that the figure on which the program was based seriously underestimated the level of national unemployment. Having the unemployed perform useful tasks if they were able to do so was a consistent New Deal philosophy, and it also seemed the obvious policy to both the trained welfare worker and the concerned layman.[2] "Work not dole" had long been a Kansas axiom, and no federal money had ever been spent on unemployables, the care of whom the state always regarded as the counties' responsibility. The president himself stressed that public employment should be useful in the sense that it must result in a permanent improvement in living conditions and, where possible, be self-liquidating so that the government would recoup its investment in the future. However, many social workers were horrified at the prospect of unemployables being cared for by the states and counties. They believed that Edith Abbott did not exaggerate when she denounced this policy with the words, "[G]oing back to the states really means going back to . . . the inefficiency, incompetency, and inadequacy of the system of poor relief supported by local property taxes."[3]

[handwritten margin note: federal "quit" this — had been spent on work relief]

WPA: The National Context

A lack of faith in the ability of some states to formulate the sort of work relief programs that would satisfy Washington's standards was one of the reasons why the WPA, like the CWA before it, was a federal agency. Federal control would ensure that work programs were more professional and socially worthwhile, thus deflecting the wounding criticism that increasingly called the attention of the press and voters to waste and inefficiency. One of the lessons learned from the FERA was that Washington

---

1. Franklin Delano Roosevelt, *Public Papers and Addresses of Franklin D. Roosevelt with a Special Introduction and Explanatory Notes by President Roosevelt*, Vol. 4, *The Court Disapproves, 1935*, 15–25.
2. William W. Bremer, "Along the 'American Way': The New Deal's Work Relief Programs for the Unemployed," 36–38.
3. Edith Abbott, "Don't Do It, Mr. Hopkins," 41–42.

had few sanctions when it concluded that federal grants were being misused. It was true that grants could be withdrawn, but that penalized the poor; it was also the case that offending state relief administrations could be, and were, federalized, but this was a Draconian step, and one that could only be used against the most recalcitrant offenders. The fact that all WPA appointees, from the most senior in Washington to those in charge of local offices, were federal officials was designed to ensure that good practices could be imposed upon those states that had not previously adopted them.[4]

In sharp contrast to the FERA, the WPA did not use state governments as a means of distributing funds. It was the task of sponsors, normally municipal or county government agencies, to suggest projects, construct plans, and guarantee to contribute part of the cost. After a preliminary meeting with local WPA officials, project plans were sent to the state WPA for approval and then to Washington for a final scrutiny. From a list of those deemed satisfactory, the state WPA administrator selected projects that would go ahead. The selection of projects was governed by the sponsors' ability to provide funds, usually to cover nonlabor costs either in cash or in kind, which could include the provision of office space. Indeed, the sponsors had an important role to play as their energy and expertise was crucial in the formulation of project plans, and their ability to raise funds was no less significant.[5]

Federal funds, however, were not advanced to local sponsors, or to the suppliers of raw materials; these were purchased through approved federal purchasing channels. The project workers received their wages in cash directly from Washington through Treasury checks. Under the FERA, federal funds were supplied to the governor for disbursement, and through the influence of field representatives and other monitoring devices a careful watch was kept on possible malpractice. By involving Washington more directly, it was hoped that the WPA would minimize any failure to maintain high professional relief standards.

The rules for prospective applicants were clear: among them was that all had to be unemployed, over eighteen years of age, and immediately available for assignment. However, unlike the CWA, unemployment alone was not sufficient to guarantee eligibility on a WPA project. At least 95 percent of all workers on projects had to be certified by an approved public relief agency as not only out of work but also in need of relief.

4. Arthur E. Burns and Edward A. Williams, *Federal Work, Security and Relief Programs*, 55–57.

5. Donald S. Howard, *The WPA and Federal Relief Policy*, 146–50.

Moreover, there was no escape from the scrutiny of social workers, who were used as investigators not only for the initial certification but also to conduct the regular six-month reviews into the financial status of each WPA employee. Although the vast majority of welfare professionals preferred relief work to charity, they were opposed to the means-tested relief that all New Deal agencies, with the exception of the CWA, embraced.

In order to spread the available work relief among as many clients as possible, only one member of a family group could be employed by the WPA, though family members could enroll in other agencies, such as the National Youth Administration (NYA) or the CCC. In practice, therefore, WPA jobs were normally reserved for heads of households, or a designated priority worker, who would usually be male. Single persons were not generally considered for WPA employment, but women with dependent children were eligible, if they were employable and certified in need. The emphasis on fitness for work was not designed to disqualify the physically handicapped who were capable of employment. Applicants with disabilities were supposed to be specifically allocated work duties that they could safely perform. The rule that at least 95 percent of the persons working on projects had to be paid from project funds and certified in need of relief secured the maximum number of places for the most disadvantaged. It left little scope, however, for recruiting from among the employed, vital workers who had scarce skills, for example, management expertise. Finally, as the WPA was a federal initiative, no residence requirement for workers was stipulated, but all had to be U.S. citizens.

Although the level of direct federal involvement was greater under the WPA than it had been when the FERA was the leading relief agency, local influence remained strong in both administration and financial provision. Indeed, the WPA has to be seen as a federal, state, and local partnership. For example, it was the local relief agency which assessed each applicant and decided on eligibility for WPA employment. If an applicant was considered eligible, the unemployed needy worker was referred to the WPA, which was empowered to accept or reject referrals. The selection, the planning, and the operation of projects, most of which were initiated by counties, or towns, or state agencies like highway departments, closely involved the localities. Moreover, the hope was that as sponsors shared in the cost they would have a vested interest in each project as it moved from the planning stage toward successful completion. Before January 1, 1940, there was no rule stipulating exactly how much sponsors should contribute. However, from that date Congress ruled that the aggregate contribution of all sponsors in any state must be at least 25 percent of the cost all projects. One serious disadvantage of this ruling was that it penalized

poor localities where the sponsors could not afford to make such a substantial contribution.[6] The vast majority of WPA projects were local, and more than 80 percent involved some sort of construction work with the building or repair of highways, streets, and public buildings to the fore.

Congress again wrestled with the problem of constructing a work relief wage structure that was sufficiently high to boost the morale of those employed and which would also inject purchasing power into the still-depressed economy. At the same time, there was a clear view among policy makers that remuneration should not dull the incentive to move to private sector jobs when they became available. Nor should payment be so generous that the employment of the maximum number of those eligible was compromised. After debating these sometimes contradictory aims, Congress introduced a monthly "security wage," paid biweekly in cash, which, like the PWA, took into account occupational and regional variations. The result was a monthly wage schedule that ranged from $19 for an unskilled laborer living in the southern states, to $94 paid to workers with technical or professional skills who lived in the high-cost urban areas in the north and west regions.[7]

John Stutz under Fire

In all states the new post of WPA State Director was seen as a position of great importance, and in Kansas many leading Democrats were determined that this key appointment should not be given to John G. Stutz. No doubt Kansas Democrats cast envious eyes across the Missouri river to Boss Tom Pendergast's Kansas City. There, the seamless political unity between the relief administration and City Hall seemed to have created an extraordinarily favorable situation where New Deal largesse could be maximized and much political credit gained.[8] In March 1935, Kansas Democratic representatives in Congress called on Harry Hopkins, who was responsible for selecting all WPA state directors, and requested that Stutz be removed from his FERA post for showing political favoritism to Republicans. They also placed before him the names of some local Democrats whom they supported for the new key WPA directorship.[9] In the

6. Ibid. 148–49.
7. The wage issue is thoroughly covered in ibid., passim; see also, Arthur E. Burns and P. Kerr, "Survey of Work-Relief Wage Policies," 711–24; Arthur E. Burns and P. Kerr, "Recent Changes in Work Relief Wage Policy," 56–66.
8. Lyle W. Dorsett, "Kansas City and the New Deal," 410–15.
9. *Wichita Beacon*, March 13, 1935.

past Hopkins had always defended Stutz against these sorts of attacks because he had such a high regard for the Kansas man's professional excellence. Indeed, press reports in Kansas stressed the confidence that Hopkins had in Stutz; a confidence so firm that there was a widespread conviction that Stutz was safe.[10] However, the 1935 campaign to get rid of John Stutz differed from previous attempts in that it was both sustained and it involved political heavyweights. While minor county figures could be ignored, their seniors could more easily put effective pressure on Washington decision makers.

In late May the press reported that local Democrats had chosen Omar Ketchum, a former mayor of Topeka and defeated candidate in the 1934 gubernatorial contest, as their candidate for the WPA post.[11] One of Ketchum's most ardent advocates was Senator George McGill, whose denunciation of Stutz as an official who played politics with relief and who favored Republican job seekers proved powerful.[12] But McGill's attack on Stutz for political impropriety, while at the same time advancing the cause of an active Democrat to head the WPA, lacked credibility. Ketchum soon withdrew his candidacy when Hopkins informed him that he was too prominent in Kansas politics to be considered.[13] This left Evan Griffith, a thirty-seven-year-old lumberman from Manhattan, the state's re-employment director, as the most favored Democrat nominee.[14] On June 1, Hopkins nominated Griffith as Kansas Works Progress Administrator. The press was quick to point out that one significant result of this struggle to influence Hopkins was that Guy T. Helvering, formerly Democratic state chairman and at the time U.S. Internal Revenue commissioner, had emerged as the chief dispenser of Kansas national political patronage.[15] He had been the most vigorous prosecutor of Griffith's case and had persuaded Hopkins to dump Stutz and appoint his man. Indeed, Helvering's position was succinctly put when he was quoted in the press: "[T]he key positions in this project in Kansas will go to men in sympathy with the administration and the works program."[16] Governor Alf Landon's denunciation of the appointment of Griffith as injecting partisan politics into relief was predictable, but he also took the opportunity to express his great

10. *Kansas City Star,* March 18, May 22, 1935; *Topeka State Journal,* March 20, 1935; *Wichita Beacon,* March 20, 1935.

11. *Topeka Daily Capital,* May 25, 1935.

12. *Wichita Sunday Eagle,* May 26, 1935.

13. *Topeka State Journal,* May 30, 1935.

14. Evan Griffith, a World War I Veteran and graduate of Kansas State College, had been elected mayor of Manhattan in 1931.

15. *Topeka Daily Capital,* June 1, 1935.

16. *Abilene Daily Chronicle,* July 6, 1935.

regret that someone with such an impressive track record as Stutz must, after September 5, confine himself almost entirely to the supervision of direct relief.[17]

Kansas Democrats were overjoyed. Their firm belief was that key positions in the new work relief program should be filled with officials who were supporters of their party, the national administration, and the New Deal. They rejoiced too in the knowledge that Stutz, who in the past had extracted himself from so many tight spots, now had his influence considerably reduced. Moreover, as one of the first tasks facing Evan Griffith was the appointment of six district WPA directors, Kansas Democrats were highly relieved that their lobbying had proved effective. These posts could now be offered to Democrat sympathizers who would be totally supportive in the run-up to the 1936 election.

An examination of the national picture shows that the state emergency relief administrator continued as head of the WPA in fourteen states. This had the advantage of maintaining continuity, but it could not, of course, guarantee excellence. In the vast majority of these cases the relief administrator was acceptable to the local Democrat political elite, and it was politics that served as the litmus test rather than talent. There can be no doubt that political intervention not only prevented some good appointments, but also permitted many poor ones. Stutz's failure to head the WPA in Kansas can be explained entirely by his past Republican sympathies and the fear that his political affiliation, though not official, was never fully subdued. Hopkins knew Stutz personally and was fully aware of his administrative and personal qualities, as were members of his staff who had always been full of praise for Stutz's professional integrity. A better man did not oust Stutz; many informed neutral observers held the view that he was beaten by a candidate whose main advantage was a location in the right political camp. FERA Regional Field Representative Harry J. Early wrote to Aubrey Williams expressing regret at the departure of a man who had done an excellent job and would now not be "able to render this administration a service which it needs."[18] It is also interesting to note that the authors of an authoritative independent study of work relief during this period were full of praise for Stutz's qualities and less than complimentary about his successor.[19] That such a dispassionate and highly regarded analysis should single out this incident for comment gives fur-

17. *Kansas City Journal-Post,* June 2, 1935; *Topeka State Journal,* August 9, 1935.

18. Earley to Williams, June 21, 1936, FERA State Files 1933–36, KS 406.1, RG69, NA.

19. Arthur W. MacMahon, John D. Millett, and Gladys Ogden, *The Administration of Federal Work Relief,* 273.

ther support for the view, if it were needed, that Stutz had lost a political battle.

The Contraction of the Kansas Emergency Relief Committee

The changes imposed by the introduction of the WPA had the effect, in Kansas, of dismembering a state welfare system that was extraordinarily stable and held in national high regard. Since early 1933, the core of Kansas's relief organization had been the unification of all public welfare service in a single county agency. As a result, Boards of County Commissioners, which had a statutory responsibility for relief of the destitute, were already using county funds to take care of unemployables, and they were also responsible for federally funded work relief. It should be remembered that Kansas never used federal funds for assisting unemployables; all federal money was directed toward work relief. In Kansas, poor commissioners were expected to be both professionally qualified and highly experienced, a combination of qualities that should have ensured smooth change to a new structure. The emphasis that Kansas officials had placed on work relief enabled county relief administrations to submit to the WPA for approval carefully constructed work programs that had been prepared and run by effective state and county engineering departments. Good organization enabled the KERC to provide the USES and the WPA with the necessary occupational classification of nearly eighty thousand males and females from the relief rolls. The long-standing aims of the KERC had included an emphasis on rehabilitation rather than emergency relief, a recognition that training was essential for those involved in relief work, and a stress on work relief for those capable of labor. Although the structure that the KERC imposed was not without its flaws, compared with the majority of states it had significant strengths. Could this organization be restructured in a way that would ensure that these considerable strengths were retained? Would the new structure be a material improvement on that which it replaced? Could the KERC and the WPA work effectively together during the period of transition, or would Stutz and Griffith be engaged in bitter conflict?

The FERA instructed the KERC to terminate its work program on September 5, and by the end of 1935 many of these work projects were operating under the aegis of the WPA. Although the WPA was now responsible for the employable unemployed, the state administration still investigated each applicant for relief and sent those who met the criteria to the WPA. A continuing source of resentment on the part of the KERC

was that the WPA did not contribute to the cost of certifying those assigned to it; neither, in fact, did the RA, the FSA, or the NYA. The cost of certification for relief in Kansas was estimated at $10–$12 for each new case and $6.50 for a reopened case.[20]

Another irritation, though not one confined to Kansas, was the imprecision surrounding the term *unemployable.* The word was never clearly defined by the WPA, whose officials had the responsibility of determining who among those referred to it was employable. This was an important issue because any definition that maximized the number of "unemployables" had serious implications for the counties' case load. The Kansas claim was that before the introduction of the WPA, the state had a diversified work relief program, one aim of which was to employ a variety of people, including the physically unfit. In other words work relief projects had been constructed with the needs of the caseload in mind. However, the reality of WPA recruitment was that the project took priority, not the caseload; as a result, employment was not available for many who fell below a high standard of physical fitness.[21]

These problems were articulated clearly by the Labette County poor commissioner in a letter to his WPA district administrator. The administrator had threatened to purge the WPA in his region of men he described as "unemployables" because of an unacceptable number of accidents and compensation claims. The poor commissioner made the point that WPA foremen had discharged some men with disabilities on the grounds that they were "unemployable" when in reality they had been thoughtlessly allocated the wrong sort of job. Older workers or those with disabilities could be given suitable tasks, for example, working as flagmen, but this required not only careful planning on the part of foremen but also a willingness on the part of project planners to accept responsibility for those who were willing to work but who were not fully fit.[22] The WPA in Kansas did not accept that help for the less able worker was part of its mission.

Once the WPA was given the responsibility for work relief, it was clear that the KERC would need to reduce staffing levels. By early September, approximately 20 percent of all KERC personnel, including 22 percent of social workers, had been released. A month later the reduction was greater than 40 percent. As caseloads were now significantly reduced, the positions of poor commissioner and case supervisor were combined in the

20. *KERC Bulletin* 355, January 1936, 277–78.
21. Ibid., 275.
22. Walter C. White, Poor Commissioner Labette Co., to Ben S. Hudson, January 24 1936, Stutz Papers, 327:1:6.

95 smallest counties, an amalgamation that produced a marked saving in administrative expenses.[23] The early staffing reductions were undertaken within an atmosphere of uncertainty, as KERC officials were not convinced that the WPA would be able to take over its full responsibilities to the unemployed immediately as it planned. A serious drought in July and August had caused an ominous increase in the relief load, which seemed unlikely to diminish during the following month. In addition, the publicity surrounding the WPA had aroused a high level of public expectation, and, as with any new relief initiative, there was bound to be a rush of early applications, all of which had to be investigated. A real possibility existed that a reduced number of staff would have to cope with an unreasonably large number of clients. This was also a time of acute personal unease for many care workers who were worried about their own positions, as were clerks, stenographers, and others who believed that they would be adversely affected by the new structure.[24]

The WPA in Operation

When the KERC cut staffing levels, quality and commitment had priority in choosing who would remain. However, KERC officials who were concerned that the shift of work relief responsibilities to the WPA could not be done entirely smoothly soon had their worries confirmed. The WPA was able neither to transfer sufficient KERC work projects quickly enough nor to create enough of its own, to cope with all the able-bodied unemployed. Both Griffith and Stutz appealed to Washington for federal funds to continue work relief after September 5 under the supervision of the KERC, but to no avail. Direct relief was essential to those who had been unable to secure WPA jobs, and that reliance remained until December, by which time the WPA had absorbed its quota of workers. Dole recipients were apprehensive as severe hardship threatened, especially for

23. *KERC Bulletin* 355, 511–12. The supplementation of salaries for poor commissioners and county case supervisors was limited to counties with heavy caseloads: Cherokee, Crawford, Cowley, Labette, Leavenworth, Montgomery, Reno, Sedgwick, Shawnee, and Wyandotte. In all the remaining counties the poor commissioner had also to be qualified as a county case supervisor, thus combining both positions. The county had to pay a monthly salary of up to $125 for the combined office. All counties had to maintain a qualified relief administration, including a properly qualified county case supervisor with sufficient assistants. *KERC Bulletin* 277, October 3, 1935, 1–2.

24. Charles Z. Gillam to John Stutz, Minutes of Supervisors Meeting—KERC, August 17, 1935, Stutz Papers, 327:2:15; Edna Swingle to H. Marvin, Report on Shawnee Co, KERC, August 16, 1935, Stutz Papers, 327:2:15.

families who had to equip their children for the new school year.[25] Even at the very end of 1935 the KERC found itself overburdened, as the new WPA agency had not been able to provide jobs for all eligible unemployed. Large numbers of relief clients had been certified for WPA work but were unassigned. In Wyandotte County approximately twenty-five hundred unfortunates were in this position; in Sedgwick County, one thousand; in Crawford County, eight hundred; and in Shawnee County, nine hundred.[26] A more detailed analysis of the figures demonstrates clearly how considerable numbers of employables continued to be a direct relief charge. On December 31, 1935, the number of employable cases in receipt of public assistance reached 17,311. This gross figure can be disaggregated in the following way: 11,666 employables had been certified but not assigned to the WPA; 1,398 had been assigned but had not yet received their WPA checks; and 1,158 were employed on WPA or other public projects but were receiving supplementary relief as their wages were judged insufficient to care for their families. That left 2,405 who were not eligible for WPA certification as their cases had been cleared after November; there were also 877 rural clients whose cases were being considered by the RA and, finally, 307 WPA employees who were receiving general relief as they were temporarily disabled.[27] In the early weeks of the WPA, Stutz, in response to a query from Frank Bane, director of the American Welfare Association, had stated that Kansas would be able to assist its unemployables, but, if it had to make provision for an appreciable number of employables, the state would be subject to financial strain from November 1935.[28] This concern became a reality. Because of inadequate funding, the WPA was never able to take care of all needy employable cases, and as a result, many Americans were unable to avoid the shame of dole payments. In a desperate attempt to avoid a looming problem, the KERC advised counties that if they had more able-bodied unemployed than their WPA quota, they should ask for it to be increased.[29] Several pursued this course but with negligible success.

In 1936 this strain continued though it was marginally reduced by the announcement, in January, of three thousand additional WPA jobs.[30] However, during the calendar year 1936, the counties spent $474,000 on

25. *Topeka Daily Capital,* August 21, 1935; *Topeka State Journal,* August 26, 1935.

26. *Topeka Daily Capital,* December 31, 1935.

27. *KERC Bulletin* 355, 272, 274.

28. Frank Bane to Stutz, October 1, 1935; Stutz to Bane, October 4, 1935, Stutz Papers, 327:1:5.

29. *KERC Bulletin* 304, December 25, 1935, 1–2.

30. *Topeka Daily Capital,* January 18, 1936.

locally funded work relief projects and $1.2 million on direct relief to families and single individuals who had been classified as employable and therefore eligible for WPA work. The allocation of direct relief to assist employables represented a not-inconsiderable 22 percent of total local public relief expenditure. In every month throughout 1936, the employable caseload receiving assistance from county funds was greater than the unemployable. Many of the employables had been certified but not assigned to the WPA; others who were assigned to the WPA, or the RA, had to receive supplementary county funds because their federal payments were judged inadequate.[31]

During each month of 1936, county relief administrations assisted an average of 10,240 employables who had been certified to the WPA; the RA monthly average was 6,392. Moreover, under the unified system, relief was given in every Kansas County on the basis of assessed need, with no constitutional or statutory limitations as to kind or amounts.[32] For example, WPA and RA clients were entitled to claim supplementary help when their remuneration was deemed inadequate, as it had been in 1934 for some CWA employees. However, the consequence of this relatively generous public assistance provision was a considerable and unanticipated burden for the counties, all of which had to operate within an agreed relief budget. As a result of WPA supplementation, other direct relief clients had to accept less than their budgets indicated they needed to maintain an adequate standard of living. County expenditure was also inflated by the demands of sponsorship for WPA projects.

The crucial point is that the WPA did not eradicate dole payments. In 1936 the total amount spent on locally funded public relief in Kansas was $3.1 million; of this, $1.6 million was allocated to unemployables and $1.5 million to employables who were not supposed to be a local responsibility. Fortunately for men and women who were forced onto the county relief rolls by inadequate WPA funding, direct relief in Kansas was administered more generously than in the vast majority of states. Especially fortunate were single employables who were never excluded from county assistance in Kansas, as they were in many other states, on the grounds that they should secure work for themselves. All applicants who met the residence requirements, and where investigation showed a need for relief, were considered for it. If federal support was not available, state law obliged the counties to provide for the destitute, though for the hardest

31. Supplementation payments varied widely across the country. In some states all relief was denied to employables. Howard, *WPA and Federal Relief Policy,* 168–71.
32. *KERC Bulletin* 380, 30–32. All the figures for 1936 are from this source.

pressed that assistance fell short of the minimum required for comfort. However, while the supplementation of inadequate WPA wages was praiseworthy from a social work viewpoint, it may have persuaded recipients that work relief was preferable to private sector employment, thus thwarting one of the key principles of the WPA.

In spite of all the difficulties outlined above, average relief payments from county funds became more generous in 1936. The yearly average amount of work and direct relief per family rose from $100.20 in 1935 to $162.48 a year later. On average, unemployables received more than employables because the former were less capable of caring for themselves. During 1935, there were 83,097 applications for public assistance, of which 33 percent were rejected. In 1936 there were 94,074 applications, and 24 percent of these were rejected after investigation by social workers who, during the course of their enquiries, made approximately 282,000 home visits and conducted 415,000 office interviews. The largest monthly caseload in 1935 (43,399) occurred in September, when the seasonal flow of farm labor returned to the relief rolls, while the lowest case load (35,216) occurred in July, showing the influence of agricultural employment in Kansas. During the course of 1936, an average of 5,278 cases each month were closed when it became clear that clients had become self-supporting and public assistance was no longer necessary.

Work Relief and the Wage Problem

A significant departure from FERA practice was the WPA's abandonment of the budgetary deficiency method of calculating work relief wages. The budgetary deficiency principle had led to serious inefficiencies on work relief projects, since workers had to be employed for different times in order to make up their varied budgets. The turnover of the workforce, together with its complex work schedules, led to formidable management problems and, in the end, to operational inefficiency. Furthermore, the frequent investigations required by social workers to determine the number of hours to be worked in order to achieve the appropriate budget were costly. The WPA wage—popularly known as the "security wage"—was not based on the needs of the recipient, nor on family size, nor on the number of dependents. Like private sector or CWA remuneration, individual circumstances were not taken into account when deciding the level of pay.

One advantage of this new approach was an end to the costly and exhaustive social inquiries that determined the budgetary deficiency wage

and the resentment that many felt at these intrusive investigations. However, Congress frequently changed the WPA wage structure, and the confusion that often resulted was a spur to relief-worker unrest. For example, when the WPA commenced in May 1935, all states were grouped into four regions (reduced to three in June) for the purposes of wage determination, with Kansas placed in region two. Region one had the highest cost of living and was therefore entitled to pay the highest wages, while region four had the lowest cost of living and pay. There were, however, further complex determinants to the calculation of pay. Monthly earnings for each WPA employee depended not just on the region but also on the degree of urbanization in each county (there were five bands), and on the level of skill required for each job (there were four levels). There were also minimum (120) and maximum (140) hours of work per month. Although hours formed part of the overall employment package, the president specifically ordered that work relief pay should not be expressed as an hourly rate. He believed that hourly rates could give an illusion of inadequate pay and were not as significant as the flow of income from continuous earning.[33]

If two Kansas counties are used as examples, the early WPA wage model becomes less mystifying. Shawnee County fell into the second band of urbanization, because in 1930 Topeka had a population of between 50,000 and 99,999. WPA rules stipulated that an unskilled worker, the lowest paid, would receive a monthly security wage of $42. Workers in the highest paid group—professional and technical employees—could expect $73 each month. On the other hand, Galena, the largest municipality in Cherokee County, had 4,736 inhabitants, so WPA workers received monthly security wages applicable to counties where the largest municipality was under 5,000 residents. As a result workers in the highest paid group received $48 and the lowest $32.[34] The lowest monthly security wage was supposed to represent a subsistence standard of living for the region, to which were added differentials representing levels of skill. However, men and women engaged in identical tasks, perhaps working only a short distance apart but with significant pay differentials determined by location, were bound to be discontented once they became aware of the differentials. Moreover, because high levels of urbanization were associated with higher work relief pay, many destitute families migrated to Shawnee, Sedgwick, and Wyandotte counties and eventually became eligible for relief.[35]

33. MacMahon, Millett and Ogden, *Administration of Federal Work Relief*, 151.
34. Howard, *WPA and Federal Relief Policy*, 860–62.
35. *Topeka Journal*, November 12, 1937.

Choosing an appropriate work relief wage structure was a persistent New Deal problem, and the WPA was no exception. Mindful of the practical problems facing WPA administrators, politicians sensibly opted for a model that simplified the complexities of real life. However, in doing so they created a new set of difficulties that, it seemed, could only be corrected by further legislation. Changes in the classification of counties, regions, and wage rates sometimes won a short-term political victory for those who had advocated them, but such alterations also led to confusion and even conflict. Congressional redefinitions could convince malcontents that vigorous agitation might result in beneficial change for the group that they represented.

One early problem sprang from the president's disingenuous insistence that WPA wages were not to be expressed as an hourly rate when it was natural for all to make that calculation. A vigorous correspondence conducted by E. W. Latchem, secretary of the Building Trades Council located in Coffeyville, Montgomery County, illustrates the concern of organized labor, and even the unemployed, with early WPA wage policies. Latchem, after some basic calculations, pointed out that the hourly rate of unskilled WPA workers was not only below the local union prevailing rate, but also less than the rates paid under the CWA and the PWA. Moreover, he claimed that men with large families would earn less under the WPA than they had under the FERA and would be unable to supplement their income with odd jobs because of the full-time commitment the WPA demanded. There was no doubt in the minds of the workers he represented that the low hourly WPA rates would drag down wages in the private sector. Indeed, some detected in the WPA a conspiracy to deliberately reduce all wages. A suggested solution was a reduction in the hours required to earn the "security wage," and Latchem was convinced that the state had the freedom to make this downward adjustment.

Organized labor was not mollified by the arguments advanced by either local WPA man Ben Hudson or Nels Anderson, director of the Labor Relations Section of the WPA. Both countered that WPA work was not permanent and therefore could not be compared directly to private sector jobs; moreover, WPA pay was not calculated according to a prevailing local wage rate and higher rates for work relief inevitably would lead to fewer positions for project workers. In May 1936, Latchem declared that the Hodcarriers and Building Laborers Local 193 and Teamsters and Chauffuers (*sic*) Local 535 had called on relief workers who were employed on Federal Highway 166 to strike.[36] This is an excellent example

36. Hudson to Latchem, August 9; Latchem to Griffith, August 17; Latchem to Whar-

of one of many pockets of discontent caused by some real and some imagined issues relating to WPA wages. It was pursued with particular vigor
because Coffeyville was a center of organized labor activities in Kansas.
However, while relief workers and organized labor were agitating for
higher pay, Evan Griffith, the State Works Progress Administrator, was ad-
vocating lower wages and a higher WPA quota.[37] His reasoning struck a
chord in Washington.

The public did not have long to wait for the first radical change in WPA
wage policy. The existing wage structure was under constant attack, and
it was soon subject to a series of minor modifications by the WPA on some
of its own projects. More significantly, the Emergency Relief and Appropriations Act (1936) retained WPA pay differentials based on skill, location, and the extent of urbanization, but the act stipulated that payment
should not be less than the prevailing hourly rates for private work of a
similar nature. Organized labor gave its strong support to this new policy, believing that WPA rates would no longer exercise a depressing effect
on their members' pay. WPA earnings, however, were still determined by
the published schedule of monthly payments. The result was that, like the
FERA "budget deficiency" payments, those employed on projects worked
different hours according to their skills to earn their "security wage."
Workers on higher hourly rates earned their wage faster than the lowly
paid, making the efficient management of projects difficult or virtually
impossible. In 1938 Congress made a further modification, altering the
minimum wage rate to make it consistent with the provisions of the Fair
Labor Standards Act. The effect of this legislation was marked in the
southern states, but it had no significant impact on Kansas.

Congress recognized the administrative difficulties that project managers faced in the implementation of this wage structure, but their collective concern was roused by the stories of highly paid skilled WPA workers exploiting the advantage of the few hours they were employed each
month by taking additional private jobs, sometimes at lower than WPA
rates. Congress had never satisfactorily defined what it meant by the prevailing wage. Was this always the union rate, or simply the wage that was
paid locally, which could be less? WPA officials abandoned an attempt to

---

ton, September 9; Latchem to Hopkins, September 9; Latchem to Griffith, September
9; Anderson to Latchem, September 24; Latchem to Griffith October 26; Latchem to
Williams (AFL Washington, D.C.) October 27, all 1935; Latchem to List&Clark (Con-
tractors), May 14; Latchem to Hudson, May 23; Latchem to Wardens, May 23, all 1936.
WPA Central Files, Kansas 641, Coffeyville, Box 1344, RG69, NA.

37. Griffith to Nels Anderson, March 13, 1936, FERA Central Files, Kansas 641, Box
1344, RG69, NA.

produce a schedule of prevailing wages when they discovered that at least twenty-two federal agencies running projects had set their own highly varied prevailing wage rates. It was decided that this task was best left to WPA state offices.[38] The inevitable result was a variety of local rates, as can be seen by using a single county as an example. In Sedgwick County during the spring of 1937, the standard hourly rate for unskilled manual workers working 120 hours each month was 41 cents; for intermediate workers, 53 cents; and for the skilled, 66 cents. The monthly earnings for workers in each of these categories were $49.20 for the unskilled, $63.60 for the intermediate, and $79.20 for the skilled. However, skilled workers were divided into different categories and paid different rates. The result was that brick layers on projects in Sedgwick County worked 70 hours at an hourly rate of $1.13, while electricians worked 79 hours at $1.00 per hour, painters 105 hours at 7 cents, and plumbers 88 hours at 90 cents to earn their monthly security wage. There were also separate hourly rates for nonmanual workers of varying skills, for professionals, for foremen and timekeepers, and for the owner-operators of teams, trucks, and equipment.[39] Project managers everywhere faced formidable difficulties in keeping all groups of workers fully employed and their projects brought efficiently towards completion.

The Emergency Relief Appropriations Act of 1939 cut short the wage debate by abolishing the prevailing wage rate policy and reverting to a standard working month of 130 hours for all. The act also ruled that no one was to work longer than eight hours per day, or forty hours per week. Regional and skill differentials were retained, but the former was to be based solely on cost-of-living differences.[40] Initially the imposition of the 130-hour rule led to some isolated protests in Kansas. In early July 1939 all nine WPA construction projects in Crawford County, employing nearly sixteen hundred people, had ceased operation, as had two in Cherokee and one each in Butler and Greenwood counties. Within a week, however, all resistance had crumbled, and fewer than twenty-five men had their employment contracts terminated because they had been absent from work for more than five days.[41] In September, Clarence Nevins was able to respond to a questionnaire from Col. F.C. Harrington, who had re-

38. MacMahon, Millett, and Ogden, *Administration of Federal Work Relief*, 156.

39. "Regulations Relating to Monthly Earnings, Rates of Pay, Hours of Work and Conditions of Employment on Force Account Projects," WPA, State Administrator's Order No. 52, April 16, 1937, FERA Central Files, Box 1353, RG69, NA.

40. Burns and Kerr, "Recent Changes in Work Relief Wage Policy," 58–61.

41. Nevins to Fred R. Rauch, July 7; Nevins to Rauch, July 10; John E. Brink to C. Gill, July 12; Nevins to Rauch, July 17, all 1939. All in WPA Central Files, 1935–44, Kansas 640, Box 1344, RG69, NA.

placed Hopkins as WPA Administrator, that the 130-hour rule had improved efficiency on projects and that worker reaction was favorable.[42] In 1941 Congress, not surprisingly, exempted WPA workers employed on defense contracts, or other emergency work, from the restriction of maximum working hours.

Legislators intended to make WPA pay more generous than that given by the work relief agencies that preceded it, but less rewarding than pay for comparable work in the private sector. Because Congress was anxious to avoid the accusation that the WPA was hoarding labor, all project workers were obliged to maintain an active registration with a public employment agency designated by the USES, in this case the Kansas State Employment Service, so that a move to private employment could easily be facilitated. However, it was possible for workers employed continuously on WPA projects to have a lower weekly wage than a private sector worker but a higher income over a longer period as a result of continuous employment.[43] A congressional majority was opposed to continuous WPA employment and also supportive of a rotation of jobs among the eligible unemployed. They were able to ensure, through the Emergency Relief Appropriations Act (1939), that workers who had been employed on WPA jobs for eighteen months or more would be dismissed and could not be re-employed for thirty days.[44] Unfortunately, many WPA workers found that having been removed from their jobs under this rule they could not be immediately reassigned later because their county's quota was full.[45] This legislation, from which veterans were exempt, was not modified until the Emergency Relief Appropriations Act (1942).

Movements in either wage rates or monthly pay were of little significance to the many men and women who were eligible for WPA employment but unable to secure one of these prized positions. Congressional funding—guided on the one hand by information on the number of families with an employable member on relief, and on the other by a need to restrict spending in order to curb the deficit in the federal budget—largely determined the WPA funding in each state. However, there had been a serious misjudgment in calculating the number of potential WPA workers, and even at their most munificent, allocations were never sufficient to provide work relief jobs for all those qualified to hold them. These able-

42. Nevins to Harrington, September 20, 1939, ibid.
43. Howard, *WPA and Federal Relief Policy*, 165–67.
44. Ibid., 515–27.
45. As was the case in Douglas County. E. T. Black, Board of County Commissioners, Douglas County, to Capper, October 21, 1939, FERA State Files, Kansas 641, File C-D, 1940, RG69, NA.

bodied, together with others in need who were disqualified from WPA jobs for a variety of reasons, became general relief cases. In other words, in spite of Roosevelt's expressed dislike of dole, direct relief for the able-bodied was still an essential part of America's fight against the depression. This was especially true during the serious recession of 1937–38, when unemployment and farm misery rose with unexpected rapidity at a time when WPA funding was being reduced. Although Roosevelt responded to this economic crisis with an increase in welfare spending, the ability of the able-bodied to obtain satisfactory general relief was crucial in the battle against deprivation in Kansas.

In Cherokee County, WPA wages were low and private sector jobs were scarce. The county struggled to take care of its unemployables in the face of a shrinking tax base and the impositions placed upon it by the Cash Basis Law, but the cost of caring for those who had been assigned to the WPA but had not succeeded in securing a place on any project was a crushing additional burden. Moreover, when social investigation demonstrated that WPA pay was insufficient to take care of a large family, desperately poor counties found it impossible to fully supplement the deficiency. The reaction of officials in Cherokee County, and in other hard-pressed counties, too, was to appeal against any cut in WPA places and to ask for higher work relief wages. Sometimes they pursued both options simultaneously, though usually without success.

In April 1936, for example, Senator Arthur Capper supported the objection of Cherokee County commissioners to a reduction in WPA employment because they knew that the result would be a rise in the demand for direct relief. Their plea fell on stony ground, as did repeated requests to move Kansas into the geographical group with the highest wage rate. A Washington official patiently explained that a contraction in congressional funding was responsible for a fall in WPA employment in all states. More optimistic than the county commissioners, he claimed that as the weather improved, the PWA, the Bureau of Public Roads, and other federal agencies would employ large numbers of idle men. He also anticipated that the current business expansion would continue, thus creating many more jobs.[46] In October 1937, Cherokee County commissioners, and those of its equally deprived neighbor, Crawford County, once again requested more WPA jobs as both faced the serious possibility of being unable to provide adequate relief during the winter months.[47] Not long

46. Capper to Hopkins, April 10, 1936; Westbrook to Capper, April 14, 1936, FERA State Files, Kansas 641, File C-D, 1940, RG69, NA.

47. Long to Hopkins, October 22, 1937, FERA State Files, Kansas 641, File C-D, 1940, RG69, NA.

afterward the Crawford County Commissioners stated publicly that funds were so short that some legitimate relief cases had been rejected, and others had been restricted to an allowance that represented only 20 percent of each family's minimum needs. The county could raise no more funds for poor relief as it had reached the limit of its bonded indebtedness and claimed that a major cause of its difficulty was in caring for nearly one thousand families over the previous eighteen months, a number of whose heads had been assigned to the WPA but had never been employed. Moreover, a shortage of caseworkers meant that families had to wait several weeks before a judgment on their eligibility could be given.[48] This is a further illustration of the limitations of the Kansas welfare model that thrust responsibilities onto counties that did not have the resources to cope with increasing hardship.

The experiences of employables who were eligible for WPA work differed significantly between counties. Practically all WPA-operated projects required initiation and sponsorship by state and local public agencies. Some, but not all, counties responded to the challenge by creating excellent projects, which provided useful work and an outcome of clear public benefit. Another important prerequisite for WPA approval was that a share of the costs, especially the nonlabor costs, was borne by the sponsor. Securing sufficient WPA work relief depended very heavily on the enthusiasm, energy, imagination, and wealth of local sponsors. Failure to generate successful projects inevitably limited the number of WPA jobs available. When a local financial crisis occurred, the number of WPA placements was restricted, as was the ability of counties to supplement an inadequate "security wage." For poorer counties the unpredictable fluctuations in WPA funding and the difficulty in financing projects often led to insurmountable problems in caring for their destitute.

The WPA and the Farmer

In the summer of 1935 a survey of seventeen northwest counties revealed a widespread, but not universal, disquiet concerning New Deal relief policies. Farmers in particular resented what they saw as generous relief payments, which exerted an inflationary pressure on farm wages, causing them to rise to punitive levels for hirers. The same men often dismissed the various New Deal welfare initiatives contemptuously, as both

48. Crawford County Board of County Commissioners, March 8, 1937, FERA State Files, Kansas 641, File C-D, 1940, RG69, NA.

too easily obtained and also as a typical response from city politicians who were keen to spend taxpayers' money in order to buy themselves popularity.[49] The widespread acceptance of policies that were viewed as pauperizing was seen as further evidence that the present population lacked the steely resolve of their forebears.[50] Although many farmers throughout the state would have agreed with these sentiments, there were exceptions. One of the surveyed counties, which expressed a favorable view of relief policies, was itself petitioning for assistance a few weeks later. Rooks County was badly affected by drought, which had destroyed crops, raised the price of feed, and scorched gardens, the fruits of which were supposed to support families through the winter. There were very few employment opportunities either on the farm or off it. In May 1935, 272 farm families in need of assistance had, in line with national policy, been transferred from work relief to the Homestead Rehabilitation Program and consequently dropped from the relief rolls. The result was a mixed blessing, as several of these families were forced further into debt at a time when the future of farming seemed particularly bleak. Some despairing operators abandoned farming and moved to nearby towns or villages; they, and also others who remained behind, petitioned relief officers for assistance.[51]

Could the WPA assist farmers in distress? Several states opposed employing farmers on WPA projects, believing that there were already a number of other programs available to help them. At the very least it seemed prudent to ensure that farmers had exhausted all possible alternatives before turning to the WPA, especially as grant or loan agencies had been specifically developed to help farmers stay on the land where they would not compete for scarce work relief jobs. It was widely recognized that one of the main reasons for migration from the open country to villages or towns was a desire to be near a relief agency.[52] However, a great obstacle to farmer participation in the WPA was that it was difficult to classify operators as needy unemployed. Apart from exceptional cir-

49. A. D. Edwards, *Influence of Drought and Depression on a Rural Community: A Case Study of Haskell County, Kansas,* 96.

50. An Index to Social and Economic Conditions in New Kansas District 5, June 1, 1935, Stutz Papers, 327:2:10.

51. Board of County Commissioners, Rooks County, to A. Capper, July 30, 1935, FERA State Files, 1933–38; Kansas Official File, June–September 1935, RG69, NA.

52. In Barber County, for example, migration was traced to several causes: the continuing drought, a tendency for land owners to farm the land themselves rather than rent, and the desire to be near the relief agency. Rural Relief Studies, Bureau of Agricultural Economics, "Survey of Current Changes in the Rural Relief Population," June 7, 1935, RG83, NA.

cumstances there is always work to be had on a farm, and the WPA was created for the jobless; few would have seen the farmer in the same light as the unemployed nonfarm worker.[53]

These were, however, exceptional times. Drought-induced crop failures and the attendant dust storms had a devastating effect on the land, especially in the western part of the state. Wheat farmers, in particular, had high fixed costs and were vulnerable to prolonged adverse weather. As the drought worsened, more farmers applied to County Relief Offices where caseworkers referred them to the local Resettlement Office. Men rejected by the RA, or its successor, the FSA, as unsuitable for loans or grants were returned to the County Relief Office and then sent, via the poor commissioner, to the WPA if they were physically able to perform manual labor. Unfortunately, work relief was usually more difficult to organize in sparsely populated rural areas than it was in urban areas. A particular problem was that as the depression continued, the most obvious local construction projects had been completed, and further work relief for rural dwellers could involve lengthy and costly travel. One suggestion was to employ farmers on their own farms, as had occurred during the early days of rural rehabilitation. They could busy themselves repairing machinery, removing dust drifts, and be ready, if the rains ever came, to plant their crops. The reply from Washington was a firm rejection. WPA employees could only work on approved projects, which had to be sited on public, not private, land.[54] In Nemaha County the situation was so dire that the county commissioners were obliged to continue their own work program, financed by the poor fund, for men assigned to the WPA but unable to secure positions. There was also great concern in Decatur County, devastated by three successive crop failures, that two federal highway projects that were about to commence would be manned by WPA employees switched from their existing tasks rather than recruited from the army of able-bodied unemployed that was a growing charge on a county without the resources to care for them.[55] In July the county commissioners of Sherman and Graham counties reported burnt pastures, rapacious grasshoppers, and high living expenses. They called for government funds for

53. Howard, *WPA and Federal Relief Policy*, 502–10.

54. Resolution by Southwest Ks Highway Officials Association, August 31, 1936; J. C. Mahaffey (WPA) to Capper, September 12, 1936, FERA Central Files, File 201:33, Box 293, RG69, NA.

55. Edna Swingle to Esther E. Twente, Nemaha County, September 5 1936; RH Ms 327:3:21, Stutz Papers; Board of County Commissioners, Decatur County, to Hopkins, February 25, 1936, FERA Central Files, Kansas 641, Box 1344, RG69.

work projects and for substantial grants where it was not possible to get work relief underway.[56]

In the late summer of 1936 Washington offered Kansas, and the drought-affected region as a whole, a lifeline by creating 325,000 extra WPA jobs for farmers and farm laborers in the driest states. Past policy had emphasized rehabilitation grants, but Congress justified this U-turn by explaining that if the farmers did not get work relief they would be forced to accept demoralizing direct relief. It was a stark fact that the drought had created crisis conditions in parts of the Plains, but whether a lack of rain or the impending election was the catalyst for action is impossible to say. The recipients of this manna from Washington were not too concerned about motivation. They welcomed the initiative but expressed their concern that assistance would be available for only a few months. To qualify for a WPA drought assignment position, farmers and laborers had to be certified by the county relief administration as in need, to have been rejected by the Resettlement Administration, to live close to the work project, and to have sufficient time to complete the proposed tasks. The relief work made available was suitable for men only.[57]

Hastily concocted and hurriedly implemented, the drought relief policy soon led to tensions between local relief organizations and the WPA. To obtain the full credit for this initiative, and to implement local quotas before they were lost, WPA officials were anxious to assign these new jobs as quickly as possible, even if this meant dispensing with the usual meticulous social investigation of applicants. In Ellis, Geary, Riley, Pottawatomie, and Wabaunsee counties, for example, WPA officials informed the county commissioners that their poor commissioner could be bypassed, as the WPA was a work program, not a relief program. They asked that lists of farmers who were thought by the commissioners to be in need be sent to the WPA without delay. This was an opportunity both for patronage and for saving administrative costs, a combination which was irresistible to some local relief organizations. However, in counties where there was an effective and strong-willed poor commissioner, the county commissioners were told that it was illegal to dispense relief in Kansas without a full investigation of the circumstances of the applicant. Sometimes a visit from the state case supervisor could strengthen the professional resolve of a weak poor commissioner, or give additional support to

56. Capper to Hopkins, July 27, 1936; County Commissioners, Graham County, July 6, 1936, FERA Central Files, File 201:33, Box 293, RG69, NA

57. Circular from Estelle Childe (WPA, Topeka) to Poor Commissioners, County Managers of Reemployment Offices, Rural Resettlement Advisors, August 18, 1936, Stutz Papers, 327:3:21.

an effective official, as in Geary County where eventually a decision was made to appoint an additional caseworker to deal with the sudden influx of relief applications.

While some counties strictly observed the letter of the law, in others it was ignored. An unattributed critique, which bears the clear imprint of John Stutz, subjected the drought relief program to a scathing analysis. Kansas had a quota of just over five thousand drought relief farmers who had to be put to work on the WPA in a very short time. A number of the district WPA directors, according to this analysis, assigned unrealistic quotas to some of their counties and then put pressure on commissioners to fill these positions almost immediately. Marion County was given a quota of more than 100 but had so few relief farmers that county officials used men who could spare the time from their farms for WPA work though they were not in need of assistance. Smith County had a quota of 336, far in excess of its needs, while neighboring counties, where the drought was just as severe, were awarded only half this number. WPA and RA administrators criticized officials in Ellis and Saline counties for failing to solicit sufficient applicants to fill their allocated WPA places. In Finney County, WPA officials used lists of persons who might be expected to ask for relief during the winter of 1936–37 to assign men without them first being certified as in need of relief. Using the returns of the county relief administrations for 99 counties during the period August 1–21, this paper reports that only one-third of the federal quota of drought relief farmers were relief clients eligible for public assistance. Indeed, in some counties, men who had private sector jobs actually found their way onto WPA payrolls. It appears, therefore, that in a significant number of counties this program was a federal public works program in a drought area rather than public assistance to needy persons.[58]

Even though Stutz was unlikely to be enamored of a scheme that ignored the highly professional structure he had imposed on Kansas's welfare practice, it seems clear that the drought program was poorly planned. On the other hand, there was an emergency under way, and rapid action, which involved bypassing established bureaucratic procedures, could be considered not only excusable but necessary. As a political initiative the provision of additional WPA jobs was a success, but by all other criteria, it emerges flawed. The drought program was popular with participating

58. "Which Is It, a Drought *Relief* Program or a Federal *Public Works* Program in a Drought Area?" Stutz Papers, 327:3:23. This five-page critique is unsigned, but it is clearly the work of John Stutz, and it was produced in late 1936. The *Kansas City Star*, September 20, 1936, mentions the report and gives Stutz as its author. See also *KERC Bulletin* 363, September 10, 1936, 1–2.

farmers because WPA cash wages were considered much more generous than either RA grants or direct relief, and farmers' delight could be translated into votes in the November elections.[59] In any case, the farmers' gains were short-lived. In late November, much to their chagrin, Washington began to remove them from the WPA; on December 15 the Emergency Drought Program came to a close. Farmers whose prospects were considered sufficient for subsistence became the responsibility of the RA. However, operators who worked on the land but who would normally earn more than half of their income from nonagricultural employment were eligible for WPA work, as were farm laborers.[60]

As soon as the possibility of WPA participation was withdrawn, furious farmers petitioned their local and national political representatives, claiming that they needed work relief to provide an adequate standard of living for their families and to maintain what little livestock they had left. Moreover, many farmers were saddled with crippling debts worsened by the price falls in the worst years of the depression; they wanted paid work, not more debt.[61] Washington's response was to explain that the transfer of people receiving drought relief from the WPA to the RA was agreed national policy and was proceeding in an orderly manner. Officials maintained that sufficient funds had been made available to the RA to enable that agency to render the appropriate assistance. The clear message was that the RA, not the WPA, was in the best position to help farmers complete their long-term rehabilitation plans. However, to ease concerns, the RA made a minor concession to farmers who were badly affected by drought and unable to secure WPA employment, agreeing that they would not be subjected to a new investigation into their financial circumstances.

According to Washington, constructive help from the RA would provide the prerequisite for permanent rehabilitation in a drought area.[62] However, the fact that little had changed since August to ease the drought in Kansas gave additional ammunition to those who denounced the WPA drought program as a cynical political exercise. By that time, however, the election had been won. An indication of their continuing exasperation was provided by nearly three hundred Shawnee County farmers, who, as-

59. Howard, *WPA and Federal Relief Policy,* 510, 588.
60. *KERC Bulletin* 378, December 12, 1936, 1–2.
61. Petition, W. Pierson, President of Pottawatomie County Farmers Union, November 22, 1936; Wire, B. J. Sheridan, Editor and Chairman of County Democratic Committee, Paola, November 27, 1936; Congressman Frank Carlson to Hopkins, December 8, 1936; Senator McGill to Hopkins December 9, 1936; FERA Central Files, 1935–44, File 201:32, Box 292, RG69, NA.
62. A. Williams to McGill, December 11, 1936, FERA Central Files, File 201:32, RG69, NA.

sisted by the Kansas Allied Workers, a Topeka-based union for the unemployed, occupied the courthouse in January 1937, claiming that they
were not given the relief work to which they were entitled. Even this interesting and unusual combination of rural and urban protest came to
naught, and the farmers were told, after receiving their final WPA checks,
to contact the RA.[63]

In 1937 the drought was still serious in the western third of the state,
and destitute farmers continued to express their clear preference for WPA
work over grants or loans from other federal agencies.[64] However, the
previous difficulties remained: WPA quotas did not allow all unemployables to work, farmers often lived a long way from work projects, and because agricultural conditions would rapidly change if rains fell, cultivators needed to be able to return to their fields quickly. In some drought
counties, a small number of farmers were employed under a special quota, but the generous expansion of WPA jobs for farmers, which had occurred in 1936, never returned to the Plains. One effect of the drought was
that it reduced harvest work, though where such employment was available, some men were prepared to leave their WPA jobs to go to the fields.
The hourly rate for harvest labor was less than WPA rates, but farm pay
generally included meals, and in some cases lodging.[65] However, the
majority of WPA workers believed that it was risky to leave projects for
temporary harvest work, as there was no guarantee of re-engagement,
certainly not immediately, when the harvest was ended. The drought
counties provided few private employment opportunities, a hardship that
was especially problematic for women. Indeed, for a majority of females,
the only paid work available was domestic service, at rates of remuneration so low that it was impossible to provide for dependants.[66]

More Political Conflict

The public manner in which Stutz had been rejected as head of the
WPA, and the fact that he was widely perceived to favor the Republican

63. *Topeka State Journal,* December 28, 1936; January 6, 1937; *Topeka Daily Capital,* December 31, 1936; January 5, 1937; *Kansas City Times,* January 6, 1937.

64. Clarence G. Nevins, State Administrator, WPA Kansas, to David K. Niles, March
2, 1937, Central Files, Kansas, 1935–44, File 640 Kansas, RG69, NA; Nevins to A.
Williams, May 29, 1937, Central Files, Kansas, 1935–44, File 201:32 Ks, RG69, NA.

65. Nevins to Niles, July 15, 1937, FERA Central Files, Kansas 641, File Da-D2, Box
1346, RG69, NA.

66. Field Supervisor, Salina, Kansas, September 1939, FERA Central Files, Kansas
640 (1939–40), File 640, Jan. 1939, RG69, NA.

cause, exacerbated tensions. A further complication was the position of Gov. Alf Landon, who became FDR's Republican challenger for the 1936 presidential campaign and thus added an extra dimension to the political battle. Accusations of playing politics with relief were commonplace in every state, but in Kansas the Democrats had an extra incentive to show that federal agencies, such as the WPA, were not only effective but would continue to be so. Given the relationship between the WPA and the KERC, it was difficult to extol the virtues of the former without denigrating the work of the latter, a task that was very attractive to Stutz's enemies.

One of the earliest signs of political conflict occurred in November 1935, when an attack by Harry Hopkins on relief in Kansas was widely reported in the press. Hopkins accused Kansas of having "never put up a thin dime for relief," adding that Landon had managed to balance the state budget by "taking it out of the hides of the people." His verbal assault on Landon included the charge that the governor had made no attempt to raise additional revenues from the state for relief purposes.[67] This was the first time that a senior member of the Washington administration had concentrated fire on Landon, who was then just emerging as a potential Republican presidential candidate. While Landon refused to be drawn into any debate, Stutz, a man never to surrender meekly to criticism, was quick in his denunciation of Hopkins's charges.

In a lengthy wire, which he released to the press, Stutz pointed out that state and local governments in Kansas, despite experiencing a devastating drought, had contributed 26 percent of all work and work relief costs, which was approximately the national average for such payments. Furthermore, local political subdivisions had paid in full the relief costs for unemployables; Kansas had never spent Reconstruction Finance Corporation or FERA funds on direct relief, with the exception of payments to transients on federal programs. It was efficient management that had enabled the counties to deal so effectively with their problems during a period of financial stringency. This forceful rebuttal ended with the tongue-in-cheek suggestion that it was possible that Hopkins had been misquoted. If so, he would now be able to set the record straight.[68] Stutz was narrowly correct in his statement, but in an especially perceptive memo to Aubrey Williams, a colleague pointed out that the failure of the state of Kansas to contribute to the relief program according to its ability was of legitimate concern to the FERA. In the first place, this action forced a heavy financial burden onto the counties, as was apparent from the fact

67. *Kansas City Times*, November 1, 1935.
68. Stutz to Hopkins, October 31, 1935, Stutz Papers, 327:1:5; *Topeka Daily Capital*, November 3, 1935.

that almost one-third of local funds raised for relief came from the sale of bonds, and another significant portion came from the diversion of funds previously earmarked for other purposes. Second, Congress had stipulated in the Federal Emergency Act (1933) that the ability of both states and localities to contribute to the relief program should have been exhausted before federal funds were made available. It was, this memo stated, the state government's duty to share poor relief responsibility with its political subdivisions.[69] There can be no doubt that although the Kansas model for welfare responsibility was effective in counties with a sound tax base and a well-run administration, clients were seriously disadvantaged in the poorest counties, even if their administrations observed the highest professional standards.

Nevertheless, Hopkins soon began to distance himself from his reported comments. He expressed surprise that his remarks had been interpreted as political, conceding that whereas the state of Kansas had spent little on relief, the counties and cities had provided well for the needy. It was also clear, he agreed, that the state legislature had taken all appropriate steps to meet the requirements of the federal government. Although Hopkins did not respond to Stutz's wire directly, he did withdraw his substantive accusations.[70] Why did Hopkins get involved in such a squabble? *New York Times* columnist Arthur Krock provided the explanation. At a press conference, the primary purpose of which was to give Hopkins the opportunity to lambaste an old adversary, Gov. Eugene Talmadge of Georgia, a journalist asked a question about Landon's ability to balance the budget. Hopkins was innocently lured into what Krock described as a "tactical blunder."[71] This incident brought into the open Washington's apprehension about the successful management of relief in Kansas. It also ensured that the Sunflower State's relief agencies would have a high profile if Landon were to lead the Republican challenge in 1936.[72]

Many KERC/WPA conflicts, whether major or minor, were played out in public, which is not surprising as both sides enthusiastically leaked information to the press. In early 1936 the *Topeka State Journal* ran a headline proclaiming a "Row between J. G. Stutz and Evan Griffith." Stutz had written to Griffith complaining that 120 WPA employees in Morris County had been laid off and were applying, along with other employable relief clients who had been unable to secure WPA positions, for direct relief.

69. L. L. Ecker to Williams, November 2, 1935, FERA State Files 1933–36, Kansas File, October 1935, RG69, NA.

70. *New York Times*, November 8, 1935.

71. Ibid., November 6, 1935.

72. Ibid., November 10, 1935.

Stutz argued that other states had been able to negotiate increased WPA quotas while it appeared that in Kansas WPA jobs were being reduced. He urged Griffith to redouble his efforts to secure an additional WPA quota so that employable men and women could be removed from the relief rolls.[73] This is a clear example of Stutz using the press to put pressure on Griffith and to expose what he saw as clear deficiencies in the WPA. The fact that Stutz now had a vested interest in exposing the shortcomings of the WPA, and was quite willing to do so, did not go unnoticed in Washington. He became identified as an opponent of the WPA, and a potentially powerful one at that.[74]

Political squabbles were, of course, commonplace. Local politicians often railed against the regulations imposed by the KERC, especially when their freedom to appoint poor commissioners was restricted by rules that imposed minimum educational standards and levels of experience. W. P. Rettiger, Democratic county chairman of Chase County, expressed his anger that "[W]e had to give the job [of Poor Commissioner] to a Republican that had a college degree. Why not let Democrats handle their own business? We do not need J.G. Stutz to tell us what to do with federal money."[75] As the 1936 election drew closer, the political current gained force. State Case Supervisor Eli Hulbert commented that in a year where many commissioners were forced to seek re-election, their attitudes and actions could not be considered "normal." He noted that some became more aggressive and others more timid, but all required careful handling. Many county commissioners whose funds were almost depleted instructed their Poor Commissioners to ensure that the available finance was spread out until after the election, in order to avoid the public hostility that would follow a bond issue. As a result, poor commissioners often found themselves in grave difficulties, as even the most conservative plans could be thrown awry. Predictions of relief demands were notoriously prone to error. For example, when WPA projects finished and there were no others to which those eligible could be directed, large numbers of clients legitimately demanded help from their county at very short notice. Sometimes clients were given an RA grant for only one month, and once that was exhausted recipients were forced back onto county assistance.[76]

73. *Topeka State Journal,* January 17, 1936; Stutz to Griffith, January 17, 1936, Stutz Papers, 327:1:6.

74. Foster to Hunter, January 28, 1936, Federal Relief Agency Papers, Group 24, Box 57, Hopkins Papers.

75. Rettiger to Hon. Randolph Carpenter (D), December 1935, FERA State Files, 1933–36, Kansas File, Dec. 1935, RG69, NA.

76. Hulbert to Esther Twente, May 22, 1936, Memo Re 5th District, Stutz Papers, 327:3:21.

In Graham County, Hulbert was convinced that a decision by the commissioners to dismiss two case aides, contrary to his advice, was motivated entirely by political expediency.[77] In Linn County a caseworker detected an assertive Democratic influence. Curiously, although the Linn County commissioners were prepared to appoint a new case aide, the gender of the post holder concerned them. It was reported that they "would rather have a man but said that if the SCS [State Case Supervisor] thought it was better that they had a woman they wanted one that looked like a man."[78] Perhaps it is fortunate that the result of this recruitment exercise is not known. In Woodson County, the County Democrat chairman tried to force the poor commissioner to certify for assignment to the WPA an individual known to him; the poor commissioner, having examined the case, rightly declined and after further pressure declined again.

The press regularly raised other political rumblings. For example, it was reported that WPA workers were forced to join Democrat clubs, make political donations and display political posters. There was editorial outrage at reports that the foremen on some WPA projects had been selected on political grounds and at the manner in which WPA representatives took every opportunity to act as boosters for the president.[79] There is, of course, nothing surprising here, and examples of political pressure could be found in every state. However, in judging editorial comment one needs to be aware that the vast majority of Kansas's newspaper owners and editors were rock-solid Republicans who strongly supported the Landon cause.[80] It is unlikely that dispassionate reporting and independent assessment were the guiding values of the Kansas press, especially during the election period.

Unemployed Organizations: Anger and Action

Protest and pressure were not confined to the members of the main political parties. Agitation against lay-offs and the WPA's failure to employ all those certified, as well as complaints against wages and hours of work, became increasingly common, and even more so when the unemployed

77. Hulbert to Twente, August 6, 1936, Memo re Graham Co., Stutz Papers, 327:3:21.
78. Miss Austin to Miss Twente, September 14, 1936. Report on Linn County, Stutz Papers, 327:3:21.
79. *El Dorado Times,* September 16, 1936; *Kansas City Star,* August 2, 1936; *Garden City Telegram,* October 3, 1936; *Kansas City Times,* October 16, 1936.
80. James C. Duram, "Constitutional Conservatism: The Kansas Press and the New Deal Era as a Case Study," 432–47.

organized into groups whose purpose was not merely to write letters of protest and to demonstrate peacefully but to undertake direct action. At times, violence, or the fear of it, led to high levels of stress for relief administrators. In December 1935, following an all-day conference, the United Action Committee, which purported to represent the state's unemployed, called for a "hunger march" on Topeka to take place on February 1. In the meantime they presented a list of demands to Governor Landon, calling on him to convene a special session of the legislature to coincide with their demonstration. Among their demands was a guarantee that the WPA would employ all the unemployed at a union wage, that farmers should receive help through an end to foreclosures, and also the provision of interest-free loans and that "there should be no discrimination against Negroes." However, attempts by the United Action Committee to attract the support of the Kansas Federation of Labor were unsuccessful.[81]

In January 1936, one hundred demonstrators occupying the Bourbon County courthouse faced a tear gas barrage and the threat of National Guard action. They were protesting what they believed was an unfair distribution of the state's WPA jobs and low WPA wage rates. The Bourbon County commissioners were in no doubt to blame for this violence: it was Evan Griffith who had failed, in their words, "to provide jobs for these people."[82] The removal of Lyle O. Armel, the Shawnee County poor commissioner, and his staff was a demand of the Kansas Allied Workers, a Topeka-based union of the unemployed, when their representatives appeared before the county commissioners in January 1936. They were presenting the views of a meeting attended by approximately three hundred unemployed who believed that Armel and his colleagues could easily be replaced by men and women chosen from within their own ranks.[83]

In January 1937, an attempt was made to create more WPA jobs for needy younger men by removing from the rolls all persons aged 65 years and over, a policy advocated by Governor Walter Huxman in his gubernatorial appeal to the electorate.[84] The hope was that the complaints of those ousted would be moderated, because in July they would be compensated by Old Age Assistance payments emanating from the Social Security Act. However, as soon as the removal of 373 older workers in sixteen counties commenced, a vigorous campaign against this plan emerged. The discharged workers were supported by the Kansas Allied

81. *Topeka State Journal*, December 16, 1936.
82. *Kansas City Times*, January 18, 1936; see also *Topeka Daily Capital*, January 18, 1936; *Iola Register*, January 17, 1936.
83. *Topeka Daily Capital*, January 6, 1936.
84. Walter A. Huxman Address, October 27, 1936, Stutz Papers, 327:1:13.

Workers and by the Farmer Labor (Party) Union, a similar organization based in Girard and Pittsburg. Not surprisingly, they also had the seventy-two-year-old Senator Capper firmly on their side.[85] Soon the Crawford County courthouse at Girard was occupied, and similar action was threatened for Columbus, Fort Scott, and Topeka. Faced with such opposition, the WPA backed down. A senior official, Corrington Gill, explained to Senator Capper that as the old-age assistance support that was supposed to be available for distribution in July would not now come on stream for at least several more months, the individuals who had been removed from the WPA would, if still assignable, be reemployed on projects.[86] Nevertheless, any favorable readjustments to policy following threats, strikes, and sit-ins provided unions of the unemployed with enhanced status in their communities and proved a valuable recruiting boost.

Organizations of the unemployed became even more agitated during 1937, when the national contraction in funding led to a reduction in WPA jobs in every state. As unemployment mounted during the recession of 1937–38, the numbers attracted to groups that would march, strike, and lobby in favor of more relief work grew. This was a nationwide phenomenon inspired by the growth of organized labor and a rise of militancy among relief workers.[87] In Kansas several themes were beginning to emerge. Striking relief workers usually called for all projects to be closed, or tried to bring about closure themselves by picketing, on the grounds that if every eligible man and woman could not be put to work, then none should work. The strikers did not always get the support of their employed colleagues when they called for it, though a show of force often overcame reluctance. The unemployed also demanded that the limited funds available for WPA work should be spent immediately on work relief wages. The hope was that when the money ran out, the ensuing crisis would be so serious that Congress would be compelled to find more. County relief offices were deeply concerned about the implications of strikes leading to WPA project closure, since idle workers and their families would request assistance from already depleted local coffers.

During the spring of 1937 various groups anxiously followed the news

85. *Topeka Daily Capital,* January 29, 1937; March 21, 1937; April 2, 1937; *Topeka State Journal,* February 2, 1937.

86. Gill to Capper, April 17, 1937; Edith Foster (Regional Director Div. of Employment) to Lucy Williams Brown (Administrative Assistant, WPA), April 1, 1937, Central Files Ks. 1935–44, Ks 641, Ca-Ch, 1938, RG69 NA; *Pittsburg Sun,* April 3, 1937; *Topeka State Journal,* March 29, 1937.

87. David Ziskind, *One Thousand Strikes of Government Employees;* William H. and Kathryn Coe Cordell, "Unions among the Unemployed," 498–510.

from Washington concerning WPA funding. Once it was clear that a reduction was inevitable, speculation mounted as to exactly what this
would mean for Kansas. The KAW called mass protest meetings, and
there was widespread support among the unemployed for the view that
if the state's allocation were reduced, the available sum should not be
managed by a reduction in quotas. Instead, the money should be allocated to all clients immediately for as long as it lasted.[88] Clarence Nevins was
particularly concerned about the effect of a WPA quota reduction on
Shawnee County, which had twenty-one hundred men and women on
WPA projects and a further seven hundred who, though eligible, could
not be placed. A proposed reduction in quota by 15 percent, he thought,
would have a disastrous impact on local relief.[89] Governor Huxman and
other senior officials met representatives of the unemployed, but their explanation that the source of the problem was a cutback in congressional
funding did not have a calming effect. Nor did the governor's promise
that he would write President Roosevelt requesting additional funding.
Militant KAW demonstrators carrying placards inscribed, "We All Work
Or Nobody Works," demanded that provision be made for workers who
were laid off by the WPA and could not secure private employment. It was
difficult to see how this demand could be met without seriously over-
committing county relief resources.[90] Not surprisingly, there were also
threats to march on WPA offices from groups in Crawford and Cherokee
counties.

The decision, made in July, to lay off 115 women from a WPA Topeka
sewing project had immediate repercussions. The discharged females, together with supporters from the KAW, descended on the Jackson Street
sewing room and prevented the women who still had jobs from working.
The sewing room was occupied briefly, but on eviction a group of protesters moved to the State WPA Head Quarters on Kansas Avenue and
confronted officials, who explained that they only had sufficient funding
to employ the 142 women who had been retained. Officials agreed to examine the records of the women who had been discharged from the project to see if, as the protesters claimed, discrimination had informed the
choices. The protesters withdrew after giving WPA administrators a
week's grace to undertake the investigation. Eventually, WPA officials reported that they had uncovered no evidence of unfair practice in identifying those workers who had been laid off. The jobless women, who then

88. *Topeka Daily Capital,* May 23, 1937.
89. Ibid., June 19 and 21, 1937.
90. Ibid., July 20, 1937.

asked for direct relief including help with rent and utility bills, were informed that the rules of the County Social Welfare Board stipulated that they must wait for two weeks after their last WPA checks before making a relief application.[91]

Sudden discharges from the WPA, usually caused by cutbacks in funding, were often a source of simmering resentment, more so than if workers came to the end of a project and found that there was no more work for any of them. A legitimate complaint raised by the KAW was that workers were selected for discharge by a foreman who had no idea of the domestic circumstances of the individuals he contemplated releasing. Layoffs were based either on the efficiency of the laborer, or suspected favoritism, rather than social need. Clarence Nevins recognized this problem and agreed to a demand from the unemployed that foremen would consult KAW representatives when layoffs were contemplated; he also set up appeal boards to investigate charges of discrimination.[92]

Strikes, protests, and occupations, or the threat of them, by organizations of the unemployed became more common, though where such actions took place they were more successful in releasing frustration than meeting their aims. For example, a march by more than two hundred unemployed from Crawford and Cherokee counties on the Chanute WPA office resulted in a brief occupation. The protesters' demands included the resignation of three officials. To achieve that end, they expressed their determination to picket the office for six months if necessary. However, after a few days the strike ended ignominiously following police intervention.[93] KAW supporters who conducted a sit-down strike that involved the occupation of the Shawnee County relief headquarters showed more determination during March 1937. Their demands included the negotiable—for example the reinstatement of some discharged workers—and the impossible, including a hike in WPA wages and a commitment on the part of the commissioners to spend all their funding allocation immediately. The occupation lasted for nine days, at which point the strikers withdrew to give the commissioners time for consideration, although the determination to reoccupy the building if satisfaction was not forthcoming remained. The tactic of withdrawal accompanied by the threat of return was a standard way of ending, sometimes temporarily, unresolved strikes. In this case, after their period of grace, the commissioners refused to give in to any of the demands of the demonstrators. However, a few days lat-

---

91. Ibid., July 21, 22, 23, 24, 25, and 31, 1937; *Topeka State Journal*, July 21, 22, 23, and 24, 1937.
92. *Columbus Daily Advocate*, August 6, 1937.
93. *Pittsburg Headlight*, July 26, 1937; *Chanute Tribune*, July 27, 28, and 30, 1937.

er Lyle O. Armel was removed from his position as Poor Commissioner, and since he was considered a foe of long standing, the KAW was able to claim that their direct action was a success.[94]

On August 18, 1938. a group of nonassigned WPA workers occupied the courthouse at Girard, demanding not only more WPA employment but also the transfer of the state to a higher wage region. They threatened to close down all county projects if their demands were not met immediately. The demonstrators then approached workers on WPA projects and asked them to drop tools and join a strike, which most did. However, almost immediately, some Pittsburg men rebelled against the strike, seeing no reason why they should sacrifice their own wages to help others. Although the demonstrators redoubled their efforts and strove to close the projects that had reopened, some work continued. Senators Capper and McGill called for an increase in the Kansas quota and even a transfer to a more favorable wage district, which the protesters interpreted as an indication of support, though it was, in fact, a costless political gesture by the two men. Eventually ten of the demonstrators were arrested, and on September 8 the strike was called off. The political ardor of the protesters had cooled when Clarence Nevins agreed to talk to them, even though he was able to articulate only some vague suggestions for improvement. This episode shows that the organized unemployed were not always successful in persuading fellow relief workers to join strikes, and that demonstrations could be highly disruptive to relief administrations and often frightening to those closest to them. Roughly at the same time as these disturbances, Kansas was given an increase in its quota, as Congress agreed with the president that the effects of the serious 1937–38 recession could only be countered with additional federal spending, and hope revived that there would be WPA jobs for all.[95]

In February 1939, the *Topeka Journal* raised the specter of communism. The newspaper claimed that the Workers Alliance of America, which had seven thousand members in Kansas and was popular with WPA workers, could have communists among its leadership. This article concluded that U.S. democracy would not be safe until "WPA feeding grounds for communist leaders is closed." However, the journal drew comfort from its belief that the trend toward an insurance-based social security program would ultimately undermine the need for a work relief program; once the

94. *Topeka State Journal*, March 26, 27, and 29, 1937; April 2, 5, 1937; May 25, 1937; *Topeka Daily Capital*, March 29, 30, 1937; April 3, 5, 1937; May 25, 26, 1937.

95. *Pittsburg Headlight*, August 24, 25, 29, 30, and 31, 1938; September 1, 2, 3, 5, 6, 7, 8, and 12, 1938; *Pittsburg Sun*, September 3, 6, 7, 8, and 23, 1938; *Topeka Daily Capital*, September 6, 7, and 9, 1938.

WPA collapsed, so would the Workers Alliance.[96] Even before 1939, conservatives, members of the business community, and a significant proportion of the population at large had developed a vigorous opposition to work relief and were also contemptuous of what they saw as the feeble efforts of the relief workforce that, in any case, they regarded as part of a corrupt system of political patronage. The accusation of communist influence can be seen as part of a concerted attack on the WPA.

Democrat Triumph—Republican Defeat

A highly significant dispute between the WPA and the KERC began in September 1936. The protagonist was Ben S. Hudson, a WPA district director, who accused the KERC of having administrative costs far in excess of the WPA. As usual, Stutz was quick to mount a defense. After Griffith refused his request to examine WPA records so that he could assess the validity of Hudson's claim, Stutz redirected his demands to Harry Hopkins, whose failure to respond promptly induced the Kansan to intensify his campaign.[97] KERC records were open for public inspection, Stutz noted, and until the spring of 1936 federal records were equally available, but since then, secrecy had prevailed. Governor Landon's press headquarters issued a fifteen-page document in support of Stutz's position and containing transcripts of all the relevant correspondence.[98] Hopkins's immediate reaction was to accuse Stutz of putting himself in the hands of the Republican National Committee. He then argued that WPA records were open to anyone who had a legitimate reason to examine them, but they were not available to individuals who would exploit them.[99] Hopkins did not indicate into which of these categories John Stutz fell, but as can be expected, Landon accused Washington of imposing censorship, born of a fear of opening the books.[100] Eventually, Hopkins asked a senior Washington aide, Corrington Gill, to examine the charges. Gill's carefully worded judgment concluded that the administrative expenses of the KERC and the WPA were not directly comparable, and that arguments about them were irrelevant. He ended, somewhat disingenuously, by claiming that the statements to which Stutz had initially objected were not made by a WPA official, but had appeared in the editorial columns of the

96. *Topeka Journal,* February 20, 1939.
97. Stutz to Hopkins, September 18, 1936, Stutz Papers, 327:1:6.
98. *Wichita Eagle,* October 5, 1936.
99. *Emporia Daily Gazette,* October 6, 1936.
100. *Dodge City Globe* and *Kansas City Journal-Post,* October 6, 1936.

Fredonia Daily Herald. This gave Stutz an easy target, as Ben S. Hudson was the newspaper's owner and editor.[101]

No doubt stung by Landon's participation in this Stutz campaign, Griffith hit back. He publicly accused Stutz of the extravagant spending of federal funds on some lavishly produced and extensively circulated bulletins the KERC had issued. The compilation of these reports was, in fact, a major FERA project, and the issue was whether the costs allocated to it had been excessive and whether Stutz, who was state relief administrator, should have authorized the expenditure. A close Washington colleague, Howard Hunter, who attributed the idea to Guy T. Helvering, favored using the accusation of excessive expenditure as a line of attack, and Harry Hopkins seized on his suggestion with enthusiasm. In the course of a telephone conversation with Hunter, Hopkins exclaimed, "[C]an you make that stand up? If they ever break that on Stutz and Landon it would kick him [*sic*] in the face. I'll work that out from here, you do so from your end."[102] If an expenditure of $350,000 on the production, printing, and distribution of KFRC bulletins was to be the main assault on the Kansas relief administration, then that body must have functioned in a remarkably honest and highly professional manner. Nevertheless, Howard Hunter supported Griffith's attack in a telegram that, on the one hand, complimented Stutz for doing a good job as head of the KERC, but on the other castigated him for having administrative expenses that were among the highest in the country. The well-aired issue of the state of Kansas never having made a contribution to relief expenditure also reappeared.[103] If more substantive evidence against Stutz had been available, there can be no doubt that Democrats in Washington and Kansas would have used it; they would have been overjoyed if Stutz, and by implication the budget-balancing Landon, could have been successfully accused of systematic corruption, inefficiency, and a lack of financial control.

As the election date grew closer, Stutz became publicly identified with the Landon campaign and was no longer considered the dedicated professional administrator defending his integrity against attack from career politicians. Former Democrat governor Harry T. Woodring, who had recruited Stutz to the KERC in 1932, now announced that he regretted the appointment.[104] Walter A. Huxman, the Democrat candidate for the gov-

101. Press Release, October 8, 1936, Stutz Papers, 327:1:13; *Emporia Daily Gazette* and *Kansas City Star*, October 8, 1936.

102. Hopkins to Hunter (transcripts of telephone conversations, Kansas No. 74), October 8, 1936, Hopkins Papers.

103. *Topeka Daily Capital*, October 11, 1936.

104. *Topeka State Journal*, October 12, 1936.

ernorship of Kansas in 1936, showed how much Stutz had alienated those who were fighting for Roosevelt's re-election when he promised that if he was victorious at the polls he would remove Stutz from his position at the KERC with all possible speed. Huxman also claimed that because Landon had failed to bring the benefits of old-age pensions to Kansas, approximately four thousand men and women aged over sixty-five were working on WPA projects. He promised to cooperate with the national government if elected, so that the over-sixty-five-year-olds would receive their rightful pensions, thus freeing up four thousand WPA places for younger unemployed applicants.[105] Benefiting from Roosevelt's overwhelming victory, Huxman triumphed; on January 11, 1937, Stutz presented his resignation as executive director of the KERC to the new governor.[106] Omar Ketchum and Evan Griffith were both mentioned as possible replacements, but the man eventually chosen as Stutz's successor was Jerry E. Driscoll, a prominent lawyer from Russell County and one-time sports journalist with the *Kansas City Post*.[107] Driscoll began his period of office by issuing an open letter to all Kansas newspapermen in which he stressed his intention to give the counties "home rule" in relief matters. With the co-operation of the press and a more liberal attitude on the part of the KERC toward the county commissioners, Driscoll hoped that the conflict of the recent past would be brought to an end.[108]

Landon and Stutz were not the only prominent Republican casualties. E. M. Leach was ousted from his post as Sedgwick County Poor Commissioner after only a brief period in office. He had been appointed in July 1934 by a civic and business committee who saw in him a man with the qualities necessary to restore confidence in a relief system that had been severely shaken by the Wichita riot in May of that year. The poor commissioner, however, soon made enemies. His use of private detectives to spy on "Red activities" enraged labor groups, and payments made to his "spies" using fictitious names to preserve their anonymity led to an appearance before a grand jury in February 1935. His subsequent exoneration did not improve an already deteriorating relationship with the Board of County Commissioners. In a lengthy correspondence with Aubrey Williams and others, Leach detailed the destructive intrusions orchestrat-

105. *Topeka Daily Capital,* October 16, 1936; Election Statement by Huxman, October 27, 1936, Stutz Papers, 327:1:13.

106. *Topeka Daily State Journal,* January 11, 1937.

107. *Leavenworth Times,* November 22, 1936; *Kansas City Journal-Post,* February 13, 1937.

108. Open letter to Managing Editors from Jerry E. Driscoll, January 29, 1937, Stutz Papers, 327:1:8

ed by his enemies, which progressively undermined his position and those of some senior colleagues.[109] In his defense, it must be said that the principle accusation against Leach, that Wichita was becoming a soft touch for relief scroungers, was not substantiated.[110] Indeed, there is no reason to doubt that Leach's conduct was other than competent, and Field Representative T. J. Edmonds commented favorably on the efficiency of the Sedgwick County Relief Administration.[111] Leach's successor was Wichita businessman and prominent Democrat R. A. (Dick) Morris.[112]

The first year of Walter A. Huxman's governorship saw major changes in the organization of welfare provision in Kansas that were a direct result of the Social Security Act, which was passed in August 1935, though Congress made no appropriations for it until February 1936. The Federal Social Security Board was organized in October, and the act that created it made substantial funds available to states to assist their aged, blind, and dependent children, if deemed needy. To qualify for federal funding, states had not only to make a financial contribution, but each had also to produce a welfare plan and create a single agency that would administer the new program. The KERC duly submitted a plan for consideration by the Federal Social Security Board in December 1936, and there seemed no reason to doubt that approval, under the state-existing laws and appropriations, would be given. However, when the board met with John Stutz, members who had no problems with the proposed administrative structure raised their concerns about the degree of local autonomy in the administration of state relief. The Kansas constitution placed the duty of caring for the needy on the counties, and the state had no mandatory powers to compel them to provide certain types of assistance. Moreover, there was considerable doubt whether the state of Kansas was legally empowered to raise and also to spend taxpayers' money for the provision of relief.[113] This was unacceptable to the board. The risk of being unable to comply with the provisions of the Social Security Act necessitated a special session of the legislature, which convened in July 1936 and agreed to submit two constitutional changes to the electorate. The first asked that the state be given the power to directly assist the needy, while the second asked voters to support a state old-age-benefit scheme. Both propositions re-

109. Leach to Hopkins, September 10, 1935; Leach to Stutz, September 10, 1935; Leach to Williams, September 11, 1935. All FERA State Files, 1935–36, Kansas File, June–Sept 1935, RG69, NA.

110. *Evening Eagle,* July 10, 1935.

111. Edmonds to Hopkins and Nunn, September 25, 1934, Box 57, Hopkins Papers.

112. *Wichita Beacon,* July 10, 11, 14, 15, and 17, 1935; August 31, 1935.

113. *Emporia Gazette,* February 19, 1936.

ceived substantial backing at the 1936 election, and the Federal Social Security Board finally approved the Kansas Social Welfare Act; it became operative on August 1, 1937.[114]

The new act created a State Department of Social Welfare, which replaced the KERC. Its chief administrative officers were the five part-time members of the State Board of Social Welfare (changed to three full-time members in 1939) who were responsible for determining policies and also had overall charge of four categories of public welfare: old age assistance, aid to the blind, and aid to dependent children, and general assistance for those who did not qualify for aid under the three other categories.[115] To fund the proposed changes in welfare policy, the 1937 state legislature embarked upon a number of radical tax initiatives. A new retail sales tax of 2 percent imposed a charge on all sales of tangible property to the final consumer, and upon other items, like meals. In addition, a compensating tax was levied on the use of goods purchased outside the state to act as a disincentive for out-of-state purchases. It was anticipated that the substantial sums raised by the imposition of these two new taxes would provide additional revenue to the counties for social welfare and for schools. On their part, the counties were instructed to broaden their tax base by reducing property tax levies once these funds had been received. As the retail sales tax was difficult to avoid, it was a more certain revenue raiser than the property tax, or income tax. Moreover, since a tax was paid each time a sale took place, income flowed to the state in a regular stream rather than in six monthly intervals. The acceptance by many Kansans that 3.2 beer should not be considered intoxicating paved the way for a cereal malt beverage (beer) tax, which also raised considerable revenue for the state, some of which was diverted for welfare spending.[116] Finally, the unemployment compensation tax on the payrolls of employers with eight or more employees made Kansas compliant with federal legislation. All the

114. James W. Drury, *The Government of Kansas*, 271–72.

115. The federal government matched local funds for assisting the needy aged, the blind, and dependent children, provided the minimum administrative and professional standards laid down by Washington were met. These included the need for a single administrative agency, the provision of a statewide plan, and financial participation by the state.

116. Peter Fearon, "Taxation, Spending, and Budgets: Public Finance in Kansas During the Great Depression," 241–43; Kansas Legislative Council, *Summary History of Kansas Finance*, Research Report No. 60, October 1937, 8–19; State Board of Social Welfare in Kansas, "A Study in Public Assistance and Other Phases of Social Security: The Kansas Social Welfare Program" (Topeka: Bureau of Public Relations, October 1938): 37–39; State Board of Social Welfare, "Report of Social Welfare in 1937" (Topeka, 1938): 11; *Kansas Social Welfare Journal* 1 (March 1938): 10–11.

money raised was used to fund the unemployment provisions of the social security legislation.

Nineteen thirty-seven was a transitional period in public assistance. Taking the year as a whole, $25.6 million was distributed in public aid to Kansans, with 84 percent of the total provided by the federal government, mostly to fund work programs, 14 percent by the counties, and 2 percent by the state. However, if the $4.5 million spent just on public assistance is examined, change is apparent. From January through July all funding came from the counties, with the KERC acting as the monitoring authority. For the last five months of the year, the federal government, the state, and the counties, under the supervision of the State Board of Social Welfare, met expenses jointly. During the August to December period, $2.2 million was distributed to clients, but Washington now provided 21 percent of the funding, the state 24 percent, and the counties only 55 percent. By December the federal proportion had risen slightly as more cases had been transferred from general assistance to other public assistance categories. Unfortunately, it is not possible to judge from the figures available the extent to which clients' needs were being met by the payments they received.[117] By late 1937, the county welfare administrations found that their funds for care of the disadvantaged came from, in order of significance, the real property levy, sales tax distribution, the cigarette tax, and income from the sale of bonds. However, the state now made a regular monthly allocation to the counties from sales tax receipts, and the federal government helped meet the cost of categorical assistance programs. In 1938, for example, total public assistance payments in Kansas amounted to $9.3 million. Of this the federal government provided 29 percent, the state 27 percent, and the counties 45 percent.[118]

The new administrative structure adopted in 1937 transformed boards of county commissioners into county Boards of Social Welfare and gave them responsibility for determining eligibility for relief. The county board was made up of three commissioners, and county directors who supervised and administered the county welfare service replaced poor commissioners. More than four hundred case workers, now called home visitors, interviewed and reviewed clients on a regular basis, constructed deficiency budgets, and offered a full social work service. In counties where the casework load was particularly burdensome, case supervisors managed home visitors by offering advice, assisting in decision making,

117. *Kansas Social Welfare Journal* 1 (March 1938): 15–22.
118. State Board of Social Welfare, *Report of Social Welfare in Kansas,* No. 2 (1938): 20–21.

and equalizing casework services. County offices referred eligible persons to the WPA, to the NYA, or to the FSA for subsistence grants; organized the distribution of commodities for the Surplus Marketing Administration; made decisions on assistance for medical cases; and selected youths for the CCC. Applications for general assistance were made at the County Social Welfare Office in the county in which the applicant had settlement, though a transient family requiring emergency assistance would also use this route. General assistance help was usually given in the form of grocery, fuel, or clothing orders, or, where appropriate, medical care; sometimes a cash grant was available, or wages were paid for work on county projects. As relief was always given on a budgetary deficiency basis, there were significant variations across the state as social workers took living costs into account. The State Board of Social Welfare did not operate a work program, and statewide responsibility in this area was left to the WPA, though the counties had the responsibility of generating sponsorship to cover expenditures on equipment, materials, and supplies for WPA projects.[119] It is clear, however, that families receiving general assistance, especially if the head was classified as employable, had a smaller proportion of their needs met than clients who were on WPA payrolls, or even those who were the recipients of other types of assistance.[120]

The state department tried to maintain the high standards of professional expertise that had long been the characteristic of welfare staff. The adoption of a merit plan in 1939 that was designed to standardize personnel and management selection was an important part of this search for excellence. Of the 105 county directors in late 1939, fifty-seven were male and forty-eight female. Just over 60 percent of these men and women had college degrees, and 30 percent had undertaken graduate training. Surprisingly, almost half the directors had been schoolteachers, and most of them had received higher salaries in the classroom than as welfare administrators. The monthly salaries of Kansas directors ranged from a low of $90 to a high of $250, and there was a strong possibility that a substantial recovery in educational employment would prove irresistible to many. Of the nineteen case supervisors, fourteen were women. All the case supervisors had college degrees, nearly 40 percent had graduate experience, and their monthly salaries ranged from $100 to $200. Very few case supervisors had been teachers; most had started out in public welfare and remained in the profession. Finally, about 60 percent of the home

119. Kansas Legislative Council, "Social Welfare Experience in 1938, 1939 and 1940," Spencer Research Library, Kansas Collection, University of Kansas.

120. *Report of Social Welfare in Kansas*, No. 4 (1940): 10–11

visitors had college degrees, and just over half had been teachers.[121] Unfortunately, this source does not provide a gender division for home visitors, but it is clear that the expansion of welfare staff during the depression provided additional and welcome employment for many women.

The Old Age Assistance program excited immediate interest because many people regarded it, mistakenly, as a pension entitlement rather than relief. The news that the federal government would meet half the cost of this program up to a maximum of $15 was eagerly translated into a monthly pension of $30 for all those qualifying by age. In fact, Old Age Assistance gave help only to those over sixty-five years who, having both been properly assessed and satisfied residence requirements, were judged in need. Moreover, the grant that each received was not only dependent on the funds available, but also determined on a budgetary deficiency basis. Regular re-investigation was carried out to identify any changes in the recipients' financial circumstances. Approximately seventeen thousand Kansans aged sixty-five years and older were receiving public assistance, but a failure to understand the rules relating to Old Age Assistance led to county welfare staff being inundated with applications from elderly people who had never been on relief. The result was that as late as December 1937, 20 percent of applications had not been processed. Counties had a vested interest in moving relief cases to this new scheme as quickly as possible, since the federal government paid half the cost of the grant and the state paid up to 30 percent of the remainder. In late 1937 the average monthly Old Age Assistance grant was nearly $19, a far cry from the anticipated $30.[122] However, averages masked significant variations in individual payments caused by differences in the cost of living between counties. Taking November 1940 as an example, the average payment in the county with, presumably, the lowest cost of living was $14.21; the highest paid $24.84.[123]

The Aid to the Blind program was funded in exactly the same manner: Washington agreed to meet half the cost up to a monthly maximum of $15 for residents who qualified on medical grounds and who were in need. By late 1937, participants in this program received, on average, nearly $21 each month. There was far more public sympathy for the plight of the elderly, as the Townsend movement showed, and the blind than for dependent children or the able-bodied unemployed. Indeed, powerful lobby

121. Ibid., No. 3 (1939): 10–12, 50–55.
122. State Board of Social Welfare, *Public Assistance in Kansas,* Division of Public Relations, Circular No.1 (August 1937): 3–6; State Board of Social Welfare, *Report of Social Welfare in 1937* (Topeka, 1938): 22–25.
123. State Board of Social Welfare, *Report of Social Welfare in Kansas* 4 (1940): 12

groups pressed the case for converting the means-tested relief granted to the aged and the blind into generous pensions. The Aid to Dependent Children initiative suffered because it had few champions and was funded less generously. Washington contributed only one-third of the assistance costs rather than one-half and, as a result, the counties were more likely to economize here than elsewhere. However, federal policies in these fields forced states that had not already done so to adopt good welfare practices and also offered a sufficiently powerful incentive for legislatures to adopt new tax-raising powers in order to fund the programs. It is also worth noting that a majority of those assisted by relief programs for the aged, the blind, and dependent children were unemployables, the very group that was supposed to be cared for by the states alone.[124] All payments were in cash.

More needy cases were located in the General Assistance category than in any other. Unemployables, eligible adults who could not obtain a place on the WPA, many children, and transients were forced to seek general assistance. There was no federal financial assistance for this group; the counties contributed 70 percent to their relief costs, and the state the remainder. This was, however, the area where many counties chose to make drastic economies, realizing that while taxpayers were prepared to help the "deserving poor," they had little sympathy for others. In 1937 some counties began an economy drive and refused to accept cases where there was an employable adult, unless very small children were present. As a result, the average amount of grant for each month from August through December, approximately $15, was lower than for each of the three other welfare categories. However, great care needs to be exercised when comparing the remuneration from different types of assistance. General assistance, for example, included supplementary payments to the recipients of other categorical assistance grants and also sums to cover the counties' share of the costs of institutional care. Moreover, the proportion of single persons in each group differed significantly, and the average family size among general assistance recipients was larger than for clients who relied on other forms of assistance.

Nevertheless, it seems clear that general assistance payments were far from generous, and this inevitably led to the migration of many destitute people, some from out of state, to counties where they believed work was more readily available and relief given more generously. Counties facing in-migration became resentful, especially as their service to existing cli-

---

124. *KERC Bulletin* 288, "A Study of Relief Cases in Kansas Covered by the Federal Social Security Act," October 1, 1935, 5–12.

ents was placed under so much pressure that standards fell. Unfortunately, considerable numbers of children and adults who, with the appropriate social welfare assistance could be rehabilitated, were neglected.[125] Fear of indigents crossing the state line eventually led to a tightening of the settlement laws in April 1939. From that date, eligibility for general assistance required residence in Kansas for five out of the previous nine years, in addition to one year of continuous residence in the county to which the application had been made.[126]

Unfortunately, with John Stutz's departure from office, his personal papers cease to be of relevance to a study of the provision of relief in Kansas. Nevertheless, although Stutz had been removed, the political battles continued. For example, the members of the State Board of Social Welfare vigorously defended themselves against charges in a Topeka newspaper that they, the director, R. B. Church, and deputy director Lester Wickliffe had all been appointed because of their support for the Democrat party.[127] However, the newly appointed members did not stay in their posts long. The State Board of Social Welfare had not received the approval of the State Senate by the time Governor Payne Ratner succeeded Huxman in January 1939, and the new governor was quick to make his own appointments.[128]

The "Roosevelt Recession"

From a low point in 1933, employment in Kansas rose during the decade to a peak in 1937, but that peak was considerably below the levels that had been reached before the depression took hold. Payrolls suffered an even steeper decline, and the gap between this measure and the index of employment remained throughout the decade. The 1937–38 economic slump put sustained recovery into reverse, and even by 1940 many sectors of the economy had not reached the employment levels that had been established three years earlier. Payrolls also contracted, reflecting an inevitable squeeze on wages.[129] The outcome of the "Roosevelt recession" was that more people needed the help of both federal and local relief administrations.

By early 1938 it was clear that a number of counties would be unable to

125. State Board of Social Welfare, *Report of Social Welfare in 1937*, 20, 27–28.
126. Kansas Laws, 1939 Supplement to General Statutes of 1935, Art. 3.
127. *Topeka Daily Journal*, September 1, 1937.
128. Neil Guy to Dean Snyder, November 12, 1938; Report of Field Visit by Neil E. Guy, November 7, 8 and 9, December 12, 1938, FERA State Files, RG69, NA.
129. Kansas Commission of Labor and Industry, *Report of Labor Department* (1941): 54.

meet their share of payments to the needy from current resources. A special session of the legislature, meeting in the spring of that year, established a Social Welfare Emergency Fund. The fund was created by appropriating $350,000 from retail sales tax revenues and a further $250,000 from the surplus that then existed in the social welfare fee fund. The state used this substantial sum to help fifteen particularly distressed counties. In the summer of 1938, many counties that had submitted their welfare budgets for 1939 to the State Board of Welfare were horrified when the board refused to accept them on the grounds that the provision made for assistance was inadequate. The counties vigorously challenged the board's right to take such a stand, maintaining that they did not have the resources to provide the level of care that the board thought was the minimum. Eventually the counties submitted revised budgets, and the legislature, recognizing the seriousness of the problem, continued to support the Social Welfare Emergency Fund beyond its 1938 expiration date.[130] In 1939, $1 million was available for distribution to twenty distressed counties that had either already levied their legal maximum for welfare purposes, or had raised the equivalent from a combination of levy and bond issue. Payments to claimants were, of course, subject to the restrictions imposed by the Cash Basis Law.[131] The Emergency Fund was eventually abolished in April 1941, but state assistance was still available for especially needy counties from a new agency, the Equalization Fund.

An examination of expenditure on general relief presents another means of assessing the local effect of the 1937–38 slump. However, any such analysis must take into account a marked seasonal cycle, with a peak for assistance during the winter and a trough during the summer, when more farmwork was available. Moreover, it must also be noted that, on average, relief payments became progressively more generous after 1935. Just using August as an indicator, the number of cases receiving general relief during that month for each of the years 1937–40 was, respectively, 15,735, 15,478, 18,938, and 18,705.[132] A clear rise in the number of cases in 1939 was maintained during 1940, but, curiously, not during the recession itself. The average sum spent on each case during August for each of the

130. Board of Social Welfare, *Report of Social Welfare in Kansas* 2 (1938): 41–43. The counties assisted in 1938 were Allen, Bourbon, Cherokee, Cowley, Crawford, Ford, Graham, Labette, Leavenworth, Linn, Montgomery, Sedgwick, Seward, Shawnee, and Wyandotte. Nearly half the funding went to Sedgwick and Wyandotte counties.

131. Board of Social Welfare, *Report of Social Welfare in Kansas* 3 (1939): 77.

132. Theodore E. Whiting, *Final Statistical Report of the Federal Emergency Relief Administration, WPA*, 387, 394. More detailed county figures can be found in various issues of *Kansas Social Welfare Journal*.

above years was $13.80, $14.42, $14.43, and $15.94. In addition, surplus commodities were distributed to the needy with a value of $2.9 million in 1938, $2.8 million in 1939, and $3.9 million in 1940.

A detailed analysis of general relief expenditure is difficult because the fund was used for so many purposes, and the information collected on those who received assistance was patchy. In July 1938, an examination of cases that received only general assistance is revealing, even though the exercise was confined to twenty-five counties. In a month normally considered good for employment, approximately two-thirds of the 1,561 cases were considered employable. A more detailed survey involving all counties taken in November 1940 showed that there were 26,021 cases receiving general assistance; of those, 18,557 relied entirely on the general assistance budget. Those entirely reliant on general assistance were divided into employables and unemployables, using as a yardstick which of them was eligible for referral to the WPA. It appears that nearly 60 percent of family cases and 20 percent of singles could be considered employable. The family cases included twenty thousand children under sixteen years of age who, because the family head was employable, were not eligible for aid to dependent children assistance. The fact that these families endured hardship may have given their heads an additional incentive to secure private employment, but in the meantime suffering was a fact of life.[133] It would be difficult to oppose the view that clients entirely reliant on general relief had every incentive to secure private employment and failure to do so indicated a scarcity of jobs rather than indolence.

There were, of course, particularly disadvantaged parts of the state. In July 1938, for example, 13 percent of the Kansas population received some sort of public assistance, WPA wages, or farm security grants, but for Cherokee County the figure was 32 percent; for Crawford County, 29 percent; and for Labette County, 23 percent.[134] In February 1939, 16 percent of the total population was receiving public assistance in one category or another, and Cherokee County (31 percent) and Crawford County (29 percent) were again among the worst affected. However, they were now joined by a number of rural counties: Graham County (38 percent), Smith County (33 percent), Decatur County (28 percent), and Phillips County (27 percent).[135] These figures indicate a high level of rural distress. In November 1939, D. J. Saia, county commissioner for Crawford County, wrote a pleading letter to Roosevelt, vividly drawing the president's attention

133. Board of Social Welfare, *Report of Social Welfare in Kansas* 4 (1940): 12–16, 37–39.
134. *Kansas Social Welfare Journal* 1 (August 1938): 19.
135. Ibid. 2 (April 1939): 7.

to local misery as acute as "in the closing days of the Hoover Administration." The families of unemployed coal miners were "barefoot, cold, ill and hungry"; riots and bloodshed were predicted unless immediate action was taken.[136] After a decade of hard times, there was still a distressing familiarity in the pleas from southeast Kansas.

Though counties in the southeast region were in a perpetually depressed state, others joined them from time to time. In the fall of 1939, for example, WPA investigators commented on the parlous state of agriculture in Kansas and emphasized the link between the cash income of farmers and the misfortunes of many small businesses.[137] In January 1940, Frank Long, Shawnee County's welfare director, expressed his concern at the recent decline in private sector jobs that had led to increases in general relief expenditure. He was adamant that the cause of persistent local unemployment was drought. "Farm conditions generally are the worst they have ever been known in Shawnee County," he wrote. A lack of water, rough feed, and winter pasture had a devastating effect on farmers who had wanted to keep their livestock through the winter. These animals had been sold off, often at a loss, and with them went the jobs of many farm laborers. In addition, the Santa Fe Railroad, the county's principal employer, had begun to lay off workers and put others on short time. This pattern was also increasingly evident among local meatpacking companies. As a result, the county was compelled to send about one hundred new and reopened certificants to the WPA each month, and referrals to the FSA had also been large. He added that the county had resisted the certification of employable rural people but was forced to do so when it became clear that drought had savaged private employment opportunities.[138]

Absolutely, the heavily populated Sedgwick and Wyandotte Counties dominated expenditure on general relief. In 1939 the state of Kansas spent $4.1 million on general assistance, of which approximately $731,500 was allocated to Sedgwick County, $367,000 to Wyandotte County, and $225,000 to Crawford County.[139] However, as we have seen, sometimes boards of county commissioners found it necessary to supplement the re-

136. D. J. Saia to President Roosevelt, November 21, 1939, WPA Central Files, Kansas 641, Box 1349, RG69, NA.

137. Report on Employment Conditions in Kansas, September, October, November, 1939, WPA Central Files 1935–44, Kansas 640, January 1939, Box 1344, RG69, NA.

138. Frank Long to John E. Brink, January 6, 1940, WPA Records, Central Files 1935–44, Kansas 640, Box 1344, RG69, NA.

139. Kansas Legislative Council, "Social Welfare Experience in 1938, 1939, 1940," n.d., Table vi, Spencer Library, Kansas Collection.

muneration of those on federal programs, including categorical assistance. Clients on categorical relief were helped, in the main, with medical and hospitalization costs, but claims for emergency hardship needs such as burial expenses, food, clothing, and rent were not excluded. Destitute families and individuals reliant on the counties for survival endured a miserable existence. While all federal programs, whether work relief or categorical assistance, paid in cash, those on general relief were assisted mostly in kind. General relief allocations were given on a budgetary deficiency basis after an assessment by social workers, which many clients resented.[140]

Help for the Nation's Youth: The CCC and the NYA

A number of New Deal–inspired research projects provided evidence of the particular difficulties that young people encountered on entering the labor market. The search for work was extremely competitive, and hirers were attracted to workers with skills and experience, a rational preference but one that disadvantaged youthful job seekers. Moreover, high wages, which the administration had encouraged through, for example, the President's Reemployment Agreement authorized by the National Industrial Recovery Act, and by support for the growth of organized labor, served to price many of the young out of jobs. In the spring of 1935, three million people aged sixteen to twenty-five years were on relief, a figure that represented approximately 14 percent of the total cohort. The most disadvantaged youth had relatively low levels of education and little vocational training that would have been attractive to prospective employers. There was clearly a need to assist the young before idleness eroded their enthusiasm and damaged their health.[141]

The CCC, which had proved to be one of the New Deal's most popular experiments since its establishment in 1933, was unaffected by the changes in welfare organization that had been introduced in 1935. Young men continued to work on activities designed to counter the effects of persistent drought and also to provide leisure facilities for the state's population. An analysis of Corps recruitment by the KERC during January and April 1937 produced an interesting insight into the program's operation. Of the 658 men selected in the January call, 168 sent allotments to families

140. Ibid., 4–5.
141. *The Public Papers and Addresses of Franklin D. Roosevelt*, Vol. 4, *The Court Disapproves, 1935*, 284–85.

receiving WPA wages, 179 to families who were receiving assistance from other federal programs, 145 to families who were only receiving county relief, and 206 to families who were receiving relief from both the federal government and counties. Because families could obtain relief from more than one federal program, the inevitable duplication in these figures makes an initial interpretation difficult to reconcile with basic mathematics. Nevertheless, the fact that 168 young men made allotments to families who received no federal or county relief and 307 sent money to families who were eligible for, but did not receive, county relief was a striking revelation. As all CCC men were supposed to be selected from, and send their allotments to, families on the relief rolls, it was clear that this regulation had been breached. That so many families who were eligible for county relief were not receiving it was a complete surprise to welfare officials. The report on the April enrollment also showed that 16 percent of the enrollees sent allotments to families who did not receive county relief, even though they were entitled to it. This remained an unresolved puzzle to the officials who analyzed the data. A great majority of the 1937 intake, as was the case in other years, was under twenty years of age, had less than a high school education, and had been unemployed for between seven months and two years.[142]

In 1938, the background of those enrolled was similar to other years, with 45 percent coming from urban homes, 27 percent from rural nonfarm homes, and 18 percent from tenant farms. Only 10 percent of the intake was from owner-occupied farms.[143] This distribution is not surprising as unemployment, which was a key element in selection, is usually an urban phenomenon. There was, however, concern among relief officials when the state found it difficult to meet its recruitment quota, and, as a result, some young men and their families would continue to be a charge on the county relief budget.[144] Indeed, a number of social workers believed that the CCC quota assigned to Kansas was too generous and had led to the enrollment of unsuitable candidates who either failed to show up at the camps or quit the Corps before the end of their six-month contract.[145] The state of the economy played a significant role in influencing recruitment levels. In 1938, a particularly depressed year, Kansas had no difficulty in meeting its target. However, by early 1941, an improving economy con-

142. *KERC Bulletin* 387, February 24, 1937, 2–5; *KERC Bulletin* 393, May 17, 1937, 1–5.

143. *Kansas Social Welfare Journal* 1 (May 1938): 4; ibid. 1 (October 1938): 26.

144. *KERC Bulletin* 387, February 24, 1937, 5; *Topeka Capital,* April 27, 1937.

145. Report of Field Visit by Neal E. Guy, September 2, 1937, Records of the CCC Division of Selection, Correspondence with State Selection Agencies, Kansas File, 1937, RG35, NA.

tributed to both disappointing recruitment and a high rate of camp desertions. In addition, competition from the NYA, which offered a superior training program through work and vocational trade centers, further undermined the Corps. State Supervisor for CCC Selection Paul V. Brenner actually requested a reduction in the Kansas quota in 1941 and also expressed his concern at the lack of cooperation between agencies that had led to an unhealthy competition to recruit young people.[146]

The educational program offered to Corps members was sufficiently attractive to generate an 85 percent participation rate by 1936.[147] Just two years later, deserving enrollees could acquire a range of education certificates demonstrating expertise in oral and written communication as well as practical skills like driving, cooking, and mechanics.[148] Unfortunately, these education and training programs were normally available to enrollees only after they had finished an arduous working day, yet the practical skills listed above were of far greater relevance to young people, who would soon be searching for nonfarm employment, than the planting and forestry work on which they were usually engaged. The educational programs run by the CCC cannot be judged an unqualified success.[149]

The perceptions and the reality of camp life influenced recruitment, reenrollment, and the level of desertions. Corps members who positively hated camp life would take any employment available in order to escape, while some would petition to leave, and others just absconded. It must be conceded that sometimes army culture and practices were not suited to the successful management of civilian residential sites. In 1941, for example, the company commander at Marysville Camp in Marshall County disciplined four Hispanics for persistently speaking Spanish after he had ordered that English alone was to be spoken in the camp. However, after a vigorous protest he was swiftly demoted and transferred, making it clear that there were no regulations that restricted enrollees to the English language.[150]

More disturbing was the disciplinary action imposed on a group of African Americans at Lone Star Camp. Four members of this camp for

146. Brenner to Persons, January 27, 1941, Records of CCC Division of Selection, Correspondence with State Selection Agencies, Kansas File, 1941, RG35, NA.

147. *KERC Bulletin* 380, 29.

148. *Kansas Journal of Social Welfare* 1 (October 1938): 4.

149. John A. Salmond, *The Civilian Conservation Corps, 1933–42: A New Deal Case Study*, 168; Richard Allen Lester, *Economics of Labor*, 382.

150. Chas W. Myers, CCC Company Commander, Marysville to Brenner, October 14, 1941; Brenner to Parsons, October 16, 1941; Lieutenant Miller to McEntee, n.d., Records of CCC Division of Selection, Correspondence with State Selection Agencies, Kansas File, 1941, RG35, NA.

blacks were accused of attending a gambling party, which was also graced by the presence of their commanding officer from whom, allegedly, some money was stolen. The young men were disciplined without being advised of their rights and in spite of each having a strong letter of support from their camp superintendent. CCC Assistant Director James J. McEntee ordered an investigation, and his agent's verdict is worth recording in full. "Had these enrollees been white," he wrote, "I would not have hesitated one minute to recommend to you that they be reinstated, but I was of the opinion doing this might cause them as well as the others to want to run the camp." The letters of recommendation turned out to be merely a device to help the men secure jobs after the termination of their CCC service.[151] The tone in which the report was couched gives the clear impression that this treatment of African Americans was not considered unusual.

The CCC neglected women, except indirectly as members of families who benefited from remittances. However, the wider positive effects of this agency should not be ignored. In 1936, for example, the CCC provided employment for approximately twenty-four hundred nonenrolled people in Kansas. These included reserve officers who ran the camps, technical experts who supervised the work programs, and numerous educational advisors and others who helped manage the wide range of activities that had been made available.[152]

Kansas gained much from the energies of CCC workers. For example, the Soil Conservation Service supervised all CCC erosion work on private land and was able to demonstrate to farmers that fields terraced on the contour would hold water and check erosion. Cooperation with local farmer organizations, a feature of CCC operations, was a means of spreading good practice. Everyone appreciated the emphasis on water conservation and the improvement in recreational amenities. For young men who enjoyed camp life, the CCC was a rewarding experience, but as the economy moved toward rearmament, the NYA's vocational programs seemed increasingly more attractive to young Kansans.

In spite of the public satisfaction with the CCC, a new agency that targeted young people was established in June 1935.[153] The NYA, under the guidance of Executive Director Aubrey Williams, was instructed to develop a program for sixteen to twenty-five year olds without family re-

151. McEntee to Collier, April 30, 1937; Collier to McEntee, May 2, 1937, Records of CCC Division of Investigation, Camp Inspection Reports, Kansas 1933–42, RG35, NA.
152. *KERC Bulletin* 380, January 1937, 28.
153. In July 1939, the NYA was transferred from the WPA to the Federal Security Agency (FSA).

sponsibilities, who were neither in regular full-time schooling nor in paid employment. The NYA was intended to support young people who were excluded from the CCC—for example, females, young people who did not want to be separated from their families, and those who wished to continue in formal education.[154] Indeed, the FERA college-student aid program was terminated, and the discharge of its remit passed immediately to the NYA. Each state was obliged to establish a State Youth Administration, to be assisted by local directors and advisory committees. Anne Laughlin, a graduate of Ft. Hays State College and highly experienced in youth problems, was appointed NYA director for Kansas in July 1935, a post that she held for seven years.[155]

The NYA student aid program was designed to fund part-time employment for needy school, college, and graduate students aged sixteen to twenty-five years, so that they could be encouraged to continue their education. The NYA also financed the part-time employment of youths between the ages of eighteen and twenty-five who had quit school, so that they would benefit from the training element in their work experience. In addition, a positive emphasis on vocational guidance was encouraged. Although the NYA prioritized education and the promotion of democratic values at a time when totalitarian regimes overseas were increasing in popularity, the president and his Washington officials viewed it primarily as a relief program with Harry Hopkins, the WPA administrator, acting as line manager to Aubrey Williams.[156] Indeed, it was also proposed that the WPA should employ more young people from relief families on projects, though on a part-time basis, so that three youths would take the place of one adult worker.[157] As there were approximately forty-five thousand young people in Kansas during 1935 who were not at school and who could be classified as unemployed, idle youth constituted a serious

154. John A. Salmond, "The New Deal and Youth," 141–53. This chapter is a fascinating comparison of the CCC and the NYA.

155. At the time of her appointment, Laughlin was state vice-chairman of the Democratic Party. However, when she sought to renew that position, Aubrey Williams advised strongly against it, stating that those in administrative positions should have no party political alignments. Laughlin to Brown, August 10, 1936; Brown to Williams, August 12, 1936; Williams to Laughlin, August 14, 1936, Records of Deputy Executive Director, Administrative Correspondence with State Directors, RG119, NA.

156. Richard A. Reiman, *The New Deal and American Youth: Ideas and Ideals in a Depression Decade*, 123–31.

157. Williams to Laughlin, October 2, 1935, Records of Deputy Ex. Director and Deputy Administrator, Admin Correspondence with State Director: Kansas Aug 1935–Dec 1938, Records of Deputy Ex. Director, Admin Correspondence with State Directors, RG119, NA.

problem and any initiative that would prevent young people from entering the labor market unprepared was potentially attractive.[158]

The NYA in Kansas was committed to decentralization, and at a very early stage, high school and college councils were established across the state to advise on the general direction of the student aid program. Officials appointed by schools selected young people whom they considered to be in need of assistance and agreed to keep the appropriate records on them. Council recommendations enabled NYA funds to be targeted toward the resolution of acute problem areas, like drought-stricken counties where support for farmers' children was essential for youth to continue their education.

Within a year approximately seven hundred high schools participated in the student aid program, where paid work—for example, in home economics departments, or in libraries, or in general maintenance—encouraged young people to remain in the classroom. Those attending college, including graduate students, benefited from similar campus-based employment. In addition, by early 1936 nearly forty freshman colleges had been organized so that young men and women who would not normally have gone to college could have an additional year of education in a field that held their interest. Those at college could earn, on average, $15 per month when school was in session, while the graduate student monthly average was $20. During the fiscal year ending in June 1939, for example, the NYA school aid program helped 7,837 high school students, including just over 400 African Americans. At the same time, the college program assisted 2,584, of whom 61 were graduate students.[159] Annual funding fluctuated sharply, but even when Congress was relatively generous, as it was in fiscal 1939–40, the annual per capita total expenditure in high schools was only $32.60 and in colleges $101.70.[160] However, these modest sums helped students with the purchase of clothing, lunches, and ed-

158. The most informative source on the operation of the NYA, and one on which this section depends, is "A History of the National Youth Administration in Kansas, 26 July 1935–3 July 1943," Records Created during the Liquidation of the NYA, Final report of the NYA for the State of Kansas, Records of the War Manpower Commission, RG119, NA. This source is a typescript with no date for submission and will be cited "A History of the NYA." The figure of forty-five thousand unemployed youth is taken from "A History of the NYA," 6, but it should be used with caution in the light of a comment by Laughlin in 1937. She conceded that Kansas did not have the appropriate statistical information to participate in an NYA census of unemployed youth. Telephone conversation between Richard R. Brown and Anne Laughlin, December 7, 1937, Records of Deputy Executive Director, Correspondence with State Directors, RG119, NA.

159. "A History of the NYA," 86–89.

160. Ibid., 95.

ucational supplies, encouraged college enrollments, and enabled the fabric of cash-starved institutions to be improved.

Local advisory committees were also crucial to the operation of the out-of-school work program. These committees provided the labor and the plans for suitable projects, while co-sponsors, often from the public sector, supplied both supervision and materials. In Smith County, for example, road signs were constructed in a woodcraft shop, library books were catalogued and repaired, and a civic recreation center was constructed. Some counties sponsored park beautification schemes; others had sewing-room projects or the upgrading of golf courses and other leisure facilities on NYA projects that were very similar to those of older WPA workers. In Jackson County, the majority of NYA workers came from the Pottawatomie Reservation. When defense work became a priority after 1940, the armed forces and the Rock Island Arsenal quickly became heavily involved in the program as co-sponsors.

Starting in September 1935, the NYA also developed resident centers, initially for women. The first of these were Camp Wood in Elmdale, close to Emporia, and Camp Washita, located at Rosedale, near Kansas City, both for white females; Camp Bid-a-Wee in Wichita accepted only African Americans. After a six- to eight-week period in a camp receiving instruction in a range of social and academic subjects, it was hoped that the young women would readily find employment. The project was, however, not a success, partly because the training was insufficiently structured to make the young women attractive to employers. Social workers hoped to eradicate these problems with a new residential initiative, Camp Towoac, which was created at Zarah, near Kansas City. Here women maintained the camp, did their own laundry and cooking, and undertook regular supervised work, usually making tennis nets. When the camp closed in October 1937, it had operated for nine sessions and had given work experience to more than one thousand young women.[161]

Although the majority of those working on NYA programs lived at home, camp experience had convinced welfare staff that the most constructive way to help some unemployed young people was to use resident centers, where imaginative and relevant training programs could be provided. By late 1940, four full-time resident centers provided employment

161. The camp, which had previously been a country club, had extensive grounds, though the accommodation for residents was spartan. The young women lived in cabins during their four-month stay, but the operation was soon considered too expensive. Dinwiddie to Twente and Stutz, November 20 and 22, 1936, Stutz Papers, 327: 3:21.

in sheet metal, radio repair, welding, and related activities for approximately 850 young men, of whom about 100 were African Americans. In 1937 the first part-time resident center was established at Kingman where, during each month, women lived at the center for two weeks and then returned home for the same period. While living at home they traveled to the center every day for work. By late 1940, nineteen semi-resident centers provided supervised employment, mostly in activities related to office work, domestic service, and the catering trade, for about 1,000 young women. However, the demands of the war economy soon shifted the interests of females away from the service sector and toward acquiring skills in, for example, aircraft welding and woodwork, where the pay was considerably higher. Indeed, the resident centers for both men and women were quick to move into defense work, and the first war production training center opened in Topeka during the fall of 1940.

Employment on NYA projects was limited to no more that eight hours each day and forty hours per week, with a monthly maximum of one hundred hours. In January 1940, youths working on nonresident projects were paid, on average, 26 cents per hour and worked, on average, 55.5 hours in each month. Monthly earnings for those in resident centers were higher, but deductions made for subsistence and medical care resulted in a similar net wage. In order to ensure that NYA work did not become a substitute for private sector employment, each youth was counseled after nine months that at the end the year he or she would have to leave, even if a job was not available. The resulting high turnover of NYA workers enabled a considerable number of young people awaiting assignment to have their chance at a period of employment and training.[162] In addition, a vocational guidance program, which was an important part of each state's NYA remit, was established under which serious attempts were made to inform young people about the employment opportunities available to them and also to guide them toward an appropriate solution to their current difficulties. In the course of 1936, for example, NYA representatives interviewed approximately fifteen thousand young people gave them occupational counseling and guidance. In June 1938, local businessmen and women spoke to five thousand young people about the possibilities available to them in a wide range of private sector enterprises.

New Dealers deserve praise for prioritizing the problems facing young victims of the depression, and the NYA was an effective means of providing support for those fortunate enough to be accepted in the various

---

162. In September 1940, for example, 4,087 males and 1,448 females were waiting for assignment to the NYA. "History of NYA," 46.

programs.[163] However, Congress was miserly in its allocation of funding for this deserving cause. In fiscal 1937–38, for example, Kansas received $3.7 million, of which two-thirds was spent on work projects and the remainder on student aid. In March 1938, nearly forty-five hundred young people were employed on work projects, and ninety-four hundred received student aid. In other words, fourteen thousand youths shared a total wage bill of only $120,000.[164] Nevertheless, in spite of these shortcomings the NYA boosted school and college enrollment and therefore provided more employment for teachers and more funds for educational institutions. Furthermore, the work experience and the counseling offered to disadvantaged young men and women was far more relevant to them in both peace and war than that available from the more generously funded CCC.

163. See, for example, the research findings in Selden C. Menefee, *Vocational Training and Employment of Youth,* and Albert Westefeld, *Getting Started: Urban Youth in the Labor Market.*

164. Betty and Ernest Lindley, *A New Deal for Youth: The Story of the National Youth Administration,* 273; "Helping Kansas Youth," *Kansas Social Welfare Journal* 1 (July 1938): 8–9,16.

6

Conclusion

What Was Radical about New Deal Relief?

While campaigning during the gubernatorial election of 1934, Alf Landon was happy to record his satisfaction with much of the New Deal. He told listeners that he was a strong supporter of direct assistance to farmers who were afflicted by drought, high debts, and low prices. As for relief, the pragmatic Progressive Republican had much in common with Hopkins and Roosevelt. For example, Landon was a powerful advocate of work relief and also had a visceral dislike of what he believed to be the debilitating effects of dole payments. The governor was convinced that a rigorous means testing of all relief applicants was essential to determine who was genuinely entitled to local or federal assistance. In campaign speeches he stressed that his administration had cooperated fully with the federal government in its attempts to assist both the needy unemployed and distressed farmers. One advantage of this policy, he told his audiences, was that the state had always received its full share of federal relief money, and he pointed out that Kansas had been quick to change state laws that might have acted as a barrier to a full participation in national relief and recovery measures. Moreover, Washington had identified the state's relief administration as one of the most efficient in the nation. Even though he portrayed himself as a budget-balancing and tax-cutting governor, he assured the public that if he were to be re-elected, the close working relationship that he had profitably forged with Washington would continue.[1]

1. *Emporia Gazette*, September 22, 1934; *Topeka Daily Capital* and *Topeka State Journal*, both October 12, 1934.

Two years later the tone had changed. By then Landon was the Republican candidate for the White House, and one could not expect a ringing endorsement of his opponent's policies. Moreover, he had seen his trusted ally, John Stutz, denied the post of state WPA administrator, which helped form his firmly held view that the politicization of relief had become inevitable once the appointment of senior WPA staff required Senate confirmation.[2] Landon believed that the WPA had, on the one hand, created an army of permanent relief clients and, on the other, had forced many needy unemployed onto state relief rolls. It is worth noting that in 1932 the Republican platform had stressed the importance of maintaining high wages in the fight against the depression. By 1936 the attraction of high wages had been replaced by commitment to reduce business costs and to return the responsibility for relief to the states and localities.[3] Landon was quick to attack spending he considered excessive and was determined to ensure that the state's budget, or, indeed, the spending of any of its taxing units, did not move into deficit. The governor still retained his affection for the Civilian Conservation Corps and supported the help given to farmers, especially via the provisions of the Soil Conservation and Domestic Allotment Act and the various initiatives introduced to ameliorate the effects of the drought. He was critical of the commercially oriented standards adopted by the FCA and felt that credit should be given to farmers far more liberally. However, as none of these farm programs required a state contribution, either in the form of matching funds or sponsorship, they must have had a particular appeal to the fiscally conservative governor.

New Deal welfare policy was characterized by high levels of spending, a commitment to means testing, and an unshakable faith in the benefits of work relief. Federal expenditure on relief was a truly revolutionary aspect of this era. Between 1933 and 1939 Congress distributed nearly $16,400 million to the states in nonrepayable grants for relief purposes. The WPA was by far the most costly agency, absorbing almost 40 percent of total expenditure. The FERA accounted for 16 percent and the CWA for nearly 5 percent. Given these figures it is easy to see why Congress could not have provided sufficient funding to employ all those who were eligible for WPA work even if it had wished to do so. Wallis and Oates have calculated that in fiscal 1934 alone, Washington directed more than $2,100 million in grants to the states and local governments for relief of the needy.

2. Alfred M. Landon, *America at the Crossroads*, 36–42; Donald R. McCoy, "The New Deal Through Alf Landon's Eyes," 64–65.
   3. Kirk H. Porter and Donald Bruce Johnson, *National Party Platforms, 1840–1964*, 340–46, 366–70.

To put this sum in perspective, they point out that in 1933, $2,000 million was 4 percent of GNP.[4] In other words, national relief spending was extraordinarily munificent by historical standards. It was also extremely generous by international standards. In 1938 social spending in the U.S. amounted to 6.3 percent of GDP; in Nazi Germany the figure was 5.6 percent, and for the United Kingdom, 5.0 percent.[5] Relief spending during the Great Depression was indeed a noble experiment in assistance to the nation's needy and a bold departure from past practice.

Most of the relief programs demanded local financial participation, insisted on the means testing of applicants, and required states to accept the imposition of minimum administrative standards.[6] The FERA initially required all states to follow a rigid formula that enabled them to secure one dollar of federal money for every three that had been spent on unemployment relief over the previous three months. Later, state contributions were set at the discretion of the administrator. We can note great similarities between philosophy of the RFC and the FERA. Both agencies were determined that each state must contribute what it could afford toward the relief effort. Furthermore, from its inception the WPA also demanded significant contributions to its programs from local sponsors. This aspect of New Deal relief policy was fundamentally traditional.

One notable outcome of increased federal funding and fiscal scrutiny was that states were obliged to fundamentally restructure their tax systems so that sufficient revenue was raised to avoid Washington's support being placed in jeopardy. Congress and New Deal officials were united in their view that the states should not shirk the responsibility they had toward their own destitute. In Kansas the early drive to improve the efficiency with which existing taxes were collected, and the decision of the legislature to impose new ones, was influenced by the need to satisfy the RFC, though the realization that a heavy reliance on property taxes could no longer be sustained also played a role. Thus, in 1933, the Republican-controlled legislature embraced individual and corporate income tax. In 1937, encouraged principally by the need to meet the requirements of the Social Security Act (1935), Kansas embarked on a major fiscal restructuring. The introduction of the Cereal Malt Beverage (Beer) Tax, a Retail Sales

Income Tax 1933

Social Security Act 1935

4. John Joseph Wallis and Wallace E. Oates, "The Impact of the New Deal on American Federalism," 163–68.

5. Edwin Amenta, Ellen Benoit, Chris Bonastia, Nancy K. Cauthen, and Drew Halfmann, "Bring Back the WPA: Work, Relief, and the Origins of American Social Policy in Welfare Reform," 3, 16; Edwin Amenta, *Bold Relief: Institutional Politics and the Origins of Modern American Social Policy*, 4–5.

6. The Civilian Conservation Corps, which was financed entirely by Washington, was a major exception.

1937-Sales Tax

1933- cash basis law

Tax, and the Unemployment Compensation Tax raised state revenues considerably. These New Deal–inspired tax changes contained significant elements of reform, and the state's move away from a dependence on property taxes toward a model that recognized the ability to pay rather than the ownership of wealth as an important factor in achieving equity should be applauded. However, local government remained reliant on property taxes for almost three-quarters of its revenue.

Unfortunately, sales taxes have regressive elements, and this must be taken into account when assessing the socially positive aspects of fiscal change. Moreover, although many Kansans were delighted that the "cash basis" law adopted in 1933 had imposed such strict controls on expenditure that all ten thousand taxing units in the state avoided fiscal distress during the following year, this was not the universal blessing that its supporters imagined.[7] This fiscal innovation prevented taxing units from undertaking expenditure unless they had the funds to cover it. In Kansas, where an enormous amount of welfare responsibility was thrust on the counties, the poorest of them were seriously constrained by the Cash Basis Law. In Cherokee and Crawford counties, for example, structural unemployment was endemic, and the local tax base, still heavily reliant on the property tax, was grossly depleted. The relief administrations in these counties had to care for large numbers of needy unemployed who could not secure positions in federal work relief programs and also had to supplement the relief wages of clients with large families whose earnings were judged inadequate. Fortunately, the Social Welfare Emergency Fund, which the legislature established in 1938, directed substantial sums to the hardest pressed counties for the next few years.

Nevertheless, social workers, often operating under extremely stressful conditions, had to deny relief to many single applicants and give miserly sums to others because their budgets were insufficient to deal with the problems that they faced. Counties mired in poverty could not provide to many relief clients a quality of service that reached the minimum standard, either in the provision of material benefits or in continuing casework support. The poorest counties also faced the most difficulty in finding sponsors for work relief projects and were usually handicapped in drawing up a range of attractive proposals because of a shortage of appropriately trained staff. It is not surprising that social workers and commissioners in the most distressed areas were frequently accosted by angry and riotous mobs.

The relationship between the states and the federal government in the

7. *Topeka Daily Capital,* June 12, 1935.

provision of relief was close. The RFC, the FERA, and the WPA, for example, allocated funds to the states but did not supervise their internal
distribution, though after 1939 the WPA became more centralized. State
relief stations assessed clients for eligibility, and the localities provided
and paid for a continuing social casework service. In other words, important administrative responsibility remained in the hands of local relief
administrations, even under the WPA. Although Congress advanced
funding for relief on an unprecedented scale, that body was prepared to
give a great deal of financial freedom to the states in determining their allocation priorities.[8] Indeed, for some lawmakers state control over social
spending was essential if they were to give their support to costly legislation. The states and local government were also linked to Washington
because they were obliged to underwrite a significant proportion of the
costs of work relief projects, though they could choose which projects suited them best.

Although there were great similarities in the way in which the FERA
and the RFC operated, they differed dramatically in several ways. Significantly, FERA grants replaced RFC loans. Furthermore, the FERA admirably sought to impose minimum administrative standards for the distribution of relief, whereas the RFC had been primarily concerned with
the ability of borrowers to repay their debts. The FERA tried to move
states away from unimaginative leaf-raking tasks and encouraged the development of more meaningful work projects. The FERA emphasized the
benefits of cash payments to work relief clients when many states relied
heavily on demeaning grocery and fuel orders. The RFC began the process
of forcing states to collect relevant social and economic data and forward
it to Washington regularly. However, the FERA demanded even more information. Field agents played an essential part in the fight to impose best
social work practice on state relief administrations, and they also played
a crucial role in keeping their Washington masters informed of the progress being made toward that end. Kansas had taken some bold steps to-
wards modernizing both its tax structure and welfare organization before the FERA had published the details of the administrative reforms it
wished to impose on states. Nevertheless, FERA pressure forced Kansas
even further down the road toward reform, especially in the field of systematic data gathering and in the recruitment and training of social workers. Support from Washington was also crucial as John Stutz and his colleagues strove to ensure that appointments to administrative positions

8. John Joseph Wallis, "The Birth of the Old Federalism: Financing the New Deal,
1932–1940," 157–59.

recognized the supremacy of practical experience and educational standards over political allegiance.

The reports of field agents between 1933 and 1935 give the clear impression that the Kansas relief administration was a microcosm of what welfare professionals were trying to create throughout the country. Why was Kansas singled out for such lavish praise? How did the state gain the admiration of seasoned critics so quickly? Any answers to these questions must acknowledge that depression unemployment was not as severe in Kansas as it was in many other states. Moreover, the state's population was relatively homogeneous, and as the majority of relief clients were white, racial tensions were minimized. Kansas residents never displayed the hostility to relief, or the determination to flout federal regulations, that was evident in some other states.[9] There was also a significant net out-migration of population during the 1930s, which may well have lessened the strain on welfare services. There can be no doubt, however, that agricultural distress, which was deepened by years of devastating drought, hit the farm population hard, and examples of extreme suffering are not hard to find. However, Congress was prepared to spend large sums of money to help distressed farmers. Indeed, many Kansans found federal intervention during times of hardship more than acceptable if the aim was a revived farm sector.

The high quality of relief administration in Kansas owed a great deal to the experience, skill, and tenacity of John Stutz. Stutz had high professional standards and made a vigorous attempt to impose them throughout the state. He had the foresight to recognize the importance of appointing trained and experienced staff, developing relevant training programs, disseminating clear instructions on best practice, resisting political interference, and gaining the respect of fellow professionals, most notably federal field officers. He also had in Landon a governor who gave him the freedom to manage. Under Stutz's influence, the state was able to make effective applications to the federal government for funds at a time when the quality of submissions must have been a significant determinant for success. Indeed, the Republican administration in Kansas never complained that the state had been discriminated against in the allocation of national relief resources. The development of a first-class transient program is a striking example of the state's professional approach toward the provision of relief. High-quality care offered to outsiders can be seen as a compassionate response to people who had few supporters in their newly adopted localities. A marked improvement in state relief administra-

9. Anthony J. Badger, *The New Deal: The Depression Years, 1933–40*, 193–96.

tions was an important reform element in the New Deal, and Stutz is the key to understanding the successful professionalization of relief in Kansas during the 1930s.

However, as the analysis of Wyandotte County in Chapter 3 shows, even in Kansas there were, periodically, serious deficiencies in the administration of county relief. Such observations do not nullify the positive remarks made about Stutz and his welfare team; rather, they illustrate the unprecedented problems facing social workers and their managers throughout the country. The complex investigations required to assess eligibility, especially using the budgetary deficiency system, created a formidable workload worsened by the periodic surges in the numbers of new applicants and frequent fluctuations in funding. Attempting to transform a ramshackle relief system that relied on imperfect information and was often corrupt would be difficult if the exercise were confined to a handful of states, but when these deficiencies were widespread the task defied rapid solution. In compelling states to contribute financially what they were able, in allocating funding on a monthly basis rather than over a longer period, and by imposing rules to ensure the efficient disbursement of funds, New Dealers were on the one hand attempting to protect both the taxpayer and the needy, and on the other, subscribing to traditional values by encouraging local effort. Any criticism of New Deal relief policies should take into account the serious imperfections in welfare provision that were evident before 1933, as well as the expansion of the working age population, the outcome of the devastating 1937–38 recession, the failure to generate a full employment recovery, and the complexities of farm distress. The nation faced a persistent relief problem that no one in the early days of Roosevelt's first term could have anticipated, and the people, who had lost faith in the curative power of self-help, demanded government intervention. Inaction was unacceptable.

Work Relief: An Assessment

New Deal relief policies had a clear link with measures to generate economic recovery in the sense that once the economy had been wrested from the icy grip of cyclical and structural unemployment, the need for a significant proportion of relief expenditure would be reduced. Nevertheless, relief policies could adversely affect the return to full employment by, for example, promoting excessively high wages. Spending on the WPA, or on the other work relief agencies, was not part of a sophisticated macroeconomic policy aimed at stimulating economic recovery, though the mas-

sive boost in WPA employment in 1938 was a counter-cyclical reaction to the deep recession of that year.[10] The WPA, like the CWA, the FERA, and the PWA, was an emergency work program designed principally to keep the motivation and the skills of the unemployed sufficiently buoyant so that they would be able to move into private jobs once the labor market improved. The failure of New Deal economic policies to eradicate mass unemployment had serious repercussions for relief spending and also put an administration anxious to achieve a balanced budget under constant pressure. It would, of course, be grossly unfair to criticize New Dealers for their failure to accurately predict the course of unemployment or, indeed, to fully cure it. In defense of the administration, one could point out that there were as many people working in 1937 as had been employed during the peak year of 1929. Unfortunately, during the 1930s the nation's population rose by approximately 7 percent, and, more significantly for employment opportunities, the proportion of the population aged between fifteen and sixty-five years expanded by around 12 percent. The New Deal economy was unable to create additional jobs for the six million additions to the labor force.

The outcome of WPA activities influenced the delivery of general relief in every state. As the numbers of needy unemployed remained stubbornly high and the funding Congress allocated to the WPA was insufficient to take full care of them, an additional welfare burden was thrust upon states and local political units. The WPA was designed to ensure that the fit and needy unemployed would not experience the shame of dole payments. However, the WPA was only able to accommodate about 40 percent of the number eligible for assistance under its remit. As a result, counties had to care not only for the unemployables, who, in Kansas, had always been their responsibility, but also for the fit, who were in need of public assistance but unable to get help from federal programs. Moreover, local budgets had to provide supplementary assistance where the security wage was insufficient to provide a minimum living standard.

It is important to recognize that federal agencies like the WPA had different objectives than the state and county relief administrations. Federal bodies provided work or, as in the case of the RA and FSA, loans and grants to help the recipients achieve economic independence. These agencies did not determine who was eligible for relief, nor did they provide a social casework service to families. It was the county relief administra-

10. Margaret Weir, "The Federal Government and Unemployment: The Frustration of Policy Innovation from the New Deal to the Great Society," 153–55; Peter Fearon, *War, Prosperity, and Depression: The U.S. Economy, 1917–45*, 194–215.

tions that were concerned with the rehabilitation of those who had been accepted onto the relief rolls following an investigation into the causes of their deprivation. Ideally, the county relief administration was not merely concerned with the distribution of relief to clients, but also with that additional piece of the social work equation, the return of welfare recipients to self-reliance as rapidly as possible. Both county and federal efforts were directed against the onset of dependency, but by different means. Trained and experienced social workers were required to provide a professional initial assessment of all cases and then, using casework procedures, to guide clients toward the world of self-reliance. That is why the KERC stressed the need for an effectively run, integrated social welfare service that brought together public and private agencies and other groups concerned with community problems—for example, churches and women's clubs. It was felt that considerable progress had been made toward this end by late 1936.[11] Unfortunately, from 1937 on, the KERC's downsizing, combined with the financial squeeze on general relief, resulted in a diminution in the quality of provision for many of the state's most disadvantaged citizens.

During 1936 the KERC drew attention to the fact that the employable caseload on the relief rolls was larger each month than the unemployable caseload. Many of the employables had been unable to secure WPA jobs even though eligible, while other clients were given supplementary relief from county funds because their WPA or RA assistance was deemed inadequate. The provision of supplementary assistance was a continuing burden. In 1936, for example, such help was advanced each month to 10,240 clients who had been certified to the WPA and 6,392 who were receiving assistance from the RA.[12] The exact nature of the burden falling on the states and counties because Congress failed to provide sufficient funding to employ all those eligible for WPA employment varied considerably. Unlike Kansas, some states did not give supplementary assistance to WPA employees, and others discriminated against needy employables. Indeed, as Edwin Amenta points out, Kansas was among the most generous of states for providing general relief to eligible men and women who failed to secure WPA places. This generosity was also evident in the provision of OAA pensions and ADC programs.[13]

The provision of work relief for as many as possible of the able-bodied who failed to secure WPA employment was a priority in Kansas. Writing

11. *KERC Bulletin* 380, January 1937, 9–12.
12. Ibid., 30–33.
13. Amenta, *Bold Relief,* 166–69.

in 1940, Corrington Gill noted that local work relief programs, then operating in twenty-four states, were becoming increasingly popular. He singled out Kansas, where more than 25 percent of the total number of relief
families had work relief jobs, as the state most committed to this principle. Gill was, however, skeptical of the benefits to be gained by those
working on local projects, which he was convinced were usually a return
to the old workhouse test that the FERA had sought to abolish.[14] Kansas
officials, who believed that their projects were planned with care, retained
a great faith in a high-morale-through-work philosophy, and it is quite
possible that local work relief in Kansas was more imaginatively implemented than in many other states. In fact, the thrust of Gill's assault on local relief was that it stemmed from a failure on the part of officials to recognize that unemployment was no longer an emergency phenomenon
but, he believed, a permanent feature of American life.

Another significant difference between federal and state programs was
that remuneration from the former came in cash, but local relief was often in kind. This can be illustrated by taking a single month, February
1936, as an example. During that month, public assistance in Kansas cost
$597,426, of which approximately $90,000 was paid to clients by the counties as cash. These cash payments were made to a variety of recipients in
eighty-five counties, and fifty-one of these counties paid more than 30 percent of their relief in cash.[15] One reason for the attraction of federal work
relief programs was the certainty of a cash wage for as long as the project
lasted, though local relief in Kansas was more generous with cash payments than many other states.

What benefits did Kansas receive from the WPA? The average number
of people employed on Kansas WPA projects (in December of each year)
fluctuated, in line with the national cycle: 41,366 in 1935, rising to a peak
of 41,784 in 1936, followed by a steep decline during the following year to
26,549. The serious recession of 1937–38 persuaded Congress to expand
the work relief program once again, and in December 1938 there were
37,126 WPA employees in Kansas, 26,716 in 1939, and 26,318 in 1940. By
1942, the impact of defense activity caused the figure to fall to 15,993.[16]
The absolute numbers absorbed by the WPA in Kansas must have had a
significant ameliorative effect through the purchasing power that was

14. Corrington Gill, "Local Work for Relief," 157–59.
15. KERC, "Some Important Policies of the KERC," March 14, 1936, Stutz Papers,
327:2:3. The breakdown was as follows: Transients, $851; Direct Relief, $299,939; Work
Relief, $58,074; Poor Farm, Hospital, etc., $106,460; Materials and other costs, $17,652;
County Administration, $93,704; State Office Administration, $20,744 (figures from
page 10).
16. Detailed figures can be found in Federal Works Agency, *Report on the Progress of
the WPA Program*, June 30, 1942, 26, 62, 71, 73–74, 83.

pumped into the local economy. If we consider the period from the start of the WPA through June 30, 1942, the federal government injected nearly $119 million into the Kansas economy, of which almost 90 percent was spent on wages. During the same period local sponsors contributed $39.2 million, the vast bulk of which was used to purchase materials for projects. By far the most important work relief activity was construction, which absorbed nearly 80 percent of total expenditure in the period up to the end of June 1942. Contemporaries were aware, and historians must not neglect, the very tangible gains arising from WPA projects, which must be added to the benefits to families arising from the jobs created. Kansas citizens enjoyed 19,747 miles of new and improved roads, 94 new and 134 reconstructed schools, and 170 new and improved parks. Further activity produced new bridges, lakes, viaducts, playgrounds, athletic fields, sanitary sewers, water mains, and privies. This work was consistent with the president's injunction to create useful projects and, with their construction, the quality of life for many Kansans was materially improved. Health, education, public safety, and ease of travel for market or for leisure were bettered in a way that would not have been possible without an extraordinarily generous commitment from the federal government. In its improvement of recreation services, the federal government was anticipating a lifestyle where technology reduced hours of work and increased the opportunities for leisure.[17]

The Division of Operations, which coordinated construction activity, was responsible, up to June 30, 1942, for disbursing $125.9 million from the WPA and local sponsors. Spending on highways, streets, and roads absorbed 40 percent of the total. The expenditure of the Service Division, which was the next most important subdivision, accounted for a mere $31.5 million, of which $20.8 million was allocated to activities that were subsumed under the heading of "welfare." The overwhelming majority of the women who managed to get on WPA rolls were employed on welfare projects that were heavily skewed toward sewing. There were, however, other highly beneficial and imaginative welfare projects; the school lunch program, for example, enabled WPA workers to serve and prepare meals with food supplied from a variety of sources, including WPA gardening projects, local sponsors, and the Agricultural Marketing Administration. As a result, the children of low-income families received at least one healthy balanced meal during each school day. The Housekeeping Aid Project trained women so that they could provide housekeeping services to low-income families in the event of illness or other emergencies.

17. Amy Sue Bix, *Inventing Ourselves Out of Jobs? America's Debate over Technological Unemployment, 1929–81,* 216.

Trained housekeepers were able to take care of children, and even offer basic care to the sick or incapacitated if it was needed. Through June 30, 1942, more than eleven million school lunches were served in Kansas, and housekeeping aides made nearly 590,000 home visits. Home economics classes in food preserving led to some 400,000 quarts of food being canned. In order to avoid competition with private businesses, sewing rooms were not permitted to produce garments or other forms of output for sale. However, the items that these energetic women made were available for distribution to people in need and, during the period in question, many poor families were happy to receive their share of the 5.5 million garments made in Kansas sewing rooms.

One of the accusations leveled against the WPA was that it discriminated against women, who faced particular difficulties in securing work relief employment.[18] The heavy emphasis on building and construction work created many jobs for unskilled male workers, but few opportunities for females. But even where employment opportunities did exist, women were often routinely rejected because project organizers felt that either they had insufficient employment experience, or their family commitments curtailed their availability for regular employment. There was also a strong prejudice against women, especially if married, competing for jobs when so many men were unemployed. A major obstacle to an expansion of female employment was the rule that WPA jobs were limited to heads of household. Most women found it impossible to qualify on those grounds, especially in Kansas, where few females were family heads. Moreover, the regulation limiting WPA employment to a single family member destroyed the opportunity for others to become WPA employees. In addition, because family income was assessed in judging eligibility for WPA work, wives and daughters had little incentive to search for private sector work.[19] Only women with dependent children who had been certified in need of relief were eligible for WPA employment. In January 1936, women accounted for almost 16 percent of total eligible WPA workers in the U.S. The figure for Kansas was 17.3 percent and therefore slightly more favorable toward women than the national distribution. The national statistics show that, on average, women tended to spend longer

18. Gwendolyn Mink, *The Wages of Motherhood: Inequality In the Welfare State, 1917–42*, 157–61; Alice Kessler-Harris, *Out to Work: A History of Wage-Earning Women in the United States*, 263.

19. For the country as a whole, by the end of the decade a wife whose husband had a relief job was 43 percent less likely to be employed than if her husband had a full-time job. Robert Margo, "Interwar Unemployment in the United States: Evidence from the 1940 Census Sample," 347–48.

on their WPA jobs than men and were less successful than males in securing private employment when laid off project work.[20] Moreover, males
dominated where skilled high-wage jobs were assigned. Women did not
accept this situation in silence. Indeed, their voices were at the fore in the
struggle to obtain better relief funding and working conditions. There is
ample evidence to show that they played a full part in many of the demonstrations, marches, and strikes organized by unions of the unemployed.
Moreover, their role was not always a subordinate one.

Females were uniquely disadvantaged. Usually young single people
who applied for relief could obtain assistance only from either the CCC
or the NYA. Payments from both agencies were small, and the CCC employed only males. There was also a lack of opportunity for both male and
female white-collar and professional workers. The Arts Program, Music
Projects, and the Writers' Project, all of which attracted criticism from conservatives in every state, were funded on a slightly less generous scale in
Kansas than they were nationally. Up to June 30, 1942, only 5 percent of
total WPA expenditure in Kansas was devoted to Public Activities, into
which category the above efforts fell, and less than 2 percent of funds were
absorbed by work on research and archival records throughout the state.
Detailed continuous figures on female and white-collar employment are
not available, but it is possible to take a useful snapshot of Kansas during
1936 that illustrates the significance of these activities.

On June 30, 1936, the WPA employed 7,322 people, of whom 6,146
were female, on either white-collar work or on goods production, which
took place mostly in sewing rooms. The Sewing Project employed 4,991
women; in addition, 179 women worked in nursery schools, and another
32 on a Topeka-based weaving project. Reports on numerous other activities did not make gender distinctions in listing their workers. The Federal Writers' Project employed 142, though in some counties, like Sedgwick,
many volunteered to help. *Kansas: A Guide to the Sunflower State* was the
most lasting contribution of a dedicated team of investigators employed
on the Federal Writers' Project. In Cherokee County, 348 people were employed on ten projects, including Adult and Vocational Education, Workers' Education, Commodity Distribution, Recreation, Sewing, Public
Health, Historical Record Survey, and a Planning Project that employed a
single statistician. Crawford County had fifteen projects employing 437
people, and the range of activity was similar to that of Cherokee County.
In Kansas City, Kansas, there was a citywide Negro Music Project, which
supported a concert band of 52 members made up of 32 unemployed

20. Donald S. Howard, *The WPA and Federal Relief Policy*, 278–85.

males assisted by 20 other men and boys who were not paid. There was a dance band of 10 professional musicians who had been transferred from other projects and a chorus of forty young African Americans who were members of relief families. The children of some low-income families were offered musical instruction in band instruments. The entire Negro Music Project was under the direction of an assistant supervisor who was assisted by four trained men and one woman. Some 240 people were involved in this project, though only 45 were on the payroll, and its success was made possible by exceptional leadership from the black community, coupled with the excellent recreation organization in Kansas City.[21]

Unfortunately, the rules governing eligibility made it inevitable that only a small proportion of total WPA funding became available for women, or professional people of either sex. However, it is easy to become too critical of WPA selection procedures and its emphasis on construction work. Given the values of the 1930s, it is not surprising that heads of household were targeted for special attention. Moreover, unemployment was heaviest among the unskilled, and the construction industry in particular had suffered serious job losses. As work relief projects could not produce output for sale, a concentration on construction activities, with many opportunities to provide work for the unskilled, made sense. It would, however, be a mistake to concentrate solely on these limitations at the cost of neglecting some positive outcomes. During these dispiriting depression years, thousands of Kansans acquired new practical skills on a variety of training programs, or were able to put their existing skills as clerks, actors, seamstresses, or archivists to work. Many people rescued from the scrap heap of neglect experienced an immense sense of satisfaction and pride in working for the government rather than being reliant on the dole, though exactly how widespread and how deep was the boost to the nation's morale is impossible to judge. Unlike the CWA, the WPA provided means-tested assistance, and the significance of social work investigation left clients in no doubt that they were part of a relief rather than a work program.

One frustration was persistent: the lack of sufficient funding to provide WPA jobs to all who were eligible for them. Indeed, Singleton identifies the failure to secure adequate finance for the WPA as a major weakness in the New Deal's change of direction in 1935.[22] Furthermore, annual con-

21. Division of Women's and Professional Projects, Report June 1936, Bound Volume, n.p., WPA records, RG69, NA.

22. Jeff Singleton, *The American Dole: Unemployment Relief and the Welfare State in the Great Depression*, 175.

gressional decisions on funding usually necessitated a rapid change in activity levels; fluctuations in finance made the forward planning of project work nigh on impossible. It is worth noting an example of the impact of funding contraction within a total allocation that in any case fell far short of what was needed. In the middle of 1936, when funding was especially tight, only 6,146 women had been allocated WPA jobs. By contrast, the average weekly female employment under the FERA / KERC during the period January 1–Sept 1, 1935, had been 9,596.[23]

Can the level of funding be defended, even though it was insufficient to employ all those eligible for WPA places? After all, the experience with the CWA had made members of Congress aware that work relief was not a cheap option. The issue here is not really the financial allocations to the WPA, which by historical standards were extraordinarily generous, but the failure of the economy to expand in a way that would have created sufficient jobs to absorb the unemployed and the underemployed. Men and women who were out of work needed employment rather than relief. Unfortunately, the administration did not begin to grasp some of the key elements of a recovery strategy until it was forced to confront the serious implications of the 1937–38 economic recession. During 1938 Roosevelt accepted that a budget deficit would assist recovery from the current slump, and the constraints on WPA funding were therefore relaxed. However, although a persistent budget deficit would have helped erode the numbers of cyclically unemployed Kansans, those who were structurally unemployed would have stubbornly remained. The destitute coal miners and their families in Crawford and Cherokee counties, for example, would still be mired in misery.[24] Moreover, granting the WPA sufficient resources to enable all those eligible for work relief to receive it would have required an increase in public expenditure so great that neither Roosevelt, nor Congress, could have supported it. Nor, of course, would the majority of voters. The sustained attack on work relief initially mounted by conservative Democrats and Republicans gradually attracted the sympathy of the public at large, rendering impossible an additional massive commitment to the WPA. The country had to wait for war-induced expansion to eradicate both cyclical and structural unemployment; these conditions also led to the demise of the WPA.

Given the massive significance of work relief to New Deal social policy, some further questions can be asked about the WPA's performance at

23. *KERC Bulletin* 355, 299.
24. Richard J. Jensen, "The Causes and Cures of Unemployment in the Great Depression."

both the state and the national level. Did the WPA provide a supporting framework to enable those employed on its projects to move smoothly to the private sector? Were the appropriate skills developed for those who secured project work? Was training a priority? Although these questions direct us to very important problems, the key issue is: did WPA workers search conscientiously for nonrelief jobs, or were they provided with a level of security that acted as a deterrent to private employment? In other words, did Kansas project workers prefer a steady flow of cash income from relief work to the possibility of a higher wage in a less secure environment?

It is clear that a key WPA aspiration was the maintenance of a continuous flow of workers from projects into private employment. All project workers were expected to accept any temporary or permanent private sector job offered to them if they were capable of undertaking the work and if the wage offered was not lower than the standard rate in the locality. The link between the public and the private sector was facilitated by the State Employment Service, which kept details of WPA employees up to date by renewing all registrations every ninety days. However, Clarence Nevins, who had replaced Evan Griffith as director of the State WPA in early 1937, was convinced that the Employment Service discriminated against WPA workers when private sector job opportunities became available.[25] Employers, Nevins believed, never complained about the quality of the project workers once they were hired—indeed, many wanted to add more to their payroll—but he was convinced that there was a problem with the Employment Service, which did not have full confidence in their ability. The service's explanation of a perceived discrimination was that project workers were indeed disadvantaged in the job market, but it was because they were not usually available for an immediate interview and, in addition, many were from a rural background and therefore lacked crucial industrial skills. Moreover, private employment opportunities were often for a few days' duration only, and it was senseless to remove workers from their WPA assignments for such a short period. As former project employees who lost private jobs through no fault of their

25. Evan Griffith quit his WPA post in 1937 when Governor Walter A. Huxman chose him to replace Harry Darby as state director of highways. Clarence Nevins had been a member of the KERC from its establishment. In 1934 he became floor leader for the Democratic Party in the Kansas House of Representatives. Notwithstanding his politics, Nevins expressed an admiration for John Stutz's executive leadership and gave him full credit for successfully creating a highly efficient relief administration. Nevins to Stutz, July 12, 1934, FERA State Files, Kansas File, June–September 1934, RG69, NA.

own were entitled to immediate re-employment, if still in need, the action of the Employment Service is understandable. Nevertheless, Nevins advocated the discontinuance of the ninety-day re-registration on the grounds that it was not only costly but also a constant reminder to the Employment Service of the relief status of WPA project workers.[26] It is not possible to test Nevins's hypothesis, though coming from such an informed source it cannot be dismissed out of hand. However, it is evident that when employment opportunities expanded during World War II, there was a marked reluctance on the part of the burgeoning defense sector to hire WPA workers, even in the face of serious labor shortages.

It is illuminating to examine the characteristics of WPA workers in Kansas in comparison with the national picture. In February 1939, Kansas WPA workers were older, had larger families, and had been continuously employed for longer than the national average. Looking first at age, with the national figure in parentheses, 7.4 percent of Kansas workers were aged eighteen to twenty-four years (12.6 percent) and 20.1 percent were aged fifty-five years and older (15.8 percent). If we analyze family size, 6.5 percent of Kansas WPA clients had one family member (10.7 percent), but 20.5 percent had six or more (18.2 percent). The duration of WPA employment in Kansas was greater for both men and women, with the median duration for men being 15.4 months (12.2 months) and for women 17.4 months (14.6 months). If this category is broken down further, it is evident that 58.8 percent of the state's relief workers were employed for less than eighteen months (70.0 percent), 18.8 percent for between eighteen and thirty-five months (13.1 percent), and 22.4 percent for thirty-six months and over (16.9 percent).[27] Thus we see a relatively elderly workforce employed largely on heavy, unskilled manual work. It is not a snapshot of a vigorous, efficient, highly productive group. Indeed, the impression is that the choice of work relief clients was strongly influenced by their welfare needs rather than the ease with which they could move to private sector jobs. It is fair to deduce that the heads of large families earning a security wage supplemented by contributions from local relief sources had little incentive to consider job mobility; in addition, relief workers employed on a project that guaranteed work for some time were not likely to busy themselves searching for private sector jobs.

Should we then, as Michael Darby has argued, reclassify all relief workers as employed rather than unemployed on the grounds that they no

26. Nevins to Fred R. Rauch, May 28, 1940, WPA Records, Central Files, KS 640, Box 1354, RG69, NA.

27. *Report on the Progress of the WPA Program,* June 30, 1939, Table V, 161.

longer had to search for private or public-sector, nonrelief jobs?[28] Although it is possible that some Kansas WPA workers regarded their positions as so secure that they had given up hope of finding a private job that offered the same advantages, it would be a mistake to consider all relief workers as employed. Indeed, it must be stressed that relief workers were not merely jobless, they had also been assessed by social workers as destitute. This group of men and women were unskilled, low waged, relatively ill educated, and generally the least attractive to employers. Even in good times they would have experienced intermittent unemployment, but during the depression they became part of an army of long-term unemployed. As the most marginal members of the surplus labor force, the alternative to federal work relief for them was county dole, not private sector work.

There was a massive oversupply of people willing to work. Thousands of unemployed needy people had failed to secure the WPA jobs for which they had been declared eligible, many others were unemployed but not considered needy, and still others had managed to secure part-time work but sought more hours. Meanwhile, on farms the disguised unemployed waited for an economic revival that would enable them to escape from rural poverty. The numerous unemployed who were cared for by the counties under the miserly General Assistance Program had every incentive to escape from the miserable existence they endured, but many remained jobless. The majority of WPA workers, who were considered suitable only for unskilled construction work, had very limited opportunities in the labor market, and the evidence indicates that they did not spurn private jobs when they became available. The problem both in Kansas and throughout the country was a shortage of jobs, not over-generous relief.[29] Nevertheless, it is possible that federal relief programs may have contributed to persistent unemployment by, for example, helping to keep real wages higher than would be expected, given the numbers out of work. Had real wages declined instead of rising, as they did between 1933 and 1937, then hiring would have been more attractive to employers and the number of jobless would have shrunk. It was legislation such as the President's Reemployment Agreement, the National Labor Relations Act, and the Fair Labor Standards Act that helped keep wages buoyant, rather than

28. Michael R. Darby, "Three-and-a-Half Million U.S. Employees Have Been Mislaid: Or, an Explanation of Unemployment, 1934–1941," 1–16.

29. For an effective critique of the Darby thesis, see Jonathan R. Kesselman and N. E. Savin, "Three-And-A-Half Million Workers Never Were Lost," 205–23; Robert Margo, "Interwar Unemployment in the United States: Evidence from the 1940 Census Sample," 325–49.

the WPA.[30] On the other hand, the WPA can be criticized for neglecting the training needs of the structurally unemployed. However, while a nationwide training program designed to equip the jobless with the skills they required to be competitive in the labor market would have been beneficial, it would also have been prohibitively expensive and probably vigorously opposed by organized trades unions.[31] Sadly, the only New Deal program that seriously addressed the training needs of the unemployed was the NYA, which was limited in its recruitment and existed on shoestring funding.

Skill deficiencies in the WPA labor force were immediately apparent when war demands, especially those emanating from the aviation industry, began to affect Kansas.[32] Wichita quickly became a boomtown, and Boeing, Beech, and Cessna airplane companies, in particular, began an intensive search for workers. These companies were keen to hire machinists, welders, woodworkers, and sheet-metal workers, but very few WPA workers had these skills. Furthermore, airplants sought young, fit, unmarried men who had at least completed the seventh grade of their education. It is interesting to note that very few on WPA payrolls secured places on courses run by the Wichita National Defense Training School, which provided 80 percent of the aviation industry's semiskilled needs. Of the 1,600 persons enrolled in training courses operational in April 1941, only 166 had come from the WPA rolls and the vast majority had been recruited from outside Sedgwick County. Most of the state's war-related jobs were created around Wichita, with other pockets in Kansas City and Fort Riley. This was of little comfort for the unemployed in southeast Kansas, where, in late 1940, one-third of the total WPA load resided.[33] The fact that so few WPA workers were young, that many had family responsibilities which made working away from home difficult, and that some had disabilities made them unattractive to the defense industry.[34]

The airplane companies soon began to hire many women, but their re-

30. M. N. Baily, "The Labor Market in the 1930s," 21–62; Robert Margo, "The Microeconomics of Depression Unemployment," 333–41; Robert Margo, "Employment and Unemployment in the 1930s," 41–59; Peter Temin, "Socialism and Wages in the Recovery from the Great Depression in the United States and Germany," 297–307.

31. Richard J. Jensen, "The Causes and Cures of Unemployment in the Great Depression," 553–58, 568–82.

32. Peter Fearon, "Ploughshares into Airplanes: Manufacturing Industry and Workers in Kansas during World War II," 298–314.

33. "Industrial Activity and the Need for WPA Employment (Kansas)," Report by FWA/WPA Division of Research, February 3, 1941, Central Files, Kansas, 640, 1939–1943, RG69, NA.

34. Clarence G. Nevins to Malcolm J. Miller, August 7, 1942, Central Files, Kansas, 640, 1939–1943, RG69, NA.

cruitment standards were so precise that most of the long-term unemployed found it difficult to meet them. In April 1942, for example, it was
clear that there were growing employment opportunities for female power-
machine operators. However, in response to the suggestion that women
on WPA sewing projects could be trained for these jobs, local re-employment representative Cornelia Edge was brutally dismissive. The WPA
women were "too old, some too fat, some physically unfit and the negroes
are unacceptable."[35] She knew that in early 1942, the Wichita-based aircraft companies would employ only young white women who were not
only high school graduates, but who also less than five-foot-two in height
and weighed less than 135 pounds.[36]

WPA workers did eventually move into the defense sector; indeed, by
fiscal 1942, more than one-third of the program was devoted to defense
and war-related activities.[37] However, most of the work was confined to
construction: the building of new plant and airfields and improvements
to the highway system were to the fore. Job creation was so successful that
by early 1942, Nevins proposed closing the WPA programs in central and
western Kansas to avoid the accusation of labor hoarding.[38] Although
many WPA workers did eventually secure defense jobs, they were not in
manufacturing, and this limited the possibility of moving up the skills
ladder to higher paid employment. The conclusion must be that if there
had been no war, WPA employees would have required a massive revival
in the construction industry in order for them to migrate from work relief
to the private sector. The possibility of such a construction boom without
the stimulus of war seems unrealistic.

By the late 1930s many taxpayers had become discontented with work
relief schemes, which they progressively associated with inefficiency and
political manipulation. The early conviction that the unemployed would
acquire skills and preserve their self-respect while providing a valuable
community service had evaporated. The public now perceived those
"working for the government" in much the same way that they regarded
the persistent scrounger or welfare cheat. The journalist Hubert Kelley expressed these views as early as November 1935 in a pungent article that
chronicled his investigation of the corrosive effects of New Deal relief pro-

35. Cornelia Edge to John J. McDonough, Report on Visit to Topeka, April 10–11,
1942, Central Files, Kansas, 640, 1939–1943, RG69, NA.

36. Judith R. Johnson, "Uncle Sam Wanted Them Too! Women Aircraft Workers in
Wichita during World War II," 40.

37. *Report on the Progress of the WPA Program,* June 30, 1942, 6–12.

38. Nevins to Howard Hunter, February 7, 1942, Central Files, Kansas, 640, 1939–
1943, RG69, NA.

grams. Traveling through Iowa, Nebraska, and Kansas, he claimed to have spoken, and more particularly listened, to men who not only sought relief but had also become addicted to it. They were universally portrayed as shiftless wasters whose principal aim was to avoid work but not payment. These men were unashamed of their lot; indeed, they gloried in their status, joked about it, and even organized themselves into unions in order to put pressure on poor commissioners. They did not merely accept relief but demanded it. In Salina, Kansas, Kelley saw men who looked strong and fit, owned automobiles, and had faces that had once exhibited the characteristics of pioneers but were now "tinged . . . with cunning." In sharp contrast he met worthy, upright citizens who worked hard, paid their taxes, and found it impossible to hire labor at wages that would tempt reliefers out of the pool hall.[39] By 1939 Kelley's prejudices were not confined to members of the nation's Chambers of Commerce. Moreover, his article was considered sufficiently important at the time to have been reproduced for insertion into WPA state files.

The organization of effective work relief projects in a capitalist democratic society is fraught with difficulty. The United States was not Nazi Germany, where the will of the state was supreme and the voices of opposition were soon silenced. Political realities, even where they embraced racial or gender prejudice, had to be observed and the possibilities of political gain vigorously pursued. All government-funded work relief had to take account of the importance of the private sector and avoid competition with it. This explains the prominence of construction work with an emphasis on roads, airports, courthouses, schools, public swimming pools, and the like, but, unfortunately, not private housing. In the main these projects provided unskilled laboring jobs and were not ideal for the unemployed factory worker, clerk, or shop assistant. It is hard to claim that WPA jobs actually maintained, let alone enhanced, skills, though they did help to preserve work habits. Work relief employment cannot be compared even with very similar private sector jobs, for in order to maximize employment, relief projects dispensed with as much capital equipment as possible and relied on the pick and the shovel. It was difficult to recruit efficient managers and supervisors, who were tempted by relatively well-paid private employment, to run projects that suffered from a high labor turnover, as the best workers quit as soon as other jobs became available.[40] There was mounting public criticism of idle workers who seemed to

39. Hubert Kelley, "Good Men Plowed Under," 16–17, 120–21, 135–37.

40. See Jonathon R. Kesselman, "Work Relief Programs In the Great Depression," 153–227.

spend too much time leaning on their shovels. Yet these deficiencies could easily have been a result of poor management, a low-quality workforce, and an emphasis on unassisted physical effort that could not be sustained all day. Moreover, relief needs are highest in the winter when construction work, because of severe weather, is at its most difficult for managers, workers, and machinery. Although labor productivity on work projects was below that of the private sector, this was an inevitable result of the way projects were set up and managed.

Richard A. Lester, a contemporary critic, noted that work relief could not be noncompetitive, value creating, and identical to private sector work all at the same time. If the output from work relief is something that would not normally be produced, then how do we judge it? If, for example, the private sector would not construct an airfield in a particular Kansas county, did it make sense for public money to fund its construction? Possibly, if a case for national defense could be made, but not if private sector criteria were used to judge the investment. There are other serious questions relating to the use of work relief. How could one hire effective managers for work projects when well-paid private sector positions were available? Since some relief workers were unused to the physical demands of their jobs, wasn't there a danger that the morale of the clerk employed as a laborer would be low? Were the benefits to those who owned houses located on improved streets, or close to improved parks, greater than for workers whose skills were underutilized? Lester calculated that work relief cost at least 40 percent more than direct relief, but even more if one added additional costs stemming from operating below optimum efficiency and made allowances for the possibility that some projects would not be completed. Lester believed that the benefits perceived by the supporters of work relief were greatly exaggerated.[41] Many of his criticisms delivered at the start of the WPA program were, unfortunately, equally valid at its close.

Dole was a far more effective means of delivering cash payments to the needy than work relief, but dole was anathema to both liberals and conservatives. In Britain, dole was never considered as demeaning as it was in the United States, where it would remain a stigma as long as work relief was stressed as the means of preserving respectability for the destitute unemployed. But because Congress did not allocate sufficient funding to the WPA for all those who qualified for a position, many of the unemployed were in any case forced onto local relief. In fact, the vast ma-

---

41. Richard A. Lester, "Is Work Relief Economical?" 264–76; see also Michael B. Katz, *In the Shadow of the Poorhouse: A Social History of Welfare in America*, 229–34.

jority of the jobless wanted to work rather than receive dole payments. It is, however, impossible to judge if a continuation of the dole under the New Deal caused personal anguish, though a constant emphasis on the virtue of paid work cannot have helped the morale of those assigned to the WPA but could find no places.

It is also impossible to evaluate New Deal relief policies in Kansas without taking into account the impact of various agricultural programs, though neither the recipients nor the donors would have considered the considerable help given to farmers by, for example, domestic allotment payments or debt assistance, as relief. If funding for FERA general relief and special emergency relief programs between April 1933 and December 1935 is added to that allocated to the CWA during 1933–34, the following totals emerge. Federal grants equalled $51.1 million, the state of Kansas contributed $1.3 million, and the localities $16.2 million. Between 1935 and June 30, 1941, Washington allocated Kansas $107.5 million to fund the WPA, and local sponsors raised $34.1 million.[42] In other words, the federal contribution to support these relief programs amounted to $159 million. However, between 1933 and 1940 Congress also allocated $226 million to the state to assist farmers who were entitled to rental and benefit payments as participants in the wheat allotment and corn-hog programs. These substantial cash payments were essential in keeping farmers out of relief offices, especially in the drought-stricken southwest. Moreover, states were not obliged to make any financial contribution to farm programs, nor were private sponsors required. Farmers also received further assistance—for example, with their mortgages—through the FCA, with seed and CCCorp loans, through the 1934 Cattle Purchase scheme, and from a number of other drought crisis measures. The argument here is not that farmers should have been denied help in dealing with their formidable problems, but that the sums spent on work relief should be kept in perspective. It is also evident that the public viewed assistance for farmers and for the "deserving poor"—that is, the elderly, children, widows, and those with disabilities—far more favorably than programs for the unemployed.

Cash payments for both the relief and the farm programs clearly assisted recipients who then helped to revive their local economies by repaying their debts and becoming active consumers. If Congress had not agreed to spend on such a scale, Landon's success in balancing the state's

42. Theodore E. Whiting, *Final Statistical Report of the Federal Emergency Relief Administration, WPA,* 263–64; Works Progress Administration, *Analysis of Civil Works Program Statistics,* 30–31.

budget would have been severely compromised. As New Dealers anticipated, both relief and farm spending had positive political repercussions. However, the benefits were not restricted to Democratic candidates; it is evident that many Kansas voters recognized the support that Republicans like Landon and Arthur Capper had given to many of the schemes. However, a critical acceptance of much of the New Deal was not sufficient for Landon to secure his own state, or even his own county, in the presidential election of 1936.

It is easy to dismiss New Deal relief measures as either conservative or inadequate. After all, many of the key programs built on what had gone before. There was, for example, a clear link between the RFC and the FERA. Moreover, the fact that federal initiatives emphasized the virtues of work relief and means testing in spite of the opposition from welfare professionals surely identifies the governing philosophy as conservative rather than enlightened. So may the determination of Hopkins and his colleagues to resist the strikes and demonstrations called by organizations of the unemployed. Perhaps, too, the case for seeing New Deal relief as conservative is made stronger by the way in which Republican Kansans seem so comfortable in accepting and implementing the programs. And the failure of a Democrat-dominated Congress to fund fully the WPA so that all who were declared eligible could be employed on work relief projects might be seen as an example of meanness or inadequacy. However, I think that some of these criticisms are too harsh or ill considered.

Accusations of congressional parsimony cannot possibly be sustained. The funding of the relief programs, especially the WPA, was on such a scale of generosity that it must be considered radical. In addition, the attempts to care for the victims of the Great Depression relied on more than historically unprecedented financial support. New Deal research investigations revealed that taking care of the needy was a complex matter, and a variety of initiatives were adopted to address the differing needs of the long-term urban unemployed, jobless youths, college students, the elderly, transients, unemployables, farm families, and needy rural people. Even after these investigations, there were still significant gaps in the available welfare statistics, most notably concerning the level of unemployment and the characteristics of the large numbers out of work. Given the paucity of information, the difficulties of establishing such a wide range of initiatives in every state and efficiently administering them were formidable. The New Dealers did, however, pioneer the drive to professionalize the nation's welfare services, recognizing that efficiency gains represented more effective care and value for money. Although the provision of relief became more centralized as the decade progressed, the

sheer magnitude of the problem meant that cooperation with the states remained as essential in 1940 as it had been in 1933. The relationship between Washington and the states forced the latter to systematically gather relevant welfare data and also compelled states to radically overhaul their tax systems. States, however, still retained great operational freedom. As a result, they varied considerably in the manner in which New Deal ideals were embraced and how effectively they could use the historically large sums of congressional funding to assist those in need.

Did the substantial numbers of fit men and women who were forced to live on dole payments suffer from low morale? It is hard to say. Certainly the vast majority would have preferred to work for the government, as did most of the recipients of rehabilitation loans. However, as the economic returns to individuals from employment on federal work relief projects were so superior to other forms of relief, especially local relief, this is scarcely surprising. In spite of the legitimate criticisms that can be leveled against work relief and the emphasis on means testing, it is difficult to see what the alternative was. The public feared that dole payments would lead to dependency but called for action to assist those out of work through no fault of their own. There was, however, strong public support for means testing, so that public assistance was available only for those who deserved it and only in amounts sufficient to meet minimum needs. Congress also expressed distaste for dole but would not, or more accurately, could not, fund a work relief program that would employ all those eligible. Business interests were in no mood to accept the additional tax burden that a fully funded WPA would have required. The employed and the trades unions would not support expensive training schemes that would make the jobless more competitive in the labor market. Full employment remained stubbornly elusive, as did 100 percent parity for farmers. The Kansas example shows that it was possible to administer relief in a humane and efficient manner, though not in all 105 of the state's counties. However, Kansas was fortunate as the depression did not strike the Sunflower State with the utmost severity. Nevertheless, the state's social workers and welfare administrators were often compelled to reduce relief payments and services to unacceptable levels. They also frequently faced the wrath of the deprived. An appreciation of the serious political, economic, and social problems encountered in other parts of the country makes one more forgiving of New Deal policy initiatives that were well intentioned but sometimes so flawed that they failed to deliver their maximum benefits.

Selected Bibliography

Manuscript Collections: Personal Papers

Kansas State Historical Society, Topeka
      Papers of Arthur Capper
      Papers of Alfred Mossman Landon
      Papers of Harry Hines Woodring
Spencer Research Library, University of Kansas
      Papers of Frank T. Stockton
      Papers of John G. Stutz (Stutz Papers)
Franklin D. Roosevelt Library, Hyde Park, N.Y.
      Papers of Harry L. Hopkins (Hopkins Papers)
      Papers of Franklin D. Roosevelt
      Papers of Aubrey Williams
Kansas State Archives, State Records
      State Board of Agriculture
      Kansas Emergency Relief Committee
      Minutes of Kansas Emergency Relief Committee Executive
      State Labor Department
National Archives, Washington, D.C.
      Records of the Civilian Conservation Corps RG35
      Records of the Works Projects Administration RG69
      Records of the President's Organization on Unemployment Relief
        RG73
      Records of the Bureau of Agricultural Economics RG83
      Records of the Resettlement Administration RG96

Records of the National Youth Administration RG119
Records of the Public Works Administration RG135
Record of the War Production Board RG179
Records of the Bureau of Employment Security RG183
Records of the Public Housing Administration RG196
Records of the War Manpower Commission RG211
Records of the Petroleum Administration Board RG232
Records of the Reconstruction Finance Corporation RG 234

Federal Government Censuses

Department of Commerce. *Financial Statistics of State and Local Govern-ments: 1932, Kansas.* Washington, D.C., 1935.
U.S. Bureau of the Census. *Fifteenth Census of the United States, 1930: Agri-culture.* Washington, D.C.: Government Printing Office, 1932.
———. *Fifteenth Census of the United States, 1930: Manufactures, 1929.* Wash-ington, D.C.: Government Printing Office, 1932.
———. *Fifteenth Census of the United States, 1930: Manufactures, 1929.* Vol. 3, *Reports by States.* Washington, D.C.: Government Printing Office, 1933.
———. *Fifteenth Census of the United States, 1930: Population.* Washington, D.C.: Government Printing Office, 1932.
———. *Fifteenth Census of the United States, 1930: Unemployment.* Washing-ton, D.C.: Government Printing Office, 1931.
———. *Sixteenth Census of the United States, 1940: Agriculture.* Washington, D.C.: Government Printing Office, 1942.
———. *Sixteenth Census of the United States, 1940: Manufactures, 1939.* Washington, D.C.: Government Printing Office, 1942.
———. *Sixteenth Census of the United States, 1940: Mineral Industries, 1939.* Washington, D.C.: Government Printing Office, 1944.
———. *Sixteenth Census of the United States, 1940: Population.* Washington, D.C.: Government Printing Office, 1943.
———. *United States Census of Agriculture, 1935.* Washington, D.C.: Gov-ernment Printing Office, 1936.

Kansas State Records

State Bureau of Agriculture, *KSBA Biennial Reports*
Kansas State Banking Department, *KSBA Biennial Reports*
Kansas State Budget, *Biennial Submission to Legislature*
State Coal Mine Inspection Department, *Annual Reports*

State Labor Department, *SLD Biennial Reports*
State Commission of Labor and Industry, *SCLI Annual Reports*
Kansas Labor and Industrial Bulletin
Message of the Governor to the Legislature

Federal Government Publications

Agricultural Extension Service Report, Crawford County.

An Interpretation of the Relief Provisions of the Relief and Construction Acts of 1932. An Address delivered by Hon. Atlee Pomerene. Washington, D.C.: Government Printing Office, 1932.

Asch, Berta, and A. R. Mangus. *Farmers on Relief and Rehabilitation.* WPA Research Monograph VIII. Washington, D.C.: Government Printing Office, 1937.

Baird, Edith. *Average General Relief Benefits, 1933–38.* Washington, D.C.: Government Printing Office, 1940.

Bell, Earl H. *Culture of a Contemporary Rural Community: Sublette, Kansas.* USDA/Bureau of Agricultural Economics, Rural Life Studies No. 2, September 1942.

Board of Governors of the Federal Reserve System. *Banking and Monetary Statistics, 1914–41.* Washington, D.C.: Government Printing Office, 1943.

Burns, Arthur E. *Federal Financing of Emergency Relief.* FERA Monthly Report, February 1–29, 1936.

Burns, Arthur E., and Edward A. Williams. *Federal Work, Security and Relief Programs.* WPA Research Monograph XXIV. Washington, D.C.: Government Printing Office, 1941.

Carothers, Doris. *Chronology of the Federal Emergency Relief Administration May 12, 1933, to December 31, 1935.* WPA Research Monograph VI. Washington D.C.: Government Printing Office, 1937.

Civilian Conservation Corps, *Annual Report of the Director.*

Edwards, A. D. *Influence of Drought and Depression on a Rural Community: A Case Study in Haskell County, Kansas.* USDA, FSA and Bureau of Agricultural Economics, Social Research Report No. VII. Washington, D.C., January 1937.

Ezekiel, Mordecai, and Louis H. Bean. *Economic Bases for the Agricultural Adjustment Act.* Washington, D.C.: USDA, 1933.

Federal Emergency Relief Administration. *Unemployment Relief Census, October 1933. United States Summary.* Washington, D.C., 1934.

Federal Works Agency. *Report on the Progress of the WPA Program, 1935–43.* Washington, D.C. Annually.

Geddes, Anne E. *Trends in Relief Expenditures.* WPA Research Monograph X. Washington, D.C.: Government Printing Office, 1937.

Horton, Donald C., Harald C. Larsen, and Norman J. Wall. *Farm Mortgage Credit Facilities in the United States.* USDA Miscellaneous Publication No. 478. Washington, D.C., 1942.

Humphrey, Dan D. *Family Unemployment: An Analysis of Unemployment in Terms of Family Units.* Washington, D.C., 1940.

Kube, Harold D., and Ralph H. Danhof. *Changes in the Distribution of Manufacturing Wage Earners, 1899–1939.* Washington, D.C., 1942.

Link, Irene. *Relief and Rehabilitation in the Drought Area.* WPA Research Bulletin. Washington, D.C., June 1937.

Mangus, A. R. *Changing Aspects of Rural Relief.* WPA Research Monograph XIV. Washington, D.C., 1938.

McCormick, M. Riggs. *Federal Emergency Relief Administration Grants.* FERA Monthly Report, December 1 to December 31, 1935.

Menefee, Selden C. *Vocational Training and Employment of Youth.* WPA Research Monograph XXV. Washington, D.C.: Government Printing Office, 1942.

Nicol, Mary A. *Family Relief Budgets.* FERA Monthly Report, June 1 to June 30, 1936.

President's Organization for Unemployment Relief. *State Legislation for Unemployment Relief from January 1, 1931, to May 31, 1932.* Washington, D.C., 1932.

Report of the President's Research Committee on Social Trends. *Recent Social Trends in the United States.* New York, London: McGraw-Hill Book Company, 1933.

Shawe, Earle K. "An Analysis of the Legal Limitations on the Borrowing Power of State Governments." *FERA Monthly Report,* June 1–30, 1936.

Social Security Board. *Social Security in America: The Factual Background of the Social Security Act as Summarized from Staff Reports to the Committee on Economic Security.* Washington, D.C.: Government Printing Office, 1937.

Stewart, H. L. *Changes on Wheat Farms in South-Western Kansas 1931–37 With Special Reference to the Influence of AAA Programs.* USDA Farm Management Reports No 7. Washington, D.C., 1940.

Taeuber Conrad, and Carl C. Taylor. *People of the Drought States.* WPA Research Bulletin. Washington, D.C. March 1937.

U.S. Department of Agriculture. *Agricultural Statistics.* Washington, D.C. Annually.

————. *Farm Real Estate Situation.* Washington, D.C. Annually.

U.S. Department of Commerce. *Analyses of Kansas Coals.* Technical Paper 455. Washington, D.C., 1929.

————. *Mineral Resources of the United States 1930.* Part II, *Non Metals.* Washington, D.C.: Bureau of Mines, 1932.

Vasey, Tom, and Josiah C. Folsom. *Survey of Agricultural Labor Conditions in Pawnee County, Kansas.* Washington, D.C.: USDA Farm Security Administration and Bureau of Agricultural Economics, November 1937.

Webb, John N. *The Migratory Casual Worker.* WPA Research Monograph VIII. Washington, D.C.: Government Printing Office, 1937.

————. *The Transient Unemployed: A Description and Analysis of the Transient Relief Problem.* WPA Research Monograph III. Washington, D.C.: Government Printing Office, 1935.

Westefeld, Albert. *Getting Started: Urban Youth in the Labor Market.* WPA Research Monograph XXVI. Washington, D.C.: Government Printing Office, 1943.

Whiting, Theodore E. *Final Statistical Report of the Federal Emergency Relief Administration, WPA.* Washington, D.C.: Government Printing Office, 1942.

Whiting, Theodore E., and T. J. Woofter, Jr. *Summary of Relief and Federal Work Program Statistics, 1933–40.* Washington, D.C., 1941.

Works Progress Administration. *Analysis of Civil Works Program Statistics.* Washington, D.C., 1939.

————. *Workers on Relief in the United States in March 1935: A Census of Usual Occupations.* Washington, D.C., 1937.

Zimmerman, Carle C., and Nathan L. Whetten. *Rural Families on Relief.* WPA Research Monograph XVII. Washington D.C.: Government Printing Office, 1938.

Kansas State Publications

Kansas Agricultural Experiment Station Bulletin
Kansas Emergency Relief Committee Bulletin
Kansas Federal Relief Committee Bulletin
Kansas Labor and Industrial Bulletin
Kansas Legislative Council Reports of Research Department
Kansas Relief News-Bulletin
Kansas Social Welfare Journal
Kansas State Planning Board

Other Primary Sources

Bureau of Governmental Research. "Welfare (Poor Relief) Activities of Wyandotte County, Kansas." Typescript, March 21, 1932. Copy in Spencer Library, University of Kansas.

Hein, Clarence J., and James T McDonald. *Federal Grants-In-Aid.* Special Report No. 50, Governmental Research Center, University of Kansas, n.d. Copy in Spencer Library, University of Kansas.

Kansas: A Guide to the Sunflower State. 1939. Reissued with an introduction by James R. Shortridge as *The WPA Guide to 1930s Kansas.* Lawrence: University Press of Kansas, 1984.

Kansas Emergency Relief Division, Monthly Reports.

Kansas Legislative Council. *Social Welfare Experience in 1938, 1939, and 1940.* Spencer Library, University of Kansas.

Kansas State Board of Agriculture (KSBA). *Price Patterns: Prices Received by Kansas Farmers, 1910–55.* Manhattan, Kansas. June 1957.

Kansas State Planning Board. *Inventory of Public Works: A Study of Possibilities in Kansas.* Topeka, June 1935.

Kansas Union Farmer.

Kansas Vehicle Department. "Registrations of All Motor Vehicles By County, 1931–40." Typescript. Copy in Spencer Research Library, University of Kansas.

McDonald, James T. *State Finance: Expenditures of the State of Kansas, 1915–53.* Governmental Research Center, University of Kansas. Fiscal Information Series No 5, n.d. Spencer Library, University of Kansas.

McNutt, Earnest F., comp. "Kansas Unemployed Organizations Their Programs and Activities." Typescript, October 25, 1940. Kansas State Archive.

Report of Drought Cattle Operations by KERC, May 1, 1935. Records of KERC. KSA Topeka.

Report of the Public Welfare Temporary Commission, State of Kansas. Topeka, January 1933.

Roosevelt, Franklin Delano. *The Public Papers and Addresses of Franklin D. Roosevelt with a Special Introduction and Explanatory Notes by President Roosevelt.*

   Vol. 1, *The Genesis of the New Deal, 1928–32.* New York: Russell & Russell, 1969.

   Vol. 2, *The Year of Crisis, 1933.* New York: Russell & Russell, 1969.

   Vol. 3, *The Advance of Recovery and Reform, 1934.* New York: Russell & Russell, 1969.

   Vol. 4, *The Court Disapproves, 1935.* New York: Russell & Russell, 1969.

Vol. 5, *The People Approve, 1936.* New York: Russell & Russell, 1969.

"A Study of Kansas Poor Farms." *KERC Bulletin* 307, Topeka, October 1935.

S. W. Bell Telephone Co. *Economic Survey of Kansas.* St Louis Mo., May 1930. Spencer Research Library, University of Kansas.

Under the Statehouse Dome. Our State Government. Radio Speeches of Governor Harry H. Woodring. Topeka, 1932.

Unemployment Status of Negroes: A Compilation of Facts and Figures Respecting Unemployment Amongst Negroes In One Hundred and Six Cities. New York: National Urban League, December 1931.

Newspapers

Abilene Daily Chronicle
Chanute Tribune
Columbus Daily Advocate
Coffeyville Daily Journal
El Dorado Times
Emporia Gazette
Dodge City Globe
Garden City Telegram
Hutchinson News
Kansas City Kansan
Kansas City Times
Neodesha Sun
New York Times
Norton Telegram
Salina Journal
Stafford County Courier
Topeka Daily Capital
Topeka State Journal
Pittsburg Headlight
Pittsburg Sun
Wichita Beacon
Wichita Evening Eagle
Wichita Sunday Beacon
Winfield Courier

Articles and Book Chapters

Abbott, Edith. "Don't Do It, Mr. Hopkins." *Nation* 140, no. 3627 (January 9, 1935).

————. "The Failure of Local Relief." *New Republic*, November 9, 1932.

Almond, Gabriel, and Harold D. Lasswell. "Aggressive Behavior by Clients toward Public Relief Administrators: A Configurative Analysis." *American Political Science Review* 28 (1934).

Alston, Lee J. "Farm Foreclosures in the United States during the Interwar Period." *Journal of Economic History* 43 (December 1983).

Arndt, Randy. "NCL Founder, John Stutz, Passes Century Mark." *Illinois Municipal Review*, February 1993.

Amenta, Edwin, Ellen Benoit, Chris Bonastia, Nancy K. Cauthen, and Drew Halfmann. "Bring Back the WPA: Work, Relief, and the Origins of American Social Policy in Welfare Reform." *Studies in American Political Development* 12 (Spring 1998).

Baily, M. N. "The Labor Market in the 1930s." In *Macroeconomics, Prices and Quantities: Essays in Honor of Arthur Okun*, edited by James Tobin. Washington, D.C.: Brookings Institution, 1983.

Bondurant, Claire A. "A Study of One Hundred Farm Security Administration Grant Families in Ellis County, Kansas, 1939." *Fort Hays Kansas State College Studies*, General Series Number Three, 1941.

Bone, Roy L. "Could Branch Banking Be Properly Regulated?" *American Banking Association Journal*, August 1929.

Bowman, W. W. "Rural Banks and Banking." *Kansas State Board of Agriculture, 30th Biennial Report*, 1935–36.

Bremer, William W. "Along the 'American Way': The New Deal's Work Relief Programs for the Unemployed." *Journal of American History* 62 (1975–76).

Burns, Arthur E., and P. Kerr. "Recent Changes in Work Relief Wage Policy." *American Economic Review* 31 (1941).

————. "Survey of Work-Relief Wage Policies." *American Economic Review* 27 (1937).

Calomaris, Charles W., and Eugene Nelson White. "The Origins of Federal Deposit Insurance." In *The Deregulated Economy. A Historical Approach to Political Economy*, edited by Claudia Goldin and Gary D. Libecap. Chicago: National Bureau of Economic Research, 1994.

Capper, Arthur. "What Kansas Farmers Think." *Review of Reviews* 84 (September 1931).

Clark, Carroll D. "Public Poor Relief in Kansas." *Handbook of Kansas Social Resources* (Topeka, 1932).

Cordell, William H., and Kathryn Coe Cordell. "Unions among the Unemployed." *North American Review* 240 (December 1935).

Dade, Emile B. "Migration of Kansas Population, 1930–45." *University of Kansas Industrial Research Series* 6 (1946).

Darby, M. R. "Three-and-a-Half Million U.S. Employees Have Been Mislaid: Or, an Explanation of Unemployment, 1934–41." *Journal of Political Economy* 84, no. 1 (February 1976).

Dorsett, Lyle. "Kansas City and the New Deal." In *The New Deal: The State and Local Levels,* vol. 2, edited by John Braeman, Robert H. Bremner, and David Brody. Columbus: Ohio State University Press, 1975.

Duram, James C. "Constitutional Conservatism: The Kansas Press and the New Deal Era as a Case Study." *Kansas Historical Quarterly* 43 (Winter 1977).

Fearon, Peter. "From Self-Help to Federal Aid: Unemployment and Relief in Kansas, 1929–32." *Kansas History* 13 (Summer 1990).

———. "Kansas Poor Relief: The Influence of the Great Depression." *Mid-America* 78 (Summer 1996).

———. "Mechanisation and Risk: Kansas Wheat Growers, 1915–30." *Rural History* 6 (1995).

———. "Ploughshares into Airplanes: Manufacturing Industry and Workers in Kansas during World War II." *Kansas History* 22 (Winter 1999–2000).

———. "Relief for Wanderers: The Transient Service in Kansas 1933–35." *Great Plains Quarterly* 26 (Fall 2006).

———. "Riot in Wichita, 1934." *Kansas History* 15 (Winter 1992–93).

———. "Taxation, Spending, and Budgets: Public Finance in Kansas during the Great Depression." *Kansas History* 28 (Winter 2005–6).

Fenton, F. C. "Progress in Rural Electrification in Kansas." *Kansas State Board of Agriculture 32nd Biennial Report,* 1939–40.

Gill, Corrington. "Local Work for Relief." *Survey Midmonthly* 76 (May 1940).

Grimes, W. E. "The Effect of the Combined Harvester-Thresher on Farming in a Wheat Growing Region." *Scientific Agriculture* 9 (August 1929).

———. "Farm Tenancy in Kansas." *Kansas State Board of Agriculture 32nd Biennial Report,* 1939–40.

Harris, Vivien S. "The Program of the American Red Cross in Outdoor Relief." *Handbook of Kansas Social Resources* (Topeka, 1932).

Hinrichs, H. S. "Twenty Years of Rural Electrification in Kansas." *Kansas State Board of Agriculture 35th Biennial Report,* 1943–44.

Hodges, J. A., F. F. Elliott, and W. E. Grimes. "Types of Farming in Kansas." *Kansas Agricultural Experiment Station,* Bulletin 251 (August 1930).

Hoover, Leo M. "Kansas Agriculture After 100 Years." *Kansas Agricultural Experiment Station,* Bulletin 392 (August 1957).

Howe, Harold. "Local Government Finance in Kansas." *Kansas State Plan-*

ning Board in Cooperation with Works Progress Administration and National Resources Committee (Topeka, April 1939).

――――. "Tax Delinquency on Farm Real Estate in Kansas, 1928 to 1933." *Kansas Agricultural Experiment Station,* Circular 186 (October 1937).

――――. "The Trend of Real Estate Taxation in Kansas, 1910 to 1942." *Kansas Agricultural Experiment Station,* Circular 228 (October 1944).

Howell, Fred N. "Some Phases of the Industrial History of Pittsburg, Kansas." *Kansas Historical Quarterly* 1 (May 1932).

Hunger, Edwin A. "Kansas Outstanding Leader in the Use of the Combine." *Kansas State Board of Agriculture 27th Biennial Report,* 1929–30.

Hurt, R. Douglas. "Agricultural Technology in the Dust Bowl, 1932–49." In *The Great Plains: Environment and Culture,* edited by Brian W. Blouet and Frederick C. Luebke. Lincoln: University of Nebraska Press, 1979.

――――. "Prices, Payments and Production: Kansas Wheat Farmers and the Agricultural Adjustment Administration, 1933–39." *Kansas History* 23 (2000–2001).

Jensen, Richard J. "The Causes and Cures of Unemployment in the Great Depression." *Journal of Interdisciplinary History* 19 (Spring 1989).

Johnson, Judith R. "Uncle Sam Wanted Them Too! Women Aircraft Workers in Wichita during World War II." *Kansas History* 17 (Spring 1994).

Kelley, Hubert. "Good Men Plowed Under." *American Magazine,* November 1935.

Kesselman, Jonathon R. "Work Relief Programs in the Great Depression." In *Creating Jobs: Public Employment Programs and Wage Subsidies,* edited by John Palmer. Washington, D.C.: Brookings Institution, 1978.

Kesselman, Jonathon R., and N. E. Savin. "Three-And-A-Half Million Workers Never Were Lost." *Economic Inquiry* 16 (April 1978).

Lambert, C. Roger. "The Drought Cattle Purchase 1934–35: Problems and Complaints." *Agricultural History* 45 (1971).

Lester, Richard A. "Is Work Relief Economical?" *Social Service Review* 10 (1936).

Margo, Robert. "Employment and Unemployment in the 1930s." *Journal of Economic Perspectives* 7 (Spring 1993).

――――. "Interwar Unemployment in the United States: Evidence from the 1940 Census Sample." In *Interwar Unemployment in Historical Perspective,* edited by Barry Eichengreen and T. J. Hatton. Dordrecht, London: Kluwer Press, 1988.

———. "The Microeconomics of Depression Unemployment." *The Journal of Economic History* 51 (June 1991).

McCoy, Donald R. "Alf Landon and the Oil Troubles of 1930–32." *Kansas Historical Quarterly* 31 (1965).

———. "The New Deal through Alf Landon's Eyes." *Midwest Quarterly* 6 (1964).

McFarland, Keith D. "Secretary of War Harry Woodring: Early Career in Kansas. *Kansas Historical Quarterly* 39 (1973).

Oppenheimer, Robert. "Acculturation or Assimilation: Mexican Immigrants in Kansas 1900 to World War II." *Western Historical Quarterly* 16 (October 1985).

Orten, M. D. "The Present Economic Condition of the Tri-State Zinc District." *Journal of Business* 1 (1928).

Pearson, F. A. "Money in Relation to Market Stabilization." *Report of Kansas State Bankers Association for Quarter Ending March 1939.*

Powell, William E. "The Cherokee-Crawford Coal Field of South-eastern Kansas: A Study in Sequent Occupance." *Midwest Quarterly* 2 (1981).

———. "European Settlement in the Cherokee-Crawford Coalfield of South-eastern Kansas." *Kansas Historical Quarterly* 41 (1975).

———. "Former Mining Communities of the Cherokee-Crawford Coalfield of South-eastern Kansas." *Kansas Historical Quarterly* 38 (1972).

Riney-Kehrberg, Pamela. "Hard Times, Hungry Years: The Failure of Poor Relief in South-western Kansas, 1930–33." *Kansas History* 15 (Autumn 1992).

———. "In God We Trusted, In Kansas We Busted . . . Again." *Agricultural History* 63 (Spring 1989).

Robinson, M. L. "The Response of Kansas Farmers to the Wheat Adjustment Program." *Journal of Farm Economics* 19 (1937).

Rowland, Mary Scott. "Kansas Farming and Banking in the 1920s." *Kansas History* 8 (Autumn 1985).

———. "Social Services in Kansas, 1916–30." *Kansas History* 7 (Autumn 1984).

Salmon, S. C., and R. I. Throckmorton. "Wheat Production in Kansas." *Kansas Agricultural Experiment Station,* Bulletin 248 (July 1929).

Salmond, John A. "The New Deal and Youth." In *W.P. Morrell: A Tribute. Essays in Modern and Early Modern History Presented to William Parker Morrell Professor Emeritus, University of Otago,* edited by G. A. Wood and P. S. O'Connor. Dunedin: University of Otago Press, 1973.

Schuyler, Michael W. "Federal Drought Relief Activities in Kansas." *Kansas Historical Quarterly* 42 (1976).

Sheridan, Richard B. "The College Student Employment Project at the University of Kansas, 1934–43." *Kansas History* 8 (Winter 1985–86).

Sherwood, R. H. "The Development of Strip Mining." *Mining Congress Journal* 31 (November 1945).

Smiley, Gene. "Can Keynesianism Explain the 1930s? Reply to Cowen." *Critical Review* 5 (1991).

Taylor, Morton. "Budget-Balancer Landon." *New Republic,* January 15, 1936.

Temin, Peter. "Socialism and Wages in the Recovery from the Great Depression in the United States and Germany." *Journal of Economic History* 50 (June 1990).

Walker, H. B. "Progress in Rural Electrification." *Kansas State Board of Agriculture 25th Biennial Report,* 1925–26.

Walker, Sydnor H. "Privately Supported Social Work." In *Report of the President's Research Committee on Social Trends, Recent Social Trends in the United States,* Vol. 2. New York and London: McGraw-Hill Book Company, 1933.

Wallis, John Joseph. "The Birth of the Old Federalism: Financing the New Deal, 1932–40." *Journal of Economic History* 44 (1984).

———. "Employment in the Great Depression: New Data and Hypothesis." *Explorations in Economic History* 26 (1989).

Wallis, John Joseph, and Wallace E. Oates. "The Impact of the New Deal on American Federalism" In *The Defining Moment: The Great Depression and the American Economy in the Twentieth Century,* edited by Michael D. Bordo, Claudia Goldin, and Eugene Nelson White. Chicago: National Bureau of Economic Research, 1998.

Weir, Margaret. "The Federal Government and Unemployment: The Frustration of Policy Innovation from the New Deal to the Great Society." In *The Politics of Social Policy in the United States,* edited by Margaret Weir, Anne Shola Orloff, and Theda Skocpol. Princeton: Princeton University Press, 1988.

Wheelock, David C. "Regulation and Bank Failures: New Evidence from the Agricultural Collapse of the 1920s." *Journal of Economic History* 26 (1989).

Books

Abbott, Edith. *Public Assistance.* Vol. 1, *American Principles and Policies.* Chicago: University of Chicago Press, 1940.

Alinsky, Saul. *John L. Lewis: An Unauthorized Biography.* New York: G. P. Putnam's Sons, 1949.

Amenta, Edwin. *Bold Relief: Institutional Politics and the Origins of Modern American Social Policy.* Princeton: Princeton University Press, 1998.

Badger, Anthony J. *The New Deal: The Depression Years.* London: Macmillan, 1989.

Barber, William J. *Designs within Disorder: Franklin D. Roosevelt, the Economists, and the Shaping of American Economic Policy, 1933–45.* Cambridge: Cambridge University Press, 1996.

Benedict, Murray R. *Farm Policies of the United States, 1799–1950: A Study of Their Origins and Development.* New York: Twentieth Century Fund, 1953.

Bitterman, Henry J. *State and Federal Grants-In-Aid.* New York, Chicago: Mentzer, Bush and Company, 1938.

Bix, Amy Sue. *Inventing Ourselves Out of Jobs? America's Debate over Technological Unemployment, 1929–81.* Baltimore: Johns Hopkins University Press, 2000.

Bonnifield, Paul. *The Dust Bowl: Men, Dirt and Depression.* Albuquerque: University of New Mexico Press, 1979.

Brock, William R. *Welfare, Democracy, and the New Deal.* Cambridge: Cambridge University Press, 1988.

Brown, Josephine Chapin. *Public Relief, 1929–39.* New York: Henry Holt and Company, 1940.

Browning, Grace A. *The Development of Poor Relief Legislation in Kansas.* Chicago: Chicago Social Science Monographs, No. 25, 1935.

Campbell, Christina McFadyen. *The Farm Bureau: A Study of the Making of National Farm Policy, 1933–40.* Urbana: University of Illinois Press, 1962.

Clark, Caroll D., and Roy L. Roberts. *People of Kansas: A Demographic and Sociological Study.* Topeka: Kansas State Planning Board, 1936.

Clark, John G. *Towns and Minerals in South Eastern Kansas: A Study in Regional Industrialization, 1890–1930.* Lawrence: Kansas Geological Survey Special Districts, Publication No. 52, 1970.

Colcord, Joanna C. *Cash Relief.* New York: Russell Sage Foundation, 1936.

———. *Community Planning in Unemployment Emergencies: Recommendations Growing Out of Experience.* New York: Russell Sage Foundation, 1930.

Davis, Joseph S. *Wheat and the AAA.* Washington, D.C.: Brookings Institution, 1935.

Drury, James W. *The Government of Kansas.* Lawrence: University Press of Kansas, 1970.

Fearon, Peter. *War, Prosperity, and Depression: The U.S. Economy, 1917–45.* Deddington, Oxford: Philip Allan Publishers, 1987.

Fisher, Glenn W. *The Worst Tax? A History of the Property Tax in America.* Lawrence: University Press of Kansas, 1996.

Fisher, Jacob. *The Response of Social Work to the Depression.* Cambridge: Schenkman Publishing, 1980.

Fite, Gilbert C. *George N. Peek and the Fight for Farm Parity.* Norman: University of Oklahoma Press, 1954.

Fitzgerald, D. A. *Livestock under the AAA.* Washington, D.C.: Brookings Institution, 1935.

Gill, Corrington. *Wasted Manpower: The Challenge of Unemployment.* Reprint. New York: Da Capo Press, 1973.

Goldin, Caudia, and Gary D. Liebcap, eds. *The Regulated Economy. A Historical Approach to Political Economy.* Chicago: National Bureau of Economic Research, 1994.

Grant, Michael Johnson. *Down and Out on the Family Farm: Rural Rehabilitation in the Great Plains, 1929–45.* Lincoln: University of Nebraska Press, 2002.

Hathway, Marion. *The Migratory Worker and Family Life.* Chicago: University of Chicago Press, 1934.

Hopkins, Harry. *Spending to Save: The Complete Story of Relief.* New York: W. W. Norton, 1936.

Howard, Donald S. *The WPA and Federal Relief Policy.* Reprint. New York: Da Capo Press, 1973.

Hurt, R. Douglas. *The Dust Bowl: An Agricultural and Social History.* Chicago: Nelson-Hall, 1981.

Ickes, Harold L. *The Secret Diary of Harold L. Ickes: The First Thousand Days, 1933–36.* New York: Simon and Schuster, 1953.

Johnson, Sherman. *Wheat under the Agricultural Adjustment Act: Developments up to June 1934.* Washington, D.C.: Brookings Institution, 1934.

Jones, Lawrence A., and David Durand. *Mortgage Lending Experience in Agriculture.* Princeton, N.J.: National Bureau of Economic and Social Research, 1954.

Katz, Michael B. *In the Shadow of the Poorhouse: A Social History of Welfare in America.* New York: Basic Books Inc., 1986.

Kessler-Harris, Alice. *Out to Work: A History of Wage-Earning Women in the United States.* Oxford: Oxford University Press, 1982.

Kirkendall, Richard S. *Social Scientists and Farm Politics in the Age of Roosevelt.* Columbia: University of Missouri Press, 1966.

Kline, Ronald R. *Consumers in the Country: Technology and Social Change in Rural America.* Baltimore: Johns Hopkins University Press, 2000.

Kolb, John H., and Edmund de S. Brunner. *A Study of Rural Society.* Boston: Houghton Mifflin, 1952.

Lacy, Leslie Alexander. *The Soil Soldiers: The Civilian Conservation Corps in the Great Depression.* Radnor, Pa.: Chilton Book Co., 1976.

Landon, Alfred M. *America at the Crossroads.* Reprint. New York, London: Kennikat Press, 1971.

Lester, Richard Allen. *Economics of Labor.* New York: Macmillan, 1949.

Lindley, Betty, and Ernest Lindley. *A New Deal for Youth: The Story of the National Youth Administration.* New York: Viking Press, 1938.

Lowitt, Richard, and Maurine Beasley, eds. *One-Third of a Nation: Lorena Hickok Reports on the Great Depression.* Urbana: University of Illinois Press, 1981.

MacMahon, Arthur W., John D. Millett, and Gladys Ogden. *The Administration of Federal Work Relief.* New York: Da Capo Press, 1971.

Maxwell, James A. *Federal Grants and the Business Cycle.* New York: National Bureau of Economic Research, 1952.

McCoy, Donald R. *Landon of Kansas.* Lincoln: University of Nebraska Press, 1966.

McFarland, Keith D. *Harry H. Woodring: A Political Biography of F. D. R.'s Controversial Secretary of War.* Lawrence: University Press of Kansas, 1975.

McJimsey, George. *Harry Hopkins: Ally of the Poor and Defender of Democracy.* Cambridge: Harvard University Press, 1987.

Miner, H. Craig. *Harvesting the High Plains: John Kriss and the Business of Wheat Farming, 1920–50.* Lawrence: University Press of Kansas, 1998.

Mink, Gwendolyn. *The Wages of Motherhood: Inequality in the Welfare State, 1917–42.* Ithaca, N.Y.: Cornell University Press, 1995.

Olson, James Stuart. *Herbert Hoover and the Reconstruction Finance Corporation, 1931–33.* Ames: Iowa State University Press, 1977.

Patterson, James T. *The New Deal and the States: Federalism in Transition.* Princeton: Princeton University Press, 1969.

———. *The Struggle against Poverty in America, 1930–80.* Cambridge: Harvard University Press, 1981.

Perkins, V. L. *Crisis in Agriculture: The Agricultural Adjustment Administration and the New Deal, 1933.* Berkeley: University of California Press, 1969.

Piven, Frances Fox, and Richard A. Clowerd. *Poor People's Movements: Why They Succeed, How They Fail.* New York: Vintage Books, 1979.

Poppendieck, Janet. *Breadlines Knee-Deep in Wheat: Food Assistance in the*

Great Depression. New Brunswick, N.J.: Rutgers University Press, 1986.

Porter, Kirk H., and Donald Bruce Johnson. *National Party Platforms, 1840–1964*. Urbana: University of Illinois Press, 1966.

Pressly, Thomas J., and William H. Scofield. *Farm Real Estate Values in the United States by Counties, 1850–1959*. Seattle: University of Washington Press, 1965.

Rasmussen, Wayne D. *Taking the University to the People: Seventy-Five Years of Cooperative Extension*. Ames: Iowa State University Press, 1989.

Reiman, Richard A. *The New Deal and American Youth: Ideas and Ideals in a Depression Decade*. Athens: University of Georgia Press, 1992.

Riney-Kehrberg, Pamela. *Rooted in Dust: Surviving Drought and Depression in Southwestern Kansas*. Lawrence: University Press of Kansas, 1994.

Romasco, Albert U. *The Poverty of Abundance: Hoover, the Nation, the Depression*. Oxford: Oxford University Press, 1977.

Salmond, John A. *The Civilian Conservation Corps, 1933–42: A New Deal Case Study*. Durham: Duke University Press, 1967.

Saloutos, Theodore. *The American Farmer and the New Deal*. Ames: Iowa State University Press, 1982.

Sautter, Udo. *Three Cheers for the Unemployed: Government and Unemployment before the New Deal*. Cambridge: Cambridge University Press, 1991.

Schruben, Francis W. *Kansas in Turmoil, 1930–36*. Columbia: University of Missouri Press, 1969.

Schultz, Constance B., ed. *Bust to Boom: Documentary Photographs of Kansas, 1936–49*. Lawrence: University Press of Kansas, 1996.

Schuyler, Michael W. *The Dread of Plenty: Agricultural Relief Activities of the Federal Government in the Middle West, 1933–39*. Manhattan, Kans.: Sunflower Press, 1989.

Schwartz, Bonnie Fox. *The Civil Works Administration, 1933–34: The Business of Emergency Unemployment in the New Deal*. Princeton: Princeton University Press, 1984.

Sheridan, Richard B. *Economic Development in South Central Kansas. An Economic History, 1500–1900*. Part 1A. Lawrence: School of Business, Bureau of Business Research, University of Kansas, 1956.

Singleton, Jeff. *The American Dole: Unemployment Relief and the Welfare State in the Great Depression*. Westport, Conn.: Greenwood Press, 2000.

Socolofsky, Homer E. *Arthur Capper: Publisher, Politician, and Philanthropist*. Lawrence: University Press of Kansas, 1962.

———. *Kansas Governors*. Lawrence: University Press of Kansas, 1990.

Stouffer, Samuel A., and Paul E. Lazarsfeld. *Research Memorandum on the*

Family and the Depression. New York: Social Science Research Council, 1937.

Suggs, George G., Jr. *Union Busting in the Tri-State District: The Oklahoma, Kansas and Missouri Metal Workers Strike of 1935.* Norman: University of Oklahoma Press, 1986.

Svobida, Lawrence. *Farming the Dust Bowl: A First-Hand Account from Kansas.* Lawrence: University Press of Kansas, 1986.

Taylor, Alonzo E. *Corn and Hog Surplus of the Corn Belt.* Stanford: Stanford University Press, 1932.

White, Eugene Nelson. *The Regulation and Reform of the American Banking System, 1900–1929.* Princeton: Princeton University Press, 1983.

Williams, Edward Ainsworth. *Federal Aid for Relief.* New York: Columbia University Press, 1939.

Wood, Charles L. *The Kansas Beef Industry.* Lawrence: University Press of Kansas, 1980.

Woodruff, Archibald M., Jr. *Farm Mortgage Loans of Insurance Companies.* New Haven: Yale University Press, 1937.

Worster, Donald. *Dust Bowl: The Southern Plains in the 1930s.* New York: Oxford University Press, 1979.

Zickefoose, Paul W. *Kansas Income Payments, 1900–53.* Lawrence: Bureau of Business Research, University of Kansas, 1955.

Ziskind, David. *One Thousand Strikes of Government Employees.* New York: Columbia University Press, 1940.

Index

Note: page numbers followed by *n* refer to notes; page numbers followed by *t* refer to tables.

Aid to Dependent Children (ADC), 196, 234, 235, 239, 261
Aid to the Blind, 196, 234, 238–39
AMA. *See* American Municipal Association
Amenta, Edwin, 261
American Indians. *See* Native Americans
American Municipal Association (AMA), 47
Anderson, Nels, 115, 210
Armel, Lyle O, 100, 226, 230
Army, 139, 140
Arts programs: Public Works Art Project, 119–20; WPA, 265
AT&SF Railroad, 26
Automobile ownership, 3, 161
Aviation industry, 271–72

Baker, Jacob, 105–6
Bane, Frank, 206
Banking Act of 1933, 55
Banks: confidence in, 54–55; decline in deposits and loans, 16; deposit insurance, 55; failures, 1, 10–11, 16, 35, 54; Federal Reserve members, 9–10, 55; mergers, 16, 55; national, 10; national bank holiday, 54–55; New Deal legislation, 55, 195; number in Kansas, 10–11; reorganizations, 55; state-chartered, 9–10, 55; unit banking, 10, 55; withdrawal limits, 54, 55
Barber County: effects of droughts, 189, 191; oil fields, 191; population movements, 216n52
Barter, 56–57
Beal, George, 119
Beasley, William A., 100, 117n57
Beckman, C. J., 22, 25, 28, 32, 33
Besore, Jay M., 28, 30, 33, 107
Black, Cyril, 102
Blind, welfare program, 196, 234, 238–39
Bonds, county, 38, 58, 60–61, 223, 236
Bounds, R. J., 124
Bourbon County, occupation of courthouse, 226
Bourbon County Commissioners, 226
Bowman, W. W., 10
Boynton, Roland, 45
Brenner, Paul V., 246
Brinkley, John R., 23n58, 49
Brock, William R., 61
Brown County: Native American population, 5; unemployment, 42

Budgetary deficiency: calculations, 98; determination of Old Age Assistance payments, 238; funding issues, 179; inefficiency when used in work relief, 208–9; procedures, 95–98, 208–9, 244; use by counties, 62, 237; use in FERA allocations, 71
Budgets: family, 96; state, 222, 275–76
Bureau of Agricultural Economics, 173, 188
Bureau of the Census, 13
Butler County: oil fields, 6; strikes by WPA workers, 212

Canning plants, 119, 128, 187
Capper, Arthur: support of CCC, 138; support of New Deal, 194–95, 276; on WPA, 214, 227, 230
Carpenter, Randolph, 122, 124
Case supervisors: clerical support, 83; importance, 141; interviews of CCC applicants, 139; position combined with poor commissioner, 204–5; qualifications, 94–95; responses to unemployment, 92; responsibilities, 93, 94, 97, 236–37; salaries, 205n23, 237; selection of relief workers, 82–83, 87; state, 72, 74, 82n70; training, 73–74; women, 237
Casework consultants, 118
Caseworkers: case assessment, 98; home visitors, 236–38; increased number, 118. *See also* Social workers
Cash Basis Law, 51, 53, 97, 99, 214, 241, 256
Cattle: purchase program, 178, 184, 185–87, 194; shipping from drought areas, 185, 186. *See also* Livestock
CCC. *See* Civilian Conservation Corps
CCCorp. *See* Commodity Credit Corporation
Census: of 1930, 2; of 1940, 151
Census of Agriculture, 150, 161
Census of Manufactures, 7
CERCs. *See* County Emergency Relief Committees
Cereal malt beverage tax, 235, 255
Certifying officers, 80, 93
CFRCs. *See* County Federal Relief Committees
Chamber of Commerce, Kansas, 22, 37
Chanute, 191, 229
Charities. *See* Private charities

42; proportion of population on relief, 242; work relief projects, 217

Defense industry: employment growth, 262; reluctance to hire WPA workers, 269, 271–72

Defense work: NYA projects, 250; for women, 251, 271–72; WPA projects, 213, 272

Deficiency budgets. *See* Budgetary deficiency

Deflation, 1–2, 153, 158

Democratic National Committee, Women's Division, 82

Democrats: criticism of Landon, 111, 122, 123, 124, 222; criticism of Stutz, 111, 122, 123, 124, 200, 201, 231–33; criticism of work relief, 267; KFRC members, 44, 50, 122; opposition to Stutz as state WPA director, 200–203, 221–22, 254; patronage, 201, 224, 225, 240

Demonstrations and riots: causes, 92, 102, 109, 114, 115, 209; in Crawford County, 100–101, 227, 230; demands, 102–3, 115, 229; by farmers, 155; federal aid suspensions, 100, 102, 103, 106, 113–14; federal and state responses, 105–7, 276; investigation of potential, 112–13; against relief administrators, 141–42, 146; by relief workers, 209, 210–11, 212; strikes, 114, 210–11, 212, 227, 229–30; in Topeka, 99, 100, 220–21, 226, 228–29; Wichita riot (1934), 90, 101–7, 109, 233; women's participation, 265; against WPA, 225–26, 227–28; in Wyandotte County, 115–16, 144

Depression. *See* Great Depression

Deserving poor, 17

Dewson, Mary, 82

Direct action. *See* Demonstrations and riots

Direct relief: average payments, 66, 117–18, 130, 208; case costs, 66; cash payments, 130, 262; cuts, 99; effectiveness, 274; for employables without WPA jobs, 205–6, 207, 242, 260, 261, 274–75; general assistance, 235, 237, 239, 240, 242, 243, 244; importance, 214; in-kind payments, 66, 98, 117, 130, 237, 244, 262; local funding, 130; as state and local responsibility, 196, 197; stigma associated with, 90. *See also* Dole

Disabilities, individuals with, 38, 199, 204

Discrimination: racial, 27, 145n120, 226, 272; against women by WPA, 218, 264, 266

Dobson, Bryan, 101

Dodge City, 5, 6n8, 43

Dole, negative views of, 41, 197, 214, 243, 253, 274–75, 277. *See also* Direct relief

Douglas County: economic conditions, 42; Lone Star Lake, 141, 246–47. *See also* Lawrence

Douglas County Republican Committee, 47, 124

Driscoll, Jerry E., 233

Droughts: crop failures, 125, 158, 161, 162, 174, 182, 189, 190, 217; designated emergency areas, 183, 186; economic effects, 125, 127, 149, 161–62, 172, 188, 189, 191–92, 243; effects on livestock, 161, 164–65, 185, 191; farmers on relief, 90, 182, 183, 190, 217; New Deal programs, 181–84, 194; in past, 8; rainfall amounts, 162–64, 163t, 187; survey of effects, 188–92; uneven effects, 193

Dust Bowl, 175–76, 195

Dust storms, 162, 180, 217

Eagle-Picker Company, 33

Early, Harry J., 202

Economic conditions: in 1934, 125–27; in rural areas, 195, 242–43. *See also* Great Depression; Recession of 1937–38

Edge, Cornelia, 272

Edmonds, T. J., 74, 79, 90, 111, 112, 124; on Landon, 123; praise for Kansas Transient program, 135; on Sedgwick County relief administration, 234; on Stutz, 122; on Wichita riot, 103–4, 106–7

Education: CCC program, 246; College Student Aid program, 72, 130, 131, 248; College Student Employment Project, 88; of labor force, 7; NYA program, 248, 249, 252; school lunch program, 263, 264; teachers, 88, 130–31, 252; work relief projects, 88

Elections. *See* Gubernatorial elections; Presidential election

Electricity, in rural areas, 3–4

Elks Lodges, 33, 36

Ellis County: rural rehabilitation program, 173; WPA projects, 218, 219

Ellsworth County: RFC aid, 45; road construction projects, 34; salt mining, 6

Emergency Conservation Work Program, 137–38. *See also* Civilian Conservation Corps

Emergency Education program, 72, 130–31

Emergency Farm Mortgage Act, 157

Emergency Relief and Appropriations Act (1936), 211–12

Emergency Relief and Construction Act (1932), 39–40

Emergency Relief Appropriations Act (1935), 196

Emergency Relief Appropriations Act (1939), 212, 213

Emergency Relief Appropriations Act (1942), 213

Emergency Relief Taxes, 52

Emergency Work Relief Program: administration in Kansas, 87, 89–90; county supervisors, 95; in drought areas, 182; establishment, 86; funding, 129; limits on work hours, 86; means testing, 86, 89; projects, 128, 129; termination, 196; wages, 86, 89

Employables: eligibility for WPA, 198–99; farmers, 216–17; federal programs for, 196; relief payments to, 205–6, 207, 242, 260, 261, 274–75; unable to find CWA/CWS jobs, 88; unable to find WPA jobs, 205–6, 207, 213–14, 217, 260, 266–67, 270, 274–75

Employment: classification of relief workers, 269–70; comparison to national average, 13–15; data collection, 12–13; decline, 13, 240; difficulties of youth, 244; index numbers, 13, 14*t*, 15–16; by industry, 5, 5*t*; non-farm in rural areas, 4, 151–52, 190–91; out-of-state workers, 36; payrolls, 13, 14*t*, 125, 240; workforce size, 5*t*, 260. *See also* Unemployment; Wages; Women's employment; Work relief

Employment agencies, 22

Employment committees, 23–24, 28–30, 35

Emporia: investigation of potential unrest, 112; unemployment, 34

Equalization Fund, 241

Eskridge, Lake Wabaunsee Transient Camp, 112, 124, 133, 136

Ethnic minorities. *See* African Americans; Hispanics; Native Americans

Ewing, Sherrard, 61–63, 64, 72, 74, 75

Fair Labor Standards Act, 211, 270

Farm Bill, 156–58

Farm Bureau, 156

Farm credit, RFC program, 40

Farm Credit Act, 157–58

Farm Credit Administration (FCA): debt extension services, 154, 156, 182; establishment, 156; loans, 194; responsibilities, 156, 157; standards, 254

Farm debt: average amounts, 174; Emergency Farm Mortgage Act, 157; foreclosures, 2, 12, 53, 153–54, 175; to local suppliers, 153; on machinery, 12, 153, 174, 175, 176; mortgage moratorium, 154–55; mortgages, 8, 12, 153, 174; New Deal programs, 154; refinancing, 175; of rural rehabilitation clients, 170; tax delinquencies, 30–31, 154, 175, 176

Farmer Labor (Party) Union, 227

Farmers: demonstrations, 155; diversity of experiences in Depression, 161–62, 170–71, 193; eligibility for WPA work, 216, 218, 220, 221; family spending, 150, 161, 243; interest in CWA jobs, 87, 182; lack of militancy in Kansas, 155; living standards, 170, 173; optimism, 178, 192; owners, 151, 193; population, 3, 8; on relief, 90, 126, 173, 182, 183, 190, 217; supplemental income, 151–52; views of New Deal, 215–16. *See also* Agriculture; Tenant farmers

Farmers' Holiday Association, 155

Farm income: decline, 2, 16, 30; efforts to raise, 149; importance in rural communities, 150, 161, 243; of rural rehabilitation clients, 170

Farm laborers: effects of droughts, 193; eligibility for WPA work, 220; on relief, 176, 193; unemployment, 16, 174–75, 188; wages, 87, 182, 192, 215, 221

Farm prices: buying power, 12, 152, 161; corn, 12, 160, 162; declines, 12; effects of droughts, 149; feed, 12, 161, 162, 164; increases, 125; indices, 152; livestock, 12, 187; in 1920s, 9, 152; in 1930s, 152–53; parity ratios, 152, 156; support for government intervention, 155–56; wheat, 11, 12, 158–59, 165, 174

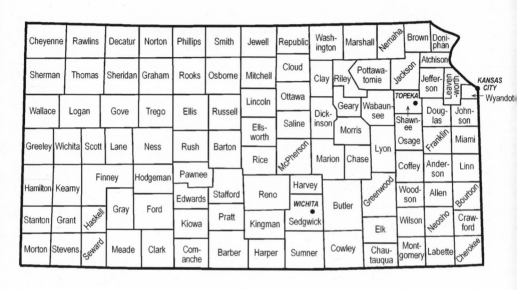

The 105 counties of the state of Kansas.

KANSAS IN THE GREAT DEPRESSION